Reiner Schürmann
Selected Writings and Lecture Notes

Reiner Schürmann

Ways of Releasement

Writings on God, Eckhart, and Zen

Edited by
Francesco Guercio and Ian Alexander Moore

DIAPHANES

Reiner Schürmann
Selected Writings and Lecture Notes

Edited by Francesco Guercio, Michael Heitz,
Ian Alexander Moore, and Nicolas Schneider

1st edition
ISBN 978-3-0358-0431-7
© DIAPHANES, Zurich 2023
All rights reserved.

Layout: 2edit, Zurich
Printed in Germany

www.diaphanes.com

Table of Contents

Edition Guidelines	7
1. The Reredos (1965)	9
2. To Live According to the Gospel (1966)	11
3. Letter to Heidegger, and Schürmann's Report of His Meeting with Heidegger (1966)	13
4. The Unknown God (1966)	21
5. A Spiritual Dimension of Technology? (1966)	29
6. Easter on Christmas: A Sermon on Love and Death (1966)	37
7. The Philosophical Presuppositions of Meister Eckhart's Christology (1967)	41
8. The Phenomenon of the Question in Theology (1967)	57
9. Peregrine Identity (1969)	95
10. Meister Eckhart, Expert in Itinerancy (1971)	123
11. Book Reviews about Eckhart (1968–1974)	135
12. To Find, at Last, the Origin (1973)	147
13. Three Thinkers of Releasement: Meister Eckhart, Heidegger, Suzuki (1974–1975)	155
14. Commentary on Professor Caputo's Paper "Mysticism, Metaphysics and Thought" (1976)	217

15. The Loss of the Origin in Soto Zen and in
    Meister Eckhart (1978)   225

16. The Law of Nature and Pure Nature: Thought-Experience
    in Meister Eckhart (1984/1986–1987)   267

17. Introduction to Lecture Course on Meister Eckhart (1993)   297

    Appendix 1: The Word of God (1964)   305
    Appendix 2: The Unknown God, Early Draft (1966)   311
    Appendix 3: Evaluation by Claude Geffré (1967)   317
    Appendix 4: Letters from Bernhard Welte (1967–1971)   321

    Sources for the Chapters   329
    Editors' Afterword   333
    Acknowledgments   417
    Index nominum   419

Edition Guidelines

References to the critical edition of Eckhart and to Heidegger's *Gesamtausgabe* have been provided in the body of the text. All other references—by Schürmann and by the editors—are to be found in the footnotes. Translations of passages for which an English edition is not supplied as the main entry in a footnote are either by Schürmann (when in quotation marks or in a block quotation) or by the editors (when in square brackets). For Bible passages, we typically cite the English translation of the Catholic Bible that Schürmann primarily used when working in French: *The Jerusalem Bible* (London: Darton, Longman & Todd, 1966). Abbreviations and other markings are as follows:

R.S.	Reiner Schürmann
No marks	bibliographical references by Schürmann
‹ __ ›	handwritten additions by Schürmann
[__]	editors' notes and additions, unless indicated otherwise
" __ [__ R.S.] __ "	Schürmann's additions to quotation
" __ [__] __ "	editors' additions to quotation
[* __ ?*]	editors' reconstruction of partially readable/audible text

Schürmann, Reiner

ME	*Maître Eckhart ou la joie errante: Sermons allemands traduits et commentés par Reiner Schürmann*. Paris: Payot & Rivages, 2005.
WJ	*Wandering Joy: Meister Eckhart's Mystical Philosophy*, trans. and commentary R. Schürmann. Great Barrington, MA: Lindisfarne Books, 2001.

Eckhart

DW	*Deutsche Werke.* 5 Vols. In *Die deutschen und lateinischen Werke*, herausgegeben im Auftrag der Deutschen Forschungsgemeinschaft (Stuttgart: Kohlhammer, 1936–2023), followed by volume, page, and line number, as well as sermon ('Pr.') or treatise titles and, when applicable, numbers.

LW	*Lateinische Werke*. 6 Vols. In *Die deutschen und lateinischen Werke*, herausgegeben im Auftrag der Deutschen Forschungsgemeinschaft. Stuttgart: Kohlhammer, 1936–, followed by volume, page, and section number, as well as sermon ('S.') or treatise titles and, when applicable, numbers.
Pf.	Franz Pfeiffer, ed. *Meister Eckhart (Deutsche Mystiker des vierzehnten Jahrhunderts*, Vol. 2). Leipzig: Göschen, 1857.

Eckhart's Latin Works in the Critical Edition

Acta	*Acta Echardiana* (LW 5: 149–655).
In Eccli.	*Sermones et Lectiones super Ecclesiastici* c. 24,23–31 (LW 2: 229–300).
In Exod.	*Expositio Libri Exodi* (LW 2: 1–227).
In Ioh.	*Expositio sancti Evangelii secundum Iohannem* (LW 3).
In Sap.	*Expositio Libri Sapientiae* (LW 2: 301–643).
Prol. gen.	*Prologus generalis in opus tripartitum* (LW 1: 148–65).
Qu. Par.	*Questiones Parisienses* (LW 5: 27–83).
S. and SS.	*Sermo* and *Sermones* (LW 4).

Eckhart's Middle High German Works in the Critical Edition

BgT	*Daz buoch der götlichen trœstunge* (DW 5: 1–105).
Pr. and Prr.	*Predigt* and *Predigten* (DW 1–4).
RdU	*Die rede der underscheidunge* (DW 5: 137–376).
Vab	*Von abegescheidenheit* (DW 5: 400–61).
Vem	*Von dem edeln menschen* (DW 5: 106–36).

Heidegger, Martin

GA	*Gesamtausgabe*. Frankfurt am Main: Vittorio Klostermann, 1975–.
NII	*Nietzsche*. Vol. 2. Pfullingen: Neske, 1961.

Silesius, Angelus

CW	*Cherubinischer Wandersmann. Kritische Ausgabe*. Ed. Louise Gnädinger. Stuttgart: Reclam, 1984.

1

The Reredos

(1965, trans. from the French by Ian Alexander Moore)

This early, untitled text, which is something of a confession or manifesto, is published here for the first time in any language. It demonstrates Schürmann's struggle with how to reconcile his faith in Christ with his growing interest in Heidegger's philosophy and in the theologically universalist scope of Eckhart's teaching of the Godhead. We have titled it "The Reredos" (a screen or altarpiece located behind the altar in a church) in accordance with Schürmann's use of this figure throughout the text.

The reredos before which I sacrifice (all of this sounds more sectarian than it is) has two panels: 1) we often say that God is someone. God is not someone. At a pinch, this affirmation could be true: "God and I are the same thing"; or this one: "God and that which is are the same thing." God is not spirit, God does not exist. It is necessary to take this more strictly than when we say: indeed, one must not attribute to God the realities that we are familiar with under names such as 'person,' 'being,' and 'spirit' as we conceive them—I mean that, in reality, all tongues [*toute langue*] must be silent before God [cf. Habakkuk 2:20]. Meister Eckhart says that the soul is above God, and God's messenger, the bishop Robinson, would like God finally to be once again 'without God.'[1] Heidegger, too, has been seized by that which is radically unknowable. I understand these authors, for the same gift has been given to all. And why should we be surprised that there are profound resemblances between the experience of the 'Tao,' of the Buddhist 'Emptiness,' of the thinker's *Es gibt Sein*,[2] etc., if it is the same divine that gives itself?

---

1 [R.S. cites a portion of the title of the French translation of John A. T. Robinson's *Honest to God*: *Dieu sans dieu*, trans. Louis Salleron (Paris: Nouvelles éditions latines, 1964). Cf. *Honest to God: 55th Anniversary Edition* (Louisville: Westminster John Knox, 2018), 75.]

2 [Heidegger's phrase, which R.S. explains as follows: "In *On Time and Being*, Heidegger asks what we think of when we say 'there is Being.' The German language does

And now for the second panel: 2) I know that I have a history, that there is an evolution of subjectivity, and that the principle of progress[3] is love. I know that by an invisible hand God gives drink to those who are thirsty; I know that he touches the heart, the hand of all men—and does so as he wishes. I know that God loves me, loves all men, and that he speaks to each human being, in a language intimate and wholly personal; that he is there at the heart of all human experience, and with all the more love as the latter becomes sin. Saint Dominic said 'my Mercy,' and I say it with him.[4] We should be able to feel, touch, and embrace this dialogue that men, so secretly, have with their Savior; this would be the most beautiful path for knowing Jesus Christ. I believe, however, that this experience of extension [*prolongement*] (of man to the Son of man), which is rather an experience of presence, is also undergone [*se fait*] in unusual ways, where the Catholic Church would scream in fear. It is not we who decide the how of this dialogue, but Jesus Christ who knows, better than we do, the human dough and the ways of kneading it.

The return, the approach of progressive elimination, stops at a paradox. The philosophers call it the ontological difference: God 'gives' being, and at the same time he has wanted us to be able to know him [*le connaître*][5] as something 'ontic.' Each human event is mysterious, but the source of the mystery is precisely this 'rift [*faille*] in God.' And the rift is a solid rock: with God's help, I will be able to build there a life that has *meaning* [*un* sens] [cf. Matthew 16:18].

Reiner Schürmann
11 November 1965

---

not say 'there is,' but rather 'it gives,' *es gibt Sein*. This idiomatic turn of speech reveals to Heidegger Being's way to be. What is experienced when language says: *es gibt Sein*? what is given? Being is given." Reiner Schürmann, "Heidegger and the Mystical Tradition," ed. Francesco Guercio, *Journal of Continental Philosophy* 1, no. 2 (2020): 298–99.]

3 ["bonheur" ("happiness") is crossed out.]

4 [Dominic would often pray, "My God, my mercy, what will become of sinners?" See also Hosea 14:4 and Psalm 145(144):8.]

5 [*le connaître* can also be translated as "to know *it*," namely "being."]

2

To Live According to the Gospel

(1966, trans. from the French by Ian Alexander Moore)

This text, also published here in any language for the first time, appears to be a letter or message to an unknown recipient. Around this time, Schürmann was especially troubled by the Catholic Church's continued commitment to the teaching of the Council of Chalcedon (451 CE), according to which Jesus Christ should be understood as two natures in one person and hypostasis. Schürmann felt instead that a new language was needed to describe Christ's incarnation.

To live according to the Gospel free from the complications of language and misunderstandings about God. But this is no longer true at the level of 'reflected' life, because the unknown God [*le Dieu inconnu*] sends us a Son who is also unknown. I am thinking of all the difficulties we sense when talking about the Resurrection. The Council of Chalcedon said what its epoch expected it to say about God. But that was 1,500 years ago. And ever since then we repeat: one person, two natures. For us today, this seems to become an unacceptable language (this is why it is a serious failure on the part of the Fathers of the last Council[6] not to have said a word about God, Christ). According to Welte, Jesus Christ is 'that man in whom the glory of divine grace has become particularly palpable [*sensible*].'[7] He admits that he has not yet had the courage to publish this definition, but it will come. Bultmann does not speak in the past tense: 'He is the one who calls me today to convert.' You know better than I that every prospect of the future, in the sense of an accomplishment expected for the future, escapes such a formula—although it magnificently expresses the demand [*exigence*] Christianity testifies to. In any case, this seems certain: to repeat over and over again that Jesus Christ was 'man and God' can be no more intelligent than to cry out all afternoon: "great is the Artemis of the Ephesians" [Acts

---

6 [The Second Vatican Council (1962–1965).]

7 [R.S., who was studying in Freiburg with the theologian Bernhard Welte in Freiburg at the time, presumably heard this from Welte personally.]

19:28]! Instead of speaking incessantly of the divinity of Christ, we would do better to try to broaden this phrase in the sense of an immediacy within the event, of Christ to God. All of this will certainly seem completely heretical to you, but ask Father Geffré what Welte writes in the volume on the Council of Chalcedon.[8] To speak of a 'hypostatic' union has become, to say the least, a limited language.

Reiner Schürmann
16 February 1966

---

8 [Bernhard Welte, "Homoousios hemin: Gedanken zum Verständnis und zur theologischen Problematik der Kategorien von Chalcedon," in *Das Konzil von Chalcedon: Geschichte und Gegenwart*, vol. 3: *Chalcedon heute*, ed. Aloys Grillmeier and Heinrich Bacht (Würzburg: Echter, 1954), 51–80; republished as "Zur Christologie von Chalcedon," in Welte, *Auf der Spur des Ewigen* (Freiburg: Herder, 1965), 429–58. Welte speaks of the need to "move beyond Chalcedon" (457).]

3

Letter to Heidegger, and Schürmann's Report of His Meeting with Heidegger

(1966, trans. and foreword by Pierre Adler)

On January 16, 1966, Schürmann wrote a letter to Martin Heidegger in which he submitted two questions for the philosopher's consideration, and requested a conversation with him. Schürmann was a twenty-four year old friar at the Dominican Faculties of Philosophy and Theology of the Saulchoir, at Essonnes in France, where he had begun his studies in 1962 (he was to complete them in 1969 and be ordained to the priesthood in 1970, which he left in 1975). At the time, he was on a stay of study with Professor Bernhard Welte at the University of Freiburg. Heidegger responded on February 4, inviting the young man to his home in Freiburg. On March 11, the very day of the visit, Schürmann related the content of his discussion with the philosopher to an anonymous correspondent [now known to be Claude Geffré, Eds.]. The three pieces of correspondence were found tucked away in one of the numerous Heidegger volumes of Schürmann's library. Schürmann's letter is written in German, whereas the report is in French.[9]

January 16, 1966
Fr. Reiner Schürmann OP
Care of Mrs. Hofmann
Lorettostrasse 42
78 Freiburg

Dear Mr. Heidegger,

Owing to Professor Welte's encouragement, I take the liberty of addressing a request for a conversation to you. I am a Dominican, belong to the order's French district, and am at this time interrupting my studies at the order's school, Le Saulchoir near Paris, in order to begin doctoral work on the "unknown God in the thought of Meister

---

9 [We have been unable to obtain the original German of the letter, although the original French of the report is available in Jean-Marie Vaysse, ed., *Autour de Reiner Schürmann* (Hildesheim: Olms, 2009), 155–57. Eds.]

Eckhart" under Professor Welte's guidance. I am German. I shall be ordained as a priest in only three years.

There are two questions that I particularly wish to ask you. The first one concerns Eckhart's relevance to the situation in which thinking finds itself today: did he perhaps think being as self-sending, as only eventfully experienceable? Meister Eckhart's 'sole thought' is aimed at the unification of the 'separated soul' with God. Insofar as the soul lets all things be, it breaks through to the ground where the Godhead continually creates all things, and which in this breakthrough also becomes my ground. The unity is a unity of the "fabric"[10] in which God operates and I become—become son, that is. Being is thus thought as course of experience, and not represented as ontic 'standing reserve.'[11] Closer to the soul than any created thing, the "unknown God" is experienced in the event of words,[12] beyond this and that,[13] and, for that reason, it always remains a 'nil of all things.' Might not Meister Eckhart's thinking help us along in a meditation directed at being which always withholds itself and, in this very withholding, addresses itself to us?

I request that you greet my second question with particular indulgence: can the wondering silence in the face of the gift of being not recollect certain words that were first brought forth in a stutter and later 'sublated' on account of their inadequacy? And can it not consent to the event thanks to an inkling remaining from them? I have in mind above all this one word, 'thou.' The mystery of the gift could be experienced as mystery of the 'thou,' without thinking's having to fall into representation (for example, the repetition of a source of being [which is] revealed to it), while it remains within the boundaries set to it as thinking. Even in breaking through all of God's titles (such as 'the good' or 'truth'), there still subsists for Meister Eckhart the inkling of the 'thou.' Might not the proposition

---

10 [R.S.'s German letter (now lost) must have had *Gewirke* here, which in this context means less 'fabric' than 'being-at-work.' See DW 1: 114,4–5 (Pr 6, "Iusti vivent in aeternum"), where one finds *gewürke*. Eds.]

11 ['Reserve' is to be taken in the sense of 'supply' or 'stock.' It translates 'Bestand.' P.A.]

12 ['Words' renders 'Zuspruch.' This translation is in all likelihood inadequate, as 'Zuspruch' may mean speaking, encouragement, consolation, or exhortation, all of which are probably meant here. P.A.]

13 ['Beyond this and that' translates 'jenseits von allem Dies und Das.' A less literal translation would be 'beyond all concerns and things.' P.A.]

'being is given' ('*Es gibt Sein*') be expressed in the form 'thou givest being' ('*Du gibst Sein*') without injury to the mystery?

[The carbon copy breaks off at this point.]

* * *

Freiburg, March 11 [1966]

The event that I awaited eagerly and with stage-fright has just taken place: I have just returned from Heidegger's house. It was a real late-afternoon reception about the mystery of being... To begin with the folkloric aspect of the visit, I had my fill and more: a pious inscription above the door to the house ("God bless you..."); a small man, who looked like a peasant, let me in and ushered me nearly without saying a word into a room that looked rather like a blockhouse; two glasses and a bottle on a small tray; and, especially, a two-hour long discussion which ended up, at least outwardly, in complete darkness. I knew that among things country he had a fondness for those that are traditional: his writings speak of the pitcher of cool water, of the peasant's rough hands, of mud-caked clogs, and such. I now know that he also likes discussions in the dark. However, the man is so shrewd, and, above all, he has such a listening ability (in this respect, I have never met anyone as heedful of what one says) that it felt like my meager schoolboy questions were received by warm and reassuring hands.

I should note first that Hans Urs von Balthasar, to whom I had written a short letter in order to introduce myself (I have resolutely taken on the role of the monk from the East who goes from father to father) and who responded very nicely, has, for all that, somewhat disheartened me, as regards this particular issue. In his view, Heidegger hides behind an anti-Christian polemic, and by means of his "general epistemology" (this, as an example of a false interpretation, is a bit strong!)[14] hammers down any mystical impulse, and cannot thus be of any help in finding answers to such questions as

---

14 [The quotation marks around "general epistemology" and the parenthetical remark that follows it are missing from Adler's translation, which we have accordingly modified. Eds.]

are raised by, say, Meister Eckhart. It is somewhat of a pity that he said that. I take it that his own passions lie elsewhere.

I am nonetheless going to give you a bit of a run-down of what has just been said. In my letter, written nearly two months ago (he was away), I had attempted to formulate two questions, one concerning Meister Eckhart's conception of being, the other concerning the possibility of saying 'thou' to what in some of his texts Heidegger calls 'gift of being,' a phrase formed after the expression 'es gibt Sein' [literally, in English, 'it gives being'], 'there is being.' In fact, my secret hope was that I would manage to make him speak about God. (How difficult it is to relate a conversation of this sort! But I shall try.)

His starting-point still remains strictly that of a phenomenological ontology, that is to say, of an inquiry into phenomena with a view to [laying bare] what is already known, being. That is the well-known hermeneutic circle. The phenomenological gaze sees that that-which-is is, that beings are owing to being, which gives itself in them (goodness, it sounds awfully like a dissertation. The letter really flattens things out![15]). Heidegger has been wondering about this gift of being for some years. He has often been asked (happily, I did not do so) whether the 'es' in the proposition 'es gibt Sein' refers to God. He denies that it does. At this point, I introduced my questions about 'thou': is there not, in this experience of the gift, of being that is granted [*de l'être a-venant*],[16] an experience of saying 'thou'? Would it not be the case that, prior to all prayer, the saying of 'thou' is part and parcel of the being of Dasein, just as having to correspond to the ineffable gift, by the response that is required, is part and parcel of the being of Dasein? I shall not dwell on this, except to say that the outcome of this part of the conversation,[17] the longest and most interesting (and of which he himself said that in it we touched on something profound), was quite remarkable. One could sum it up as follows: the gift of being opens up within Dasein the possibility of receiving and of saying 'thou.' This 'thou' is identical with neither being nor 'es.' There is something like a series of containers (although he rejects this word): the beings are not being; rather, through beings one experiences that being gives itself; being

---

15 ["la lettre tue," more literally "the letter kills," a reference to 2 Corinthians 3:6. Eds.]
16 [Alternatively, "of being that is coming" or "ad-vening." Eds.]
17 [R.S. uses the German *Gespräch* in the original. Eds.]

is not itself that which gives being; it is rather the 'es'—the mystery—which gives it; when the possibility of saying 'thou' to more and to something other than a human being is realized, it is not this 'es' that is addressed by the 'thou,' but rather something beyond it. However, for that, a privileged experience is required which man can never obtain by his own doing, but which only this 'thou' can grant. The experience is no longer one of thought alone, but of all of oneself (those are still his own words). In this sense, philosophy does not speak about that experience. It does, however, open the paths on which such an experience may become real. In Heidegger's view, Hölderlin certainly had that experience. It is thus not a matter of the experience of faith, although what is usually designated by 'experience of faith' naturally touches upon it very closely. Incidentally, he let out a beautiful sigh: "Who can say what faith is!"

In a world that is dominated by science and technology, and which treats art as a commodity, Heidegger understands his entire philosophy as a preparation for this experience of Something Else of which philosophy itself can no longer speak. From *Sein und Zeit* to the present, the whole of his thought has solely been considering the possibilities that are to be disclosed in order for this ineffable experience to happen: "And when it is granted to one, one will no longer need philosophy." It should be specified, however, that his philosophy does not speak of a supreme being which would give itself in such a fashion: "What I am attempting to think is both smaller than traditional philosophy (which constantly speaks about God) and larger (because it opens the way to an overcoming, by way of an experience, of philosophy)."

He dreads dogmatism. For that reason he was unable to accept what I was propounding, namely, that philosophy succeed, as philosophy, in giving a verdict about a 'thou' from which Dasein would 'always already' originate. To him, it would properly amount to theology to say that man can say 'thou' to what in a granting gives itself in the 'es' only because he also harbors his origin within it.[18] For, according to Heidegger's argumentation, to consider man as always in relation to a 'thou' would, to put it coarsely, make prayer an obli-

---

18 [Trans. mod. by Eds. The French text reads: "Cela, pour lui, serait proprement de la théologie, de dire que l'homme ne peut dire 'tu' à ce qui dans un grâce se donne dans l'*Es*, que parce qu'il a aussi en lui son origine."]

gation for everyone. Indeed, if every man always already had a personal relation to this 'thou' which lies in mystery, one would be able to reproach those not respecting this 'thou,' with living in contradiction to their being. That is precisely what dogmatism does. One may thus say no more about the matter than this: philosophy's role is to open the way by which an unutterable experience may be given, but such an experience would no longer belong to philosophy;[19] it would be the privilege of the one to whom it was granted.

What he said very simply and with enormous respect for the matters under discussion, my letter makes sound awfully complicated and constructed. No doubt I am reporting it very poorly, but I believe that I have not added anything of my own. I am not going to tell you what he said about Meister Eckhart and about scholasticism, for it would take too long. I should also mention a series of remarks about the 'sacred' and about 'language' (the latter being also only the possibilizing ground[20] that Some Thing be addressed to us, but not that which allows to infer it ...). Heidegger is unquestionably a 'religious' thinker, and it is because I knew that he had spent some time at the Jesuit noviciate (I have never been able to determine whether it was ten days or ten months)[21] that I dared to start him on this trail. He invited me to come back.

Welte was extremely happy about the day he spent at the Saulchoir.[22] He told me: "If I were your age, that would be my monastery of choice." His maid is even worried that he is going to become Dominican. "They have a very candid, free, and open way about them; I was presented with intelligent questions which the theology

---

19 [Trans. mod. by Eds.]

20 [R.S. uses the German *Ermöglichungsgrund* in the original. Eds.]

21 [The actual time was closer to ten days. See Hugo Ott, *Martin Heidegger: Unterwegs zur seiner Biographie* (Frankfurt: Campus, 1988), 59. Eds.]

22 [On 7 March 1966, the feast day of St. Thomas Aquinas, Welte gave a lecture at Le Saulchoir titled "La métaphysique de Saint Thomas d'Aquin et la pensée de l'histoire de l'être chez Heidegger," later published in the Le Saulchoir-run journal *Revue des Sciences philosophiques et théologiques* 50, no. 4 (October 1966): 601–614. Claude Geffré, rector of the Dominican school of theology at the time, had invited Welte. See Martin Heidegger and Bernhard Welte, *Briefe und Begegnungen*, ed. Alfred Denker and Holger Zaborowski (Stuttgart: Klett-Cotta, 2003), 26, and Dominique Janicaud, *Heidegger en France*, 2 vols. (Paris: Albin Michel, 2001), 1:486, 2:161 ('1965' should read '1966'), and 2:281. On account of this, and of R.S.'s frequent and intimate correspondence with Geffré, we can conclude that Geffré was the intended recipient of this report. Eds.]

students from here would never raise; one senses that this place has caliber." Congratulations: you seduced him.

Reiner

4

The Unknown God

(1966, trans. from the German by Ian Alexander Moore)

This early, sermon-like article deals with the tension between the essential unknowability of God (cf. Romans 11:33–34, Acts 17:23) and Christ's own words on how to understand him. Schürmann focuses on three of these words for God: "good" (Luke 18:19), "spirit" (John 4:24), and "thou" (Matthew 6:9). The text first appeared in German in the popular Christian weekly Der christliche Sonntag *(now published under the title* Christ in der Gegenwart*). The basis for the edition here is a longer typescript in Schürmann's Nachlass, although we note divergences between it and the published version. An earlier, significantly different typescript version also exists in Schürmann's papers, which we include in translation in Appendix 2, below.*

God is always on our lips. Without thinking anything by it, we use God's name to lend weight to phrases which we have never reflected on. Could that be because we aren't at all acquainted with him? What do we know about God? Over the years, we have heard and learned a lot about him. But what of him have we experienced? Just as I can experience, in interacting with another person, that he has the same freedom, which I take for granted for myself, to do and to leave undone [*lassen*] what he wants? All of a sudden I may have felt that this other person has the power to refuse to trust me, to love something other than I do, and that I will never grasp how differently he can think, how *free* he is to accept me as his friend or to refuse to grant me his thou [*sein Du*].[23] Such an experience, in which I encounter this-one-here with complete immediacy as the free, independent other is the experience of a mystery.[24] "Truly, I will never completely understand you"—this is how we express

---

23 [Untranslatable into English, *Du*, in German, is an informal pronoun, often addressed to people one knows well, to children, to equals, or to God. The translator has opted for 'thou,' rather than 'you,' because of the theological, Buberian resonance of especially the final section of this chapter.]

24 [This sentence is missing in the printed version.]

ourselves when the unfamiliar and different breaks forth from the vicinity of the familiar. The unknown, the unknowable, flashes up among the features that we know.[25] From now on, we will be careful not to treat this person as though we had him at our disposal at every step and turn. In his freedom, his mystery has confronted us.

Has God ever confronted us in the mystery of his freedom? Have we ever experienced him in his inability to be compelled, how it breaks forth here and there from a countenance among people? Then God would have become godly for us again, would no longer be the dullest word with which we decorate our empty phrases.[26]— Let us examine for once how we speak about God. If God is to become meaningful for me in his divinity or Godhead [*Gottheit*], then each of the words that I use must possess a completely special weight of reality.[27]

Is God good?

First of all, there is the word 'good.' Yes, God is good: in his goodness he created the world, sent us his son as the redeemer, and ultimately offered me salvation [*das Heil*]. We live in a time when Christians seem to rediscover the so often quoted sentence of the Gospel, "in so far as you did this to one of the least of these brothers of mine, you did it to me" [Matthew 25:40],[28] in an entirely new way: the goodness that I show [*walten lassen*] to the poor and suffering is fundamentally already a piece of the infinite goodness of God himself. There are not two ways of being good, of which the one would belong to God and the other would be 'purely human'— just as there are not two types of love. Within my narrow limits, I succeed at being good only by virtue of the limitless goodness of God, and I am able to love only by virtue of the all-encompassing love of God.

---

25 [This sentence is missing in the printed version.]
26 [This clause ("would no longer" to "empty phrases") is missing in the printed version.]
27 [This sentence is missing from the printed version.]
28 [In the original, R.S. writes *eurer Brüder*, 'thy brethren,' rather than *meiner Brüder*, 'my brethren.']

When we try to appreciate what we are actually thinking when we assert that God is 'good,' we are first confronted with the need to put ourselves into his hands. He is worth our trust, since he has stood by us so far and will continue to stand by us. Are we really building upon God when we think in this manner? Perhaps the word that Meister Eckhart called out from his pulpit to the faithful[29] also applies to us: "Some people say: 'I have ten *malter* of grain and just as much wine this year; I firmly trust in God!' Quite right, I say, you have complete trust—in the grain and wine!"[30] We may succeed in experiencing God anew in the mystery of his freedom if we say: no, God is not good!—his goodness is of such an unprecedented kind that our word 'good' is as appropriate as it is unfit to describe this goodness.

We call someone 'good' who lifts us up, consoles us, who speaks to us with his heart. "You're a good person," we say, because we have received something, and we are right to do so. But we have received everything from God, we have received even ourselves, indeed every day we receive him in all the unexpected ways he invents to bestow himself on us. What is the point of the word 'goodness' when applied to God, since, after all, we receive more than a 'good' and since he does not just 'do good' by us? God does nothing good, he does what is godly. And his godliness is so highly elevated beyond the meaning we typically confer on our words that we would do better to be silent before God and to worship him in stillness and simplicity. Even after the coming of Christ, we should still speak of the 'unknown God,' whose true goodness is inexpressible [cf. Acts 17:22-23, 31]. Every tongue should therefore be silent before the mystery of God, since all our words, rather than striking his core, fall short of it. We burn to someday imbibe his goodness in an eternal gaze and eternal wonderment. Only then will we really know it. Today, however, we prefer to say (so that God for us may

---

29 [The printed version has "Perhaps Meister Eckhart's word" instead of "Perhaps the word that Meister Eckhart called out from his pulpit to the faithful."]

30 [DW 3: 63,6-9 (Pr. 62, "Got hât die armen gemachet durch die rîchen"). R.S. cites from Quint's translation into modern German, which appears in both Meister Eckehart, *Deutsche Predigten und Traktate* (Munich: Hanser, first published in 1955), and DW 3. He is likely using the former, as the latter was not published until the 1970s, after the composition of "The Unknown God."]

again become God) that his goodness is even better than our word 'good' is able to say.

Is God spirit?

Our faith experiences, sometimes painfully, that these words are correct: God is spirit [*Geist*], and it is not given to us to be able to encounter him like we do corporeal figures. No one has ever seen him [cf. Exodus 33:20, 23, and 1 John 4:12]. But although, indeed precisely because he is spirit, he is very close to us—closer than any object, any person can ever be. We worship him 'in spirit and truth' [John 4:24], he bestows himself on us in an unsayable, 'spiritual' experience, and we await the eternal love exchange of our ‹ awakened ›,[31] 'spiritualized' body with him. It does make sense when we say God is spirit.

There seems to be a special relationship between what we experience in us as 'spirit,' and God. However, we have to be on our guard, because it is all too easy to think of spirit as the opposite of matter. God then belongs to a spiritual region of the totality that everything material no longer has anything to do with. We thereby relegate him to the side of spirit and can hardly avoid equating everything material with the dark, ungodly, and bad. We are no longer far removed from that sinister [*unheilvoll*] two-worlds-schema, which ascribes all that has to do with the body to evil. God belongs only to a part of the world.

But we must not think of God as in opposition to materiality; there is no opposition to God in the realm of what is. The 'material' is just as much an image of God as is 'spirit'! The creator does not belong to a region of the created. He created a material-spiritual world "and saw that it was good" [Genesis 1:4 et passim]. As long as 'spirit' is still somehow imprisoned in the conceptual pair 'spirit/matter,' we should dare to utter the following sentence: no, God is not spirit—he is, rather, the primordial ground that preserves and embraces everything, spirit and matter. He speaks to us in the interplay between the spiritual and the material, without being absorbed

---

31 ['resurrected' is crossed out.]

by them. Faith understands precisely the word 'spirit' [*'Geist'*] differently than we usually do (for example in the case of the 'humanities' [*'Geisteswissenschaften'*][32] and 'natural sciences'). 'Spirit' is, for faith, only the most suitable expression for apprehending the unsayable in periphrastic words.

Our everyday thinking represents things to us; 'spirit,' too, can become such a thing. But precisely that which we are capable of representing to ourselves is not God. God, the only true God worshiped in all religions, the God of the philosophers and the God of Abraham, the Father of Jesus Christ and my Father—he is rather the one who deserves our marveling silence; the one at whom we arrive only when we have cast aside all representational thinking from our faith. When we encounter him in his Godhead in this way, God will appear to us as always 'more unknown.' We have thoughtlessly applied too many representations to God. We have grown accustomed to an image of God and have concealed his true countenance under words which we have hardly thought through.

Is God a 'thou'?

To say 'thou' to God, a simple, loving 'thou,' is certainly the surest way to avoid the danger of false images of God. 'Thou' is the most beautiful name with which we can call on God. The friends of St. Francis of Assisi were somewhat disappointed when they wanted to overhear his prayer one night and secretly followed him into the chapel: they heard him say only this one word over and over again: "thou—thou—thou—."[33]

When I say thou to someone, I experience not only him, but also myself in a new way: by finding my way to the other, I also find my way to myself. I experience that[34] the human being becomes an I only through a thou. Conversely, one will never learn to say thou who is not ready to trouble his I and put it at risk: the risk of encounter. Anyone who has never ventured to say thou, who has never succeeded in stepping before a countenance openly, has missed the

---

32 [Literally, 'sciences of spirit.' *Geist* also means 'mind' in German.]
33 [St. Francis of Assisi, "Laudes Dei altissimi," "The Praises of God."]
34 ["I experience that" is missing in the printed version.]

greatest human lived experience, indeed has missed himself. In the same way, a newborn child will suffer irreparable damage throughout its whole life if it has not had the basic experience of the thou in its mother's arms in the first few months of the child's life. All actual life is an encounter. And every actual encounter is a mystery: I cannot explain the thou, I can only utter it, listen to it, and answer it.

Every singularized [*geeinzelte*] thou is a glimpse of the eternal thou.[35] Whoever begins to say thou will not find rest until he succeeds in addressing [*anzusprechen*] the godly thou and corresponding [*entsprechen*] to it. An all-encompassing ability-to-say-thou is given to being human, and that means he is able and called on to say thou to the all-encompassing. Only because every encounter plays out on the basis of this never-to-be-extinguished primordial encounter with God does every person feel driven to ‹ reach out for a thou also among people ›.[36] Only for this reason does, in a certain way, every beloved being commit the injustice of not being God: it can never completely satisfy and fulfill our power to say thou. God alone can do this. In every friendship, in every conversation, God promises himself. Human love is nourished by the powers of the absolute, godly supply of love. I would never be able to enter into a relationship with a human thou if God had not already, since time immemorial, established a thou-relationship with me. It would not occur to us to swear 'eternal loyalty' to one another if we had not originarily already been drawn into endless exchange of love.

God is the thou on whom our being depends. But God's being does not depend on my saying thou to him. I need God in order to be, but God exists without needing me. Our life depends on God continually speaking his sustaining thou to us. He, however, has no need for our lives in order to live. He bestows his thou on us, but is himself more than this thou.

It is ‹ therefore ›[37] right to say: God is an I more than a thou; for he does not, without remainder, coincide with his thou-relationship with us. First, he says "I am the Lord," and only then "thy God"

---

35 [This sentence comes from Martin Buber, *Ich und du* (Stuttgart: Reclam, 1995), 71; trans. Ronald Gregor Smith, *I and Thou* (Edinburgh: Clark, n.d.), 75.]

36 ['to encounter a thou' is crossed out in the draft. The printed version has 'seek' instead of 'reach out.']

37 [The typescript has *wohl* ('indeed,' 'probably').]

[Exodus 20:2]. One is again also allowed to dare the sentence: no, God is not a 'thou.' He is not just the eternal pledge [*Zusage*] with which he sustains me. The God whom I encounter as a thou is 'God-for-me'; God, however, becomes truly godly again only when we have learned to say 'I-for-God.' He is more than just my counterpart; everything, after all, first comes from him, including this thou-relationship. Already before all saying thou, before all creating of the thou, he is there. Even more than 'toward him' (as toward a partner), I am 'through him and with him and in him'[38] (as through a creator and sustainer). He is God already before any relation to the world or to me.

The God to whom I say thou is the God whom I know. Thus did the existence of Jesus [*das Dasein Jesu*] entirely coincide with this thou-saying: he knew the father and was entirely 'son' [cf. Matthew 11:27]. We, however, who think we are acquainted with God and know everything about him, would do well to rediscover his mystery. Before the mystery one can only be silent; even the thou that we speak does not exhaust it.

We looked at three expressions that we could use to answer the question "What do I know about God?" By right, we should avail ourselves of them only when Christ himself speaks them to us first. For, only when we negate all the titles—'goodness,' 'spirit,' 'thou'— that we so casually impose on God; when God confronts us as an unknown God and we believe we cannot get beyond the mystery of his freedom, only then is our heart ready to receive the message of the incarnate one. Otherwise we will remain stuck to an image of God of which we will have to admit one day (for example, when the thought of death calls into question all familiar modes of representation) that his countenance no longer at all has the radiant power to redeem us [cf. Hebrews 1:3].

The paradox of the known-unknown God can be resolved [*aufgehoben*] only in a living form. For us, this means that we can overcome it only in daily imitation [*Nachleben*][39] of Christ. Yet we are

---

38 [From the Eucharistic doxology: "Per ipsum, et cum ipso, et in ipso." Cf. Romans 11:36.]
39 [This word typically means 'afterlife' or 'survival,' but R.S. seems to mean it more literally as 'living after' and 'in accordance with' Christ. Cf. 1 Corinthians 11:1 et passim, and Thomas à Kempis, *De imitatione Christi*.]

allowed to, and must, bear witness to him in human words. The greatest thing we can say now is that we have experienced God in the crucified one. Only the son is the mediator in whom we feel how terrifyingly real God is, and it is only his words which may we use and say: "God alone is good" (Luke 18:19), "God is spirit" (John 4:24) and "Father, thou..." (Matthew 6:9; 26:39). The familiar God of phraseology becomes the unknown God of mystery; only the latter can speak and attribute [*zusprechen*] to us the one true word, which is his son.

5

A Spiritual Dimension of Technology?

(1966, trans. from the German by Kate Morrison and Tim Steinebach)

On 10 July 1966, the magazine Der christliche Sonntag *(Christian Sunday), where Schürmann's "The Unknown God" had appeared two months prior, published an article by Helmut Meisner on* Gelassenheit. *One week later, the editors published the following reply by Schürmann, adding, by way of introduction: "As a supplement to the article published in the last issue about 'Gelassenheit,'[40] about inner distance from things, here follows an article that—in a concrete and practical manner appropriate to our time—underscores the commitment, the inner religious involvement, of the Christian."*

Our time is marked [*geprägt*] by technology: often enough, we hear this sentence and at every turn we note how true it is. But what does technological progress mean with regard to the judgment and the redemption and the return of Christ? This was asked only recently in this venue.

For some years now, a group of French Dominicans has been going to great lengths to find an answer to this question. Is there a 'Christian' sense—that is, a sense that concerns the resurrected Christ—in our daily 'profane' work? They all work in large companies as engineers or technicians, so they know from experience what it means to be a Christian, to be a priest, in the midst of this working world. Nowadays for all of us, 'real' life is no longer religious life but everyday life that gets by very well without God. This experience has sent them on a joint search. "I am enthusiastic about my work," says one of them, who works at the State Power Plants. "The possibilities of technology have always profoundly interested me. Is there a unity between my profession and my being a Christian? A *search* for unity, yes. What does my work for the company have to do with the coming of Christ among humans? This question

---

40 [Helmut Meisner, "Gelassenheit," *Der Christliche Sonntag*, no. 28 (10 July 1966): 221–22.]

remains quite open for me. Am I living in two worlds? Some of my comrades, who are Christians and do not simply accept the duality, overcome this impression with spiritual detours. By this I mean, for example, the objective *purpose* that my work fulfills: after all, I make electricity! So, from a human point of view, my work has its meaning; it improves people's existence. Or the *intention* that I personally put into my work: service to others, a job well done... Such detours are necessary but not satisfying. By no means do they help in forming a unity. Every Christian who works and thinks a little, must attempt to escape the dilemma for himself. That is why the priest is so important as a 'co-worker' in the workplace. People say that the task of the priest is the preaching of the Word. But fundamentally, my encounters, conversations, and so on are not the most important thing. Rather, the main thing is that the priest takes upon himself to the fullest extent the conditions of life that all people are subjected to today."

Every age needs its spiritual teacher. To be sure, the old 'spiritualities' remain precious to us: we can still learn to pray and learn to believe when we read Augustine's *Confessions*, Thomas à Kempis's *Imitation of Christ*, or Thérèse of Lisieux's *Autobiographical Writings*. But they do not help us form a unity between professional life and the life of faith. The spirituality of our time can only be a "spirituality of the profane." We also do not expect this teaching from an individual, a religious genius (even though Teilhard de Chardin has ingeniously illustrated the path to be taken, for example in his book *The Divine Milieu*), but from a group, a team.

Two Worlds?

The world we are building no longer refers us to God but only to ourselves, we who investigate and improve it. Technology—that is the power within us that is preparing to force everything under human domination. It makes the fundamental claim to be able to see through everything, to produce everything. This is what is so 'profane' about technology: under its grip, the world is desacralized. This circumstance is not to be lamented but assumed and incorporated into our faith. We are in a process that affects all levels of our existence. First, the *gaze* is desacralized. Natural events are supposed to be explained in terms of the natural sciences, mental events psychologically, social events sociologically. What occurs in these realms no longer reveals anything divine to us. The traces that lead from nature to God become sparse, unreliable. God slips out of our field of vision. Our eye now only sees the "facts." But this also means that our *image of the world*, in which we stand, is desacralized (we call "world" the mathematically fixable interlocking of natural events). God has no place therein. The technological world is not directed by God, but by conformity to inherent laws. The thought that through them a personal God could freely act on the human is not only far from us, but actually contradicts our great discovery: namely, that the world is fundamentally transparent. For Paul, the universe groans for redemption through the one who created it [cf. Romans 8:19–23]. We, in contrast, can no longer do much with the words 'creation,' 'redemption.' Industrial products are created nowadays, and people are redeemed (from misery, from war) through a more just social order, a more responsible politics...

Let us be careful not to minimize this growing independence of the world: it is not this or that domain of life that is desacralized but the *supreme values*. Our innermost expectations become 'profane.' Judaism expects an end time in which Yahweh will lead all people to Jerusalem; but, more effectively than Yahweh, international organizations, aid campaigns for developing countries, and publications of scientific results bring people together. Christianity proclaims devotion and humility and hopes for a peace only possible in Christ, but better methods of education, securing living standards, birth control and so on seem to bring about justice and peace faster than a religious way of life. The 'supernatural' way is neither as reliable nor as effective as the profane. And what is ineffective is worthless. Justice, peace, fraternity, freedom: the highest values are desacralized.

The Christian expects no less from the world than an unbeliever. Both endeavor to take from the world what it can give. But let us not be too quick to say that our hope in Christ is in harmony with the hope in progress: more than it may seem to us, even for us the 'worldly world' is moving away from the religious world. We 'live' in a technologized world and only drag the world of faith along uncritically. Our world is no longer whole; it consists of two worlds.

"There are enough," one of the aforementioned priests reports, "who consider the modern desacralization process demonic and see therein nothing but the continued rebellion of Adam against his God. Perhaps such a judgment is not entirely wrong, but it is at least impermissibly hasty. I myself believe that every event can and must be interpreted by faith. I am certain that the present desacralization of the world carries within it a call from the Lord to which we must respond."

Inner Law of Progress

The call of God reaches us in technology itself; it is not added to it somehow. A spiritual dimension is to be looked for in technology itself. Does it reveal to the believer a structure that does not first become 'Christian' via detours? Our question aims at the inner law according to which technology develops. — In a somewhat bold-sounding thesis it can be said: every instance of progress, as far as it serves the welfare of mankind, is a *paschal event*, is necessarily 'death and resurrection'—be it 'profane' or 'religious,' be it expressly intended as service to the Kingdom of God or not.

Technological development shows itself initially as 'dying.' The example of the researcher may serve as an indication for this: he must constantly be ready to question his knowledge again. He must always be able to 'die' again to the truths he discovered; otherwise, he hinders research. It is not infrequent that a scientist no longer knows how to die to his own ideas—and thus no longer 'lives' as a researcher. Every genuine instance of progress in technology means a departure into uncharted territory. In this, the 'law of technology' resembles the fate of Abraham, who was the first to set out on the path. Progress is the élan that shatters all systems that establish security. Not only to believe in progress but to cooperate in it is only possible for those who are "poor in spirit," who "hunger and thirst for justice," who can "die to themselves" [cf. Matthew 5:3, 5:6, and Romans 6:1–8]. This is one side of the transition—of the "pascha."

Progress is also a source of new life. Technology promises humans a 'better life.' Bringing the means of the technological world to perfection is to *have faith*: that more to life is possible; it is to *hope*: that progress will not be delayed on earth; it is to *love*: that all people may enjoy the new [cf. 1 Corinthians 13:13]. Technological development only pushes forward because man feels constantly attracted to the prospect of "more life" [cf. John 10:10]. The image of the future, which, even if unconsciously, is in the mind of everyone who believes in his work, has something boundlessly optimistic about it: everything will be new, "every tear will be wiped from their eyes, and there will neither be sorrow nor lamentation nor toil" [cf. Revelation 21:4]. The secret driving force of technological progress is nothing other than the confidence dwelling in the human being in what Christians call resurrection.

We should not be surprised to again find the age-old scheme of Christianity in the seemingly most mundane domain of our lives: toward glory through suffering and death. The risen Christ is present in the power of his effects, in our midst, in everything that concerns the human being. We live "in him" [cf. Galatians 2:20]: it would be much more surprising not to again find anything of his glory of grace in everyday profane existence. Certainly, the 'better life' toward which technology assists us *is* not already the Christian resurrection; but the point here is to make an inner law perceptible in technology that, far from any explicit reference to Christianity, nevertheless follows Christianity's ownmost rhythm. Technological progress runs through the same phases as our own consciously lived Christian existence: death and resurrection as a passage to a new life in faith, hope, and love.

"Heal Thyself" [cf. Luke 4:23]

Mind you, this is only the 'attempt' at a spirituality of the profane. We are by no means equating the achievements of technology with the arrival of the Kingdom of God either. A second aspect of the 'inner law of progress' should show this. Progress not only has a paschal character, it is also the *expectation of salvation*. In the domain of technology, just as in any other domain of life, salvation is always still to come. This is shown very well by the fact that technology progresses according to the same rule, even if unconsciously, as Christian existence. It secretly hopes for what Revelation calls the "heavenly Jerusalem" [cf. Hebrews 12:22 and Revelation 21:2], but it cannot build it itself. What technology promises, it cannot deliver. What human beings hope for, they cannot give themselves. Only the dreamer thinks that his self-made salvation can ever satisfy him.

One does not need to be a Christian in order to ascertain this. As a Christian, however, one can say: in technology the human being encounters the offer of salvation [*Heils*], but technology does not already 'heal' ['*heilt*'] the human being. In technology he indeed experiences the saving act of Christ in an 'anonymous' movement toward the Kingdom of God, but 'technological salvation' cannot claim ultimacy. Ultimate salvation can only be accepted by receiving. That the ironic exclamation "heal thyself" runs counter to the essence of being human is part of the experience of every life. The efforts at progress prepare the human being to receive his *ultimate* redemption in Christ.

Technology cannot ultimately heal itself. The Christian, and only the Christian, can say that it is entirely directed toward a 'savior.' Every trace of paschal death and resurrection in the world since the coming of the Lord is a trace of Christ. Perhaps in this way the path on which science and technology are progressing today leads us better to Christ, and in him to God, than do the "divine traces in nature" mentioned above. Every awakening to new faith, hope, and love—no matter how 'profane' it may be—is already a reflection of him who calls himself the perfecter of all who truly believe, hope, and love. Every healed need (and such healing is, after all, the greatest task of technology) is already a visible ray of the splendor of the invisible divine salvation.

One Single Love

To point out a spiritual dimension in technology does not mean to devalue faith. Technology is under a paschal law, and as technology it is already an indication of salvation in Christ—but this only indicates the direction in which it aims. It is not yet the reality of the Kingdom of God, but the latter is already concealed in it as something possible, even as a beginning. It finally becomes real in only one unique experience: the encounter with the risen Christ.

We have attempted to show to what extent the hope of humans for a world reshaped by technology, science, and progress does not run counter to the *faithful* hope for redemption *in Christ*. To want to perfect the world does not mean to compete with the perfection in Christ; worldly expectation is the visible garment of Christian expectation. We should not only say (to the believer): Hope in God, and it is enough; but, rather (to all humans): Hope for a better world, and it is enough. For *every* human is called into the kingdom, whether he has heard of Christ or not. Hope in the world (and work on it), and you already hope in God (and work on his kingdom). Teilhard once said: "Even if I were to lose my hope in the Triune God and his incarnate son, I would still have hope in the world."[41] We cannot demand that what lives in all humans as supernatural hope is to be felt by them otherwise than 'naturally.' Only the faithful gaze sees how far the 'unfaithful hope' really reaches. And only he who has recognized this dimension in profane hope lives consciously in a unity of faith in this world and faith in the beyond. Many nonbelievers, however, already live in this unity unconsciously.

At the beginning, we pointed out the difficulty with establishing a unity between the life of faith and the professional life. We have now started to grasp such a unity: something dynamic dwells within progress, the tip of which aims at Christ. Progress moves forward in the direction of a fullness of life, which is only intimated by it. But the Christian is permitted to call it: glory, resurrection, vision of God... A life becomes whole when it lives entirely out of this one dynamism. There is no longer a gap between prayer and work, Sunday and every day: work *is already* work for the Kingdom of God, and every day *is already* the Lord's Day.

Let us attempt to name more precisely what concurrently drives humans on in their 'profane' and their 'religious' life. The source from which both flow wholly united is none other than *love*. There is but *one* love: in it we create a better world with every effort, and it also drives us to encounter Christ in faith. It is impossible to love Christ without loving others and impossible to love others without coming closer to Christ *in the same movement*. Trying to find a principle other than love that would accomplish completeness will lead to nothing. Love does not belong to Christians, but to all humans,

---

41 [Loose quotation of *Comment je crois*, in *Œuvres de Pierre Teilhard de Chardin*, vol. 10 (Paris: Seuil, 1969), p. 120 (trans. mod.); trans. René Hague, *Christianity and Evolution* (San Diego, CA: Harvest/Harcourt, 1974), 99: "If, as the result of some interior revolution [*renversement*], I were to lose in succession my faith in Christ, my faith in a personal God, and my faith in spirit, I feel that I shall continue *to believe* invincibly *in the world.*"]

and Christ was not the first to teach, "Love one another" [cf. John 13:34]. But: love, that is Christ. He who abides in love abides in him [cf. 1 John 4:16]. That is why love is already "with the Father" [cf. John 1:1, 1 John 1:2] as that sign belonging to all of mankind, under which all situations in life let themselves be joined together. Whether it is baptized or not, provided it really lives out of the dynamic of which we spoke, love can lead nowhere else but to God. That is why we should also forgo many a strange way of speaking, which still pretends that God and the world are in competition for the favor of our love: to love humans "for the sake of Christ's love" is the psychologically quite complicated undertaking of a Christianity that seems to know nothing of John's word: "God is love, and he who abides in love abides in God" [1 John 4:16].

A Process of Transformation That Reveals the Ultimate Meaning ...

The Christian, and in particular the priest, must actively participate in the process of transformation in the world. From within, they should reveal the 'spiritual dimension of technology'—that is, the true direction of the aim of technological progress. Through their daily visible example among humans, they are to exemplify in their lives the ultimate meaning of working for a better world, namely love. They should show what love authentically is: "Love is always given by God. I do not believe that human love should be guided in two paths—one leading to God, the other leading to humans. For we will be judged by whether we have actively helped to liberate humans. It seems to me that the one who has found *agapē*—that is, who loves as Christ loved—is already saved. I think it is more important for love to grow—even covertly—than for Christ to be proclaimed to a community into which he himself has not already been carried by way of a love lived practically. Whoever feeds the hungry and washes the feet of his brothers belongs to God, whether he knows him or not. Such love is spreading. I know from experience how really contagious it can be, even in the workplace."

6

Easter on Christmas: A Sermon on Love and Death

(1966, trans. from the French by Ian Alexander Moore)

Unlike "The Unknown God," Schürmann appears to have actually delivered the following text as a sermon during the season of Advent in 1966. Since the typescript on which this edition is based bears no title, we have given it one in accordance with its themes of love, death, and eternal life. Schürmann's sermon appears here for the first time in any language.

Fourth Sunday of Advent [18 December] 1966

Lovers swear to each other: I will love you forever. They say these words, but a fissure is there in them that contradicts them. Certainly, the fissure of time: one never knows what the years will bring. But if the trust is strong, and part of the road is traveled together, their 'pact' will survive. No, there is another fissure that it would be deceitful to deny: we will love each other forever, yes, but we will also die.

The thought of death, its certainty, seems secretly to be stronger than hope. The photos that show me as an eighteen-year-old, terribly in love with a young girl, carry a sad face, or at least a grave one. Unadmitted, the conviction is there: that it is naive to hope! The end casts its shadow upon the moments that are lived the most intensely.

There are old couples who admit: it was during the war that we were most in love. Is this surprising? Death, the unceasingly imminent end of life, makes loving presence a sacred presence, to the point that artistic creation has always been nourished by this entanglement of love [*l'amour*] and death [*la mort*].

Let us talk, my love, and we will forget death.

Furthermore: love learns how valuable it is from death. I hasten to learn to love better, to exist better: the profound reason for this is the certainty I have of death. If we had within us the feeling of an unending life, would we pay the price, day after day, to live better?

And yet, do we even know death? We know the death of others; the death that looms over us always remains distant. We are certain about our death, but we do not have the experience of it.

This is why, moreover, we sing at our ease: the Cross of Christ is our glory.[42] We have no experience of death. When we speak of it, it becomes an irritating song of glory or of melodrama, if not a stupid banality: "oh yes, everyone must die."

The most precious gift that the feeling of death can give us is to force us to smile about ourselves. Briefcase in hand, bowler hat on head, with a hurried step, the man of importance disappears at the turn of the street; James Bond awaits him there.—This is melodrama, I know, but not without significance. Death is nothing, literally speaking, but it has this strange power of annihilating everything that gives consistency to our days. It is not wrong to say that it is present at the heart of life.

* * *

These few days that still separate us from Christmas are saturated with hope. We repeat to ourselves: Jesus Christ has come, he comes—in each human life, in each Mass—and he will come at the end of the world. "I am with you always; yes, to the end of time" [Matthew 28:20]; we believe it, we hope for it.

But is the life of Christ in us strong enough to vanquish the certainty of death? Jesus lives, he is there at each moment of our existence. But so little do we experience him; thus, were not Hemingway and Marilyn Monroe right to hasten their death?

It is necessary to say that Christmas is no match for the reality of death. The genealogies that we will read, the titles of 'King,' 'Son of God,' 'Messiah': all of this expresses no more than a presence among us. An admirable presence, to be sure, but one that is insufficient.

---

42 [Cf. Philippians 2:6–11, thought to have been a hymn in the early church; repeatedly set to music.]

If God became incarnate only to dwell among us, who will contradict Faust when he cries out: two souls dwell, alas, in my heart…?[43] The Buddhists are right, then; at least they do not treat the sacred as a historical individual or as a morsel of bread.

If God became incarnate only to dwell among us, death will continue eternally to betray our most sincere generosities.—This is why, in celebrating Christmas, we must have a thought for Easter as well. He who will be born will also be the one who will vanquish death, has already vanquished it.

In a village not far from the Mediterranean, a young man has just died. At a public square, typically deserted at this hour owing to the heat, small groups gather. Two women above all, who have become unsightly by the pain, are inconsolable. For them, suddenly, death has entered in its true countenance: the end, the end of an existence. Even when Jesus turns up, Martha and Mary do not stop mourning Lazarus [John 11:1–44]. The simple presence of the Master is not enough to reassure them. It is still necessary for God to manifest himself, through him, as the vanquisher of death. Only then is the arrival of the Son of God welcome.

Because God has resurrected his Son on Easter morning, Christmas can no longer be the sacrament of the simple presence of God. His birth for us, in us, is from now on a birth that saves. God coming to save us from death: if this is Christmas, it is truly a Christian celebration for us. Saved from death, our existence will dare to hope, without having to silence the inner feeling of its unfolding in the shadow of the end.

God exists: it is great to know this, and every day we must experience it again. God is near: we are right to celebrate Christmas with the most pomp and splendor possible. But when the certainty of death comes to verify our existence, only the following affirmation will enable it to resist the ordeal: God saves.

---

43 ["Zwei Seelen wohnen, ach! in meiner Brust." Johann Wolfgang von Goethe, *Faust*, part 1, line 1112.]

7

The Philosophical Presuppositions of Meister Eckhart's Christology

(1967, trans. from the French by Karl von der Luft)

This early paper was written in conjunction with Schürmann's studies at Le Saulchoir and, less directly, at the University of Freiburg. It is the earliest extant draft for what would eventually become Wandering Joy. *For comments on it from Schürmann's teachers Claude Geffré and Bernhard Welte, see Appendices 3 and 4, below.*

In the history of ideas, Meister Eckhart appeared at an instant when a peak had already been reached and when the blossoming of new ideas which one had just witnessed were beginning to be systematized, according to the needs of the school. He arrived too late to participate in the gigantic effort of construction which gave rise to High Scholasticism, and too early to inaugurate a new era of thought. Meister Eckhart was probably still able to know Albert the Great. In any case, his intellectual universe was permeated by St. Thomas. As Provincial and then as Prior of the convent of Strasbourg he preached Thomas' doctrine to the Dominican nuns who were then numerous in the Rhine valley.

Nevertheless, Meister Eckhart is not a commentator on Saint Thomas. He instead appropriates some of the latter's fundamental intuitions and makes manifest in them those extreme consequences which Saint Thomas himself was no doubt too prudent to recognize. Even in his language, Meister Eckhart attaches himself to paradox, rejecting any ambition to establish a school. Meister Eckhart is too original an author for there to be an Eckhartism. He thus leaves to the side, in the Thomistic edifice, everything that does not serve his personal intuition.

1) The intuition of Meister Eckhart

This fundamental intuition is difficult to grasp and impossible to explicate. It is a path that thought must take and which demands to be followed by existence itself. This is why Heidegger calls Eckhart the *"Lese- und Lebemeister"* [master of letters and life] [GA 13: 89].

In sermon No. 2, Eckhart says: "May man become void as he was when he was not—*Der Mensch soll ledig werden wie er war, da er nicht war.*"[44] The first stage of the itinerary proposed by Meister Eckhart is 'divestment' [*'dépouillement'*] or 'detachment' (*Abgeschiedenheit*). To become void as I was when I was not yet; to become what I was, i.e. nothingness—this is what this thought commits one to. The same sermon uses other expressions for this reality: 'to become a virgin'; 'to become free of all images.' I must leave [*laisser*] all creatures in order to choose the itinerary into God.[45] "Where the creature ends, God begins to be" (Pr. 6)[46]—such expressions are philosophical rather than spiritual affirmations. To void oneself of all creatures is to think the created properly as created, thus in its dependence relative to the creator. Creatures are nothingness because of their being created: "All creatures are pure nothingness. I am not saying they are little things or valueless: they are pure nothingness. That which has no being is nothingness" (Pr. 4).[47] Creatures have no being; their being resides in God: "all creatures grow green in God" (Pr. 56).[48]

I will become "void as I was when I was not" by abandoning in me all that belongs to the created. This *'Gelassenheit'* [releasement]

---

44 [Unless otherwise indicated, R.S. cites and translates from Josef Quint's translation of Eckhart into Modern German: Meister Eckehart, *Deutsche Predigten und Traktate* (Munich: Hanser, 1963); we shall provide pagination for the 1979 edition (Diogenes Taschenbuch). The sermon numbers sometimes differ in DW. R.S.'s French renderings have been translated directly into English. Cf. Eckehart, *Deutsche Predigten und Traktate*, 159. DW 1: 25,2 (Pr. 2, "Intravit Iesus in quoddam castellum").]

45 [Cf. Bonaventure's *Itinerarium mentis in Deum* (Journey of the Mind into God, 1259).]

46 [Eckehart, *Deutsche Predigten und Traktate*, 180. DW 1: 92,7 (Pr. 5b, "In hoc apparuit").]

47 [Eckehart, *Deutsche Predigten und Traktate*, 171. DW 1: 69,8–70,2 (Pr. 4, "Omne datum optimum").]

48 [Eckehart, *Deutsche Predigten und Traktate*, 413. DW 3: 247,5 (Pr. 72, "Videns Iesus turbas."]

wherein I let be what is without attaching myself to it, without claiming to make it exist when God alone makes it exist, this attention to the divine being [*être*] in each and every created being [*étant créé*] is only possible because the spirit is capable of turning back upon itself. "The more the soul is clear, naked, and poor, the less it has in it of creatures; and the more it is void of all things that are not God—the more also it becomes God and grasped in God and one with God" (DW 5: 32,8-11 [*BgT*]). The second stage of thought—certainly not chronologically, but in the order of discovery—is the recognition of a similarity, even an identity: the identity of myself [*le moi*] turning back upon itself and God. The man who detaches himself from the created resembles divine simplicity, and "similarity results from unity [..., R.S.] this is why neither the one nor the other will cease [i.e. neither man nor God, R.S.] until they be united in the One" (DW 5: 33,1-4 [*BgT*]).

There is a power in man that is capable of grasping God as he is in himself. Meister Eckhart insists on this very often. "In this power, God is like an ember or a flame, with all its riches, all its sweetness, and all its delights. [..., R.S.] it is a force in the spirit [..., R.S.] a guard of the spirit [..., R.S.] a light of the spirit [..., R.S.] a spark. Now I say: it is none of these, but nevertheless is something that is elevated above them higher than heaven is elevated above the earth. [..., R.S.] This is free of all names and void of all forms [..., R.S.] one and simple as God is one and simple [..., R.S.] the castle in the soul [..., R.S.] elevated above all particularity" (Pr. 2).[49]

There are many texts which treat this similarity and unity between the ground [*fond*] of the soul and God: "Here, the ground [*abîme*] of God is my ground and my ground is the ground of God" (Pr. 6);[50] "the soul takes its being immediately from God, and this is why God is closer to the soul than it is to itself; this is why God is in the ground of the soul with all his divinity" (Pr. 11).[51] If Meister Eckhart thinks the creature in its bond of entitative dependence with regard

---

49 [Eckehart, *Deutsche Predigten und Traktate*, 162-63. DW 1: 35,5-42,1 (Pr 2., "Intravit Iesus in quoddam castellum").]

50 [Eckehart, *Deutsche Predigten und Traktate*, 180. DW 1: 90,8 (Pr. 5b, "In hoc apparuit").]

51 [Eckehart, *Deutsche Predigten und Traktate*, 201. DW 1: 162,4-6 (Pr. 10, "In diebus suis").]

to God, one could say that he thinks man in a unity—an entitative identity—with him. The being of man is the being of God because God has put a power in the ground of man, a power that is not created and that is God himself.

What does this mean? All that is created is finite; but man escapes this condition by the grace of the spirit: this is the phenomenon of the infinity of the spirit, *'quodammodo omnia'* [in a certain way all things], which is at the origin of the doctrine of detachment; for only the intelligence, receptive to all that is, can void itself of all images in order to receive God. The mysticism of Meister Eckhart is a mysticism of the intellect. He distinguishes indeed a third faculty of knowledge beyond sensibility and reason, a faculty "which grasps God in his pure, proper being [..., R.S.] which grasps him without clothing [*in seinem Kleidhaus*, R.S.]" (Pr. 12).[52] This knowledge also precedes the will: "Knowledge [*bekantnisse*] holds the key, it opens and bursts in and finds God unveiled, and tells its companion, the will, of what it has just taken possession [..., R.S.]. Knowledge precedes" (Pr. 3);[53] and "[knowledge, *vernünfticheit*] looks into the interior of the divinity and penetrates into all its angles" (Pr. 40).[54] It transports man into "the pure being of God, and this is the pure being of the spirit" (Pr. 35).[55] It would thus be false to speak of a 'spiritual creature,' for that which is spiritual is not created, but divine. The notions 'created,' 'finite,' and 'nothingness' are thus opposed to the notions 'uncreated,' 'spirit,' and 'being.' To these latter, God is present without mediation.

But as soon as it is established, this kinship at the level of the spirit must be broken [*cassée*] anew. This is the third and final stage: the supreme power in man does not care about the Father, the Son, or the Spirit; it passes over the goodness, the truth, the mercy, and even the being of God. It breaks [*rompt*] (*durchbricht*) all this and goes even beyond God. This movement is admirably described in

---

52 [Eckehart, *Deutsche Predigten und Traktate*, 210. DW 1: 183,4 (Pr. 11, "Impletum est"). Literally "in his dress room" or "closet" (*kleithûs*), where he is naked.]
53 [Eckehart, *Deutsche Predigten und Traktate*, 166. DW 1: 52,9–12 (Pr. 3, "Nunc scio vere").]
54 [Eckehart, *Deutsche Predigten und Traktate*, 348. DW 3: 178,3–179,1 (Pr. 69, "Modicum et iam non videbitis me").]
55 [Eckehart, *Deutsche Predigten und Traktate*, 320. DW 3: 322,6 (Pr. 76, "Videte qualem caritatem").]

Sermon No. 32, which treats the divine ideas, i.e. the creation in God before it emanates from him: "When I still remained in my first cause, I had no God and I was the cause of myself."[56] This expression 'causa sui,' traditionally reserved for God alone, clearly shows that this passage concerns the unity of all things in God wherein they subsist as eternal ideas. To conceive in this way the created before it is actually created is to think of it as identical with God; but this identity is an identity of the 'not yet' which has as its sole purpose to manifest the origin of all things as they are. God, creatures, myself, all primitive images (*Ur-bilder*) were equal in God. Although images of different things, they were identical at the beginning [*principe*] of creation and they were God. For all that is in God is God. But Meister Eckhart goes further still: "Before there were creatures, God was not yet God."[57] God became God only when the world emerged from its origin. "When I emanated from God, all things exclaimed: God is."[58] And: "If I were not, God would not be either; it is I who am the cause of God being God."[59] And yet, in this origin in the divinity, beyond 'God,' the soul retains the power of returning. In this sense, it is more than God. "This is why I pray to God to render me quit of God, because my essential being is beyond God."[60] And Meister Eckhart ends this sermon by reassuring the nuns who listen to him: "It is not necessary to know this."[61]

The intuition of Meister Eckhart concerns this identity with the divinity in view of which man must detach himself and let that which is be. We will see that his concept of identity has nothing static or 'metaphysical' about it in the sense of a substantial coinci-

---

[56] [Eckehart, *Deutsche Predigten und Traktate*, 304. DW 2: 492,3–4 (Pr. 52, "Beati pauperes spiritu").]
[57] [Eckehart, *Deutsche Predigten und Traktate*, 305. DW 2: 492,8–9 (Pr. 52, "Beati pauperes spiritu").]
[58] [Eckehart, *Deutsche Predigten und Traktate*, 308. DW 2: 504,5 (Pr. 52, "Beati pauperes spiritu").]
[59] [Eckehart, *Deutsche Predigten und Traktate*, 308. DW 2: 504,2–3 (Pr. 52, "Beati pauperes spiritu").]
[60] [Eckehart, *Deutsche Predigten und Traktate*, 308. DW 2: 502,6–7 (Pr. 52, "Beati pauperes spiritu").]
[61] [Eckehart, *Deutsche Predigten und Traktate*, 309. DW 2: 504,3 (Pr. 52, "Beati pauperes spiritu").]

dence, but that he thinks of it on the contrary as an accomplishment and an event—he would say: a 'birth.'

2) The birth of the Son

a) The birth of the Son in the soul

The soul that takes the divinity beyond God, that takes it in its unity and in its 'desert' (*in seiner Einheit und in seiner Einöde; in seiner Wüste und in seinem Grunde*" [in its oneness and in its wasteland; in its desert and in its ground], Pr. 11[62])—this soul becomes "as it was when it was not." It 'becomes' so: this is to say that the identity with the One ought not to be represented as the simultaneous presence of two things subject to the same 'ontic' conditions, but as an actuality (*ein Gewirke*)[63] which ravishes the very being of man in his truth, in an 'energetic' identity. "The spark in the soul [..., R.S.] maintains itself ceaselessly in the being of God. God gives himself ceaselessly to the soul in a perpetual becoming. [...This spark, R.S.] is always new and young as in a never-ending becoming" (Pr. 21).[64] It is this becoming which Meister Eckhart calls Filiation: "Ceaselessly the Father engenders the Son" (Pr. 7).[65] The return to original unity, which is the truth of the human being, is here expressed in terms of birth. For when God emerges out of this primitive unity in order to create, he gives birth to himself as Father and to man as his son. This is why the soul is called to become what it already is: one with the Father via the birth of the Son in the soul. The soul itself cooperates in the eternal filiation in God, its principle being beyond God the Father or the Son. Cooperating in the birthing of God, it is thus even more than the locus of the Son's birth: the soul is the Father. In the primitive unity, anterior to God and to the soul,

---

62 [Eckehart, *Deutsche Predigten und Traktate*, 206. DW 1: 171,14–15 (Pr. 10, "In diebus suis").]

63 ['Fabric,' from *wirken*, 'to operate,' but also 'to weave.' R.S. seems to have in mind a gathering (*Ge-*) of being at work (*Wirken*). Cf. DW 1: 114,4–5 (Pr. 6, "Iusti vivent in aeternum"), where one finds *gewürke*.]

64 [Eckehart, *Deutsche Predigten und Traktate*, 249. DW 1: 349,4–8 (Pr. 20b, "Homo quidam fecit cenam magnam").]

65 [Eckehart, *Deutsche Predigten und Traktate*, 185; 186. DW 1: 109,7; 112,1 (Pr. 6, "Iusti vivent in aeternum").]

there is "one life alone and one being alone and one actuality alone" (Pr. 7).[66]

"When I emanated from God, all things exclaimed: God is." The profound sense of such an affirmation is that God engenders me for himself and engenders himself for me: I participate in that paternity which makes God be, just as much as it makes the created be. Because I am Son, I am also Father. To be born by God is both to be birthed and to give birth. God is birthed when he engenders a being [*être*] capable of turning back upon itself—turning back upon *him*, that is, by actively accepting to be [*d'être*] and by recognizing that he who begets *is*.

> In eternity the Father engenders his Son equal to himself [..., R.S.] To this I add: he has engendered his Son from my soul. Not only is my soul with him, and he with it as his like, but he is inside it; and the Father engenders the Son in the soul in the same manner in which he engenders him in eternity and not otherwise. He must do this whether it pleases him or not. The Father ceaselessly engenders the Son, and I say further: he engenders me as his son, and as the same son. I say still more: he engenders me not only as his Son, but he engenders me as himself, and himself as me [*er gebiert mich als sich und sich als mich*, R.S.]. (Pr. 7)[67]

The supreme affirmation which can be made of God is that he begets. What can be said of God can also be said of the soul, just as much a mystery as God is himself, and indeed the same mystery as God. The soul that has emerged from the unity of divinity is not only begotten—I am not only Son—but it begets in its turn—I am also Father. Both the eternal identity before creation between me and the divinity and the energetic identity after creation between the soul and its principle lead beyond filiation. The birth of the Son is not the last word Meister Eckhart has to say within the framework of Christianity; he speaks of it only in order to prepare for the mystery of paternity in the soul:

---

66 [Eckehart, *Deutsche Predigten und Traktate*, 185. DW 1: 109,11 (Pr. 6, "Iusti vivent in aeternum").]
67 [Eckehart, *Deutsche Predigten und Traktate*, 185. DW 1: 109,2-10 (Pr. 6, "Iusti vivent in aeternum").]

> "*In principio*": this word makes us understand that we are an only Son whom the Father has eternally engendered in the hidden darkness of the eternal 'concealment' [*Verborgenheit*, R.S.] and who is nonetheless immanent at the first commencement of the emptiness [*Lauterkeit*, R.S.] which is a plenitude of all emptiness. Here I have reposed eternally and slept in the hidden knowledge of the eternal Father, immanent and not emerging out of it. Out of this emptiness he has eternally engendered me as his only Son in the image of his eternal paternity, that I might be Father and engender him from whom I was birthed. (Pr. 23)[68]

We touch here on the other side of the mysticism of the intellect: *nous* for Aristotle is not only receptivity, *tabula rasa*, detachment and emptiness, as Meister Eckhart would say; it is also spontaneity, activity, *energeia*. It is in this sense that we must understand the passages of the sermons related to the begetting of God in the detached soul: Eckhart pushes an Aristotelian and Thomistic intuition to the extreme, to the point of translating it into the theological terms of Father and Son, principles secondary to a soul which is, just like the divinity, originally one. When Meister Eckhart speaks of the "two sons of intelligence," he refers explicitly to Aristotle: "One [of these two sons] is possibility; the other is actuality. A pagan master says: the soul in its power [i.e. intelligence as possibility, R.S.] has the ability to become all things. In the power of actuality, it resembles the Father and engenders all things into a new being [*être*]" (Pr. 51).[69]

The ultimate unity which precedes paternity and filiation, both in the divinity and in the soul, is the one origin of the one divinity and the one soul: "I affirm against God, angels, souls, and all creatures [*trutz Gotte, trutz den Engeln, trutz den Seelen und allen Kreaturen*, R.S.] that they cannot separate the soul from God at the place where it is the image of God" (Pr. 52).[70]—We will have to come back to the

---

68 [Eckehart, *Deutsche Predigten und Traktate*, 258. DW 1: 382,3–383,1 (Pr. 22 "Ave gratia plena").]
69 [Eckehart, *Deutsche Predigten und Traktate*, 394. DW 2: 220,2–221,1 (Pr. 37 "Vir meus servus tuus mortuus est").]
70 [Eckehart, *Deutsche Predigten und Traktate*, 399, modified. DW 2: 329,5–6 (Pr. 43 "Adolescens, tibi dico").]

question of knowing [*savoir*] in what sense this unity is cognizable [*connaissable*].

b) *The birth of the Son in history*

So far, we have examined the German works of Meister Eckhart exclusively. It is significant that he treats the historical Christ only in the part of his work, in the Latin language, that was intended for teaching in the faculties of theology. The historical Jesus appears in this author only in a scholarly context.

The principal text on the Incarnation is found in the commentary on St. John: "God the Word, the Son, assumed a human nature in order to teach us that we can become sons of God" (LW 3: 240, no. 288 [*In Ioh.*]). The first sentence of the text gives the two motives that Meister Eckhart assigns to the Incarnation: God became man in order to instruct us in a new revelation, and in order to constitute us as Sons of God. He adds a third motive elsewhere (Pr. 23): God wished to show himself passible and to ransom humanity by his suffering.[71] However, the principal motive does seem to be that of filial adoption (whereas for St. Thomas the principal motive is the redemption of sin). It is remarkable that Meister Eckhart, in order to explicate his thought on the Incarnation, appeals to the distinction between nature and person. Our text continues: "It is to be noted that God the Word has assumed a human nature and not a human person" (LW 3: 241, no. 289 [*In Ioh.*]). Then he gives five determinations of his concept of nature: 1) it belongs univocally to all of us and to Christ; 2) it is more intimate to each man than he is to himself; 3) it is the principle of the love of neighbor; 4) it loves God in every being [*être*] more than it loves itself; 5) it is a cause of joy for all those who belong to Christ.

The Incarnation of the Word is the condition for the possibility of its birth in me, for in it God has assumed human nature, i.e., that which is most intimate to each being [*être*] and that which in it loves God. If he had assumed only a person, this assumption would not concern us. That is why Meister Eckhart often repeats: "*Christus naturam assumpsit, non personam*" [Christ assumed (or took on) a

---

[71] [Cf. Eckehart, *Deutsche Predigten und Traktate*, 257. DW I: 378,1–379,1 (Pr. 22 "Ave, gratia plena").]

nature, not a person] (e.g. S. XX ["Attendite a falsis prophetis"], no. 199 [LW 4: 184]; S. VI ["In hoc apparuit gratia dei"], no. 57 [LW 4: 56–57]; S. XXV ["Gratia dei sum id quod sum"], no. 263 [LW 4: 240]). In his defense at the Cologne trial he insists twice: "*Deus assumpsit prima intentione hominem, naturam scilicet, non personam*" [God assumed, in his first intention, man, namely a nature, not a person] (cited in LW 4: 184, note 4 [S. XX, "Attendite a falsis prophetis"]).[72] Let us note that in this question too his Christology diverges from that of St. Thomas (IIIa P., q.4 a.4: *assumptio ista terminatur ad personam* [the assumption terminates in a person"]).[73] The reason for this is the fact that he [Meister Eckhart] places the principal accent on the birth of the Son in me, which requires that I 'void' myself of everything that touches the person. God is the 'natural' place of all things (cf. *In Ioh.*, nos. 199 to 208 [LW 3: 168,1–176,9]) in whom they tend to rest as in their origin. Human nature, assumed by Christ "*ut vere, proprie et per substantiam sit homo*" [in order that he be man truly, properly, and substantially] (S. LII, no. 523 [LW 4: 437 ("Induimini dominum Iesum Christum")]), is henceforth the locus of divine filiation. The grace of the Incarnation has already brought human nature back into the primitive One; this is why each man is called to divest himself in his person of what it has of the created and to return to what it has of the spiritual, the uncreated. The spiritual nature, assumed by the Word, becomes the principle of return to the One. "It is therefore given to each man to become Sons of God, '*per substantiam*' [substantially] in Christ, '*adoptive et per gratiam*' [by adoption and grace] in himself. […] For this Word penetrates even into God, being at the beginning [*principe*], in the Father, in the bosom of the Father, in his source and in his hidden abyss, i.e. in his intellect, in the simplicity where he returns entirely upon himself [*ubi se toto redit super se totum*, R.S.]" (ibid.) [LW 4: 437–38]. This text seems to us to be typical: proceeding from the Christ of history it goes immediately to the Word subsisting with the Father, and then to the 'source' anterior to the distinction between Father and Son, in order to bring this source together with the reflexivity of the intellect.

---

72 [Now in LW 5: 335, no. 68 (*Acta*).]

73 [From a question in the *Summa theologiæ* on "Whether the Son of God should have assumed a human nature abstracted from all individuals."]

Detachment acquires its true significance through the concept of person. The experience of the birth of the Son in the spiritual nature comes at the cost of detachment from 'the instinct of possession' (this is how one could translate the Middle German *'eigenschaft'*; Quint translates: *Ich-Bindung* [I/ego-attachment]; cf. e.g. Pr. 2 DW 1: 25,8 ["Intravit Iesus in quoddam castellum"]).[74] Nature will thus become what it already is: the locus of divine filiation. Christ is Son of God by the very fact that he constitutes us as Sons of God: "We must not imagine that Christ is Son of God by this filiation or this image, and that the just and deiform man would be Son of God by some other [filiation or image]" (*In Ioh.*, no. 119, LW 3: 104). Meister Eckhart here reveals his profound way of thinking about the historical Christ. He is less interested in [*s'attache moins*] reflecting on Christ's ontological constitution, and is content to underline that in him God has taken back human nature into his bosom. In Christ, as in the Christian, it is God who acts; Christ does not have a superhuman 'causality' any more than the Christian does. If causality is necessary (Meister Eckhart does not think in these schemes which flatter the imagination), then Christ and the Christian legitimately participate in that [causality] which belongs to God. And Meister Eckhart comments on the verse of St. John [John 16:28]—"I issued from the Father and came into the world"—by saying: "*per creationem, non tantum per incarnationem*" [through creation, not only through incarnation] (S. XXV, 1, no. 253, LW 4: 231–32 ["Gratia dei sum id quod sum"]). Creation and Incarnation are linked by a continuum at the level of divine filiation. One could say that Meister Eckhart's thought is 'Christian' not so much because he interrogates the ontology of the incarnate Word, but because he proposes a path to existence that is an 'imitation of Jesus,' a *kenōsis* of the Christian. He seeks less the intelligibility of the historical God-Man than the intelligibility of what in modern terminology one might call the moment of conversion. He leaves it to "*doctores meos collegas*" [my professional colleagues] (*In Ioh.*)[75] to answer the question "Who

---

[74] [Quint's translation is in DW 1: 434. Cf. Eckehart, *Deutsche Predigten und Traktate*, 159.]

[75] [The reference ("*doctores meos collegas*") is rather to a passage in Eckhart's defense at Cologne regarding the uncreated aspect of the soul. See LW 5: 548 (*Acta*), as well as *ME*, 56–57; *WJ*, 28 and 228n44.]

was Jesus Christ?"—in order to answer all the more abundantly this other question: "How is Jesus Christ present in my life?" His answer has nothing heretical in it: whoever in detachment dies to his own person will be reborn as Son of God. And he does not hesitate to express this new birth in terms of identity with God.

3) The philosophical presuppositions of this Christology

We have already had occasion to analyze some of the philosophical concepts characteristic of Meister Eckhart's thought, such as 'nature' and 'person,' 'energetic identity,' 'divine ideas,' 'detachment,' etc. We will therefore restrict ourselves here to the concept of time, the concept of being, and the concept of knowledge.

a) The concept of time

We have seen that Meister Eckhart does not offer a more developed notion of history than do his contemporaries. He even goes so far as to classify 'time' on the side of 'creatures,' thus on the side of non-being: "*Deus non est in tempore, in divisione, in quantitate, in aliquo habente magis et minus*" [God is not in time, in division, in quantity, in anything that has a more or less] (*In Ioh.*, no. 206, LW 3: 174). Time can touch neither the soul nor God. Time is what grows old, but the birth of the Son is always new; this birth is consequently outside of time: "*Quia creatio exterior subiacet tempori quod facit vetus, sic generatio filii, quae fit in spiritu non subiacente tempori, non est vetus, sed nova*" [Whereas exterior creation is subject to time which makes old, the generation of the son, which takes place in the spirit which is not subject to time, is not old, but new] (*In Ioh.*, no. 323 [LW 3: 271]). And he interprets the verse from the Epistle to the Galatians—"When the fullness of time came, God sent his Son" [Galatians 4:4]—in a very personal sense: "*plenitudo temporis est ubi nullum tempus est*" [Fullness of time is where there is no time] (*In Ioh.*, no. 293 [LW 3: 245]; cf. Pr. 4 ["Omne datum optimum"]). "*Nullum tempus*" is directed at something that is not time, that is opposed to time. The contrary of time, for Meister Eckhart, has two names: eternity and moment. While speaking of the birth of the Son in the soul, he will often say that it takes place in the moment, conceived of as the irruption of the eternal into the temporal. The '*nunc*' of the eternal embraces all the fullness of time. "What belongs to being [*être*], to time or place, does not touch God [..., R.S.] but if I consider the now, it embraces all times. The now in which God created the world is as close to our present time as the now which I pronounce in this instant; and the last day is as close to this now as the day that was yesterday" (Pr. 10).[76] "When the soul stands in the day of eternity, in an essential now, the Father engenders his only Son in a present now, and the soul is rebirthed to God" (Pr. 11).[77]

This notion of time (to which Kierkegaard and Bultmann would doubtless feel quite close) makes Meister Eckhart belong to another intellectual world than that of the Middle Ages. (Let us recall the sentence that Professor Welte pronounced at Le Saulchoir on St. Thomas' Day, 1966: "The trial at the papal court of Avignon against the Meister's theses gives the impression of a trial initiated by being itself against the one who boldly outstripped its destiny."[78]) His Christology thus reveals such an existential turn that one would be justified in having Meister Eckhart say: I exist as a Christian to the extent that I detach myself from my person in the moment and give birth in myself to the Son of God.

b) *The ontological difference*

God is the *esse* of creatures. They do not have their own being, but receive their being from God. Meister Eckhart thinks of being as constantly given. He who gives being [*être*] to beings [*étants*] is not himself a being, but still remains in the most intimate part of every being: "*Est quidem Deus in quolibet, ut illud ens est, in nullo autem, ut illud est hoc ens*" [Indeed God is in everything insofar as it is a being but in nothing insofar as it is this being] (*In Ioh.*, no. 206 [LW 3: 174]). Insofar as the being is a being, God is in it, but insofar as it is such a being, God is not in it. (We see to what degree the distinction mentioned above between nature and person is the result of

---

76 [Eckehart, *Deutsche Predigten und Traktate*, 195. DW 1: 142,10; 143,8–144,3 (Pr. 9, "Quasi stella matutina").]
77 [Eckehart, *Deutsche Predigten und Traktate*, 206. DW 1: 171,8–10 (Pr. 10, "In diebus suis").]
78 [Bernhard Welte, "La métaphysique de Saint Thomas d'Aquin et la pensée de l'histoire de l'être chez Heidegger," *Revue des Sciences philosophiques et théologiques* 50 (1966), 614.]

a reflection on being: insofar as I am nature, God is in me; insofar as I am person, God is not in me). It is quite surprising that Meister Eckhart has been reproached for a pantheism that he himself refutes: *"Deus non est pars aliqua universi"* [God is not some part of the universe] (*In Ioh.*, no. 207 [LW 3: 175]), no more than [he is] the totality of the universe, "which is in relation to God what nothingness is in relation to the sum of the universe" (*In Ioh.*, no. 220 [LW 3: 185]). God is not being [*être*] pure and simple (as he is for St. Thomas), but he makes that which is be. While commenting on Peter's question—"Rabbi, where are you staying?" [John 1:38]—he says that God *"est ubi et locus omnium"* [is the where and the place of all things] (*In Ioh.*, no. 199 [LW 3: 168]). The demonstration subsequently employs a syllogism of which the major premise seems to be taken from Martin Heidegger and the minor from St. Augustine. Between being [*être*] and beings [*étant*], there is no mediation, *"hoc est maior"* [this is the major (premise)]; being is that outside of which everything that is remains restless [*inquiet*] as if it were far from its natural place, *"hoc est minor"* [this is the minor (premise)]; therefore: God is the place of all things (*In Ioh.*, no. 205 [LW 3: 172]) in whom they are *"ut illa sunt entia"* [insofar as they are beings] (*In Ioh.*, no. 206 [LW 3: 174]).

Every being is constituted as such by the divine *esse* which makes it be and by a privation or negation which makes it such a being. Beings do not give themselves being; this is because there is a difference in them between being which constitutes and the beings which are constituted. It is this difference that permits Meister Eckhart's anthropology to identify the ground of the soul (spiritual, thus infinite, thus not a being) with the ground of God. The soul, because it is intellectual, becomes a giver of being. Man is himself the locus of the ontological difference since it does not suffice to say of him that he is a created being: "the being of God is my life; and if the being of God is my life, the being of God must be my being" (Pr. 7).[79] Being is thought of as an ineffable gift of which no particular being is the source and about which man can only question himself.

---

79 [Eckehart, *Deutsche Predigten und Traktate*, 184. DW 1: 106,1–3 (Pr. 6, "Iusti vivent in aeternum").]

c) The role of intellect

It is not impossible that Meister Eckhart should be the first thinker to have abandoned the schema—so convenient for representation—of a hierarchical cosmos. If this could be demonstrated, we should be less hasty in cataloging Meister Eckhart, as we habitually do, among the late Neoplatonists. His mysticism of the intellect is already, as we have seen, of profoundly Aristotelian inspiration.— To the cosmos of degrees of being, our author opposes a cosmos centered on the one who makes it be: man. For, because of his intellectual nature, man creates the beings whose being resides in God: "all creatures are transported into my intellect so that in me they are intelligent [*vernünftig*, R.S.]" (Pf.: 56) [DW 4,2: 768,41–769,42 (Pr. 109, "Nolite timere eos, qui occidunt corpus")]. Only when the creature has attained its perfection in a spiritual being [*un être spirituel*] does it really exist as a creature: as that which subsists only through another. Intellect is thus constitutive of the non-spiritual creature, and man deserves to be called the center of the created universe.

This creative function of intellect has its foundation in such an immediate relationship with God unattainable by a philosophy of degrees of being. What the latter philosophy will be obliged to expound 'by analogy,' Meister Eckhart can affirm 'by identity.' Human intellect, in the deepest part of itself, is identical, in the sense stated, with the intellect of God. Meister Eckhart's intellectualism is not, like that of St. Thomas, an intellectualism of participation, but rather an intellectualism of union. Meister Eckhart's paradoxical expressions, so it seems to us, follow from his rejection of a world ordered according to degrees of participation in a First [*Premier*], a rejection which gives to his concepts not an analogical but a univocal purview.

The third characteristic of intellect is negativity. The ground of the soul, which is the ground of God, is unknowable: "What the soul is in its ground (*Grund*), no one can know" (Pr. 8).[80] Precisely because man will never be entirely detached from his person, will never be

---

[80] [Eckehart, *Deutsche Predigten und Traktate*, 190. DW 1: 124,4–5 (Pr. 7, "Populi eius").]

'humanity' (cf. Pr. 38),[81] only a 'spark' in him is divine. In other words: in man there is always a portion of negation or privation, opposing his true nature and the origin in him of the ontological difference. God, on the other hand, he who is *"negatio negationis"* [negation of negation] (*In Ioh.*, no. 207 [LW 3: 175]), is one. More than a philosophy of being, Meister Eckhart's philosophy is a philosophy of the One; in this sense, it is less 'positive' and more dialectical than that of St. Thomas (cf. Pr. 22: *"Eins ist ein Verneinen des Verneinens und ein Verleugnen des Verleugnens"* ['One' is a negation of negation and a denial of denial]).[82] This dialectic is expressed at the level of intellect by the doctrine that, on the one hand, God is what is most intimately present to the mind [*l'esprit*]—that he even 'is' the mind, since the true being of intellect is the being of God in it—but that, on the other hand, this profound unity is radically unknowable. More than any philosophy of being, this philosophy of the one is apophatic. God is unknowable for three reasons, Sermon no. 55 explains: "What we need to know must be known from its cause, or from its mode of being, or from its efficiency. This is why God remains unknowable, because he is not caused by anyone [..., R.S.] he is outside of all modality [..., R.S.] and inoperative, namely, in his hidden being."[83] (Cf. also Pr. 9: "God acts beyond being, offshore where he can evolve; he acts in non-being."[84]) The best that man can do in the face of the unfathomable silence of divinity is to be quiet in his turn (cf. Pr. 57).[85]

---

81 [Cf. Eckehart, *Deutsche Predigten und Traktate*, 334–39. DW 2: 6–18 (Pr. 25, "Moyses orabat dominum").]

82 [Eckehart, *Deutsche Predigten und Traktate*, 252–53. DW 1: 363,1–2 (Pr. 21, "Unus deus et pater omnium".)]

83 [Eckehart, *Deutsche Predigten und Traktate*, 408. DW 3: 381,4–382,1 (Pr. 80, "Homo quidam erat dives").]

84 [Eckehart, *Deutsche Predigten und Traktate*, 196. DW 1: 145,5–6 (Pr. 9, "Quasi stella matutina").]

85 [Eckehart, *Deutsche Predigten und Traktate*, 419. DW 4,1: 335–67 (Pr. 101 "Dum medium silentium").]

8

The Phenomenon of the Question in Theology

(1967, trans. from the French by Francesco Guercio and Lucas Wright)

In his first year of theological studies at Le Saulchoir (which were preceded by three years of courses in philosophy), Schürmann wrote an essay on "the phenomenon of the question" for Fr. Bernard Quelquejeu's Methodology of Theology class. Taking his cue from Proclus' question of foundation and Heidegger's question of being—while touching upon Meister Eckhart's teaching on the Son's begetting in the soul—Schürmann points out the distinctiveness of philosophy vis-à-vis theology and explains what "thinking while believing" is. Prior to Schürmann's text, one finds a short preface by his friend and fellow Dominican Philippe Nouveau.

Preface
(by brother Philippe Nouveau)

If you have been lost in a Japanese city or a *favela* of Rio, you know the value of a friend who speaks your language and truly knows the area. More precious still is one who will communicate the song of another people, who will invent new words where their soul will vibrate.

Proclus, Saint Thomas, Meister Eckhart, Heidegger... we are grateful to the guide, to the friend, who leads us toward you and beyond you toward the mystery that you display in the distance.

He calls himself a philosopher and not a theologian. But do these polemics at the bottoms of the valleys still matter on the summits? We prefer, in silence, to listen to his song from across the river and to watch the sea with him as the evening sun sets upon it.

Schürmann's Text

§1) A Suspicion

"May the day perish when I was born,
and the night that told of a boy conceived.
[..., R.S.] Why did I not die new-born, not perish as I left the womb?"
(Job 3:2–4; 11)

"Jesus said to the blind man: 'Do you believe in the son of man?'
'Sir,' the man replied 'tell me who he is so that I may believe in him.'
Jesus said to him: 'You are looking at him, he is speaking to you.'
The man said: 'Lord, I believe,' and prostrated before him." (John 9:35–38)

Faith lives off the vitality of questions that provoke it, that it provokes. It becomes possible when they are deepened, it is beautiful when they are simplified, it dies under the implacable 'to what end!' of the spirit that no longer questions. "Why are we born into this life?" "Where do we come from and where are we going?" "Who is he who created me, who has saved me?" Faith is a life for the one who does not cease [*laisse*] to question.

To believe, for a Christian, is to adhere to a positive, supernatural given (Congar), this is to say, to a person who reveals himself and to revealed truths. To believe, while striving to comprehend one's faith, is: "on the one hand, to take possession of the given, apart from which nothing would be; on the other hand, it is then the fermentation, dilation, fructification, exploitation of this given in the intellect, which is lured by this new object."[86] Theology, the 'science of God,' poses questions, supposes questions, but these arise from and pertain to an objective given which serves as their platform. 'Put everything into question' is an attitude contrary to faith. In theology, there are 'questions'; the diverse 'treatises,' *quæstiones* of the mediaeval Summas, are there to manifest its profoundness and fecundity. But are they radical to the point of letting themselves be

---

86 Marie Dominique Chenu, *La foi dans l'intelligence* (Paris: Éditions du Cerf, 1964), 116.

reduced to a single question that would thus be the question of all [*question du tout*]?

A suspicion arises: if theology poses and supposes certain questions, would it be because it has always already responded to certain other questions? Theological science would thus appear as an entanglement of questions, limited to the exploitation and the fructification of the given, and of responses, outside of which one could place oneself only on pain of leaving the community of believers. Is there a place in 'dogmatic' theology for the question of all? Or is this question reserved for philosophy? Which is the philosophical question?

Two stages of philosophical thought will help us to discern what the question of all is: *The Elements of Theology* by Proclus,[87] and a text by Heidegger.[88] This double analysis of the phenomenon of the question will permit us to again take up our disquieting suspicion: namely, that for the believer to pose the question of all means to exit the theological domain.

Part 1:
The Phenomenon of the Question

I) Proclus: The Question of Foundation[89]

§2) The Experience of the Multiple and the Gift of Unity

With Proclus, Neoplatonism reaches a synthetic summit that, by virtue of its extreme formalism, also seals its end. In the 5th century, the reverential task of investigating such a venerable tradition was too great to allow for an original thinking—Proclus inaugurates the scholasticism of Neoplatonism. His thinking is bound by every sort of authority whose superiority is respected when approaching wisdom: the writings of Plato are 'illumination' (*eklampsis*); they have

---

[87] Diadochus Proclus, *The Elements of Theology*, ed. E. R. Dodds (Oxford: Oxford University Press, 1933). [We shall provide pagination for the 1963 edition. Cited in our text as Stoich. prop. followed by proposition and page numbers.]
[88] Martin Heidegger, *Die seinsgeschichtliche Bestimmung des Nihilismus*, in *Nietzsche II* (Pfullingen: Neske, 1961), 335–98.
[89] For this exposé of the doctrine of Proclus, we made use of, among other texts, twelve articles by Jean Trouillard from different Francophone journals.

to be received, can be commented on, but it would be blasphemy to critique or interpret them. The Proclean commentary on the *Parmenides* begins with these words: "I implore all of the Gods and all of the goddesses [..., R.S.] to kindle the living light of the truth in me [..., R.S.] and to open the doors of my soul so that it may receive the divine doctrine of Plato."[90] The words of Plato are 'divine' (*ta theia*) and, in this respect, they are not different from the Chaldean and Orphic oracles that Proclus also comments on as abundantly as he does the dialogues of Plato. Philosophical traditions and religious practices are means by which the unique truth makes itself understood.

The *Stoicheiōsis*, a doctrinal exposé presented as the 'summa' of Neoplatonic thought, interrogates the relation between the one and the multiple. The one, the real foundation of generation and becoming, is thought of as the origin of the multiple; as the real conclusion of the movement of knowledge, it is also its end. The origin and the end are present in the multiple by means of images: the emanation from the primitive unity can be deciphered in the image that the hierarchical cosmos is; the return toward this unity, in the human intellect, recapitulates the order inside of which and over which this intellect is exercised. We would like to show, taking our cue from *Stoicheiōsis*, how the first movement, the *exitus*, introduces us to the experience of a gift, and how the second, the *reditus*, raises a question. Our aim is to make the unique philosophical question emerge in thought, a question that—if it is preserved as a question—must fall silent before a unique event in which it knows itself as given [*se sait donnée*].

The world, the image of the *exitus*: everything that is only is by virtue of another that makes it be. It is from this other that the former receives every property; the world is not itself its origin. A difference distinguishes that which is from that which makes be: the difference is that of making be. The *exitus* is the principle of difference; or rather, participation is the principle of difference. The multiple participates in a first. The formal principle of the cosmos is that it participates; the real principle is a first in which it participates. The

---

90 [*Procli philosophi Platonici opera inedita*, ed. Victor Cousin (Frankfurt am Main: Minerva, 1962), 617.]

imperfect multiple participates in the simple perfection of the first. The latter is *amethekton*, it does not participate in anything; it lets emanate from itself that which is participated, *ta metechomena*, this is to say: being, life, and intellect; they make what is, *ta metechonta*, be (Stoich. prop. 24 [28-29]). The emanation of which the cosmos is the image goes through three phases. The undivided one engenders the principles or ideas that in turn engender the multiplicity of beings. Every inferior rank is contained in the superior *kat'aitian* [causally], the superior in the inferior *eikonikōs* [in the manner of an image]. The making be [of the many by the one] is not a simple positing [of the many] in existence, but a coming-forth [*pro-venir*] which goes through phases.

That which comes forth refers to that from which it comes forth. Not only do things say what they are; to the philosopher, they say their 'being as coming forth' ['*être-pro-venant*']. The world is a cosmos only because it does not contain in itself its principle of order (*taxis*); participation is a principle of difference and a principle of order between the first and the world. The world subsists 'because of' a first without which nothing could subsist in it; to say that objects are found in the world is to say that the world is their place. Yet, the world has not given to itself the perfection of being the place for that which is. If the world is the 'place' of what is, what lives, and what is intelligent, it enters into relation with them. Participation is the principle of difference between the world and things. The world is not the sum of that which it contains; as the order of that which is, it gets its perfection of order from another. If there were a simple and pure identity between the world and its principle of order, there would only need to be, strictly speaking, one single thing in the world. To experience the three regions of being, *on*, *zōē*, and *nous*, is again to grasp a certain unity, the unity of order. The experience of the multiple refers back beyond the world of ideas, and from this fact even refers back beyond science, physics, biology, and ontology: the world refers back to a first from which it possesses its order.

Philosophically, it is not so much the passage from the multiple to the one that creates a problem (even an 'empiricist' such as Kant will be constrained to carry this out, albeit as a postulate of a first, a regulator of ideas only), but rather the passage from the first—the principle of order—to the first—the principle of being. Or in other words, how do we pass from the phenomenon of order and the intuition of participation to the thought of causality? A new intuition seems to be required: that of appearing, contra being-present [*l'être-présent*]; that of coming-forth in movement, contra being-established [*l'être-établi*]; or that of emanation, of being-'given' [*l'être-'donné'*] in the sense of an unceasing gift, contra fixity, contra 'being'-given ['*être'-donné*] in the sense of a state of fact that has been set in place once and for all. The first is a cause because the multiple ap-pears. The *exitus* is thought of as an emerging that is never achieved, not as an arrival of a primitive ground that would have been produced in mythical time. Causality, because it is thought of through the schema of 'ideas,' is also thought of as ceaselessly making that which is be, that which lives live, that which thinks think.

It is possible to think of the first as the principle of order without appealing to the intermediate phase of the world of principles or ideas. It is not possible to avoid thinking of the first as the causal principle without falling into the univocity of an undifferentiated world and, thus, without negating the experience of multiplicity. To thin out the real distinction between being, life, and intelligence and hence between the diverse ways of participation would be, for Proclus, to misunderstand the terrifying fissures in the world; denying the anteriority of unity with respect to the three subsisting ideas (*authypostata*, Stoich. prop. 40f. [42f.]) would be tantamount to denying in them the foundation of efficient causality. The order of the world refers back to a first from which it emanates, causality in the world refers back to a double movement of emanation. Without this double *proodos* (Stoich. prop. 25 [28–31]), the multiple would only appear like the slight inequalities on the surface of a ball. When Proclus affirms that the ideas or causes do not communicate among themselves, he introduces the reader to a profound experience of the multiple: "Every efficient cause engenders the principles that immediately or mediately follow it while it itself remains what it is (*menon auto eph'heautoū*)" (Stoich. prop. 26 [30–31]). These efficient causes come forth (*pro-viennent*) from the separate One, just as the spokes come from the singular hub of a wheel; they meet in it but without the hub being mixed up with them or with one of them. The *archē kai aitia* [principle and cause] is *mē on, mē zōē, mē nous* [non-being, non-life, non-intellect]; it is *haplōs hen* [simply one] (cf. Stoich. prop. 11 [12–13]).

The one is separate from the ideas, which are causes of that which is. It [the one] is the non-cause beyond causes, the non-being beyond being; but it is not nothing. The one cannot be represented in a thought that imagines multiplicity in the world according to the ways of causal emanation; to the inferior principles, the superior principles are surrounded by a mystery; the One, a plenitude radically separate from the knowable principles, is a radical mystery. We can say of it [the one] only this: it makes the causes of that which is be, it founds that which founds. The one yields itself to thought only according to its function, which is to give and to found.

The unheard-of novelty of the experience of the multiple in the thought of Proclus is equaled only by the unheard-of novelty of the gift that founds. The phenomenon of multiplicity is rending for thought, that thought which dares to follow the path indicated by multiplicity; but multiplicity also reserves for thought the consolation of unity regained:

Wo aber Gefahr wächst,
naht das Rettende auch. (Hölderlin)

[Yet where danger grows,
That which saves also draws near.][91]

§3) *The Phenomenon of the Question*

That which is only is because it is given; the one is thought of as the foundation that makes be, that lets be. This determination of the one is however nothing more than a functional determination. Before the being of the one, thought must halt. The spiritual soul can know its origin only in the silent recognition that it itself is not by virtue of itself. Nevertheless, the spiritual soul can interrogate what prohibits it from knowing its origin otherwise than in its originating function. Thought, by recognizing the horizon that is attributed to it, is amazed by this horizon and by the fact that that

---

91 [R.S. misquotes Hölderlin here. The third and fourth verses of Hölderlin's poem "Patmos" instead read: "Wo aber Gefahr ist, wächst / das Rettende auch" (But where danger is, there grows / also that which saves). Friedrich Hölderlin, *Sämtliche Werke und Briefe*, ed. Michael Knaupp, 2nd ed. (Munich: Carl Hanser, 2019), 447 et passim.]

is its horizon, unsurpassably. The soul that returns upon itself must cease thinking of its origin; it begins to think of its own destiny. The mystery of the origin refers the soul back to the mystery that it is itself for itself. In this way, it [the soul] brings to completion the order of dependence with regard to the first; participation and return, *exitus* and *reditus,* are the two wings of a single and selfsame law established between the one and the multiple. The cosmos, the unfolding between the one as *archē* and the one as *telos*, is brought to completion in the activity of the *psychē*, the mediator between unfolded variation and originary simplicity. In the movement of the totality of the world, going from unity to unity by passing through the multiple, the second phase—that of reduction and concentration—falls to the spiritual soul. The reductive concentration collides with an enigma: namely, what is this horizon with which the soul collides as with a limit?

To return upon oneself as upon a mystery of limitation is to experience a nothingness. The soul interrogating itself (*to pros heauto epistreptikon* [that which reverts upon itself], Stoich. prop. 43 [44–45]) touches upon a nothingness, a relic within itself of the multiple which is its condition. In the silence before the unsayable gift of being and of thought, the question of the soul's horizon emerges on the surface of the soul. The horizon makes for a question [*fait question*].—The soul experiences disquiet; the information that it gives itself—namely, that the horizon is what it is because it is given—is disquieting [*inquiétante*]. The human mind [*L'esprit humain*] is disquieted because the question that it poses is that of the foundation. A question to which we desire to be able to respond and that refuses this response is disquieting. The nothingness in the mind poses the question and already supposes it. The question that arises from nothingness is not one question among others. The comprehensible positivity within the horizon and the unknowable negativity beyond it are interrogated by this question simultaneously with the horizon itself. The question is that of all, the properly philosophical question.

The soul, the principle of the *epistrophē* [reversion] of all that is, interrogates all that is and interrogates itself. In the movement of the *reditus*, the soul, being *pantē panta* [all things all throughout], poses the question of all which it [the soul] is *psychikōs* [psychically]. The radical question may be thematized in different ways: "What is the sense of all things?" "What about the destiny of the mind?" "Why is there anything rather than nothing?" "What is this point of departure from which I pose this question that I am posing?"—the question itself is still only circumscribed.

It [the soul] must however be one. The reflexivity of the soul, mediating the return to the one, cannot be determined by the multiple; this is necessary because of its cosmic role: the soul must be one with regard to the act and with regard to the object. Proclus emphasizes the fact that thought, in the *epistrophē*, touches upon a unity of object, act, and being, which is at the origin and at the end of thought: "Every intellect, in the act of comprehension, knows that it comprehends [..., R.S.;] it knows, at the same time, the known thing, itself as that which is in the act of knowing, and itself as the object of the act of knowing" (Stoich. prop. 168 [146–47]). When thought folds back upon itself, it experiences a unity that does not come from itself and that it can only approach by the question. How would thought judge at all if it could not, in every judgment that it makes about things, be placed prior to the propositions it judges? And once its judgment is issued, it still has the ability to question: is what I say true? The mind thinks by taking as its point of departure a unity which never will fall under its thought. Unity is necessary for thought. Without this unifying regulation, every act of knowing would be multiple in itself, and all things would only be known according to their multiple appearances. This unity is also real (Proclus at least does not doubt it); it is the image of the unknowable one beyond the subsisting ideas.

The reflexive constitution of the mind verifies what the multiple constitution of the real had already revealed: that unity is 'given' in a perpetual coming forth out of a first which transcends, on the one side, the order of the cosmos and, on the other, the activity of the mind. The first unity is real: it is the 'transcendent' which one can worship; and it is necessary: the 'transcendental' that determines everything that is by the mediation of the intelligent soul.

It is possible now for us to approach the phenomenon of the question with more precision. The thinking that experiences the multiple interrogates the unity beyond which, at least as regulation of knowledge, it cannot pass. The question is inseparably that of the foundation of the multiple and that of the foundation of thought. Returning upon itself, the soul experiences in itself the image of unity. However, the latter, because of its imperfection as an image, imposes silence upon the soul. The question concerning the foundation becomes the question concerning the mystery: what about this silence? Thought touches upon something that is anterior to all that is. The anterior that *makes be* and *makes think* is that which *makes for a question*. The unknowable 'making' is disquieting.

* * *

II) Heidegger: The Question of Being

§4) The Forgetting of the Question of Being

As with Proclus, Heidegger comes to a moment in the history of thought where a certain tradition reaches its end: German idealism. Kant, Hegel, and Nietzsche indicate a way[92] for his thinking, a way that it borrows and recapitulates. In contrast to Proclus, Heidegger does not build a scholasticism of German idealism, but rather interrogates the tradition with regard to what it has not thought. Proclus venerates his predecessors as divine authorities. Heidegger interrogates his predecessors regarding whether they have not proceeded under the claim of a 'divine' whose authority they had misunderstood. That which gives, and gets one, thinking [*donne à penser*] seems to take away the path upon which thought thinks. Furthermore, this path comes to us, perhaps, from origins further back than the last century; idealism, the 'ism' of ideas, the reign of ideas, did not only begin in Germany after 'the Enlightenment.' The philosophical tradition interrogated by Heidegger is the Western tradition in its entirety. Why has the West thought as it has thought?

A particularly significant witness of Western thought (Thomas Aquinas would have been still more significant) has shown us that this thought interrogates the foundation which 'makes' all that is. Thought from the side of things, the foundation can be functionally determined as that which founds. That which is, because it is multiple, is not through itself; that which is, because it receives its

---

92 Cf. the beautiful title of the book by Otto Pöggeler on Heidegger: *Der Denkweg Martin Heideggers* [Martin Heidegger's path of thinking] (Pfullingen: Neske, 1963).

unification from the soul, is by virtue of another. This other 'certifies' that which is; the other that founds is certain. Western thought poses the question concerning the 'reason' for that which is. Reason 'poses' all that is, it also imposes silence; the certain foundation that provides moorage to all things is unknowable, but it founds. The 'certification' of that which is founded by and through the foundation is certain, not the foundation itself. The thought of 'reasons' only obtains certainty about the foundational relation, not about the subject that founds. This is why this thought is restless. The 'restless heart' of S. Augustine[93] illustrates the primacy of the certainty of the relation over that of the subject of the relation. What is anterior to that which is founded transcends that which is founded. Transcendence is deployed in the science of the transcendent—'what is Being itself [*l'Etre même*]?'—and in the science of the transcendental—what about beings [*l'étant*]'? What is anterior is at once the first in which all participate and that which is most commonly participated in. In the West, thinking, when it poses the philosophical question, thinks of the foundation of that which is insofar as it is.

To this 'philosophical' question, Nietzsche responds that there is nothing of being.[94] It is a statement, not the opinion of a gloomy mental lunatic. Nietzsche states the death of that which made be: Who is Being itself? The one who is dead. What about beings? The

---

93 [Augustine, *Confessions*, 1.1.1.]
94 Friedrich Nietzsche, *The Will to Power*, ed. Walter Kaufmann, trans. Walter Kaufmann and R. J. Hollingdale (New York: Vintage Books, 1968), 14 (§15): "The most extreme form of nihilism would be the view that *every* belief, every considering-something-true, is necessarily false *because there simply is no true world*"; *The Will to Power*, 4 (§4): "For why has the advent of nihilism become *necessary*? Because the values we have had hitherto thus draw their final consequence; because nihilism represents the ultimate logical conclusion of our great values and ideals"; *The Will to Power*, 528 (§1020): "'nihilism' (the penetrating feeling of—'nothingness')"; *The Will to Power*, 13 (§12, B): "The *faith in the categories of reason* is the cause of nihilism. We have measured the value of the world according to categories *that refer to a purely fictitious world*"; *The Will to Power*, 36 (§55): "This is the most extreme form of nihilism: the nothing (the 'meaningless'), eternally!"; *The Will to Power*, 7 (§1): "Nihilism stands at the door: whence comes this uncanniest of all guests?" [Here and in the next note, R.S. cites only the German from Friedrich Nietzsche, *Werke in drei Bänden*, ed. Karl Schlechta (Munich: Hanser, 1956), vol. 3.]

will to will. Zarathustra teaches the eternal recurrence[95] as the foundation of that which is; the certifying relation of the transcendent to the transcendental has vanished.—Heidegger asks how this terrible discovery by Nietzsche[96] can manifest the claim under which Western thought is always already thinking. Heidegger's goal is as follows: welcome in thinking the negation of philosophical thought—a negation that first took place through Nietzsche, but also and above all through modern technology and science—and question what is unthought in it. For a century, that which is has seemingly lost its foundations. This loss is the disappearance of something whose appearing went without saying in another epoch. It is at the moment in which the disappearance of 'reasons' occurs that thought asks about their destiny: where did the power of foundations that 'reasons' no longer seem to possess come from? How is it possible that what founded everything for centuries could fade away? Must one say that a piece of the universe failed? The universe would have rested on this piece—now lost—up until our age; what is this loss that is capable of shaking the repose of the universe? What is lost is more than one 'reason' among others. By asking 'by reason of what,' reasons fulfilled their function of serving as reasons. Here we have the question of alienated reason that searches to explain the disappearance by means of what has disappeared. The destiny of that which is unthought is fatal. The explication of beings must cede to the thinking of being.[97]

The destiny of Western thought is our abandonment [*délaissement*] by being.[98] Busy with explaining that which is, why it is, by reason of what it is, Western thought has forgotten to pose the ques-

---

95 Nietzsche, *The Portable Nietzsche*, ed. and trans. Walter Kaufmann (New York: Viking Penguin, 1982), 563 (*Götzen-Dämmerung*, "Was Ich den Alten verdanke," §5): "I, the teacher of the eternal recurrence."

96 And by Kant (the transcendent and the transcendental become ideas of the subject) and by Hegel (they coincide in Spirit) ...

97 Martin Heidegger, *Einleitung zu:* »*Was ist Metaphysik?*«, now in GA 9: 377: "The attempt to pass from the representation of beings as such into the thinking of the truth of being." Cf. "Introduction to 'What is metaphysics?'" in *Pathmarks*, ed. William McNeill (Cambridge: Cambridge UP, 1998) 286. [Here and in other notes below, R.S. cites only Heidegger's German, which unless otherwise indicated has been translated directly into English.]

98 Ibid., now in GA 9: 378: "unsere Verlassenheit vom Sein." *Pathmarks*, 287.

tion of being; being is the unthought of the tradition. The disappearance that terrifies our century and that pushes it into the multiple efforts to establish security by production, journalism, intellectual competencies, and artistic fashions is more than the loss of a piece of the universe: being itself fades away, *"das Sein selbst bleibt aus"* (NII: 353).[99]

Heidegger thinks the insofar-as of the philosophical question. This question represents being as that which is insofar as it is. Yet, it does not think the insofar-as. It thinks of beings as transcendental or transcendent and thus brushes against the question of being so as to better be able to think of beings (what is God, the totality of the world, the subject, spirit). However, the thinking of beings only thinks of being to the extent that it serves its discourse about that which is. For it [the thinking of beings], being is an *a priori* (NII: 346).[100] By this is meant that being is thought of as anterior to beings. By this is also meant that being is thought of from beings and in view of beings. The philosophy of the *a priori* invokes being only in order to 'certify' beings. It interrogates the totality of that which is and interrogates itself regarding this totality. Its interrogation regarding beings and regarding itself searches for the foundation: of the world upon a first, of the soul upon a certitude—image of the certain reality of the first. Philosophy, in the order of things and in that of knowledge, appeals to being, but it does not think being. Being, in the philosophical question, remains concealed. Proclus experiences that there are beings—the cosmos and the human soul—founded upon what he calls non-being. But, in this way, Proclus divides the unique question of being into disciplines that conceal the forgetting of being because the word 'being' figures in each of them: henology (the one is not nothing), cosmology (the world is in virtue of that which makes be), and anthropology (the soul leads all things back to their true being). The *theion* [divine] 'is' not being; however, when a thinker or an epoch declares the death of the *theion* and that a world blindly lives this death, it becomes clear that, in the various disciplines, the word 'being' was misleading. Perhaps the 'piece' that assured the relation of foundation—and that we would have

---

99 [Cf. Martin Heidegger, *Nietzsche IV: Nihilism*, ed. David Farrell Krell, trans. Frank A. Capuzzi (New York: Harper & Row, 1982), 214.]
100 [Cf. Heidegger, *Nietzsche IV*, 208.]

lost—is the doctrine of analogy; phenomenologically the declaration suffices: when Nietzsche announces the death of God, he announces the disappearance of a relation.

> Things fall apart, the centre cannot hold (Yeats)[101]

The relation that links things to their 'centre' is the insofar-as. After centuries of specialization in different branches of the knowledge of beings, it becomes urgent to pose the question of the insofar-as, to 'overcome' [*'dépasser'*] the forgetting of being.

Heidegger thinks of the insofar-as as the withdrawal of a concealment. To think of beings as beings is to remove them from the obscurity where they are held. The withdrawal of the veil gives, and gets one, thinking; being as unveiling gives, and gets one, thinking. Every thinking that interrogates that which is regarding its reasons for being, regarding its order or its cause, must be called a thinking of beings. That which thinks the insofar-as not in view of an explanation of things, but rather for the very unveiling that it [being] 'is,' is called a thinking of being. The insofar-as of the philosophies of beings is the unthought unveiling. Philosophies develop within the withdrawal of the veil—they forget the unveiling.

§ 5) *The History of Being*

This destiny—the veiling of unveiling—is a historical destiny. Its fatality does not seize a solitary mind; the history opened by the Presocratics and closed by Nietzsche is the unique history of the destiny of the thinking of being. Proclus (who is not a great philosopher and whose scholastic ambition makes the analysis easier) is a good witness of this forgetting of being: he interrogates beings, the cosmos, or the human soul or the totality of that which is; his search for the foundation leads him to think of an unknowable unity, the source of the causes of that which is and the terminal point of the latter's return. His thinking is a thinking of beings that, by its apophatic element, brushes against the question of being, but without posing it for itself (by the way, the French expression *poser une*

---

101 [William Butler Yeats, "The Second Coming," in *The Poems*, ed. R. J. Finneran (New York: Macmillan, 1983), 289.]

question attests also to the fact that the thinking of beings is lost in 'positions'). The forgetting of being becomes present when the foundation of that which is is no longer called *theion*, but rather *nihil*. Since Nietzsche thinks of everything as founded upon 'nothingness,' he does not pose the question of being any more than Proclus does. But, unlike the ancients, he no longer adores the supreme being [*étant suprême*] that founds, because this being is dead. The difference between the Neoplatonic *hen* and Nietzsche's *nihil* is a difference of life and death. The *hen* and the *nihil* say the same, although between Proclus and Nietzsche something has happened to the same, something that had the power to happen from the origins. The failure of the same comes about in thinking and poses the question of origins: what about, at the origin of philosophy in Europe, the thinking of being?

In the beginnings of Greek philosophy, being is thought of as *alētheia*, that is, as a withdrawal from concealment: 'truth' removes from concealment that which remained confined therein by *lēthē*. The 'privative' is the liberation of what was obscure: being lets that which is be; it takes that which is out of concealment, and unveils it in truth; it sets it out of itself, lets it ec-sist, in freedom. The truth of being is freedom that is thought of as the ex-position of beings in their unveiling.[102]

Heraclitus asks the question, "How can someone take shelter in the face of that which never sets?"[103] The question does not seek a response; it is surprised by the search for a shelter [*abri*][104] that would protect one from the always new advent. Heraclitus, read by Heidegger, thinks of that which withdraws from thought in order to find refuge in an unthought. In the face of what does man seek to take shelter? In the face of that which never sets, that which is there, unyielding, always already. Being-there [*l'être là*] [however,] penetrates into the shelters; how could man evade an unveil-

---

[102] For this interpretation of truth, cf. Heidegger, *Vom Wesen der Wahrheit*, 15 et passim, now in GA 9: 192f. Cf. "On the Essence of Truth," in *Pathmarks*, 147 and passim.
[103] Diehls, 22 B,16; cf. Heidegger, *Vorträge und Aufsätze* 257f., now in GA 7: 273f. Cf. *Early Greek Thinking*, trans. David Farrell Krell and Frank A. Capuzzi (San Francisco: Harper & Row, 1984), 109.
[104] [With *abri* R.S. renders Heidegger's *Unterkunft*, see NII: 357; cf. Heidegger, *Nietzsche IV*, 217.]

ing that is originary?—In such reading of the fragment, Heraclitus thinks of man's relation to that which never fades away: to the primitive unveiling; and he thinks of man by starting from this relation. Here, man is not thought of as 'founded' by this new relation that is inaugurated always already, but rather is the being-there of the unveiling, the place of that which never withdraws itself. In another fragment,[105] Heraclitus calls that which is so unveiled 'fire.' The world is fire—this appeared clearly even before men established knowledge of it. The fire Heraclitus speaks of was not invented by the gods or by men; to remain sheltered from this fire is beyond their power. Would the gods then not be almighty? The relation of men and of gods to that which is unyielding is nothing other than the unveiling itself inasmuch as it brings together and wards gods and humans. The unveiling of being wards that which is; the thinker is the guardian of this warding. The question of being must never be forgotten; it and the one who poses it bear the burden of warding the unveiling. The thinker is the guardian of being.

Plato[106] himself also thinks the unveiling: *alētheia*. That which unveils is named 'the idea' by him. The world, a shadow of the ideas, is drawn together and warded by something that the world itself is not: the Supreme Good draws together and wards; through the ideas, it makes that which is be. Unveiling thus signifies in the perishable the 'trace' of that which does not perish, the spark of light in the shadow of the cave. The idea appears in the things that it transcends. The idea is transcendental, transcendent by participation in the supreme good that illuminates it. The being of beings resides in another world, and it is only thought of by starting with beings, by 'ascent' ['*remontée*']. The idealism of Plato is oblivious to the primitive unveiling of truth, because he poses the question of being starting from the appearing of beings. The guardian falls short of his task by prostrating himself before an invisible source of truth; he represents the insofar-as of beings in a separated world of ideas emanating from a first good. The idea becomes the master of the unveiling, truth becomes the accuracy of the gaze that discloses an 'intelligible' content. Since Plato, the question of being has

---

105 Diehls, 22 B,50.
106 Cf. Heidegger, *Platons Lehre von der Wahrheit*, now in GA 9: 203–38. Cf. *Pathmarks*, 155–82.

withdrawn behind the question of beings whose multiplicity refers back to a simple and ordered world and whose insofar-as disquiets thought, which, instead of thinking the former in itself, certifies it by means of transcendence. From now on, thinking in the West will be the search for causes. Man is no longer the place of the unveiling of being; he is the one who, being capable of God,[107] is made to fit with the totality of that which is. Mind and world: the unique question of being is broken apart into two scientific branches: the science of the subject (anthropology) and the sciences of the object (ontology, cosmology, theology). The two types of disciplines are connected by a theory of knowledge: the truth of the primitive unveiling that had been thought by the ancients has become adequation between intellect and its vis-à-vis (*Gegenstand* ['object' or, literally, 'that which stands against'] expresses this opposition between intellect and *res* well). Kant drives the breaking apart of the phenomenon of the question to its disastrous climax: the schematism of knowing erodes receptivity, the three transcendental ideas erode the spontaneity of the mind. The philosophy of ideas, although at its origin thought of as henology, suddenly makes manifest by its final pulverization the inability of the originary one to sustain the unique question of man which is the question of being—an inability characteristic of the originary one from the beginning. The dislocation of the final epoch reveals the forgettings of the initial epoch.

Heidegger does not claim to comprehend and repeat—according to the criteria of the history of ideas (this expression is also significant: the unique history of being becomes manageable, 'interesting,' to the extent that it falls into the inauthenticity of the investigation of ideas)—or to interpret the thought of the writers in whose company he thinks: "We do not seek force in the already-thought, but rather in an unthought of which what is thought receives the space in which to unfold. [..., R.S.] The unthought interlaces the tradition primitively, unfolds ahead of it, without however being thought in itself and as that which inaugurates initially."[108] In thinking in the company of Heraclitus and Plato, or of Kant and of Nietzsche, Hei-

---

107 [Cf. St. Thomas, *S.Th.* I^a, II, q. 113. a. 10 referring to St. Augustine's description of the soul as "capax Dei" (De Trin. 14, 8, 11).]

108 Heidegger, *Identität und Differenz*, 44–45, now in GA 11: 57–58. Cf. *Identity and Difference*, trans. Joan Stambaugh (New York: Harper & Row, 1969), 48–49.

degger interrogates the tradition regarding what it does not think of, but which makes it think the way it thinks. The 'making' of the making-think is no longer here a 'making' of foundation, but rather of a primitive unfolding in the sense in which Heraclitus speaks of the 'fire.' Heidegger's hermeneutics is entirely governed by the thought of the unthought of philosophy.

Between the beginning of philosophical thought in Greece and Nietzsche, through the different epochs of thought, a single destiny has come about for the West, that of abandonment by being (*Seinsverlassenheit*, NII: 355).[109] A unique destiny marks a unique *epochē* (NII: 383)[110] of the history of being: Heraclitus inaugurates it, Nietzsche brings it to completion, and Heidegger thinks this unique epoch that is dominated by the abandonment by being.

The thinking of Proclus bears witness to this abandonment; the question that it poses is that of the first, the generous unity out of which everything comes forth, as well as the attractive unity toward which everything tends through the reflexivity of the human soul. Being is only thought of there as participated in *eikonikōs* by what comes forth from being *kat'aitian*; it is not thought in its own terms. The transcendent one, *archē* and *telos* of the cosmos, and the transcendental one, the omnipresent image of divine simplicity, is mysterious as it 'pro-duces' more than the soul can think of; the soul does not 'comprehend' what makes be because it is comprised by it. The soul is disquieted by it because the nothingness that it experiences in itself is opposed to its search for certainty regarding the 'anterior' that makes that which is be, that which lives live, and that which thinks think.—I would like to have shown the following: the mystery that is thought of by a philosophy of beings— hence, all Western philosophy—is not to be depreciated or levelled or ridiculed when one learns to see that it is represented as the unknowable foundation of the totality of that which is; this representation has on the contrary engendered admirable theologies that brush against the question of being, such as the theology of Meister Eckhart. But when the tradition touches upon the mystery of being, it thinks of it in view of totality, even of the one who poses the ques-

---

109 [Cf. Heidegger, *Nietzsche IV*, 215.]
110 [Ibid., 239.]

tion of being. It thinks of being [*l'être*] so as to best think of a being [*un étant*]. In this way, the mystery of being becomes the mystery of man, or the mystery of the world, or the mystery of God. Only a thinking that poses the question of being for itself, albeit by starting out from the one who poses it, but not in view and service of him, will set itself on the path of the mystery that is no longer that of a being, but rather of being.[111] The reciprocal implications of the mystery of man and of the mystery of God have haunted philosophers and theologians throughout the Western tradition, but also the poets, as attested by this beautiful poem by Rilke (to whom, one will understand without much effort, Heidegger prefers Hölderlin):

> Ich kreise um Gott, um den uralten Turm,
> und ich kreise jahrtausendelang;
> und ich weiß noch nicht: bin ich ein Falke, ein Sturm
> oder ein großer Gesang.
>
> [I circle around God, around the ancient tower,
> and I circle for thousands of years;
> and I don't yet know: am I a falcon, a storm
> or a great song?][112]

§6) *The lingering abode of Being*

A 'step backwards' (NII: 368)[113] should be undertaken that will open to thinking the clearing where the unveiling, wrested from its forgetting, comes to unfold itself. The forgetting of the unveiling indicates a way that leads one in the vicinity of a region where the abandonment by being lends itself to thinking [*se laisse à la pensée*]. Late in the refusal of being by being, thinking enters into the lingering

---

111 Cf. Heidegger, the first paragraphs of *Sein und Zeit*, e.g., p. 7, now in GA 2: 10: "The working out of the question of being accordingly means: making a being—the questioner—transparent in its being." Cf. *Being and Time*, trans. Joan Stambaugh, revised and with an Intro. Dennis J. Schmidt (Albany: SUNY, 2010), 6.
112 Rainer Maria Rilke: *Das Stundenbuch, I: Das Buch vom mönchischen Leben*, "Ich lebe mein Leben" (Leipzig: Insel, 1948), vol. I., p. 9.
113 [Cf. Heidegger, *Nietzsche IV*, 225.]

abode [*demeure*][114] of this refusal (we say 'late' from the perspective of the history of being). It [thinking] opens a place for abandonment, where, as abandonment, it [the refusal] is given to thought. The place is the lingering abode where both the 'late' of the forgotten question and the primitive unveiling unfold themselves; it is the place of the ad-vening [*ad-venir*] that being itself is (NII: 357).[115] This advent is the event of the gift of being. If the advent comes about [*survient*] as a not-yet and if it remains fatally veiled, it is however an interpellation in the very heart of the forgetting.[116] Thinking, if it corresponds (*entspricht*) to the interpellation (*Anspruch*) of the advening (*Zuspruch*), finds the way that leads it toward its lingering abode. The lingering abode of man: the yawning gap that being is. The lingering abode of the event of the advent of being is being itself. It is the lingering abode of man who always already is held under the advent, as the withdrawing of concealment or as concealment, of the unveiling that the question of being is. 'Lingering abode of being' means: the lingering abode that the question of being is for man.

One of the names given to this lingering abode is language. Language [*langue*] unfolds itself essentially in an advent anterior to every exchanged speech [*parole*]. But language refuses itself to instances of speech [*aux paroles*]; the event of the advent of language eludes representation in words just as the advent of being eludes representation by beings. The utterances of speaking [*énoncés du parler*] veil the lingering abode that language is; this veiling also belongs to its essential unfolding. The step backwards leads in the vicinity of the lingering abode where language gives itself. The gift of language is this event where the poet (*Dichter*) gathers together [*rassemble*] (*verdichtet*) the ways of gods and of humans, of heaven and of earth.[117] Hölderlin already wrote:

---

114 [With the French noun *demeure* R.S. renders Heidegger's *die Bleibe* (NII: 357). The German verb *bleiben* means 'remain,' 'abide,' while the French *demeurer* means both 'remain' and 'inhabit' or 'dwell.' In order to express both meanings delivered by *demeure*, it is rendered here as 'lingering abode.']
115 [Cf. Heidegger, *Nietzsche IV*, 217.]
116 Cf. Heidegger, *Vorträge und Aufsätze*. p. 183, now in GA 7: 193. Cf. "... Poetically Man Dwells...," in *Poetry, Language, Thought*, trans. Albert Hofstadter (New York: Harper & Row, 1971), 213.
117 Cf. those pages, among the most beautiful by Heidegger, on the *Geviert* [fourfold] in *Unterwegs zur Sprache*, 159–216, now in GA 12: 147–204. Cf. *On the Way to Lan-*

Viel hat von Morgen an,
Seit ein Gespräch wir sind und hören voneinander,
Erfahren der Mensch; bald sind wir aber Gesang.

[Much has from the morning on,
Since we are conversation and listen to each other,
the human experienced; soon though we will be song.][118]

Always already, language gathers together; it is the lingering abode of man where in the thinking of or in the forgetting of being, he corresponds to the advent. Language, thought, and being say the Same.

Man: the shelter that being claims so as to give itself in a 'there,' an advening [*avènement*] of the unveiling in the lingering abode of language.

Being, which in this way advenes in the event of the gift, while refusing itself in the withdrawal of the unveiling, is the promise of itself (NII: 369f.).[119] Being promises itself to thinking by making the question of unveiling emerge therein. The promised lingering abode shelters man as in a mystery. In the fatal forgetting that is the lot of the Western tradition, the mystery of the promise nevertheless gives itself. The 'late' of this promise is our lingering abode in the history of being that is the history of this mystery. The lingering abode that the question of being is, is historical (cf. the words *Geschick* [destiny, sending], *Geschichte* [history]): the event of the gift of being advenes as sent from history.

The history of the question of being gives man the task of gaining the soil of the fatherland. Hölderlin writes:

---

guage, trans. Peter D. Hertz (New york: Harper & Row, 1971), 57–108.
118 Cited by Heidegger in *Unterwegs zur Sprache*, 182, now in GA 12: 171; Heidegger continues, "The song is the celebration of the advent of the Gods—the advent in which all falls silent." Cf. *On the Way to Language*, 78. Some decades before Heidegger, Franz Rosenzweig had already written similar lines, on the *Zwiegesang* [duet], in *Der Stern der Erlösung*. [Cf. F. Rosenzweig, *Der Stern der Erlösung*, ed. A. Raffelt (Freiburg i.B.: Universitätsbibliothek, 2002), 255: "But the redemption of the soul in things and of things through the soul happens in the like-breathing duet of both [*Zwiegesang*], in the sentence that chimes together out of the voices of both words. In redemption, the great And closes the arc of All." Cf. *The Star of Redemption*, trans. from the 2nd ed. of 1930 William W. Hallo (New York: Holt, Rinehart and Winston, 1970), 229.]
119 [NII: 369f. Cf. Heidegger, *Nietzsche IV*, 226f.]

> Warm ist das Ufer hier, und freundlich offene Thale,
> Schön von Pfaden erhellt grünen und schimmern mich an. [..., R.S.]
> Freilich wohl! das Geburtsland ists, der Boden der Heimat,
> Was du suchest, es ist nahe, begegnet dir schon.
> Und umsonst nicht steht, wie ein Sohn am Wellen umrauschten
> Thor und siehet und sucht liebende Namen für dich,
> Mit Gesang ein wandernder Mann [..., R.S.]
>
> [Warm is the shore here and friendly the open valleys,
> Beautifully lit up with paths, gleam verdantly toward me. [...]
> But of course! It is the land of your birth, the soil of your homeland,
> What you seek, it is near, already comes to meet you.
> And not in vain does he stand, like a son, at the wave-washed
> Gate, and sees and seeks loving names for you,
> With his song, a wandering man][120]

The shores of the fatherland are warm, everything that the son loves is near it; he knows the names of things, he is greeted at the doorway of town. The lingering abode that the history of the mystery of being is for man is his fatherland.

The fatherland heals man of the forgettings and of the errancy on the ways that lead nowhere. Both the anxiety that accompanies the thinking of being and the restlessness that accompanies the thinking of beings are appeased: that which heals (*heilt*), salvation (*Heil*), opens also to the sacred (*heilig*), and to repose (NII: 393-94).[121] The lingering abode that, for man, is the question of being heals the inauthentic security of beings by preparing a holy lingering abode whose peace saves. Lingering abode, fatherland, and mystery say the Same.—The thinking of beings is an impious thought. 'That which' gives being is sacred. Being must be thought of as the play

---

120 Cited by Heidegger in *Erläuterungen zu Hölderlins Dichtung*, 10-11, now in GA 4: 10. [We have used Hoeller's translation of Hölderlin in *Elucidations of Hölderlin's Poetry*, trans. Keith Hoeller (Amherst, NY: Humanity Books, 2000), 27.] Heidegger continues, ibid. 23 [GA 4: 24]: "The nearness that now prevails lets what is near near, and yet at the same time lets it remain what is sought, and thus not be near [..., R.S.] The nearness to the origin is a mystery." [Cf. *Elucidations of Hölderlin's Poetry*, 42.]
121 [Cf. Heidegger, *Nietzsche IV: Nihilism*, 248.]

of the advening or the gift of the event of unveiling.[122] Being is given in time. It belongs to being to temporize itself in time. Being and time say the Same. In a rare privileged experience, the Same (in Heidegger's eyes, Hölderlin was one of those to whom this grace—*Huld*—was granted) lets itself be experienced in the life of a man. The gift of the Same opens up in being-there the field where a 'thou' can be received and can be said [*se dire*]. 'Thou' is thus not fused (one would need to say: Thou art not thyself fused—how difficult it is to escape representation!) with being or with that which gives being. Being is not itself that which gives being, it is given. When the 'thou' comes about, granting itself [*s'accordant*] from elsewhere than a being-with-beings [*un étant-avec*], it comes neither from being nor from that which gives being: Thou art not that which gives being. Thou only canst grant the light in which this experience comes about. When thou grantest it, philosophy ceases; the ineffable experience is unthinkable, is addressed not merely to thinking (and as Heidegger has confessed, here is his profound intention ever since the publication of *Sein und Zeit*); the thinking of being must prepare for this experience, but it does not manufacture or capitalize on it [*ne la monnaie pas*]. In a world dominated by the sciences, technology, and art as merchandise, the thinking of being is a preparation for this experience of Something Else [*un Autre-Chose*] of which philosophy itself can no longer speak.

The thinking—even apophatic thinking—of beings, haunted as it is by its need for establishing security, uses the first foundation to explicate the world. The thinking of being prepares man to let himself be used by the ineffable 'Same' that does not serve up any certainty. In experiencing thee, I fall silent—or I sing:

...soon though we will be song.

---

122 Cf. the expression *es gibt Sein* in the lecture "Zeit und Sein" that was given in Freiburg im Breisgau in 1962 and is still not published. [Now in GA 14: 9; cf. *On Time and Being*, trans. Joan Stambaugh (New York: Harper & Row, 1972), 5, and n. 1.]

Part 2
The Phenomenon of the Question in Theology

I) Theology—Science of the Mystery?

§7 The Suspicion Reinforced

What is the relation that theological thought has to the thinking of being? Would the question of being, the lingering abode of man, be the *ancilla* [handmaiden] of theology just as the philosophies of beings were for the scholastics? Or would it rather encompass theology in the manner of a genus of which it [theology] would be a specific question? Or again would theology already be the thinking of being which the thinking of beings, progressing to a new level of experience of sensible things, would necessarily forget because "no man has ever seen God" [1 John 4:12]?

Theology, science of God, cannot claim to think the mystery of the lingering abode that the question of being is; for theology, 'mystery,' 'lingering abode,' and 'fatherland' signify the 'mystery of salvation,' 'lingering abode of the Church,' and 'fatherland of the fulfilled Kingdom.' The science of God does not say the mystery of being.—The phenomenon of the question in theology seems thus to differ from the phenomenon of the question in philosophy, just as the question of beings differs from that of being. Our initial suspicion is reinforced: theology, asking about God the creator and the savior, about the Church and the Kingdom, cannot pose the question of being. Its proper intelligibility prescribes to theology another method of questioning. The intelligibility of theology, because the latter poses the question of the reciprocal implications of the mystery that is man and the mystery that is God, falls under the exact definition of the thinking of beings—as Rilke's verses attest. Theology would not therefore pose, properly speaking, 'the' question of mystery, but it would pose questions whose scientific character would end up consecrating the belonging of theology to the thinking of beings. Theology would naturally and necessarily be 'informative' and 'metaphysical' (in Martin Heidegger's sense of the term). In other words, scientific theology, abandoning initiation into the unique mystery, would enter into competition with other knowings of the real, by coordinating certain realities of which it would be the noetic correlate.[123]

However, although informed by the scientific method, theology nonetheless asks about the unique mystery of God of which man who believes will never accept saying that it is only a metaphysical representation of the 'greater' mystery of the question of being. What exactly does the scientific status of theology signify and what is the mystery that it thinks?

§8) Saint Thomas: Theology, 'Science' of God

Saint Thomas Aquinas deals with the scientific status of theology at the beginning of each of his two Summas: the identification of *sacra doctrina* [sacred doctrine] with the *scientia Dei* [knowledge of God] (*S.Th.* Ia 1, 2) is key; it founds a relation of subalternation between the knowledge that proceeds by taking as its point of departure principles known in the light of faith (one should translate *lumen superior* as 'light of faith') and [the knowledge that proceeds by taking as its point of departure] those known by the natural light of intelligence. The first type of science perfects the second by constituting a doctrinal body whose formal element [*le formel*] is nothing less than a vision of things that makes theological knowledge akin to that of the blessed and of God himself. By means of faith, human intelligence is superelevated by God in such a way that it can adhere with certainty to truths that exceed it. This is why theology does not deal with the singular (*S.Th.* Ia 1, 2, ad 2) but with principles: God and the theologian know all things by their principles!

The *Summa contra Gentiles* begins in a similar fashion. To the question: "Is it fitting that the truth concerning God, and which natural reason can attain, be proposed to the faith of men?" (I *C.G.* 4), this text responds with a double affirmation: it is fitting that a supernatural revelation proposes to belief the truths concerning God that

---

[123] It is on the basis of such a strong opinion of theology that Karl Jaspers declares the localization of transcendence among the realities of the world unthinkable and thus impossible: "It is unthinkable that the actuality of transcendence would become a reality in the world in such a way that as an acting God, it would, from this historical point, have a bodily effect on the world, localized in space and time, distinguished from all other realities, none of which are God or acts of God." *Der philosophische Glaube angesichts der Offenbarung*, now in *Karl Jaspers Gesamtausgabe, I. Werke*, Bd. 13, ed. Bernd Weidmann (Basel: Schwabe, 2016), 224.

are accessible to human intelligence (*ad quam rationis inquisitio pertingere potest*), as well as the truths that exceed the power of intellectual investigation (*quæ omne ingenium humanæ naturæ rationis excedunt*).[124] The revelation of these latter truths is necessary, because "once one proposes to man facts that exceed his intellect, the opinion that God is something beyond everything that man can think is confirmed in this man" [I *C.G.* 5].—A systematic thinking thus becomes possible: in possession of the foundation that exceeds it, human intelligence is capable of establishing links, relations, passages between the different givens which—be it via nature or by supernatural revelation—are available to it. Revelation, a foundation of new relations of 'fittingness' ['*convenence*'] between facts of knowledge and of believing (that which the text of the *Summa Theologica* calls *principia* such as the origin and the end of man, his situation under the Creator's gaze, intra-Trinitarian processions, etc.), at the same time founds a new science: all things are more knowable in their causes than in themselves; to know, by intervention of the First that makes what is be, the 'cause' of the universe is to know everything that is, in a 'sapiential' vision. Theology, because it knows, by way of revelation, the unknowable 'reason' of that which is, will never be 'disquieted,' in the sense that metaphysics is disquieted by foundations. What metaphysics seeks, theology possesses. The latter won't be anxious either—anxiety is born of the question of being that theology does not pose.[125]

What does this ambition of theology to establish an objective, rigorous system—with contents deduced from first principles that are intelligible or revealed—mean? In the final analysis, it signifies a quasi-definition of God: the second question of the *Summa Theologica* also comes to demonstrate God's being, the point of the pyramid of the *scibile* [the knowable] and the light of all 'science'; because of

---

124 [R.S. adds *naturæ* to the quotation.]
125 In the Bible, although there is an anxiety that arises from authentic fear of Jahweh (e.g. Isaiah 8:13: "It is Yahweh Sabaoth, whom you must hold in veneration, him you must fear, him you must dread"), the feeling of anxiety is nevertheless vain (e.g. Ecclesiasticus 40:1: "Much hardship has been made for every man, a heavy yoke lies on the sons of Adam from the day they come out of their mother's womb, till the day they return to the mother of them all") and even indicates the wickedness of men (e.g. [Proverbs 28:1]: "The wicked man flees when no one is after him"; cf., also, the whole chap. 17 in the Book of Wisdom).

its scientific ambition, theology must define its object and its light as *ipsum esse subsistens* [subsistent being itself]. Theology is a science whose formal object is that which is revealed [*le révélé*] insofar as it responds to a necessary operation of the mind. The material object of this science is not revealed, but rather 'proved.'[126] Formality alone is revealed: God, whose existence is demonstrated and certain, is also the one who saves in Jesus Christ. The science of God is materially natural, and formally supernatural.

Proclus had already made us understand the following: God, whose existence is certain, albeit unknowable in his essence, founds the unity of the real and the unity of the knowledge of the real. Revelation, engendering a new type of science, does not alter this relation to the foundation, nor the intelligibility put to work in order to account for it. The new formal element that revelation brings forth is the source of a new type of relation between that being which founds [*l'étant-fundement*] and that being which is founded [*l'étant-fondé*]: the relation of salvation in Jesus Christ. But from the point of view of the phenomenon of the question, there is a homogeneous passage from the thinking of beings to theological science. Revelation comes to enrich the foundational relation between God and man with a new 'formality'; it also comes to consecrate the alterity that presides over this relation. The one who saves is not the one who is saved; a 'mediator' only arises between two 'beings' ['*étants*'].

One may object that the question, "does theology as a science belong to the thinking of beings or to the thinking of being?," is a sophism. By means of the response we give to it—that theology is a thinking of beings that is enriched by a supernatural formality—such a question would serve to illustrate a polemical intent conceived for specific ends, namely, that theology presents itself to philosophy as 'sacred metaphysics.' This is not at all our intention. But isn't it remarkable that theology puts to work an intelligibility that makes the simple phenomenon of the question—which in 'scientific' theol-

---

126 One is not surprised to see this affirmation confirmed by S. Augustine's itinerary; *Le Monde* of March 18, 1967 published the review of a book that situates S. Augustine's discovery of the images of the Trinity in creation *before* his conversion. [Jean Lacroix, "Saint Augustin," reviewing Olivier Du Roy de Blicquy, *L'Intelligence de la foi en la Trinité selon Saint Augustin: Genèse de sa théologie trinitaire jusqu'en 391* (Paris: Études augustiniennes, 1966).]

ogy is that of a relation between God and man—more akin to the thinking of beings than to the thinking of being? By the way, St. Thomas' deliberate philosophical syncretism provides a clue: from St. Paul to Karl Rahner, theologians have moved at ease within the limits of different thoughts of beings, all of them striving to explicate a foundation upon which Christian revelation casts the ultimate light. Also, as soon as a thinking dares to relinquish the schemas of metaphysics (the legal proceedings instigated against Meister Eckhart at the papal court of Avignon superbly testify to this hold that the forgetting of being exercises over thinking, a hold insurmountable in theology), it is condemned as 'detrimental.' All the way up to the usage of *Sein und Zeit* by certain contemporary theologians (theology 'uses' every philosophy and leads it into the truth), this verdict that hangs over theology deforms thinking: unmindful of Heidegger's initial project (which we have sketched above at the end of §5), these theologians are intoxicated by the existentialist categories, 'reinterpreting the given' by taking as their point of departure the ontic-ontological and *Geschichte-Historie* [history-historiography]. However, they do not sense the blunder they commit in again reducing Heidegger's project to a 'thought concerning man'; it is only in connection with certain of his more recent writings (in order to be able to continue to hold forth on 'Heideggerian *Verstehen* [understanding] and theology' and similar subjects, they distinguish an 'early' Heidegger from this 'second Heidegger') that their misunderstanding has become evident to them. They qualify the content of those writings as 'poetry' and return to the 'seriousness' of the existentiell-existential.

'Theology of being': a contradiction in terms. Every scientific theology is constrained to move within the limits of the thinking of beings. It is essentially the 'science of fittingnesses' concerned with harmonizing the multiple beings, 'facts,' of the given in a single doctrine. Theology thus occupies a 'position'[127] among other sciences; one can exit this position and then be found at fault. Here we have another characteristic of the thinking of beings: in the thinking of being there is neither default nor error; in the thinking of beings

---

127 See P. Marie-Dominique Chenu, *Position de la Théologie* [in *Revue des Sciences philosophiques et théologiques* 24 (1935): 232–57.]

there exist prohibited paths that lead the one who takes them to the expulsion from the community of those who guard the right path; 'anathemas' are only possible in the thinking of beings.—Outside the Christian West that is dominated by the forgetting of being, there is however a thinking that, without succumbing to the hold of the science of beings on it, thinks the God [*pense le Dieu*]. The first book of the story "The Ox and Its Oxherder," told in China since the time of ancient Zen Buddhism, ends as follows:[128]

> The emperor asked a great master:
> 'What is the first meaning of holy truth?'
> Dharma responded:
> 'Wide ranging lingering abode. Nothing holy.'
> The emperor asked again:
> 'Who is the one standing before me?'
> Dharma responded:
> 'I do not know.'

§9 *Lumen Gentium*: The Theology of the 'Mystery'

Christian theology, while claiming to be ranked as 'science,' is also an introduction into a 'mystery.' Perhaps in considering not 'systematic' theology, but rather 'mystery' theology, we will find a more positive solution to our suspicion.

The first chapter of the dogmatic constitution *Lumen Gentium* treats 'the mystery of the Church.'[129] The meaning of the title is explained in the first lines of this text: "the Church is in Christ like a sacrament or as a sign and instrument both of a very closely knit union with God and of the unity of the whole of humankind" (LG 1,1 [modified]). Church–Christ–God–Humankind: the mystery of

---

128 *Der Ochs und sein Hirte: eine altchinesische Zen-Geschichte*, trans. H. Buchner, K. Tsujimura, (Pfullingen: Neske, 1958), 134. [Although contained in this edition, the dialogue R.S. translates actually comes from *Biyan Lu* or *The Blue Cliff Record*.]

129 [See *Lumen Gentium* in English translation on the Vatican's website https://www.vatican.va/archive/hist_councils/ii_vatican_council/documents/vat-ii_const_19641121_lumen-gentium_en.html accessed on December 13, 2022. R.S. cites from the French translation by Pierre Thomas Camelot, OP, *Unam Sanctam*, 51 (Paris: Les Éditions du Cerf, 1965). The *Lumen Gentium* was promulgated on November 21, 1964.]

which the constitution speaks is one of a relation between different 'dimensions' ['*grandeurs*']. The Christian mystery is that of the manifestation of God's plan in Jesus Christ. This manifestation creates a body: the Church is the 'fact' that re-presents the mystery of the manifestation. Finally, this mystery was willed 'for' someone: humankind is the gangue in which the crystal that the Church is takes shape. The latter's mission is to transform and to bring that crystal to completion. "The Church, or, in other words, the kingdom of Christ now present in mystery, grows visibly through the power of God in the world" (LG 1,3).

It is important here to show in which language the believer expresses himself when he speaks of the Christian mystery. Now, even through symbols—such as 'sheepfold,' 'edifice,' 'field,' etc.— this language formally recalls the 'mystery' as we have analysed it in Proclus' text. 'Mystery' signifies a being knowable in its function but unknowable in itself. To say that Christ is the summit or the point of creation in which the latter is summed up in its entirety, is to use schemas that are properly speaking metaphysical. When the Council speaks of the Church as a mystery, it sides with the destiny that we mentioned when we spoke of the medieval *quæstiones*: 'the' mystery is broken apart into multiple stages of salvation: God sends a savior, Christ saves, man is saved, the world must be saved... there are Christian mysteries. The constitution confirms this view: "we, who have been made to conform with Him, who have died with Him and risen with Him, are taken up into the mysteries of His life, until we will reign together with Him" (LG 1,7). Categorial theology divides the unique mystery into 'amazing facts.' The words employed by theology ('being,' 'science,' 'mystery') take on an analogical sense, but, notwithstanding, theology does not escape the forgetting of being. Theologians indeed insist on the unity of the mystery when they introduce a treatise about the one God (cf. *S.Th.* Ia 1,7 ad 1: "*licet de Deo non possimus scire quid sit, utimur tamen eius effectu* [..., R.S.] *loco definitionis*" [granted we cannot know of God what he is, nonetheless we make use of his effects... in place of a definition]). Also a whole tradition, called 'negative,' insists on this aspect of the unknown God, hence on the unique mystery. But, for negative theology, isn't respecting what is radically beyond [*l'au-delà radical*] the human mind already to escape the destiny of the forgetting of being?[130] Apophaticism does not think of being any more than kataphatic theology does; as we have said, it brushes against the question of being when it is amazed by the unknowable foundation of that which is and by the insurmountable horizon of the intellect.

Excursus on the Thought of Meister Eckhart

It seems to us that Meister Eckhart's thinking goes further than ordinary apophaticism: to the nuns of the Rhine Valley, Eckhart preached the identity between the ground of the soul and the ground of God: "before there were creatures, God was not yet God. When I emanated from God, all things spoke: God is. And if I myself were not, God would not be either: That God is God, of this I am a cause. If I were not, God would not be God. This is why I pray God to rid me of God, for my essential being is above God."[131]

This text certainly says that God in himself is unknowable; he is only known when the world is held before him, a world for which he then becomes 'God.' Here, 'God' is thought of as a correlate to 'creature': creatures obtain their being from God and he lets himself be invoked by them to be 'their God.' But beyond this distinction of the created and the uncreated, the soul resides always already in a primitive ground that is anterior to all creation and to all dichotomy that the former entails. Man's essential being is beyond God; there is, in Meister Eckhart's thinking, the discovery of a mystery of identity (perhaps one ought to say of univocity, so as to distinguish it from the analogy of 'domains of being') by virtue of which that very thinking is raised beyond negative theology. The identity of which his sermons speak is expressed in terms of event (*ein Gewirke*). Far

---

130 It is in this that the thinking of Professor Bernhard Welte is perhaps a bit optimistic when he writes ([«La métaphysique de Saint Thomas d'Aquin et la pensée de l'histoire de l'être chez Heidegger,"] *Revue des Sciences philosophiques et théologiques*, Oct. 66: 610): "The statement 'Deus non est in genere [God is not in a genus]' signifies that he is not in any way a being [..., R.S.]. In this statement, one touches upon the Being [*l'Être*] that is no longer any being [*étant*] nor the being of any being [*l'être d'aucun étant*]."

131 [R.S. provides reference to Josef Quint's translation of Eckhart into Modern German: Meister Eckehart, *Deutsche Predigten und Traktate* (Munich: Hanser, 1963); we shall provide pagination for the 1979 edition (Diogenes Taschenbuch): 305; 308. DW 2: 492,8–9; 504,5; 504,1–3; 502,6–7 (Pr. 52, "Beati pauperes spiritu"). The sermon numbers sometimes differ in DW. Here, R.S. rearranges Eckhart's text.]

from being represented as the simultaneous presence of two beings subject to the same conditions, it [identity] is thought of as a 'begetting': ceaselessly God begets in the soul united to him "one life alone and one being alone and one actuality alone [..., R.S.] The Father ceaselessly engenders the Son, and I say further: he engenders me as his son, and as the same son. I say still more: he engenders me not only as his Son, but he engenders me as himself, and himself as me [*er gebiert mich als sich und sich als mich*, R.S.]" (Pr. 7).[132]

Eckhart takes a further step forward when he thinks of this 'energetic' identity between the ground of the soul and the ground of God in a reciprocity of begetting:

> "*In principio*": this word makes us understand that we are an only Son whom the Father has eternally engendered in the hidden darkness of the eternal 'concealment' [*Verborgenheit*, R.S.] and who is nonetheless immanent at the first commencement of the emptiness [*Lauterkeit*, R.S.] which is a plenitude of all emptiness. Here I have reposed eternally and slept in the hidden knowledge of the eternal Father, immanent and not emerging out of it. Out of this emptiness he has eternally engendered me as his only Son in the image of his eternal paternity, that I might be Father and engender him from whom I was birthed. (Pr. 23)[133]

In the identity of begetting between God and the spiritual soul, the filiation is reciprocal. In Proclus, the unity of act, of subject and of object, was a unity of intelligence, inaugurating a 'theory of knowledge' by means of its scission; perhaps the experience of identity that Meister Eckhart delivers to us is not far from the event, the gift of the unique mystery, which made Hölderlin sing, and the Dharma master be silent.

The texts of Vatican II do not speak of God or of the birth of Christ in the soul of the believer (nor, for that matter, do they speak of love, faith, or hope). The council has presented anew the relations between the bishops and Pope, between the Roman Church and the world, between Catholics and Protestants—yet, would we not touch

---

132 [Eckehart, *Deutsche Predigten und Traktate*, 185. DW 1: 109,7–11 (Pr. 6, "Iusti vivent in aeternum"). Here, R.S. rearranges Eckhart's text.]
133 [Eckehart, *Deutsche Predigten und Traktate*, 258. DW 1: 382,3–383,1 (Pr. 22 "Ave gratia plena").]

here upon the same phenomenon of breaking apart and forgetting the unique question that we have already encountered in the form of modern sciences, in speaking of the question of being and of questions of beings? This theology of 'relations' is perhaps the culmination of the medieval theology of 'fittingnesses': the breaking apart of the unique mystery into increasingly numerous mysterious entities (the French translation of *Christos*, *'le' Christ* ['the' Christ], still manifests this tendency to objectify into 'entities,' preceded by an article...) would have thus found its fulfillment in the slogans on 'dialogue.' From the point of view of the form of thought, *relations of fittingness* are not far off from *relations of dialogue*; but all theology of mysteries is indeed far from the thinking of the unique mystery.

Perhaps the current forgetting of the unique mystery will one day give rise to a new prophet in theology, just as the manifestation of the forgetting of being in the last century prepared a 'step back' toward the thinking of being and toward experiencing its gift.

II) The Leap into the Concreteness of Faith

§10) The Suspicion Overcome

Theology is occupied essentially with concrete questions that are raised by faith in the salvation offered by God in Jesus Christ. Faith casts a new light, a new 'formality,' on that which is, and in this way, it gives access to a new order of questions. To think while believing [*penser en croyant*] is to make a leap into the concreteness of this new order, and to accept that the mind limits itself to the elucidation of the connections between these new questions. To believe is also to die to the unique question whose advent is man's lingering abode.[134]

---

134 To tell the truth, this lingering abode certainly does not withdraw itself: it is called 'Jesus Christ' and from now on requires another type of thinking. Different authors have tried to confront the thinking of the mystery of the question of being with the thinking of the mystery of the salvation of God: Bernhard Welte, for six years, has been developing the idea that the history of being 'is' already the history of salvation. At first, he was content with a purely interpretative rapprochement ("Theology must, I believe, learn to understand the witnesses on the basis of the *epochal understanding of being* that has in each case given birth to them" [*Auf der Spur des Ewigen: Philosophische Abhandlungen über verschiedene Gegenstände der Religion und der Theologie* (Freiburg:

Herder, 1965), 416], inspired by Heidegger ("The thought of the epochal history of the understanding of being was prompted in me by Martin Heidegger's concept of the history of being. It was however formed independently of the latter" [ibid., 417[n4]]). In his later work *Heilsverständnis: Philosophische Untersuchung einiger Voraussetzungen zum Verständnis des Christentums* (Freiburg: Herder, 1966), Welte goes even further: the comprehension of being is already the comprehension of salvation (the second part is entitled "Seinsverständnis als Heilsverständnis" [comprehension of being as comprehension of salvation]); since the two comprehensions are 'epochal,' the mystery of the history of being temporizes the mystery of the history of salvation.

Heinrich Schlier opts for the rapprochement between the experience of what we have sketched at the end of §6 and the experience of the encounter of the resurrected Christ: "In the event of the history of Jesus Christ, God declares himself definitively [..., R.S.]. The word [*Wort*] of this happening articulates itself in the interpreting answer [*auslegenden Ant-wort*, literally 'counter-word which lays out'] of those who apprehend it [..., R.S.]. The transmission of God through Jesus Christ to the world enters into the transmission of those who have experienced it" (*Besinnung auf das Neue Testament* [Freiburg: Herder, 1964], 42).

Karl Rahner still represents 'absolute being' [*l'être absolu*] as a correlate of the human spirit. His analysis of the structures of the spirit has led him to read in it an opening to transcendence. Although it does not 'posit' a revelation of this very transcendence in a human being, this opening allows for its appearance—when it comes about in history and is announced by preaching—to be neither impossible nor absurd. In the finite spirit, there is an expectation [*attente*] for the infinite with which it is not contradictory that God gives himself to that finite spirit under a man's countenance. Using his anthropology *Geist in Welt* [*Spirit in the World*], completed in 1936, Rahner has developed this 'hearing capability' in *Hörer des Wortes* (Munich: Kösel, 1963), in which he writes (115) [*Hearers of the Word*, trans. Michael Richards (New York: Herder and Herder, 1969), 92, modified]: "It is of decisive importance to our study, however, to see that man's transcendence toward the absolutely luminous being that is completely knowable is at the same time at least openness before a God who deals freely with man [..., R.S.]. If this is the way things are, then knowledge of God as absolute being [*Seins*] is simultaneously a having to reckon with a possible action of God that goes beyond the act that has already taken place in the free positing of the finite spirit. Then man has always been essentially the listener for a possible revelation of God." More recently, the role Rahner has attributed to philosophy is that of being a 'preparation' for hearing the word of God: "Philosophy is necessary and useful for the proclamation of Christianity when it suffices for our actually sufficient hearing of revelation. But it only does this if we acquire it anew in and out of our own spiritual situation, which is actually ours here and now" (*Schriften zur Theologie*, vol. 6 [Einsiedeln: Benziger, 1965], 102).—It thus seems that Rahner wants philosophical thought to be kept in the function of a 'preparation for faith.'

Heinrich Ott takes from Heidegger the most beautiful thinking 'on the way': from the thinking of being, the thinking about God can learn that it has to wander from one experience to another (*ein 'erfahrendes Denken,' 'er-fahren'* comes from: gaining by moving on routes). He writes, on the role of 'systematic' theology: "Essential thinking

To think while believing, is it to abandon the unique spontaneous question of thinking as we have made it emerge along the way? We ourselves were until now content with considering the intelligibility or the form of thinking actualized in philosophy and theology. These were shown to be radically divergent: the question—if however it is one question—that theology poses is not the question of being. Heidegger writes: "for anyone for whom the Bible reveals divine truth, questioning about being will always be a 'doing as if,' although he can still be interested in the question of philosophy; to take seriously the phenomenon of the unique question, amounts for the believer to renouncing his faith. A 'Christian philosophy' is thus a misunderstanding and a piece of wooden iron."[135] Faith and philosophy unfold in two mutually exclusive orders of questions. We would like to now abandon the methodological debate and ask whether the life of faith always already overcomes an insoluble dilemma of self.

It must be underscored first of all that faith is never something acquired or possessed in the manner of an object. It is perpetually becoming. Ceaselessly, God invents new ways of arousing faith; ceaselessly the believer must will it. Faith, the free act of a man in search of a life project, is subject to the time of this freedom and subjects this freedom to itself by temporizing it; the ages of faith are as much the ages of freedom under the advent of God as those of God in the free becoming of man. To believe in Jesus Christ is to seek to better believe in him. In the itinerary of a life, faith appears as mixed with what it is not and, nonetheless, makes it such that it is the faith of such freedom. The presence of Christ in St. John's life was not the same as that in the life of Saint Paul; the life projects and, thus, the risks and the victories of faith immediately differ from one disciple to another. Since faith is never something acquired, it is determined differently according to the freedom of every believer.

---

does not arrive at results; it remains on the way, is experience, encounter [..., R.S.]. It corresponds to a claim. To be sure not every thinker and not every epoch stand under the same claim, but rather, each great thinker has his path" (in *Der späte Heidegger und die Theologie*, ed. James Robinson [Zurich: Zwingli, 1964], 130 [*The Later Heidegger and Theology*, ed. James M. Robinson (New York: Harper & Row, 1963), 108, modified]). [In this note, R.S. supplies quotations only in German.]

135 [Heidegger, *Einführung in die Metaphysik*, now in GA 40: 8–9. Cf. *Introduction to Metaphysics*, trans. Gregory Fried and Richard Polt, 2nd ed. (New Haven: Yale University Press, 2014), 8.]

If, *de jure*, faith excludes disquiet and anxiety, it will never eliminate them from the existence of the believer; it will even render them more painful in placing them under the sign of the love of God. Faith, because it is always becoming, will also always be disquieted and anxious.

Wishing to determine faith entirely by the formality of that which is revealed thus seems to go against the faith which is lived. The believer lives as much off the divine light in himself as off his questioning of being. Existence that believes [*l'existence croyante*] always implies an intrinsic relation to the existence that does not believe: the two are merged in a single adventure that is thus the adventure with God, of Paul or of John. If the theologian knows God and all things according to their principles, the believer knows God in the singularity of his own life as a believer. The only God that Israel is allowed to invoke is the God-with-Israel [*le Dieu-avec-Israel*]; and he speaks to his people not only in his temple and through the accomplishments of the law, but also at Sodom and in the unfaithfulness to his precepts. God remains faithful throughout men's fidelity and infidelity.—The act of faith is entirely an act of a man whose steps the light of grace comes to 'guide' (Luke 1:79), and whose feet, shoes, and soles are those of the unique question that man poses, the question of being. This simultaneity however, to repeat, is not linked to the very structure of the act of faith (which is sufficiently described when one affirms that it is "the act of the intellect adherent to divine truth under the command of the will that is moved by God by grace" *S.Th.* IIa, 2, q. 2, a. 9), but rather to its *de facto* accomplishment in a living, searching existence. Far from diminishing the place of faith in the heart of man, it [the simultaneity] sharpens its zeal. To believe in God and to continue to carry within oneself the unique question that the question of being is, is to search for God with still more love.

Is the encounter with Christ the event that Heidegger's thinking prepares for by introducing man to the fatherland that, for him, is the question of being? To describe the event of the free gift in this way would be to fall into the dogmatism and the manipulation of mystical experiences. Let us say rather that faith can prepare for a privileged experience that is like an introduction to the vision of God. In this experience, the simultaneity of the questions of faith and of the philosophical question would be abolished, whereas the faith which is lived 'ordinarily' would keep that simultaneity as such. To live while believing, for us, is to believe while posing the radical question which is not a question to God. To live while believing is to grasp God "by the hands of faith that hold one in the night" (an expression of St. Augustine).[136]

"The phenomenon of the question in theology," if 'question' means the question of being and 'theology' means the science of God, is a contradiction in terms that verifies our initial suspicion. "The phenomenon of the question in the life of the believer" overcomes this suspicion provisionally; the leap into the concreteness of faith is not a leap outside of the lingering abode that the question of being is for man. But when the provisional shall cease before the power of glory, every question and every anxiety shall be struck dumb in the silence of the one who willed them the better to be loved, and this silence shall live off of song and laughter.

---

136 [Cf. Augustine, *Sermones*, 375C, "Tractatus de Quinta Feria Sanctae Paschae": "In die tribulationis meae Dominum exquisivi manibus meis nocte coram eo" [In my day of tribulation, I searched for the Lord in the night with my hands held out before Him"; cf. Ps. 77:3.]

9

Peregrine Identity

(1969, trans. from the French by Michael Portal)

Here we include the epigraphs, introduction, and conclusion of an early, markedly different version of Schürmann's Wandering Joy: Meister Eckhart's Mystical Philosophy *(1972). Schürmann submitted this early version to Le Saulchoir as a final thesis in 1969, titling it "Identité pérégrinale: Le concept de détachement dans les sermons allemands de Maître Eckhart" ("Peregrine Identity: The Concept of Detachment in Meister Eckhart's German Sermons"). In it, Schürmann focuses on Eckhart's preaching of detachment as an imitation of Christ's self-emptying on the way of the Cross. The detached thereby undergo a practical transformation of existence that Schürmann calls "peregrine identity with the origin," i.e., with the Godhead at the source of the Trinity. This early version also contains valuable remarks on conversion, on letting-be as a solution to the violent, "Promethean attitude" of our age, and on St. Francis as the one who "most visibly put into practice the doctrine of detachment."*

Illuminated by the Spirit,
baptized in fire,
whoever you are,
you are the throne of God,
you are the home, you are the instrument,
you are the light of the Godhead,
you are God,
God, God, God!

Saint Sergius of Radonezh[137]

---

[137] [From the so-called canticle of St. Sergius (penned in Italian by Fr. Divo Barsotti, a portion of which can be found on the outer chapel wall of the Comunità dei figli di Dio in Settignano, near Florence). R.S. gives a French translation, rendered into English here.]

The beginning of living beings is ungraspable;
we grasp the middle; but their destruction too
is ungraspable: does this warrant tears?
This one contemplates life as a wonder;
that one there speaks of it as a wonder; another
listens to talk of it as a wonder; and when
all has been heard, none yet understands it.
Also, science is worth more than perseverance,
but contemplation is worth more than science.
Detachment is worth more than contemplation;
and very close to detachment is beatitude.
For what we name detachment, know, Oh son,
that is Union itself.

Bhagavad-Gita[138]

Introduction

a) Too many words press themselves into our ears.
Too many words today press themselves into the ears of those who want to talk about God. They come to us from a cultural past, but also from the way in which everyone cohabitates and talks with themselves. As if it went without saying that God, man, the world, that friendship and prayer, could not unfold without recourse to words!

On the banks of a lake surrounded by fir trees, I say: "This lake is surrounded by fir trees." I pronounce these words, and already the immediacy is ruptured. We can certainly take refuge in painting and slow down the cascade of words with the help of forms and colors that address themselves to the retina. But here again, 'canvas', 'oil', 'jade green', 'Autumn', 'Black Forest' … they are all there. Wherever I turn, words have already arrived before me.

The technician, it is true, rejoices; it is thanks to the welcomed power of words that he organizes, transforms, manufactures what

---

138 [English rendering of R.S.'s modified translation of the French in *Bhagavad-Gîtâ*, trans. Émile-Louis Burnouf (Paris: Libr. de l'Institut, 1941), ch. II, vv. 28–29; ch. XII, v. 12; and ch. VI, v. 2.]

he calls the universe of objects. However, when it is not about a world of things to be dominated, but about a human being to know and love, the prompt usefulness of words will appear more ambiguous; they open to us their range of nuances which have proven themselves, they mediate knowledge, arouse attachment... but how to not feel them as a prefabricated straitjacket? Through them, we are forced to dissect the simple into consonants, vowels, syllables. The most serious things are the simplest, but the simple is unsayable. On the other hand, the perfectly taciturn person does not know or love anybody, because to know and to love is to still have recourse to words. To seek words is necessary; to find them is impossible.

It is before the God [*le Dieu*] that every word becomes decidedly intolerable. There is not a single word, even the most discreet, the most thought through, the most marveled at, that is not an unadmitted blasphemy. We would have to invent a new way of speaking of God, this one without words, but reuniting them all in a concentrated surge of meaning. The crowd of syllables would then be rejected as a heap of residues now useless, bothersome.

To escape from the tyranny of words by fleeing from the words themselves: would this be the only condition for the lake to become a lake again for us and nothing else, and for the God to become God again? I can of course refuse to speak, refuse to listen to what is said around me, and withdraw from the market of concepts and slogans; I will be able to create a kind of lunar landscape around me where there would be nothing left except, in the center of a great mental void, precisely the image of the lake, of the God; immediacy will be bought at the price of two words that remain: 'lake' and 'God.'

The mind [*esprit*] devoid of all articulable content, the Emptiness acquired at the end of a long ascesis, would this not be the secret of the immediate experience of God? But if nothing is worth saying or thinking, at the edge of the lake, under the gaze of God, then this 'being devoid of all saying and all thinking' will not itself be abolished as void; if it is the void that has the last word, it is not the void; it is not devoid of all words. In the same way, if it is pure feeling—as some have taught—that has the last word, it is not pure feeling.

Faced with the invading army of words, one will not be able to take refuge on the islands of Emptiness, of pure experiencing, or of any other non-word; the trans-lation toward the elsewhere of words is still carried out thanks to their help, and one would have proven the omnipresence of what precisely one had wished to abandon once and for all. We are besieged by words, it is useless to attempt an escape.

Immediacy 'before' words is a deception. It is within language that we must seek it. If this is so, perhaps there will be words 'in' and through which immediacy will deliver itself, servants who are vigorous and nonetheless self-effacing whose only job is to make us see? If the refusal to speak cannot compel God to come and cheer us up, if speaking is necessary, then what is there to speak about? What we are asking for are new words, but at the door of which wordsmith will we beg for them? And then, even then, will the endeavor be able to deliver on its promises? Because the new words will soon be old.

One of our elders taught us the words 'totality' and 'absolute spirit.'[139] It only takes two decades for another to rise up and serve us 'philosophical crumbs,'[140] destroying the very nerve of the vast work that was beginning to enchant us. Words age faster than their makers.

Finally, our groping nevertheless meets with something solid: a founding word [*parole*] exists, and it has become incarnate. The eternal has germinated in the temporal, and as a testimony of this germination, we precisely have words [*mots*], the Scriptures. Common, banal words—'son,' 'body,' 'forgiveness,' 'breaking of bread,' 'fidelity,' 'happiness,' 'father'... —like clay vases, have been filled with a new, divine, imperishable meaning, which intoxicates with joy those who know how to listen. So, is not every search for words now a vain lack of belief? Do not the words of Revelation sound eminently 'right' since they are inspired by the unique wordsmith that is the Spirit? Is he not capable, he and his spouse, the Church, of enriching certain human words with divine meanings that prevent them from aging, maintaining them in a continuously renewed youth thanks to his creative breath?

Even more: do not the words used and thus consecrated by Scripture and the Magisterium establish the Christian as 'immediately'

---

139 [Namely, Hegel. See especially *The Phenomenology of Spirit*.]
140 [The title of a book by Kierkegaard.]

the contemporary of Christ? Faith is born of listening to words, and faith establishes immediacy.

However, this divine meaning added on top of human words poses a problem. How are we to understand the dissociation between the supernatural 'meaning' ['*sens*'] and its natural 'receptacle'? Is a 'theandric' language just another language that our ears can hear? If human speech does not itself establish the meaning that the words would like to say, is not revelation radically incomprehensible, even impossible, today? Only a language that is ours through and through will establish us in the immediacy of Christ's contemporaneity. This immediacy must be conquered on the basis of words that are from the outset rich in meaning; it is not given by the very fact that there is a sacred text.

Said otherwise: If the words of Revelation constitute a privileged region of language, they still do not establish an immediacy such that it would be sufficient to have recourse to them to receive the event of Jesus of Nazareth in all its imperishable freshness. Words, even those of Revelation, must be torn away from the decay that threatens language. The grace of the event, always inexpressible, does not give itself intact, neither outside of words nor in words. Let the Freudian critique of the word 'father,' the Marxist critique of the word 'happiness,' be a serious invitation to verify the bases of our theandrism of the language of Revelation.

The true ascesis is the apprenticeship of saying and falling silent. The immediacy with the 'lake,' with the 'God,' will be second, a continual victory over words, at the level of words. In short, the immediacy will be an interpreted immediacy.

The status of language about God today thus appears: it is entirely interpretation. No fact of language, no tradition, will be abandoned to cultural anemia. Our contemporary must incessantly become again an auditor of his own words. When an entire epoch gathers for a new beginning, one would do well to relearn how to listen. It is the quandary of the new beginning that forces the exegetical status of thought.

However, what it means to interpret an ancient author is not clear.

b) *What does it mean to interpret an ancient author?*
Can we speak of a 'true' reading of a text? Or, on what condition is the reading of a text true?

It is necessary to question the man who submits himself to the privileged experience that is reading: what happens to him when he confines himself to this hermeneutic relation that is the reading of a document written in a language whose meanings his culture enables him to understand?

What happens to him is inscribed between two limits: a surge of interest that carries him toward the text he is about to read; and the result of this reading, the accomplishment of the hermeneutic relation by which it will be closed, the reading of the book finished. Between the *terminus a quo* and the *terminus ad quem* of this relation, terms that delimit a duration, something happens.

The most banal case of the hermeneutic relation perhaps most clearly manifests what its result or goal must be. I am thinking of those cheap novels that one buys in paperback in railway stations and that offer the public a fiction of feeling at low cost. The purpose of these quickly consumable tales is precisely to bewitch by the immediacy of their comprehension; the hermeneutic exercise being simplified to the extreme, their language seems close to the daily experience of the average customer. Here is their declared ambition: to transport the reader into an elsewhere made of illusions, to assimilate us to the universe that their language opens up. Illusion enchants; it develops a new possibility of being in the world [*d'être dans le monde*]. This possibility, we have already understood, is already ours, because the world that is offered to us hardly differs from the one that we move through.

The elsewhere is what is most comprehensible here, because it immediately reflects our own experience of language. The immediacy is founded on the way the reader moves through language. Self-understanding (which always precedes reflection), understanding of the world, and understanding of language: all three conspire to enchant by way of the illusion that offers us our own reality in a more desirable light.

The traveler who, in the train, leafs through his paperbacks is thus not, first of all, with the hero of his novel, nor even in public transportation: he is first of all with himself, under a new mode. The hermeneutic experience gives us a glimpse of a reality truer than our own, it tends to abolish the latter and to replace it. Pulp fiction, by accumulating words whose immediate meaning seems to be able to do without the work of interpretation, is immediately effective with regard to our way of inhabiting language, of inhabiting the world, and thus of inhabiting ourselves.

In another cultural domain, we must say that there are books whose reading leaves indelible traces. A great literary work, which 'captivates' its reader, transforms his way of seeing and acting; in closing such a book, the reader is no longer the same person he was when he started off. It is at the time of adolescence that such works shape us most deeply.

Here is what this phenomenon shows: the reality of a text, of a word which comes to us from outside, is powerful with regards to our own reality, it is truly creative. Reading appears as a veritable transfer of reality whose condition of possibility lies in a complicity within language. Inaugurating an experience with language, the hermeneutic relation concerns the very reality of our existence.

Clearly, to read is to interpret. Reading is indeed the life of a text insofar as it addresses itself to me. And to interpret is to exist anew. All interpretations are therefore not equal: there are some that "don't speak to me" [*"ne me disent rien"*]. The reading that inaugurates in me a new reality will be a 'good' one.

What does this word mean: reality? Beyond the information of the grammarian that it derives from the Latin word *res*, the usage itself teaches us its meaning: reality—that is what we call the whole of the things which are present at hand. The word reality, as a category for the totality of the objects that are present at hand, satisfies the desire for an understanding that is oriented according to present things, as opposed to the ones from the past, which are no longer 'real.' In another epoch, these things were themselves present, present at hand, 'real.'

But what about things to come? Doesn't the future, as that which is possible and which nobody has at their disposal yet, determine our reality more radically than present things? When it comes to ourselves, possibility sometimes seems stronger than reality; this at least indicates that the equation between the present thing and reality does not account for the phenomenon sufficiently.

One could call reality the project of existence in which man, by his way of being situated in language, joins together the past, the present and the future in a unique access to himself. We use the word reality in this sense: being with oneself [*l'être auprès de soi*] is the sole condition under which things present at hand or a text become significant. 'Reality' means something else than 'fact'; on facts I can count, I have to count with them, but I possess them—by knowledge, perspective, production. Over reality I have no sway. Of what in some way exists, reality says the meaning it takes on for me. The fact is mute, reality speaks. It is a category of language. What speaks to me is real. Only the saying liberates reality. Language is what for me lets reality appear.

The word 'reality' must thus be understood in an eminently historical sense. Reality is what language [*langage*] has already said (the idiom [*langue*] in which we are born to language), what it is saying now (the meaning of things in the world), and what the impulse of saying tends to rest in (a certain project of new existence). Reality is the coming repose in which the many words will signify an existence that is totally mine. Language indicates a reality that is about to make itself appear; it is the movement that carries us toward the appearing of our own reality. In language, reality comes about [*advient*]. In the hermeneutic experience, language, reality, and the future [*avenir*] are indissolubly linked.

The 'true' interpretation is the one that opens up a future for today's people. True interpretation gives the starting point.

Interpreting an ancient author will mean auscultating the letter of his writings in order to detect new possibilities of existence. This questioning will be done according to the guiding thread of language: what in Meister Eckhart made there be talk of it and how? What has come [*est advenu*] to language? What path does his saying open up for me today?

The creative interpretation of reality verifies the mode in which I myself access language for myself. And conversely, this mode makes possible and determines the mode in which an ancient author speaks to me.—Meister Eckhart says that whoever wants to understand his teaching on 'detachment' must himself already be highly 'detached' (Pf.: 209,30) [DW 2: 109,1–2 (Pr. 30, "Prædica verbum")].

To interpret an author is therefore to let oneself be verified by him. *Verum facere,* to render true, means the contestation of a reality, suitable to provoke it in its truth. Verification is the essential contestation that makes the contested reality say what its truth is. An amalgam of metals verifies its composition by the test [*épreuve*] of fire: the truth is made by fire.

Hermeneutic verification thus takes on the appearance of a testing of the reader; the truth of a text is tested by the one who submits to its power of contestation. The interpretation is always an ordeal; the word of the ancient author splits the way in which existence is with itself. The text is the hard test of the reader.

True interpretation opens a path. There are also authors whose thought engages the interpreter more explicitly to take upon himself a certain future, whose apostrophe they translate for us. Meister Eckhart is one of them. It will principally be a matter of our own existence in the interpretation of Meister Eckhart's sermons.

We call the type of thinking that is essentially concerned with opening up a new way to existence 'imperative' thinking; it is opposed to 'indicative' thinking that apprehends the real and establishes a noetics of it. According to this convention, the first type of thinking will be attentive especially to the possible, thus to the future, or even to what is ordained [*ordonné*], the second to the actual, the present, or the given [*donné*]. Imperative thinking and indicative thinking are separate with respect to the question of being: for the first one, being is known insofar as existence takes up the path—at once condition and unique content of ontology—for the second one, being is represented as the whole of the objects grasped by the mind.—Imperative hermeneutics engages on a path where being lets itself be experienced and tested [*éprouver*] anew.

c) *Your path comes from nowhere and goes nowhere.*

To walk a path: that means, first, leaving one place to reach another. The pilgrim experiences the sequence of places and realms. When the curious consciousness questions the pilgrim, it is interested only in the two ends of his road: where does he come from, where does he go? If, to this double question, the guest passing through responds with the required precision, his stay is agreed on; he is offered lodging and maybe is recommended a shortcut or even public transport so that he can save his strength and arrive faster to a safe haven. The curious consciousness, journalistic, has learned everything about the path when it learns of its starting point, the voyager's fatherland, and his point of arrival, his destination. Between the two, the ideal would be to complete the trip in zero time. The sequence of places, which is characteristic of the route, is not considered in itself, but only according to its usefulness, whether it facilitates or slows down the journey toward the end to be reached. The path spontaneously appears as the shortest passage between two geographical points.

Such an understanding of the path is born of the concern for a 'why.' Where does the path come from? And where does it lead to? Both questions arise from a single worry, that of the why. Why the path? Anxious about causes and ends, the unprompted consciousness does not see the path itself. It only worries about the reasons for the path.

Just as there are words for everyday use—all words, as vehicles of a certain amount of information and not of a call—so too do we speak of paths for everyday use—all paths, no matter where they lead, as long as the common consciousness questions their why.

Is it an adequate understanding of the phenomenon to ask the itinerant existence to give a reason for the 'why' of the path? Only the pilgrim can inform us whether the common concerns about reasons liberate or rather obstruct the access to the phenomenon of the path. We are looking for the one who, as an expert in itinerancy, will authoritatively enlighten our understanding of the path.—But will we ask him a litany of various questions about what happened to him on the way? His answers will appear as a series of details without any apparent link. It is again the curious consciousness that demands an anecdotal account. We do not ask for many words [*mots*] about the path, but for the one word [*parole*] to be spoken to us that allows us to see.

However, we ourselves are always already engaged on a path.

Where do we come from? Where are we going? We must unlearn posing the question in this way. If we want to experience and test our essential itinerancy, we must not occupy ourselves with a concern for the why. To live without why; letting be [*laisser être*] what is, the plane trees that delimit the route, the swamp even further where we don't dare go; letting be the turns, the inclines and the declines, the noise of other travelers and also the solitude. We have unlearned how to let ourselves go [*nous laisser aller*]. The understanding of our existence as the shortest passage between two fixed points in a biography is a poor understanding of the path that we are on, and is in any case insufficient. Where do we come from? From ourselves, from nothingness, from the totality. Where are we going? Toward ourselves, toward nothingness, toward the totality.—Such answers, which want to indicate and inform, do not teach us anything about our essential wandering [*errance*].

This is the teaching of Meister Eckhart: as long as you have not learned to 'leave' yourself [*te 'laisser' toi-même*], as long as you have not learned to walk with *gelâzenheit*, you don't know how to live.

Gelâzenheit, in modern German *Gelassenheit*, designates an attitude. It is the attitude of a being who looks at objects and paths not according to their usefulness, but who accepts them in their autonomy. This attitude makes one renounce influences and provides equanimity. This word can also be translated equally as 'infinite resignation' and as 'serenity.' Both translations speak of becoming unaccustomed to possessing things and to possessing oneself. *Lâzen*, *lassen*, means 'to let,' 'to restore freedom,' 'to untie.' It is only secondarily that it means 'to abandon,' 'to reject,' or even 'to ignore.' The one who has learned to 'let-be' restores all things to their primitive freedom, he returns all things to themselves. He has unlearned enslaving them to his projects, he has despoiled himself of all affirmations of self where the mixture of curiosity and ambition inhibits him.

Four centuries later, Meister Eckhart's preaching of *gelâzenheit* served as inspiration for Angelus Silesius' verses,[141] in which the latter takes up the formulations of the Dominican, sometimes to the letter.

It is, furthermore, with regard to these sermons on *gelâzenheit* that Martin Heidegger will say that in Meister Eckhart "there are many good things to take [*prendre*] and to learn [*apprendre*]."[142]

The attitude contrary to letting-be is characterized by the 'Promethean' spirit. Prometheus is the dominator of nature par excellence: he steals a piece of the celestial fire, invents the construction of ships, and finally makes a fool of Zeus. He introduces enmity into

---

141 *Pf.*:, 12f. [DW 4,1: 412,36–415,68 (Pr. 102, "Ubi est, qui est natus Rex Iudaeorum?")] In Angelus Silesius, *Pèlerin chérubinique*, trans. Henri Plard (Paris: Aubier, 1946), 120 [*CW* 2.92: 85], *Gelassenheit* has the same meaning: "Gelassenheit fäht Gott; Gott aber selbst zu lassen | Ist ein Gelassenheit die wenig Menschen fassen" [Releasement grasps God, but to release God himself | is a releasement that few people grasp].
142 Martin Heidegger, *Gelassenheit* (Pfullingen: Neske, 1959), 36; now in GA 13: 42; cf. *Questions III*, trans. André Préau (Paris: Gallimard, 1966), 187, and *Discourse on Thinking*, trans. John M. Anderson and E. Hans Freund (New York: Harper & Row, 1966), 61–62.

the cosmos, because from then on man wants to be a conqueror and lord. The Promethean race does not consider doing the work of reconciliation, but of violence. *Gelâzenheit* means nothing to this race, which rushes into fury and cunning. While Prometheus boasts of ennobling the earth, he increases its divisions: this is his fury. Under the banner of building the world hides an enterprise that destroys its unity: this is his cunning.

Today, the Promethean will to power and the spirit of letting-be establish an antinomy in the technological universe. Prometheus reduces nature to the state of a corpse, while letting-be tends to restore it to its perfect harmony with man. By coordinating themselves as antinomies, the will to power and *gelâzenheit* determine the current effort to manage the globe.

From the living organism that it was before Prometheus rose up, the earth is converted into inorganic matter, rearrangeable according to needs, by the relationship of utility and property. The synthetic products that contemporary automated industry delivers to us reveal even on their smooth surface this cadaverous aspect, in which the relationship between master and slave culminates. These soulless objects, washable but unable even to rot, illustrate the ambiguity of the humanization of the earth: the paradox of technology [*la technique*] is that, while leading the universe toward a noble world for man, it is unceasingly hounded by the project of exploiting, dominating, making use of, and enslaving. This ambiguity is an integral part of the Promethean attitude, and is reflected in the word 'exploit' itself, since it means both to cultivate or to make valuable, thus to humanize, and to abuse for one's own benefit, to pillage by fraud.[143]

The systematic and organized reduction of the earth to a corpse, which is the rebellious face of Prometheus, the face punished by Zeus, is the extreme opposite of 'letting-be' as taught in the sermons of Meister Eckhart. For us, it is not a question of condemning Prometheus, but of teaching him to free the universe that he has

---

143 Jim Morrison (The Doors, "When the Music's Over" in *Strange Days*, Elektra EKS 74014, 1967) sings the accusation of this extinction of the earth: "What have they done to the earth? | What have they done to our fair sister? | Ravaged and plundered | and ripped her and bit her | Stuck her with knives | in the side of the dawn | and tied her with fences | and dragged her down." [In the original, R.S. includes his French translation. See the beginning of chapter 10.]

subjected. The real question is to know whether will to power and *gelâzenheit* are necessarily opposed and exclude each other irrevocably; in the eyes of the young Marx, the two attitudes are reconciled only in the communist utopia of a society without classes, a society which will see:

> the completion of the essential unity of man with nature, the true resurrection of nature, the accomplished naturalism of man, and the accomplished humanism of nature.[144]

Faced with the subjugation and extinction of nature by the Promethean will, Eckhart calls to the path where God, man, and the world, where every being, can return to themselves, far from any seizing hold of or brutalization. Eckhart's thought, from which we indeed still have much to learn, aims at liberating the master from the slave, man from the things he thinks he is handling, and at restoring the one and the other to their primitive serenity.

It is not by chance that Meister Eckhart chose to preach. He invites his listeners to come back from the oblivion of their essential freedom, and to embark on the way where it lets itself be experienced and tested anew. He calls this way 'detachment,' a concept that will serve us as a guide in exploring the new path. He thus announces a simple message, his doctrine is not esoteric or extraordinary. It concerns what is most ordinary in an existence, and what most people live. It answers the elementary questions in the apprenticeship of the craft of living:

> What about my originary freedom, and how will I regain it? How will I come back to myself?

In the execution of this program, Eckhart often resorts to paradoxical formulations. Indeed, scholastic conceptuality, too analytical

---

[144] *Manuscrits de 1844*, trans. Émile Bottigelli (Paris: Ed. Sociales, 1962), 89. [See Karl Marx, Ökonomisch-Philosophische Manuskripte, in *Werke–Schriften*, vol. 1, Frühe Schriften, ed. Hans-Joachim Lieber and Peter Furth (Darmstadt: Wissenschaftliche Buchgesellschaft, 1971), 537; cf. *Economic and Philosophic Manuscripts of 1844*, trans. Martin Milligan and Dirk J. Struik, in *Marx/Engels Collected Works*, vol. 3 (London: Lawrence and Wishart, 1975), 298.]

when it comes to giving an account of an experience of unity, offers no other approach to the One than the dialectic of antinomies. God is, and he is not. God is good, and he is not good. Man is God, and he is nothingness. Also, Eckhart does not hesitate to distance himself as much from the official thinking of his time[145] as from the traditional currents that we are accustomed to call Neoplatonic and Aristotelian. In fact, he does not fit into any tradition, nor did he generate a school. His thought, bold and disquieting, has inspired the greatest authors of Western philosophy (and we will mention a few examples) but refuses all systemization.

Is Meister Eckhart a philosopher, a theologian, an educator? It has been said that he transposes the metaphysics of his great predecessors into psychological advice; less frequently, one has emphasized the poetic character of his work—especially with the aim of warning those among his readers who would want to take literally what he says about the relationship between man and God.[146] In reality, these philosophical, theological, pedagogical, psychological, and poetic tendencies are intertwined in his work in a literary genre which it would be wrong to analyze under only one of its aspects, neglecting the others. There is in Meister Eckhart a veritable entanglement of categories. He is a philosopher, but to read him simply as a philosopher is to miss his message. He is a poet in the wake of Wolfram von Eschenbach, and, anticipating Luther, he even holds the rank of one of the great innovators of the German language, but his poetic genius should not serve as a pretext for the reader to dispense with a rigorous analysis of his assertions.—So, which categories to use? The difficulty will consist in doing justice to all

---

145 Konrad Weiss, *Meister Eckharts Stellung innerhalb der theologischen Entwicklung des Spätmittelalters* (Berlin: Töpelmann, 1953), especially 29–39, has sketched the intellectual landscape of the beginning of the 14th century, in which Meister Eckhart was embedded. In this passionate study, Weiss shows to what extent Meister Eckhart was independent of the trends of his epoch—above all, nominalism—and how he instead inaugurated the impetus of returning to the sources which would later characterize the Renaissance in the 15th century.

146 James M. Clark, *Meister Eckhart: An Introduction to the Study of his Works* (London: Nelson, 1957), dedicates a chapter to "Meister Eckhart, the Scholar and Poet," 99f. He concludes by saying: Meister Eckhart was a man of imagination, which excuses the assertions which we don't know what to do with in his work. "The tendency to take his remarks too literally is to be avoided," 104.

these various aspects which make up the face of the living Meister Eckhart, without adding to the confusion.

Another difficulty is the freedom, even the casualness, with which he treats received doctrines. After stating the opinion of one of the 'masters' (most often Albert the Great or Thomas Aquinas), he then declares: "I, Eckhart, tell you the opposite..."; or even, he concludes something he has personally developed with the warning: "what I am telling you here is contrary to the doctrine of all the great masters." Eckhart leverages philosophical and theological traditions as Romans used their historical monuments: he makes use of them as quarries for the construction of a new dwelling.

More profoundly, the multiplicity of the intellectual faces of Meister Eckhart is in conformity with the intention of his thought: by successive negations to bring man to experience the nothingness that is the true fullness. The antinomian approach, in his work, serves to introduce the believer to the 'nocturnal' experience of faith, that is to say, to the night of sensibility:

> Many people complain that they feel neither inner collectedness nor intimate devotion, nor sweetness, nor particular consolation coming from God. Such people do not understand anything. I am willing to tolerate them in this way, but it is not the best; (DW 1: 272,6–8 [Pr. 16b, "Quasi vas auri"])

the night of intelligence:

> If we grasp God in being [*l'être*], we grasp him in his forecourt, for being is the forecourt in which he dwells. As long as you still know something of him, it is not God; (Pf.: 82,7–8 [DW 1: 150,1–2 (Pr. 9, "Quasi stella matutina"); DW 3: 221,2–3 (Pr. 71, "Surrexit autem Saulus")])

the night of faith:

> Those who seek neither sainthood, nor reward, nor the kingdom of heaven, but have renounced everything, even that which is their own, it is in such men that God is glorified. (DW 1: 100, 4–8 [Pr. 6, "Iusti vivent in aeternum"])

His taste for paradox and intellectual independence contributed to his being condemned as a heretic. Only a strictly exegetical method that penetrates to the heart of his thought and reveals its articulations will allow us to say to what extent this condemnation was justified or not. There is no longer doubt today that the theologians of Pope John XXII carefully examined the transcripts of the sermons submitted to their evaluation; but it is also certain that Meister Eckhart was the victim of gross distortions of his sayings and of summary and thoughtless attacks.

The most characteristic texts of Meister Eckhart, those in which the originality of his thought and the creative genius of his language are best felt, are the sermons in German. Among these sermons, we choose one of them that particularly brings into relief the 'peregrine' character of his doctrine: the sermon "Intravit Jesus in quoddam castellum" [DW 1: 21–45 (Pr. 2)].

Only a detailed analysis of such a text, without simplification of contrasts or apologetic or accusatory biases, will make it possible to evaluate whether Michel Henry's observation is well founded:

> To those who condemned him as if, fooled by his enthusiasm and perhaps also by his love, Eckhart had, in the alleged identification of the creature with God, as it were exaggerated the feelings and ideas suggested to him by his 'mystical' soul, only one thing was lacking, the understanding of his thought.[147]

Conclusion

a) Philosophical Judgment:
From ontological difference to peregrine difference

To follow Meister Eckhart's journey to the end is to experience a new understanding of being. This understanding springs from the peregrine experience of self, of God, and of the world, and has as its sole condition of possibility resolute engagement on the path of

---

[147] Michel Henry, *L'essence de la manifestation* (Paris: PUF, 1963), 1:398. [Cf. *The Essence of Manifestation*, trans. Girard Etzkorn (The Hague: Martinus Nijhoff, 1973), 319.]

serenity. The prerequisite of the peregrine understanding of being is the conversion to serenity.

Conversion—what does it mean?

The verb 'to convert' comes from *vertere*. The one who converts turns toward something from which he had previously turned away. The return, indicated in the Latin prefix '*cum-'vertere*, means paying new attention to something: what I had turned my back on is now before my face. Thomas Aquinas, in his visual language, says *motus de contrario in contrarium* [movement from contrary to contrary].[148] Conversion is an about-face that brings about the rehabilitation of something forgotten, so that the rehabilitated thing is now invested with predilection. The law of the *vertere* means the reversal of an intentional order, the conversion is a flip-flop in intentionality. The converted is turned and poured out [*versé hors*] from his former existing. Philosophically, the conversion to serenity means not only a new way of seeing, an additional attention or intention, but it flips the whole existence of the one who chooses *Gelassenheit* and *Abgeschiedenheit*.

The conversion that sends one on the road to the origin knows only the now. It pulls itself back together [*se réssaisit*] at every moment, does not admit any 'dues' that reassure for tomorrow. Serenity only gives life to the today of conversion. The existence that commits itself in this sense becomes significant for itself, without questioning the why of the path. It leaves itself [*se laisse elle-même*], abandons itself to the duplicity of the 'already' and the 'not-yet.' It experiences this duplicity, the law of the present-absent, as the normal status of its itinerancy. That which is present while being absent, that which shows itself while veiling itself, that of which the dialectic of cataphatism-apophatism translates the sparklings, is properly the mystery. We call that which manifests itself while hiding itself a mystery.—Of itself as well as of the origin, the existence that has been converted to the mystery of serenity has a peregrine knowledge.[149]

---

148 St. Thomas Aquinas, *S.Th.* I\ª, II\ᵃᵉ, q. 113, a. 1.
149 Pierre Hadot has shown in different studies that conversion, as thought according to Plotinus, Heidegger, and Wittgenstein, although different each time in its structure, presents itself philosophically as the same phenomenon; see, e.g., "Réflexions sur les limites du langage à propos du 'Tractatus logico-philosophicus' de Wittgenstein," *Revue de Métaphysique et Morale* 64, no. 4 (October–December 1959): 483 [cf. "Re-

Today, such an existence knows that it advances on strange paths.

The man who 'leaves' himself is so freed that the world does not love him. (Pf.: 260,10f.) [DW 2: 61,10-11 (Pr. 28, "Ego elegi vos")]

The pilgrim on the road to the origin in his migrating existence will be a taciturn guest. Preserving the mystery of his path from everyday use, he walks among unconfessed farewells. To the questions of the curious and the ambitious he answers with silence. He is the foreigner in the universe of organized domination and manipulation. Originary existence has become unusual today. It must accept its foreignness, it is used to it; wandering far from the origin but being called back to it, it is always already the exiled.

Wandering is serene; it is not the wanderer who converts to the origin, but the origin, by converting to the wanderer, introduces the latter into the mystery of serenity. The new understanding that he experiences is born of listening: listening to the apostrophe that invites one to the infinite resignation of detachment.

That in his wandering, man is thus able to listen to an interpellation—what does this manifest? Does not receptivity to the coming of the origin reveal a trait of this coming itself? Serenity, it seems to us, testifies that the origin has already made itself the ally of the wanderer.

Peregrine thinking manifests man as a place where the origin becomes a call. The serene man signifies this origin. In ontological terms: he is the being [*l'étant*] that signifies Being [*l'Etre*]. But he does not give himself the privilege of this signification. The origin, by converting itself to man, converts the latter to it, and thus to himself. The origin becomes man's ally in identical conversion to himself and to it. Detachment, says Eckhart, is identically the discovery of the ground of the soul and the discovery of the ground of God.

We call peregrine difference the itinerancy under which the existence experiences Being as that which converts itself to it in order to send it on the way of its own conversion. The peregrine difference is the distance that joins man to his origin, in a detached existence.

---

flections on the Limits of Language: Wittgenstein's 'Tractatus Logico-Philosophicus,'" trans. John A. McFarland, *CrossCurrents* 20, no.1 (Winter 1970): 51-52], and "Heidegger et Plotin," *Critique* 15, no. 145 (1959): 549f.

Detachment thus takes on the function of a photographic developer [*révélateur*]. We have spoken of the Difference where being-in-God is opposed to being-with-God; or again: the One in the soul to the multiplicity of substances; or finally: being among created things to the ground of the uncreated soul. This difference is 'ontological' in that it declares itself to the questioning of beings [*l'étant*] in view of being [*l'être*]—a questioning that denounces created being, *iht*, as borrowed being, *niht*, nothingness.

The 'originary unfolding,' *wesen* in the verbal sense, in beings gives itself to be thought of as 'beingness' ['*étantité*'],[150] that is to say, as nothing. Thus the meditation on the nothingness of the created and on the origin, *wesen*, reveals an amphiboly of being, *wesen*, which in beings gives itself to be thought of as entity, *iht*. Being appears as double.

Far from being added to being, this ambiguity or duplicity is for Meister Eckhart the very meaning of what is; the Difference is 'being itself.' The ontological difference does not, therefore, propose two things for representation, so that we would compare them according to their respective greatness and conclude: Being, *wesen*, is greater than the entity, *iht*. Eckhart refuses precisely that creatures are "small or anything: they are pure nothingness." [DW 1: 69,8–70,1 (Pr. 4, "Omne datum optimum").]

Nothingness is being itself insofar as it has retreated into the entity. Meister Eckhart thinks the 'ontological' difference not to better think man, God, the world, but instead to think the origin: the source and the estuary, the bed and the stream, the desert and the solitude where the Three originate. The ontological difference, for him, is the break [*brisure*] between the entity that gives to the Three the appearance of being, although they are nothingness, and the Being of the origin that retreats into the mystery and thus also veils itself with nothingness.

The 'peregrine' difference gives being to be thought as it calls to man on the path. The peregrine difference, no more than the ontological difference, is not thought in service of man. It is thought in service of the origin. But it says more than ontological difference: it

---

150 See above, page 90. [R.S. refers here to an earlier passage of his text not included in the translated excerpts here. A later version of the passage can be found in *ME* 142–43; *WJ* 83–84.]

says the itinerancy that the origin inflicts on existence. It says the destiny of the man who lets himself be converted [*se laisse convertir*]. The metaphysics of duplicity fades behind the peregrinating existence. His peregrination leads the detached man nowhere, but it makes him experience the attraction of the origin.

If detachment is thus the condition for the origin to manifest itself as a call, this implies that between man and the origin there opens a difference within which the interpellation can resound. Detachment manifests this difference. The peregrine difference gives the origin and man to be thought as reunited in the call. 'Peregrine difference' says more than 'ontological difference': what it also says is the *dynamis* proper to the origin to attract toward itself whoever lets himself be converted.

Identity by conversion and by call is inseparable from the difference where the demand is made on existence to renew itself entirely. The ontological difference opens to man a space where he can think; the peregrine difference opens to him green meadows where he can live.

The ontological difference separates what is originary from what is not originary; the peregrine difference separates that which in man is already 'in' the origin from that which is still only with the origin. The showing [*monstration*] of a not-yet, preaching, suggests the difference between the given [*donné*] and the ordained [*ordonné*]: Everything is not yet as it should be, the exhortation to return to the origin is possible and necessary.

To conclude and to illustrate the mutation of ontological difference into peregrine difference as an interpretation of Meister Eckhart invites us to think of it, we shall briefly consider the itinerary of Francis of Assisi. It is undoubtedly he who, a century before Meister Eckhart, most visibly put into practice the doctrine of detachment.

In his 'Testament,' Francis of Assisi writes:

> There was no one who showed me what I ought to do, but the Sovereign himself revealed to me that I ought to live according to the form of the Holy Gospel.[151]

---

151 "Nessuno mi mostrava che cosa dovessi fare; ma lo stesso Altissimo mi rivelò che dovevo vivere secondo la forma del santo Vangelo." Fra Francesco d'Assisi, "Testamento" (1226): 14, in *Scritti*, ed. V. Facchinetti (Milan: Vita e Pensiero, 1921), 98. For

This sentence, taken from the document that has been called "the most solemn manifestation of his thinking,"[152] contains the principal elements of an understanding, through conversion, of the peregrine difference.

Let us note first of all that Francis' statement must be understood in reference to a specific event in his life. According to the first accounts of this life, the scene to which the notation of the Testament refers is situated in the spring of the year 1207.[153] Francis had embraced the project of betrothal to 'Lady Poverty' for a little less than two years, and for some months he had been living near the small church of San Damiano, away from the city and separated from his family. It is known how his father, after vain attempts to make him return close to him, decided to repudiate him definitively. However, he wanted to recover the money he had given to his unworthy son for the reconstruction of the old chapel where he then spent his days.

It was in this context and before the bishop's court that the decisive event took place. The father, Pietro Bernardone, demanded the sum he considered his due. The bishop reminded the young Francis that if he wanted to marry poverty, he had to return the donations made for the "restoration of the house of God." It is only then, free from the shackles of a debtor, that he would be truly poor.

The court was usually held on the steps of the cathedral. In front of the city's notables, the bishop, and his own family, Francis declared: "Not only will I give him back the money that belongs to him, but with a joyful heart I will also give him back my clothes." Then he undressed, laid everything he had on at his father's feet, and to the assembled citizens he proclaimed [*protesta*]:

> Listen well: until now I called Pietro Bernardone my Father, but since I have formed the project of serving the Lord, I am giving him back this money that caused him so much grief, with all these clothes that I pos-

---

the conversion of Francis, see *Die Schriften des hl. Franziskus von Assisi*, ed. Kajetan Esser and Lothar Hardick (Werl: Coelde, 1956), Exkurs 3: *Busse*, 199f.
152 Paul Sabatier, *Vie de Saint François*, 42nd ed. (Paris: Fischbacher, 1914), 385.
153 *Franz von Assisi: Legenden und Laude*, ed. Otto Karrer, 3rd ed. (Zurich: Manesse, 1945), 586.

sess belonging to him, and from now on I will say: our Father who art in heaven, and no longer: my father Pietro Bernardone.[154]

The bishop then covered him with his cloak, understanding, as the *Vita* of Ceprano adds, that he had just witnessed a great mystery.[155] Another *Vita* comments in the manner of a midrash: "Naked, the man of God then conformed himself with Him who was stripped on the cross."[156] The trial of Assisi is the celebration of the marriage between Francis and 'Lady Poverty.'

"Until now ... and from now on": the revelation of the path that Francis was to follow, even though it had been prepared for two years, appeared as suddenly evident. It is in the 'now' of conversion that Pietro Bernardone was destituted of his paternity and that the marriage between Francis and the Chosen Woman was sealed. In our vocabulary: the understanding of the call that opens a path is granted in the moment. The peregrine identity with the origin comes about as a sudden event.

On the other hand, we can talk about a revelation only after the fact. "The Sovereign himself reveals to me ..."; when the origin converts itself to us in order to call us to detachment, we can only say that the revelation 'was made.' 'It' was thus granted.

He who speaks of a revelation speaks identically of the path that is his already at the time of his testimony; the point of departure has already been taken when the revelation reaches language.

Let us remember the Eckhartian theory of the *bîwort*; the word [*parole*] forever hidden where a life is said, becomes a 'conjunction' with the Word [*Verbe*]. It is a way of expressing, according to what happens in language, the reversal that revelation inflicts on the one who lets himself be converted.

"... that I ought to live according to the form of the Holy Gospel": when the origin becomes word, or revelation, it indicates and opens a

---

154 *Franz von Assisi*, ed. Karrer, 47f.
155 *Acta Sanctorum*, Oct. II, Antverpiae 1788, 729, col. b. [Cf. Tommaso da Celano, *Vita di San Francesco d'Assisi* (Rome: Tipografia della Pace, 1880), vi, 36.]
156 Iulianus De Spira, *Vita sancti Francisci*, in *Analecta Franciscana*, vol. X (Florence: Collegio S. Bonaventura, 1926–1941), 340: "Iam se vir Dei nudus in cruce nudato conformat." The editors point out: "Hic conformitatis cum Christo conceptus novus est in Iuliano" [Here the concept of conformity with Christ is new in Iulianus], which perhaps confirms the role that we attribute to this episode.

way. From now on you will live according to what has been revealed to you. It is characteristic of the phenomenon of conversion that in the experience of the 'from now on,' the word manifests its effectiveness on existence in the form of a *praxis* that is urgently demanded. Everything happens as if the origin apostrophized the convert: "You will go away and you will do..." The one who has experienced the apostrophe of the origin feels in a hurry to quit his country.

At the core of wandering, the call to return resounds. Already we inhabit the originary word that calls us back close to ourselves. Already the itinerancy evolves 'in' the origin that has come to us; on the way to the origin and already in it, the converted existence inaugurates the peregrine identity with the Solitude from where it comes and to where it returns.

b) Theological Judgment:
From negative theology to abnegative theology

In a theological reading, detachment means the loss, undergone by the believer, of any external or internal support to his faith. As we have said, the detached man experiences the failure of God represented as a counterpart to subjectivity or as a counterpart to the world.

One can ask oneself, in fact, what the disappearance of God in the anonymity of the origin means for a Christian.

Generally speaking, two understandings of faith can claim to come from the Bible.

For the one, i.e., the 'personalist' understanding, believing will mean trusting in a Covenant Partner, in the God of Abraham who accompanies his people through the pitfalls of their history; this God is adorned with the most beautiful titles which all inspire confidence: the Father, the Rock, the Guardian, the Beloved...; one gives thanks to him for his faithfulness over the centuries, and one implores him to come and renew his great deeds.

Alongside this 'diurnal' invocation of the acting God, Scripture testifies to a 'nocturnal' understanding of faith. God veils himself; the rock gives way. God abandons man. Job laments that the Foundation has lost its ground, and none of his personalist theologian friends can bring back the God who has become scandalous. Christ himself, when he speaks for the last time of the Father, will loudly exclaim his desertedness.

Why did I not die new-born, not perish as I left the womb? Why were there two knees to receive me, two breasts for me to suck? [..., R.S.] Why give light to a man of grief? [..., R.S.] Why make this gift of light to a man who does not see his way? (Job 3:11–12, 20, 23)

Why have you deserted me? (Mark 15:34)

To experience that the question of why is an empty question is to do an apprenticeship in nocturnal faith. Such is the pedagogy of Meister Eckhart. He requires the believer to discard all external laws and prescriptions, liturgical practices, states of life, to renounce expressions about God and even to renounce God himself—in short, to abandon every last support of his faith.

The soul, in the extreme divestment of faith,

> has abandoned God and all things. You must in effect lose both the Kingdom of heaven and God; for your soul must be divested of everything that emanates from God, such that the Spirit can no longer give it anything. (Pf.: 532,8–11)[157]

The ultimate purification of faith, abandoning God for the love of God, perhaps opens a way of access to his mystery that an age without God is still able to understand.

In the God who in the course of Israel's history has fashioned a face for himself, in the God who acted millennia ago, Eckhart is completely disinterested. Judged against a dogmatics of the history of salvation, there is effectively little that is Christian about his thinking. The question remains intact, however, as to whether the logic of 'nocturnal' faith does not push the one who experiences it to the point of divesting himself even of the givens of the history of salvation.

For Meister Eckart, authentic Christian faith not only must tolerate such an entry into Christianity, but demands it: you will follow Jesus on the path of total abandonment; you will renounce yourself and you will renounce God; you will renounce the memory of the

---

157 [R.S. cites from the untitled tractate XIV in Pf., which is not in DW.]

great deeds accomplished in Jesus Christ; only then will you follow Jesus Christ on the way of the Cross.

We can still go one step further. The preaching of exinanition following Jesus is not a translation into practical language of the contents of a theology otherwise constituted as a body of theoretical doctrine; for Eckhart, theology, the *logos* about God, is nothing other than precisely the preaching of detachment or of conversion. The proclamation of this way is not an incidental duty of the theologian; rather, theology does not exist independently of the preaching of conversion.

This implies that if God fades away as a motivation for itinerancy, he also fades away as a subject matter of science. The destruction of theology as a science of God is the rigorous consequence of detachment understood as the renunciation of all supports to faith.

The question is therefore no longer whether Meister Eckhart teaches a positive or negative knowledge of God; he does not teach any knowledge, but a practice. He teaches total abnegation, the only condition on which man will be one and undivided in himself and will understand that knowledge is not the last word of faith.

> Since he desires to unite with God, to find him, [man, R.S.] must be one, separated from all things, undivided in himself, by abnegation of self. (S. XXXVII n. 375) [LW 4: 321 ("Unus deus et pater omnium")][158]

The perfectly detached man has nothing more to learn about God.

Said otherwise, and if we want, despite everything, to keep the word theology: in Eckhart, the transmutation of negative theology into abnegative theology is accomplished. Speaking of God only in relation to the journey of the converted man to serenity, Eckhart proposes an interpretation of wandering as a theological virtue [*théologale*]. The mystery of the path is precisely that nothing satisfies the spirit in search of knowing, that the point of departure as well as the point of arrival are lost in the desert, but that the experience of detachment is identically the experience of God. Divestment of self

---

[158] "Quia volens deo uniri, ipsum invenire, debet esse unus, divisus ab omnibus, in se indivisus abnegatione sui."

and divinization are a single "path without a path" (Pf.: 50,15f.) [DW 3: 486,13 (Pr. 86, "Intravit Iesus in quoddam castellum etc.")].

If such a teaching has moral consequences—for example, the renunciation of the accumulation of property—or dogmatic ones, the point of departure is not to be sought in either of these two disciplines. The entanglement of ethical, dogmatic, and ontological themes in Eckhart is practically inextricable; what is important to see is that his point of departure lies in a certain fundamental attitude of existence, which flows back to the three types of questioning. The hermeneutical key that introduces one to his thinking is serenity. From there comes the discomfort we feel in characterizing it as theological; from there also comes the extreme poverty in affirmations as taught in the Schools and by the Roman Magisterium.

The destruction of theology as a science in Meister Eckhart is the ultimate consequence of an authentically Christian experience, if Christian faith is defined first of all by the imitation of Jesus. Of God without 'God' nothing can be said; but he gives himself to be experienced through poverty and silence.

There is no doubt that, personally, Meister Eckhart was deeply Christian. But one has the right to question the Christian authenticity of his thought. The assessment is very difficult. Doesn't Eckhart claim to be able to do without Christ except insofar as he is born in us, at least without the Christ born in Bethlehem, dead and resurrected in Jerusalem, and ascended back to be with the Father?[159] Is there not in him, in addition to the destruction of the scientific status of theology, a will to overcome Christology? If this is so—isn't it a disquieting sign of spiritual *hybris* to no longer need Jesus of Nazareth?

The whole problem is to know whether the insistence with which Meister Eckhart announces the *kenōsis* of the Christian reflects and organically prolongs the *kenōsis* of the Word made flesh, or whether, on the contrary, it derives rather from the universal experience that men have of the mystery of being in general.[160]

---

159 [Cf. Luke 22:69; Romans 8:34.]

160 It is remarkable that Meister Eckhart is today considered to be a 'Master' by Buddhists as well as Christians. Some works on this dialogue between religions, as it concerns Eckhart, can be found in *Revue des Sciences philosophiques et théologiques* 53 (1969): 176f. [R.S. refers here to his review of Degenhardt, translated below in

It is true that if Meister Eckhart is little concerned with the intelligibility of the Incarnation as a historical event, it is because he is only interested in the birth of the inner man[161] as Son of God.[162] At least in his German work, apart from a few isolated remarks,[163] Eckhart is little concerned with the question "Who was Jesus Christ?" but exclusively with this other question, "How, how shall I follow Jesus Christ?" or, "How shall I become Jesus Christ?" Thus, his Christology takes on an existential twist such that one would have the right to say: I exist as a Christian insofar as in the present moment I detach myself from myself and give birth within myself to the Son of God.

But the preaching of the birth of the Word in us is not yet a Christology. It is rather a 'cipher' among many others suggesting the divinization of the detached man. So the ambiguity remains intact.

It seems to me that Eckhart's thinking, in spite of the reservations that we have articulated and that should not be minimized, is profoundly Christian in inspiration for two reasons: on the one hand, what we have called the *kenōsis* of the believer—the imitation of Jesus through detachment or a faith which knows no way but the way of the Cross—and, on the other hand, his call to active charity.

---

chapter 11.] To this should be added this episode described in a *Zen* tale featuring the emperor and Dharma, the sage:

> The emperor asked a great master:
> 'What is the first meaning of holy truth?'
> Dharma responded:
> 'Wide-ranging abode. Nothing holy.'
> The emperor asked again:
> 'Who is the one holding himself in front of me?'
> Dharma responded:
> 'I do not know.'

Der Ochs und sein Hirte: eine altchinesische Zen-Geschichte, trans. H. Buchner, K. Tsujimura (Pfullingen: Neske, 1958), 134. [Although contained in this edition, the dialogue R.S. translates actually comes from *Biyan Lu* or *The Blue Cliff Record*.]

161 [Cf. Romans 7:23; Ephesians 3:16–17.]

162 See e.g. Pf.: 3,6f. [DW 4,1: 335,1–3 (Pr. 101, "Dum medium silentium")]; Angelus Silesius in *Pèlerin chérubinique*, 70 [CW 1.61: 36]: "Wird Christus tausendmal zu Bethlehem geboren | und nicht in dir: du bleibst noch ewiglich verloren" [Should Jesus be born a thousand times in Bethlehem | but not in you, you will remain eternally lost].

163 E.g. DW 1: 378,1–2; 379,1 [Pr. 22, "Ave gratia plena"]

In fact, he devotes himself diligently to the preaching of fraternal love,[164] and if there is *hybris* in the work of Meister Eckhart, it is at least good to the extent that it leads to a mercy that acts among men. Eckhart insists so much on this active mercy that he is not afraid to distort the letter of the Gospel: between Martha the active and Mary the contemplative, he says, it is not Mary who chose the better part, but Martha:

> Mary was all filled with desire. She longed but without knowing what for, she was full of nostalgia without knowing for what. We suspect that dear Mary stayed seated [at the feet of the Lord, R.S.] rather because of the sweet feelings it gave her. [..., R.S.] Martha was so essential [*wesenlich*] that her toil did not hinder her in any way. [..., R.S.] So Christ gave her this warning and consolation that Mary would also become as perfect as Martha wanted her to be. (Pf.: 48,27–29; 53,1f.; 48,35–37) [DW 3: 483,13–15; 491,6–7; 483,19–20 (Pr. 86, "Intravit Iesus in quoddam castellum etc.")][165]

---

164 E.g. DW 1: 67,5–9 [Pr. 4, "Omne datum optimum"]; Pf.: 310,16–21 [DW 1: 195,5–11 (Pr. 12, "Qui audit me")].
165 Cf. Luke 10:41f.

10

Meister Eckhart, Expert in Itinerancy

(1971, trans. from the French by Michael Portal)

Reiner Schürmann edited a special issue of the Dominican-run journal La Vie spirituelle *on Meister Eckhart in January 1971. Although a part of his scholarly ambitions at the time—he was also, for example, preparing to submit his doctoral dissertation on Eckhart to the Sorbonne—Schürmann wanted the issue to speak to Eckhart's existential, spiritual, and transcultural appeal. Topics included death-of-God theology, Marxism, and Zen Buddhism. Schürmann even tried (unsuccessfully) to get one scholar to write on Eckhart's role in American drug culture. Schürmann's own article for the issue, translated here, is an accessible summary of* Wandering Joy.

Before I sink into the big sleep
I want to hear
the scream of the butterfly.

I hear a very gentle sound,
very near now,
very far,
very soft now,
very clear.

Come today
Come today.

What have they done to the earth?
What have they done to our fair sister?
Ravaged and plundered
and ripped her and bit her,
stuck her with knives in the side of the dawn,
and tied her with fences
and dragged her down.

I hear a very gentle sound,
with your ear down on the ground.

We want the world and we want it—now![166]

I listen to Jim Morrison, a young American pop singer, and I understand why Meister Eckhart is so alive today! "What have they done to the earth?" They—that's us. The earth, it is we who have tied her up, ripped her up. But for those who know how to listen, a very soft rustle announces itself; it says: you will possess the universe!

Your path comes from nowhere and goes nowhere.[167]

What I have understood of Meister Eckhart, the obscure, is this: His speech [*parole*] opens a way to existence, it teaches us a certain way of walking along the path. This new pace is that of a liberated man. He has stopped doing violence to things, he is a haven where his friends feel accepted. Then, he owns the earth.

What does it mean to walk a path? First, leaving one place to reach another. The traveler experiences the sequence of places. The common consciousness that questions the traveler is only interested in the two ends of the road: where does it come from, where does it go? If he knows how to respond to this double question, maybe he will be offered lodging, or even a car, so that he can reach the goal faster. The curious consciousness has learned everything about the path when it learns of his starting point, the traveler's fatherland, and his point of arrival, his destination. Between the two, ideally one would complete the trip in zero time. The succession of places, which is proper to the route, is not considered in itself, but accord-

---

166 Jim Morrison (The Doors, "When the Music's Over," in *Strange Days*, Elektra EKS 74014, 1967). [In the original, R.S. also includes a French translation: "Avant que je sombre dans le grand sommeil | je veux entendre | le cri du papillon. | J'entends un son très doux | la voilà très proche | très lointain | le voilà très tendre | très clair. | Viens aujourd'hui | viens aujourd'hui. | Qu'ont-ils fait à la terre? | Qu'ont-ils fait à notre blonde sœur? | Ils l'ont ravagée et pillée, | écorchée, déchirée, | ils l'ont plantée de couteaux | du côté de l'aurore; | ils l'ont ligotée de barrières, traînée à leurs pieds. | J'entends un son très doux, | ton oreille contre le sol. | Nous voulons la terre, et nous la voulons—maintenant!"]

167 [*Nulle part* can be translated as both 'nowhere' and 'anywhere.']

ing to its usefulness, whether it facilitates or slows down the journey toward the end to be reached. The path appears immediately as the shortest passage between two geographical points.

Where does the path come from? and where does it lead? To pose the question this way is to not see the path itself. Just as there are words for everyday use—all words, as vehicles of information and not as carriers of a call—so too there are paths for everyday use: all paths, no matter where they lead, as long as we interrogate them only as to their usefulness.

Here we are again on a quest for the one who, with authority, would open our eyes so that we might *see* our essential wandering.

Whoever I was five, ten, fifteen years ago, and whoever I will be in five, ten, fifteen years—who will show me where he comes from and where he is going? Yet, here's what Meister Eckhart says: Go your way without worrying yourself about its *why*. Leave behind [*Laisse là*] your worry about its point of departure and point of arrival. *Lebe ohne Warum.* "Live without why."

Where do we come from? Where are we going? We must unlearn to pose the question this way. If we want to *see our wandering*, worrying about the why cannot be our business. Where do we come from? From ourselves, from nothingness, from the bosom of God. Where are we going? Toward ourselves, toward nothingness, toward the bosom of God. Such questions, such answers, which would like to inform and advise, don't teach us anything, neither about the path itself, nor about where we are going. Eckhart is a voice that shouts: "Your route, it is the desert."

Learning to "let be"

Our Lord says: Whoever leaves anything for me and in my name, I will give it back to him a hundredfold, and I will also give him eternal life (Matthew 19:29). But if you leave all this in order to receive a hundredfold and eternal life, you have left nothing; and even if you had left it for a reward a thousand times bigger, you wouldn't have left anything. You have to leave yourself, and totally. Only then have you left yourself in truth. One day, not long ago, a man came to me and told me that he had abandoned great possessions, land and wealth, in order to keep his soul. Ah! I said to myself, so you actually left very little! It is blindness, madness, as long as you still think even a little bit about what you have left. If you have left yourself, only then have you left in truth. The man who has left himself is so free from everything that the world cannot suffer him. [..., R.S.] The closer he is to justice, the closer he is to freedom. He is that very freedom. [DW 2: 61,1–62,5 (Pr. 28, "Ego elegi vos")][168]

Leave yourself [*Laisse-toi toi-même*], and you will be free. As long as you have not learned this, as long as you have not learned to go your own way by letting be what is, you do not know how to live. *Letting be* [Laisser être] for Meister Eckhart doesn't mean *abandoning*. It is not about giving anything up. It is rather about breaking the habit of seizing hold of things, even if it is of yourself. The German word that Eckhart uses, *lassen*, means to give freedom back, to unbind. It is only secondarily that it means to abandon, to reject, or even to ignore. Also the word *Gelassenheit*, a key word in Eckhart's work, means serenity more than renunciation or resignation. This word means that one turns one's back on the quest for influences and prestige—that one returns to the opening up of the world, "in the side of the dawn."

Jim Morrison's poem reaches its culmination when his singers (and his audience) yell out: "We want the world, and we want it now!" Does he who 'lets be' still want something? He no longer wants *dies und das*, "this and that," he no longer wants a certain amount of things. What he wants is simple: the totality, that is to say God, that is to say nothingness. Meister Eckhart says: the will goes beyond this and that. In such a passage beyond all that is, in the breakthrough, wanting the universe and abandoning the universe will be the same thing. Whoever in this way wants the world and lets it be has already found. He restores all things to their primal self-sufficiency, he gives all things back to themselves. He has unlearned to enslave them to his projects. He learns to see them again. He has stopped "tying them with fences" (Jim Morrison).

Meister Eckhart's way: to move differently among the objects that surround us. When the desire to possess vanishes, an ease appears within man, which finally makes possible the supreme interest in beings: that each of them would be themselves, that each being

---

168 [Here and in the citations of Eckhart below, R.S.'s French has been translated directly.]

would discover the source. Only one thing matters: to loosen one's grip, to stop clinging to life's projects, to a culture, to everything that stuns the spirit, to dispossess oneself.

> Leave there all that is yours and you belong to God alone. Then God belongs to you as he belongs to himself, and he is God for you in the same way as he is God for himself, without any difference. [DW 2: 107,4–108,2, (Pr. 30, "Praedica verbum")]

Organizing the desert

> "Temptation to organize the desert around me. Actually, I no longer desire anything."[169]

In Eckhart, everything starts from there: learn to let be what is, not to alter its light by means of my desire. To speak of a man engaged in this journey will already be to speak of God; and of God, Meister Eckhart speaks in no other way than by speaking of a man on the path of letting-be. The fact that these two things in Eckhart become one is what makes him a master in itinerancy.

It is necessary to organize the desert. There are, in Eckhart, four successive approaches to union, which are as many calls to man to dispossess himself. They determine existence here and now, like the four cardinal directions. They are not phases that would follow one another like childhood, adolescence, maturity, and old age. They are not stops along the path, but rather the air, fire, water, and earth, which at every moment the traveler needs to walk.

Dissimilarity. The dissimilarity of man and God declares itself total from the outset:

> All creatures are pure nothingness. I am not saying that they are small or anything whatsoever; they are pure nothingness. [DW 1: 69,8–70,1 (Pr. 4, "Omne datum optimum")]

---

169 Jean Lorbais, *Les cicatrices* (Paris: NRF Gallimard, 1970), 272.

God is, while man is not. This sentence is to be taken in the strong sense: 'to be nothing' does not mean to deprive oneself of what one has. Eckhart means the opposite: man has nothing, he is nothingness in the proper sense of the word.

> That which does not possess being is nothingness. Now, no creature has being, because its being depends on the presence of God. Should God turn away for a moment from all his creatures, they would self-annihilate. [DW 1: 70,1–4 (Pr. 4, "Omne datum optimum")]

Creature, this designates what incessantly receives itself from elsewhere. Its being does not belong to it, but to the one who created it. The creature is pure nothingness: its life comes to it from what God, without turning away from it, lavishes on it. Let this prodigality dry up, and all things will show their true face: nothingness. In themselves they are nothingness; what they are, they are only by the grace of God's presence. I am not who I am, but I receive who I am. This dispersion of man who experiences that he has a body, a breath, a history, and yet is nothingness in himself, accounts for his foreignness.

To *leave* oneself does not mean: to retrace the blooming of one's personality, to strip off the few acquisitions that life has conceded. To *leave* oneself does not mean to get rid of the self but to realize that there is only such a personality because God incessantly gives the grace of not turning away from what he makes exist. Nothing is to be gained, your path goes nowhere. Nothing is to be lost, in yourself you are nothingness. Nothing is to be given; not that you have to *become* poor, you *are* poor, radically so. Nothing is to be taken, for all creatures are pure nothingness.

A Zen master tells us the story about a discovery that is strangely similar to that of Meister Eckhart:

> Last year's poverty was not yet perfect, this year's poverty is absolute. In last year's poverty there was still room for the word *poverty*, this year's poverty has let this word disappear.[170]

---

170 [By Kyogen Chikan, as recounted in *The Transmission of the Lamp*, 11.221.]

The poverty of last year was voluntary, the fruit of asceticism. In this year's poverty, asceticism has lost its place. The truth has finally come out: man does not have to become poor, he is nothingness from the beginning [*dès l'origine*].

What is created in man, his being as his own, is nothing. Any itch of possession, the enemy of serenity, is therefore untruth rather than moral imperfection. Such a doctrine has nothing to do with the desperate discrediting cast onto the things in general that envelop existence. Rather, it aims at educating the gaze:

> He who would know nothing but creatures need not think of sermons, for every creature is full of God and is a book. [DW 1: 156,7-9 (Pr. 9, "Quasi stella matutina")]

Meister Eckhart did not think at all that things would not deserve any attention, he thought that what is worthy of interest in them is He who gives them to appear. We must consider every creature to be on account of the Creator, and not on its own account.

Letting be now means: to let show through that in all there is, nothing but God appears...

Similitude. Maybe it would be better to say, *assimilation*. Eckhart believes that a man who resolutely follows the path he has indicated assimilates himself to God "like wood, through crackling and combustion, assimilates itself to fire."[171]

Such a man, says Eckhart, becomes like an "adverb to the Word [*Verbe*]."[172] He becomes close to the Son, the living sign of the living Son. He is entirely like the Latin word *Ecce*, Look! He says entirely: Look at the Son; he is his monstrance.

The destiny of the man who lets be: to become an adverb to the Word.

---

[171] [Cf. *ME* 153-54 and *WJ* 89-90, for a similar quotation from DW 1: 180,7-13 (Pr. 11, "Impletum est.")]

[172] [See *ME* 159 and *WJ* 89-93, for the quotation from DW 1: 154,7-155,3 (Pr. 9, "Quasi stella matutina") and further discussion. The original French *Verbe* is translated as "Word," which, unfortunately, obscures the way in which 'adverb' (*bîwort*) carries the sense of accompanying (*ad-*, *bî-*) the word (*verbe*, *wort*).]

A man speaks. Through the many words in his discourse, it is possible that a single saying [*une parole unique*] can be heard; the single saying that a speaker "means to say." The many words he puts one after another suddenly become clear. I who listen thus declare: now I see what you mean. Against the background of all that I have heard, I have made the single saying mine. I have grasped, for example, that the Sermon on the Mount speaks of God's love, even though that expression is not there. The many words [*mots*] want to say one single saying. Not a single word, but a single saying, which necessarily fragments into multiple words.

This saying can even be inscribed on a whole life; thus the life of Francis of Assisi was marked entirely by the word poverty, an ever unpronounceable saying where an existence is summed up.

Now, this saying, or this word [*verbe*], which can show through as a common thread throughout a man's whole life, must become an adverb to the Word of God, says Eckhart.

Just as Christ is with the Father, the visible sign of the Father, so man must be with the Son, the visible sign of the Son.

Dissimilarity was linked to the theology of creation; similitude is linked to Christ and the Redemption. The same is true of identity.

Identity. That we would be visible signs of Christ, says Eckhart, is still insufficient. We must be the Son himself, the Firstborn of the Father. We must beget this Son, in the Father, and beget ourselves as this only Son.

> Out of the same ground from which the Father begets his eternal Word, from there, fecund, [man, R.S.] begets together with him.
>
> He gives birth to Jesus in return in the fatherly heart of God. [DW 1: 31,2–4; 27,8–9 (Pr. 2, "Intravit Iesus in quoddam castellum")]

The *letting-be*, here, becomes fecundity. Man assists the birth of the Son in him and, by the same token, in God. A single act unites God and man: giving birth. Man returns to God what he has received from God, namely the Son.

It is usually known that Meister Eckhart teaches the birth of the Son in the "ground of the soul," or the "castle in the soul," or the "spark in the soul." In reality, he teaches much more: the birth of the Son in God and in man is one and the same birth. The identity between God and man, for Meister Eckhart, is supreme activity. In making myself entirely available to God's will, I become one with the Father, and from this unity emanates an identical incandescence, the Son. How can this be understood?

A man listens to music. Before such beautiful sounds, he becomes "all ears." In himself he reproduces simultaneously, *identically*, what his ears hear: this is what it means to truly listen. If by distraction or lack of training, the listener omits to accompany within himself the harmonies and rhythms that his ears perceive, he does not really receive the music within him. Only the one who reproduces receives. In perfect listening, there is no longer strictly speaking the soloist on one hand and the listener on the other, but only one event is accomplished: the song that enraptures.

It is the same between God and the man who has perfectly left himself. Only one event takes place: the will of the Father. There is no longer a commandment, be it that of love; a commandment, in fact, establishes a distance between the leader who gives it and the subordinate who receives it. In letting-be, man is no more distant from God than the Son is; he becomes the Son, and penetrates into the paternal heart of God.

> The Father begets his Son in eternity, equal to himself. [..., R.S.] But I say even more: he begot him from my soul. My soul is not only near him and he is not only near my soul, in similitude, but he is in my soul. And the Father begets his Son in the soul in the same way that he begets him in eternity, and not otherwise. He is obliged to do so, whether he likes it or not! The Father incessantly begets his Son, and I say further: he begets me as his Son and as this same Son. And I go even further: not only does he beget me as his Son, but he begets me as himself, and he begets himself as me, and he begets me as his own being and his own nature. [DW 1: 109, 2–10 (Pr. 6, "Iusti vivent in aeternum")]

Dehiscence. When autumn, the time of dehiscence, comes, the fruits open and give way to the grains that sow the soil.

God, man, the world—the totality of what is—appears to the eyes of Meister Eckhart like seeds that arise from elsewhere. What grants them passage? What lies uphill from this source where God and man, together, beget the Son?

The path of letting-be culminates in this ultimate imperative: Learn to leave God himself. This path leads to the desert. Before God, man, the world, is the desert.

In the desert, everything only begins—but God disappears. The desert is the vast solitude, there is no room for two in the desert. The opposition between Creator and creature is abolished there. In the desert there is no use in shouting; there is no counterpart of man toward which he can raise his hands. In the desert, the wind and the sand sweep away the tracks of the caravans; God's footsteps have been erased along with those of man.

In some texts, Meister Eckhart calls this unspeakable origin beyond God, Godhead: "God and Godhead are as distinct from each other as much as earth and heaven" [DW 4,2: 767,34–768,35 (Pr. 109, "Nolite timere eos")]. The Godhead is my true fatherland. Eckhart's thought makes us experience the failure of the representation of God as the counterpart of man.

> I pray to God that he will make me quit of God, for my essential being is above God, inasmuch as we grasp God as the principle of creatures. According to my uncreated being, I existed eternally, I exist at present, and I will remain eternally. That which I am according to my created being, will die and self-annihilate, for it belongs to the day, which is why it must perish with time. In my eternal birth were also born all things, and I was the cause of myself and of all things. If I had willed it, neither I nor all things would be. And if I myself were not, neither would God be; that God is God, of this I am the cause. If I were not, God would not be.—But it is not necessary to know these things. [DW 2: 502,6–504,3 (Pr. 52, "Beati pauperes spiritu")]

Martha has the best part

The path we have outlined has given rise, over the past seven centuries, to reservations and condemnations. There is, however, a profoundly Christian inspiration to this letting-be, understood as the renunciation of all the supports of faith.

Meister Eckhart, an expert in itinerancy, takes us nowhere else but on the way of the Cross. You will follow Jesus on the way of total surrender [*abandon*] to the will of the Father; you will renounce yourself, and renounce God: then, and only then, will you follow the Son in his abasement and dispossession.

What remains to be done when God has vanished as the goal of the journey? One must still occupy oneself with ... cooking. Eckhart attaches such a high value to an active return to daily toil that he does not hesitate to contradict the very letter of the Gospel: it is not Mary, in her intimacy with the Lord, he says, who had the best part, but Martha (Luke 10:38-43). Martha, in fact, discovered true freedom: the freedom to move among things, in the service of men.

Here again, a Buddhist text will shed light on Eckhart's experience:

> One day, an old monk came on a merchant ship to buy mushrooms. He was a cook in a Zen monastery. The young Dōgen asked him to stay on the boat for a while to talk with him about Zen. But the old monk replied, 'I can't, because I have to take care of tomorrow's meal.'—'In your monastery,' Dōgen said to him, 'surely there is someone to take care of the cooking during your absence.'—'Cooking is my study,' the monk replied, 'why should I leave [*l'abandonner*] it to others?' However, Dōgen had not fully understood this profound answer. So he insisted: 'Cooking, you say, is your study? But why not throw yourself into seated meditation or into sacred books, and leave [*délaisser*] domestic chores be?' The old monk laughed: 'Ah! young foreign student, it is unfortunate that you do not understand the very essence of study.[173]

---

173 Masumi Shibata, *Les maîtres du zen au Japon* (Paris: Maisonneuve et Larose, 1969), 173-74.

Book Reviews about Eckhart

(1968–1974, trans. from the French by Ian Alexander Moore)

In 1968 and 1969, respectively, Schürmann published reviews of Bardo Weiss's 1965 dissertation on salvation-history in Eckhart and of Ingeborg Degenhardt's dissertation on the historical reception of Eckhart. Both reviews appeared in the journal Revue des Sciences philosophiques et théologiques, *which was run by clergy affiliated, among other places, with Schürmann's Dominican school of theology Le Saulchoir. In 1971, Schürmann edited a special issue of the journal* La Vie spirituelle *(also connected to the French Dominicans), in which he reviewed several works on or related to Eckhart. Together with the Weiss- and Degenhardt-reviews, we include the most detailed and important of them here, followed by two reviews Schürmann wrote for* La Vie spirituelle *in subsequent issues.*

1. B. Weiss, *Die Heilsgeschichte bei Meister Eckhart* [*Salvation-History in Meister Eckhart*] (Mainz: Matthias-Grünewald, 1965).

Here we have a "thesis" in the twofold sense of the term: an academic work written in support of a certain interpretation of Meister Eckhart. The author has gone through the entire corpus of the Rhenish mystic, both the writings recognized as authentic by current scholarship and those that have not yet been declared authentic. One of the advantages of this careful work certainly resides in the clear separation that B. Weiss maintains at each step of his inquiry between these two types of texts, the analysis of which sometimes leads to two different, even opposed dogmatic conclusions (thus, for example, concerning the hierarchical priesthood, p. 117: none of Eckhart's authentic writings allows one to speak of an anti-hierarchical tendency in this theologian; among the texts on which scholarship has not yet been able to make a pronouncement, however, some of them "force" the spiritual primacy in Meister Eckhart's thought to the point of a pure and simple negation of the sacramentality of the particular priesthood).

The "thesis" here is that, according to W., Meister Eckhart's thought would be crystallized entirely around what the mystic calls the birth of God in the soul. Next to this fundamental idea, the facts of the

135

history of salvation would matter little, even though the theologian of the fourteenth century would be far from ignoring them or excluding them from his reflections. The reproach of "non-Christian mysticism" would therefore be shown to be a superficial reading. However, the various aspects of the "given," in the pen of the Dominican Master, would tend to become simple symbols (p. 181) or exterior and temporal "introductions" to the interior and supra-temporal event that is the birth of God in the soul of the believer, detached from all creatures.—B. W. therefore intentionally restricts himself to approaching only marginal themes in Meister Eckhart's oeuvre; the catalog he presents us with—and we have no reason to doubt that it is complete—concerns, not the central message of the speculative mystic, but rather seven chapters in the history of salvation, criteria external to his theology: original sin, the Incarnation of Christ, the Passion and Glorification of Christ, the Virgin Mary, the Church, the sacraments, the ultimate realities.

The results of these various surveys are similar. Each of them indeed forces one to acknowledge the absence of theological elaboration on the part of Meister Eckhart, a neglect of the concrete facts of the history of salvation, which eloquently indicates, should this be necessary, how much the true interest of this "excessive Thomist" lies in something other than in the economy of the history of God with men. In themselves, the details of this history "do not interest" him; he uses them to better present his doctrine of mystical union. This approach is particularly discernible when it comes to the Incarnation of the Word. Although Meister Eckhart, in his defense plea against doctrinal incriminations made by the Bishop of Cologne and then by the papal curia in Avignon, uses the very expressions of the Council of Chalcedon on this subject (the Word has become man "vere, proprie et per substantiam"[174]); although, with St. Thomas, he teaches a unique *esse* in the God-Man—all of his Christology nevertheless seems to culminate in this affirmation: "God became man in order to be born in us."[175] More than any of his contemporaries, Meister Eckhart therefore wondered about

---

174 ["truly, properly, and substantially." This quotation can be found rather in LW 4: 437, no. 523 (*S*. LII, "Induimini dominum Iesum Christum").]

175 [Cf. Weiss, *Die Heilsgeschichte bei Meister Eckhart*, 61 ("3. Gott wurde Mensch, um in der Seele geboren zu werden"); John 1:14; and LW 3: 240–41, nos. 288 ff. (*In. Ioh.*)]

the motive for the Incarnation. The doctrine of hypostatic Union, too, only illustrates this motive: among the three types of union taught by Meister Eckhart—the union between the three persons of the divinity, the hypostatic union in Jesus Christ, and the union between the soul and God—only the last is treated with an abundance of texts and by itself deflects the interest of the other two. Anyway, there will be no room for doubt: the unique coming of God into the world is impossible (p. 70); God has already come among us in creation, and there are many passages where it is very difficult to specify whether Eckhart is dealing with this first coming of God, at the origin, with that in Jesus Christ, in history, or finally with that in the soul, outside of time. In reality, only the last deserves the Christian's attention.—One can see that B. W.'s investigation, despite extrinsically revealing the gaps in Meister Eckhart's theological teaching, nevertheless brings into relief, by way of contrast, the mystic's unique idea, which our author, however knowingly, has avoided treating (confining his work to this "secondary" zone that, under the name of history of salvation, seems to us today to be of primary importance in Christian faith): the birth of the Word in the believing soul. Let us note in passing other glaring "gaps" in this High Scholastic theology: in the entire oeuvre of the German mystic, the author was able to identify two texts that speak of the Resurrection of Christ, a single text that deals with the sacrament of penance, and no text directly relating to the sacrament of marriage; admittedly, in each of these domains, it would have been necessary to take a historical inventory before being scandalized by the "oversights" of Meister Eckhart.

Despite its impressive and thorough scholarship, W.'s book nevertheless remains on the surface of the thought which he analyzes with so much care. The wealth of information is delivered to us at the expense of going deeper. On the one hand, we would have liked the author to have supported on a more elaborate foundation some of his summary statements: for example, when he deals with the substitution, present since the Middle Ages, of "individual" eschatology for "general" eschatology (p. 166) or with the "neo-Platonic hostility toward the body" (pp. 94, 165, 179) in the work of Meister Eckhart; or again when he declares that he wants to go upstream of the various theological traditions that Eckhart claims to follow in order to delimit the original elements of the latter's Mariology—work which he carries out in thirty-five lines (pp. 102–3). Likewise, among the flood of secondary literature he mentions, the author does not seem to know the contents of Lossky's great book,[176] certainly the most remarkable recent contribution to Eckhart scholarship, which he quotes four times simply as a mine of references; he would have found in it a doctrinal, historical, and spiritual interpretation of the very points in which W. contents himself with very approximate indications, for example regarding the question of the two kinds of grace, p. 164; Lossky pp. 182 ff.; or that of the exterior man and the interior man, p. 141; Lossky p. 176; or further with respect to the intellect, p. 31; Lossky *passim*. On all these points there is disagreement.—On the other hand, the dogmatic "grid" used by the author (the seven stages of the history of salvation) would itself be in need of critique. Indeed: would not a principle of interpretation that is both foreign as a category (that of the "history of salvation") and secondary in its content (in relation to the primacy of the theology of mystical union) call for a more ample meditation on each of the Christian mysteries on display? W. absorbs Meister Eckhart's system with the help of a system borrowed from modern manuals of dogmatic theology; he is content to signal the points of intersection between the two "grids," without "thinking," in the strict sense, their meaning. While we await a study on this hermeneutical difference itself—it is our destiny—we recommend this book as a clear and useful material presentation.

2. Ingeborg Degenhardt, *Studien zum Wandel des Eckhartbildes* [*Studies on the Transformation of the Image of Eckhart*] (Leiden: Brill, 1967).

Interest in the thought of Meister Eckhart since the last war has given rise to illuminating historical studies, although it has yielded only a few properly theological or philosophical works. The reason for this lack must undoubtedly be attributed to the devastation wrought under the regime of National Socialism, which one can get an idea of by rereading the chapter devoted to Meister Eckhart in A. Rosenberg, *The Myth of the Twentieth Century*. Just as, in

---

176 [Vladimir Lossky, *Théologie négative et connaissance de Dieu chez Maître Eckhart* (Paris: Vrin, 1960).]

the last century, following German Idealism's infatuation with the Thuringian Master, criticism had a lot to do in order to readjust the method of interpretation—it was above all the merit of H. Denifle to inaugurate, with his famous thesis about Meister Eckhart as a "very mediocre Thomist,"[177] the search for a more sober image of this medieval thinker—so was it necessary to proceed today to a decryption, once again, of the exact scope of the Rhenish Master's teaching. This justifies the numerous analyses, for the most part university theses, that, without claiming to engage in proper dialogue with the thought of Meister Eckhart, have contributed to a better understanding of his place in history. Let us point out that, besides these historical studies, it is today especially the Buddhists who seem to discover in Meister Eckhart's thought the source for a veritable renewal of thought. This can be seen in publications such as: Shizuteru Ueda, *Die Gottesgeburt in der Seele und der Durchbruch zur Gottheit* [*The Birth of God in the Soul and the Breakthrough to the Godhead*], Gütersloh 1965; Heinrich Dumoulin, *Östliche Meditation und christliche Mystik* [*Eastern Meditation and Christian Mysticism*], Freiburg/Munich 1966; Hugo M. Enomiya: *Zen-Buddhismus*, Cologne 1966; M. Nambara: "Die Idee des absoluten Nichts in der deutschen Mystik und ihre Entsprechungen im Buddhismus" ["The Idea of Absolute Nothingness in German Mysticism and Its Correspondences in Buddhism"], in *Archiv für Begriffsgeschichte*, vol. VI, Bonn 1960.

We would like to take this opportunity to point out that Vladimir Lossky's book, *Théologie négative et connaissance de Dieu chez Maître Eckhart* [*Negative Theology and the Knowledge of God in Meister Eckhart*], Vrin 1960 (see the reviews in this journal, 46, 1962, pp. 317–319, and 47, 1963, p. 288),[178] is, fortunately, an exception to this lack of theological and philosophical dialogue. In this book, Lossky has attempted to untangle the numerous traditions that inter-

---

177 [See Degenhardt, 175–77, and her citations of Heinrich Denifle's invective from the latter's "Meister Eckharts lateinische Schriften und die Grundanschauung seiner Lehre," *Archiv für Literatur und Kirchengeschichte des Mittelalters* 2 (1886): 417–652, 673–87.]

178 [Claude Geffré, "Le mystère de Dieu," *Revue des Sciences philosophiques et théologiques* 46, no. 2 (April 1962), and L.-J. Bataillon, "De saint Thomas à Maître Eckhart," *Revue des Sciences philosophiques et théologiques* 47, no. 2 (April 1963).]

sect in Meister Eckhart's work. One could, however, remark that Meister Eckhart's most original work is found refracted throughout his German work much more than in his Latin writings. The latter, in fact, are of a scholastic nature, written for the use of theology students; in contrast, the German sermons, even though we possess only second-hand copies, give us a reflection of the spontaneous outpouring [*jaillissement*] of the thought of this original Master. It is the German work of Meister Eckhart, and far less his Latin work, which, moreover, was almost unknown until Denifle, that earned him his role of a philosophical instigator of bold thoughts across European history. Yet L. decidedly emphasizes the Latin work of Meister Eckhart, which is less replete with paradoxes and neologisms, but is perhaps also less significant. If we have counted correctly, of Lossky's nine hundred citations of Eckhart's works, a little more than eight hundred are taken from the Latin works, and only around eighty from the German works. Perhaps we should look for the reason for this choice in the influence that the Neo-Thomism of E. Gilson has exerted on Lossky's book; such inspiration is indeed suggested by the space Lossky devotes to the analysis of the real distinction, in Meister Eckhart, between essence and existence (cf., for example, p. 106 f.; p. 137 ff.; p. 142 f.; p. 146 f.). And this distinction is obviously more often at issue in the scholastic context of the Latin works. It remains the case that L.'s study is the only recent contribution to the dialogue with Meister Eckhart that has taken up the philosophical challenge of this mystic.

The work by Miss I. Degenhardt crowns, in a way, the series of historical presentations of Meister Eckhart. She traces the history of judgments issued on his person and thinking. It is therefore a survey, not of the oeuvre itself of the medieval Dominican, but of his numerous commentators, exegetes, plagiarists, disciples, and judges, who for six centuries have never ceased to be inspired by him or to challenge him. The analysis starts from the trial before the papal court in Avignon and leads us step by step to the appraisal—obviously laudatory—of the monumental edition of his works begun in 1936: Meister Eckhart, *Die deutschen und lateinischen Werke*, ed. on behalf of the German Research Foundation, Stuttgart.—If the vast survey carried out by I. D. does not escape regrettable oversimplifications and omissions, it nonetheless offers fascinating insight into how our predecessors read and interpreted Meister Eckhart. The author seems to have deliberately excluded two authors who have, however, directly or indirectly, been influenced by Eckhart: Angelus Silesius (alias Johann Scheffler, died in 1677), whose *Cherubinische Wandersmann* [*Cherubinic Wanderer*] (*Sämtliche poetische Werke*, Munich 1952, 3rd ed., vol. 3) was translated into French by Jean Rousset: *Le voyageur chérubinique et la sainte joie de l'âme* [*The Cherubinic Wanderer and the Holy Joy of the Soul*] (extracts), Paris, G. L. M., 1949, 34 pp. The other author is Martin Heidegger, who, even though he cites Eckhart only twice in his books (*Der Feldweg* [*The Fieldpath*], Frankfurt 1962, 3rd ed., p. 4 [GA 13: 89], and *Vorträge und Aufsätze* [*Lectures and Essays*], Pfullingen 1954, p. 175 [GA 7: 178]), is nevertheless largely dependent on his thought.

3. Shizuteru Ueda, *Die Gottesgeburt in der Seele und der Durchbruch zur Gottheit: Die mystische Anthropologie Meister Eckharts und ihre Konfrontation mit der Mystik des Zen-Buddhismus* [*The Birth of God in the Soul and the Breakthrough to the Godhead: The Mystical Anthropology of Meister Eckhart and Its Confrontation with the Mysticism of Zen Buddhism*] (Gütersloh: Mohn, 1965).[179]

Certain Zen masters today consider Meister Eckhart to be the privileged partner in a dialogue with Christianity. Shizuteru Ueda is among them. Professor at the Buddhist University of Shingon [Koyasan University], then at Kyoto, he finds in the Rhenish mystic the very impulse that animates ancient Japanese mysticism. According to him, the kinship extends to what is essential: the thought of nothingness. But, at the same time, his text clearly shows the limits of the dialogue. The Buddhist cannot follow Meister Eckhart all the way. The pages that you will read here [i.e., the extracts from Ueda's book that Schürmann translated for *La Vie spirituelle*], although they trace the stages of a fundamental spiritual experience of man, nevertheless also make evident the irreducible originality of the Christian Revelation.

---

[179] [A partial English translation by Gregory S. Moss is available under the title "Meister Eckhart's Mysticism in Comparison with Zen Buddhism," *Comparative and Continental Philosophy* 14, no. 2 (2022): 128–52.]

4. Jeanne Ancelet-Hustache, *Maître Eckhart et la mystique rhénane* (Paris: Seuil, 1956) [*Meister Eckhart and the Rhineland Mystics*, trans. Hilda Graef (New York: Harper Torchbooks, 1957)].

The short book by J. Ancelet-Hustache is, without doubt, the best contribution of the past years to acquainting the French reader with the German Rhineland school and with Eckhart, on whom this school is based. As much by its historical and spiritual presentation as by its choice of texts, this work helps to give a balanced view of the Eckhartian oeuvre.

5. Vladimir Lossky, *Théologie négative et connaissance de Dieu chez Maître Eckhart* [*Negative Theology and the Knowledge of God in Meister Eckhart*] (Paris: Vrin, 1960).

The best study, quite voluminous, on Meister Eckhart is currently that of Vladimir Lossky [...]. Lossky attempts to untangle the numerous traditions that intersect in Meister Eckhart's work. Following the praises that have been showered on this work and that we agree with for the most part, we would like to identify a bias in Lossky: his scholarship is based principally on Meister Eckhart's Latin works. Now, the latter emerged in a university context, according to scholastic methods already triply secular, in the fourteenth century. Without any doubt, Meister Eckhart was more original, more personal, and spoke more freely when, in his mother tongue, he was addressing the nuns of the Rhineland who, moreover, preserved his German sermons for us. It is the texts in Middle High German, and far less his Latin corpus, that earned Eckhart the role of a philosophical instigator of bold thoughts across European history. Lossky clearly places the emphasis on Meister Eckhart's Latin commentaries; if we have counted correctly, of Lossky's nine hundred citations of Eckhart's work, a little more than eight hundred are taken from the Latin works, and only around eighty from the German sermons and treatises. Perhaps we should look for the reason for this choice in the influence that the Neo-Thomism of Étienne Gilson has exerted on Lossky's book; the principal themes studied by Lossky lead us to this belief. This bias leads the author, on the one hand, to interpret Eckhart on the basis of the *real distinction* between essence and existence and, on the other, since this analysis turns out to be adequate, to look for the true masters of the Thuringian mystic's thought among the Neo-Platonists. A thorough reading of Meister Eckhart's German texts would have made the originality of this author evident, which is irreducible to the two currents of thought so brilliantly traced by Lossky. It remains the case that this study is the only recent contribution to the dialogue with Meister Eckhart that has taken up the philosophical challenge of this mystic. One can find a summary of Lossky's theses in Louis Cognet, *Introduction aux mystiques rhéno-flamands* [Introduction to the Rhenish-Flemish Mystics] (Paris: Desclée, 1968), 50–105.

6. Masumi Shibata, *Les maîtres du zen au Japon* [*The Masters of Zen in Japan*] (Paris: Maisonneuve et Larose, 1969).

This book parades before us the impressive line of Japanese Zen masters, from the monk Yōsai, who introduced Zen Buddhism to Japan, to Shin'ichi, the author's professor at the University of Kyoto. Shibata thus reconstructs a veritable spiritual genealogy, which ranges from the disorderly epoch of the monk-warriors in the twelfth century ("Whether it is the water of the Kamo River, the luck of the dice, or the monk-warriors, none of them obeys my will" [15]—complaint by the emperor Shirakawa) to the contemporary infatuation in the United States with the doctrines of Suzuki. Each of the masters presented by the author appears in their intellectual, personal, and social aspects.

The author does not hesitate to compare their doctrines with certain Western philosophers, notably Meister Eckhart. He cites the following verses of Saichi and underscores their affinity with the teaching of the Rhenish mystic:

> It is not I who become Amida,
> It is Amida, for his part, who becomes me.
> Adoration of Amida.

[...]

> Mercy and Light are but one.
> Saichi and Amida are but one.
> Adoration of the Buddha. [156]

The second part of the book is a translation of two famous texts: the Sermon of Tetsugen on Zen, and the Sermon of Bassui on Zen. Regarding the first, Shibata again recalls the resemblances with Meister Eckhart: German thought and Japanese thought alike appear as the surpassing of theism. But, says Shibata, Eckhart has not found the practical method for arriving at the Buddhist atheism of absolute absence (p. 172). The difference between European mysticism and Zen is practical, not speculative. Seated meditation, the *koan*, motionless squatting, the tea ceremony—so many gestures useful "for erasing the relativity of time and space [172]." On the other hand, the Christian tradition seems to him to be incapable of surpassing alterity, the juxtaposition between God and man. In his introduction to Bassui's sermon, Shibata says that, as long as the "ego" and God or Buddha are posited as objects, one will never reach union. Bassui's tendency "is the inverse of mystical union or of the identification of the human will with the divine will, which is at issue in Western mysticism. Some think that Zen and Western mysticism are identical, but this text [Bassui's sermon, R.S.] demonstrates quite clearly the differences that exist between them" (pp. 211-12).

Yet how could we not read the following story as praise of the one charity (p. 21)?

> When Yôsai was living in the Kmen-ji, a poor man came to him and said: "My family is poor and there are days when they run out of fire. My wife, my children, and I are on the brink of dying of hunger. Have mercy and help us!" At that time, there was neither clothing, nor food, nor any valuable object in the monastery. Yôsai thought about it but found no solution. However, there was a piece of copper that, when drawn, was supposed to serve as the material for the construction of the halo rays of the Medicine Buddha statue. He took it, broke it, and gathered the pieces, which he gave to the poor visitor, telling him: "Go exchange this for food and relieve your hunger!" His disciples reproached him: "But that was for the rays of the Buddha! And you gave them to a layman!" — "That's true. But when I think of the intentions of the Buddha, he would offer to share even his flesh and limbs with living beings. Even if I had given the entire body of the Buddha statue to living beings dying of hunger under my eyes, I would have been in accord with the intentions of the Buddha. Even if, because of this sin, I would have to fall into a bad way, I would still help living beings who are hungry."

7. Meister Eckhart, *Les traités* [*The Treatises*], translated and introduced by J. Ancelet-Hustache (Paris: Seuil, 1971).

Ms. Ancelet-Hustache, already known for an excellent short book on Rhenish mysticism,[180] just published this translation, which will henceforth be an indispensable benchmark for reading Eckhart. She gathers together the four treatises recognized by most critics to be authentic. She has found a clear and precise language to render in French the difficult linguistic creations of the German text.

Each of these four treatises can be read as an introduction to Eckhart's religious thought. The *Spiritual Instructions*, table talk intended for novices, present themselves as an initiation into inner peace. The formulations are less paradoxical and excessive than in some of the sermons; one can sense the pedagogical care that animates them. *The Book of Divine Consolation* was written for a young and unhappy Agnes, queen of Hungary; here again, the (sometimes more philosophical) developments are intended to provide help; they aim to relieve suffering by recalling what is essential in the life of man. *On the Noble Man* sketches Meister Eckhart's anthropology: the presentation traverses six stages of the spiritual itinerary, which are so many facets by which Eckhart defines the human being. *On Detachment*, finally, shows that the emptiness [*vacuité*] of the soul as Eckhart conceives of it is nothing other than the emptying out [*exinanition*] of Christ and of the Christian on the way of the cross.

Easily accessible, of a rare literary quality (in comparison to other translations of Eckhart), and of a sometimes-shocking spiritual authenticity, these treatises make for a beautiful meditation book.

8. Meister Eckhart, *Sermons, I* (1–30), translated by Jeanne Ancelet-Hustache (Paris: Seuil, 1974).

With respect to the quality of the translation, several probings have sufficed to fill us with joy. Toward the end of the thirteenth century, the Rhineland mystics conferred on the Middle High German language a completely new status of being an academic language; although they still think in Latin, the masters seek vernacular equivalents, above all at the pulpit. Whence the importance of preaching

---

180 [Jeanne Ancelet-Hustache, *Maître Eckhart et la mystique rhénane* (Paris: Seuil, 1956). *Meister Eckhart and the Rhineland Mystics*, trans. Hilda Graef (New York: Harper Torchbooks, 1957).]

at this stage of the language's formation. Whence also the overdetermined character of their discourse. Ms. Ancelet-Hustache has done justice to this complexity of vocabulary by adopting, according to context, different French terms for the same word in the original. Numerous difficult technical terms are thereby clarified. For example, she translates *ledic* sometimes as *dégagé* [bare], sometimes as *libéré* [liberated], sometimes as *affranchi* [freed]. Although, in certain contexts, the word is associated with the opposition "virgin-wife" and thus suggests the more recent meaning of "single" [*"célibataire"*], its original sense is indeed "without hindrances" [*"sans entraves"*] in general—and not only those of marriage. Another example: regarding the verb *lâzen* and its derivatives: our translator uses *laisser* [to let or leave], *omettre* [to leave out], and *abandonner* [to abandon]. Here again we agree that the context requires each of these interpretations. Sometimes an excellent translation of a text, such as that of Ms. Ancelet-Hustache, brings to light nuances that can escape the notice of the reader of the original. This is, I think, the greatest praise that one can give to a translator.

In the gamut of possible stances on Eckhart, where does this translation situate itself? To mention only the serious interpretations, there have been spiritual and philosophical ones (Platonizing, idealist, existentialist), atheist and Buddhist ones... Eckhart seems to suit above all a certain intellectual temperament, and this temperament can be found in apparently even opposed currents of culture. Ms. Ancelet-Hustache does not make a mystery of where her interest in Eckhart stems from: it is the Christian faith that is lived in "the visible world, the everyday world" (this is the title of a lovely chapter of her introduction). Other readings of the Meister exist; one can wonder in particular whether the logic of the experience of Meister Eckhart does not lead beyond the borders of Christianity. But the orthodox reading that Ms. Ancelet-Hustache proposes can pride itself on remaining within the lineage that precisely gave birth to Eckhartian thought. One probably "reduces" [*"raccourcit"*] this thought by giving it a political or ideological coloring, but not in displaying it in its authentically Christian inspiration. That is why we welcome this translation.

12

To Find, at Last, the Origin

(1973, trans. from the French by Ian Alexander Moore)

This chapter serves as a précis of Schürmann's prizewinning autobiographical novel Les Origines *(1976; English 2006). Schürmann had been working on the project of coming to terms with his German origins in writing—"Born too late to see the war, too early to forget it"—since at least 1968, when it bore the title* Livre de errance *(Book of Wandering). The précis appeared in a special issue of the Dominican journal* La Vie spirituelle *devoted to the theme of initiation. It is not only (as might be expected given the venue) more theologically oriented than the 1976 book; it also contains valuable comments on releasement (Gelassenheit, délaissement) that Schürmann never makes elsewhere in his corpus. Schürmann's text was published with a preface presumably written by the editor of the special issue, his former teacher at Le Saulchoir Albert-Marie Besnard, O.P., which we translate here: "True initiation is characterized by the fact that, in introducing us to the heart of a Reality that surpasses us, it also makes us know who we are. 'Who am I?' The question silently plagues all of us, and it is clear that no external oracle or sickly introspection will give the answer. The answer can only be an elucidation of the ground of ourselves under a light that is actually strong enough to awaken us. In rare cases, the elucidation can occur abruptly and rapidly. Normally, it is slow and progressive. The ground of ourselves becomes clear only here and there, and sometimes just as timidly as it does in the clarity of dawn. The Christian knows well that he is a son in the Unique Son, that he is far from having penetrated the common secret of the Son and of himself. For, son in the Son of the unique Father, I am burdened with the existence that is mine, with a cross that is mine and of which I perhaps do not know the contours, by particular paths about which I hesitate or on which I stumble forward. The authors of the Middle Ages read this phrase in the Song of Songs: 'If you do not know [yourself] [Si tu t'ignore toi-même], O loveliest of women, follow the tracks of the flock...' (1:8), and they thought that no search for God could succeed unless this ignorance had been overcome. The testimony that you are about to read reminds us that, in the context and circumstances of the modern world, the same spiritual demand is made on us, and that there are plenty of reasons for its sometimes being laborious or painful. Some advice: do not read the following lines too quickly, for they will seem strange to you upon a superficial reading, but if you know how to let them say what they will, perhaps they will speak also of you?"*

"Of German origin." For ten years I lived in France, under the pointed finger of the past. Born too late to see the war, too early to forget it. In Israel, I heard something like a confession: "of Palestinian origin." In the United States, where I write these lines, again like a confession: "of African origin." Through these origins, an initiation is pursued. Those who have a presentable past, an undivided country, a language that does not evoke the orders shouted by officers in a trance, what do they know of this? "Hitler—obviously it's a painful matter, but that was a quarter of a century ago." A statement made to me on the evening of Armistice Day, after a speech by His Honor the Mayor of E...[181] Put the past in its place, i.e., in the archives? Like one puts a child in its place who bluntly tells you your truth? I must take the opposite path. Question the origin. Follow the initiation that it inflicts all the way to the end. Also all the way to the end of my desire that the origin be one. This apprenticeship is not easy to write about. It does not lend itself to an ideology. It moves one backward: sometimes in tears, more often in incredulous silence. A political initiation from the worst side, that of nationalisms, of cultural resentments, of skin irritations like measles that never stop burning. Words stick in my throat. Sometimes, to see the effect, and to laugh also: "I am Prussian." An acridity propagates in the air, a metallic taste. To have origins like others have malaria or migraines. A numbness spreads that imposes its own delays on relaxation. Like at the dentist. The shot of anesthesia in your gums. Your mouth moves into one corner. Useless to articulate your words. For thirty years I have been waiting for life to circulate normally.

What about the origin? I take this word literally: *origo*, rising up, emerging. Everyone has their origin*s*. Bourgeois, proletarian, legitimate, illegitimate, white, coffee-with-cream, yellow, black, delicate, hard-working, well-heeled or not. These things follow you. They can be read without effort. Just sit at an outdoor café. Hats, wrinkles, the intonation of the laughter, the gait of a young woman coming back from the restroom, the mount of her perm, her way of ordering an espresso, of paying the check, of looking at the passers-by... Or else our politicians on television. Their past written in large letters

---

181 [Cf. Reiner Schürmann, *Origins* (Zurich: Diaphanes, 2016), 21, where "E" is given as "Etiolles," the suburb of Paris where Le Saulchoir was located.]

on their foreheads. Origins, I say, are things to relegate to the past. Too painful, or in any case restrictive. But how to do this if the past is more present than the business of the day?

When Prince Myshkin[182] arrived in Basel, the braying of a donkey was enough to awaken him from a long slumber of epilepsy. Hakuin, the founder of a Zen school in Japan, heard the ringing of a bell, and the sound opened his mind. "I suddenly awoke." Prior to this, he says, "I was frozen in a field of ice, I was like an *idiot*, like an imbecile." The origin speaks. Braying, ringing, every insignificant noise. Then, the false oppositions collapse. A more fundamental knowledge takes over. Myshkin and Hakuin were prepared for it: the one by sickness, the other by diligent study. These were their origins, an epileptic, an intellectual monk. Behold: we are all prepared. Initiation into the originary life has begun, for a long time now. Ever since we have had origins. Yet, for the braying of a donkey to open our minds, a kind of violence is necessary. The submission to several imperatives.

"Listen!"

It is necessary to cover your ears. Too many voices shouting: "Listen to me!" I misunderstood what it means to listen. I confused it with the politeness of lending an ear, with following the effusions to the end. Remaining an auditor, I already lost the essential: the desire to have a past. A turn in life. Not because of what I have gained, but because of what I have lost. From now on, dare to be savage. I know too many who, over a beer, drift up the stream of phantasies in their memory. And who died on this path. Sordid fraternity in the face of memories hides its victims well. You take the train from Paris to Cologne, the happy convalescence of the country seems evident. "With Brandt,[183] the economic giant has become a political giant." But even when covered in fat, the origins still move.

---

182 [Protagonist of Dostoevsky's *The Idiot*.]
183 [Willy Brandt, chancellor of West Germany from 1969 to 1974.]

There are years in life when one clings to a landscape rather than a human being. These are the years that follow upon violent encounters with oneself. After puberty, after a war, after separations, after wrongs done between friends. True listening is perhaps learned there. Nature. Preferably majestic. She utters in a powerful enigma the situations that wound. And she leads back to the one desire: that all would be one. The rush to the sea, highways in the summer. If that is not an initiation! That we have so much need of the sea, of the mountains, of the forest, of solitude is an indication that we require a more primitive knowledge. An initiation into the single Origin beyond our mutilated origins. It is true that the cosmic mystery has been deflated by what we have done with it. Landscapes can only just put us on the path. Open the way to true questioning. For that matter, the news in the paper, a bus ride does the same. Too many words that leave us dumbfounded. But their very din suggests that silence is possible. That an originary freedom is there to be listened to. In any case, the point of departure is an act of aggression. Such as: "Do they still make soap and candles out of human bones where you're from?"

Rising up, emerging, awakening. The first step is not difficult. No need for a spiritual master. Perhaps for a friend. Who sometimes gets you started: "I want so much…"—"But what? Say it."—"…to no longer suffer." There is no life in which the essential questions do not sound like a bass drum; Kant said as much (though not exactly in these terms). Listening is neither a performance nor a privilege. It is a departure. But a departure can be missed. One can close oneself off to whatever reality. At least comfort is thereby assured. Reality: for Marx, class. For Freud, desire. For me, a war that I did not see. Images that have become autonomous circulate like water in a baroque fountain: a chubby-faced angel spits it out, the water is pumped up through a tube within the plaster statue, the chubby-faced angel spits it out again, it is pumped up… The water remains the same. Like the angel, mentally I gabble on.

"Leave!"

This cry is also familiar. Your pretty complexion, your convictions, your noble anguish—leave them [*à laisser*].[184] We flaunt our assets, lofty or not. And then one day, they leave you. Like an old car leaves you in the open country, on the trunk road. The difficulty does not consist in saying, "values are going away," but in making the connection: "thus, I will no longer cling." Here is the crossing of the desert. Memories, true and false, and all the other small capital fall from your hands like a newspaper. From fright or ecstasy—it is impossible to say. Thus, I will no longer cling. Crossing the single desert, that of property. Crossing the dissolution, the harassment, all the racket in my ears, the grotesquely huge specters. Leave the past. The *fact* of Auschwitz. A hard fact like black bakelite. Which does not decay.

Not to dam up the alarm rising from within. This is impossible. But to no longer wrap yourself in it. To not hold onto it. This is the crossing that counts. Crossing the nothingness that separates us from the emergence in which all things are one. We have become experts in fragmentation. East–West. My country–your country. Friend–enemy, present–past, victor–vanquished, Allies–Axis, blablabla–shut-up. One who would cease to lay hold of these oppositions would be "released" [*"délaissé"*]. He would have left [*laissé*] himself, as the mystics say. He would be liberated, free. He would know the single origin. He would live from the originary life.

Besides this imperative of releasement, there is not much to say about the origin. It is nothing. Leave your origins, whatever they may be, and you will be translated into the origin. The essential translation. Thus do we understand the "whoever loses wins" that we were taught. The origin as releasement: the single reality. But it does not furnish any security. It bears nothing, it grounds nothing. To leave things does not mean to no longer be concerned. Rather, it means not being captured. Man then no longer identifies himself with what he undertakes. What comes about, what has been,

---

184 "How I regret my arm so plump, / My shapely leg and lost time [*Combien je regrette mon bras si dodu, / Ma jambe bien faite et le temps perdu*]" (Yvette Guilbert). [From the 1918 recording of "Ma grand-mère," written by Pierre-Jean de Béranger.]

becomes a sign. The origin points out the path to us, calling us back from and reminding us of our essential forgetfulness.

Here is the second certainty. Letting go, unclenching [*Lâcher prise*], ceasing to lay hold of. Of oneself, of others, of the images of the past and the projects of the future, of God finally. This has nothing to do with desperate abandonment. On the contrary. It is a matter of supreme interest in everything that is. But to see what is, it is necessary to pull back and keep our hands off. Away from the haze, we have a future in place of apprehensions, and a heart in place of a past. Letting be [*Laisser être*]: this opens a path. An initiation, perhaps, but not a threshold crossed once and for all. Dare dispossession, with an animal patience. These words say it well: peregrination, peril, experience. Our essential peregrination, the experience of ourselves, remains perilous.

"Speak!"

The encounter with oneself that would not come to speech would be the most miserable of defeats. But also: no more words. Never. For pity's sake. If you should ask: "What do you truly desire?" The abolition of language. No more moving lips. None of that verbal elongation of the past into the present, of property into dispossession. Nudity. No more sentences, no more need for clothing. To break the collusion of all our languages with History. If speaking is necessary, reduce language to a single word: "yes." The word in which all is one. The manifestation of pure presence. Heard correctly, all words, words in disarray, suggest it. Like the origins suggest the origin. "Yes": the simple splendor [*éclat*] of what is present. The rising, the emergence in which there is neither past nor future. To lop from human speaking every grammatical form that causes pain. Mine, yours, perfect, future, interrogatives, affirmatives... All those phrases that come like fat malicious insects in the air. To flee. To erect fences made of polite formulas. A curtain of words like tear gas.

I know very well that language also generates an inverse passion. A consolation. Words of kindness. Words of truth, especially. Which heal, open our ears, invite us to releasement. I know this. Words tell the truth, but in passing. To leave them, even them. Perhaps only in extreme cases does this mean: to fall silent. More often, a shrug of the shoulders. That words would be just that, words. And that we still have to advance through a world of hands, eyes, mouths. Which entice or repel. Which compel us to language, are language. The feverish sensuality of rush hours, the face we put on in the middle of it all: language. Again a lie. An urgency, once more, to recover the incipient drift, to dispossess oneself of everything that speaks. To recognize the gap between words and the foreboded mystery. Granted, given, recognized, received just barely. To say "still alive," and then *fall silent*.

Or to speak as if on the run. Travelers and pilgrims, wanderers of all types know something about this. Traveling is not a distraction. It is to experience in our joints the multiplicity into which we are thrown by forgetfulness and exile. Traveling light, in poverty. The ancient emergence of things comes close. Continual detachment from the periphery. Becoming porous to receive the origin. Its vertical coming in the present. "Yes." The scattered abdications consumed in the piercing brilliance of the intact present. The evidence in which stasis and falling are reconciled.

I am released [*Je suis laissé*]

The edifying conclusion does not exist. But I can seriously engage in "leaving": the past to its bad vapors, desires to their rumbling, all things to what they are. Thus a lost dimension of existence is recovered. Lost insofar as we are busy with our projects, our deadlines. Lost also insofar as we purely and simply negate our projects and deadlines. The "yes" of originary freedom cannot be forced, not even by the "no" of asceticism. We recognize the fundamental gift in passing, in the fleeting instant in which ties come loose. To want the real simply because it is real—the one who has accomplished this has left the real. *He has left* [laissé] *his origins; the Origin then lets him be* [le laisse être]. This gift can be neither represented nor figured. It approaches, visits me, pronounces me. An *épreuve* in the double sense of the word: the initiate experiences [*éprouve*] his original being, but this apprenticeship is also an ordeal for him [*sa dure épreuve*]. If the aim is to escape violence, there is no use in learning history, inventing the press, or opening your eyes around you.

My origin lies in wait for me and wounds me. You see only the scars. With dizziness and love, I turn back toward it. I seek less to escape. Whatever is, so be it. Whatever was, so may it be. The origin: it does not heal, does not save. But through dispossession, it shows itself. It releases [*laisse*] everything that is. Otherwise, this would not be. It establishes me. It celebrates me. The origin in me celebrates itself, is celebrated. "What do you have to forget?"—"I no longer know."

13

Three Thinkers of Releasement:
Meister Eckhart, Heidegger, Suzuki

(1974–1975, trans. from the French by Karl von der Luft)

This long essay was first published in two parts in French in the American Journal of the History of Philosophy, *alongside John Caputo's "Meister Eckhart and the Later Heidegger: The Mystical Element in Heidegger's Thought."*[185] *Both philosophers had submitted their texts to the journal within one week of each other, and they corresponded during the revision stage to make sure there was not too much overlap.*[186] *Schürmann's text is his first extensive comparison of Eckhart and Heidegger with Zen Buddhism (see also chapters 15 and 16) and develops thoughts previously outlined in* Wandering Joy, *especially concerning the all-important theme of releasement (Gelassenheit in German, délaissement in French).*

> If I understand this man [Suzuki, R.S.] correctly, this is
> what I have been trying to say in all my writings.
> *Heidegger*[187]

> Meister Eckhart, the old master of reading and living
> [..., R.S.] from whom there is much to learn.
> *Heidegger* [GA 13: 89, 42]

In cultures as diverse as those of Buddhism, the Christian Middle Ages, and contemporary Europe, it seems that certain authors have thought of analogous experiences. Here is my thesis: in Meister Eckhart, Heidegger, and Suzuki, the understanding of being in general

---

185 [*Journal of the History of Philosophy* 12, no. 4 (October 1974): 479–94 / 13, no. 1 (January 1975): 61–80.]
186 [See John D. Caputo, *The Collected Philosophical and Theological Papers, Volume 1: 1969–1985*, 7. Their correspondence is available in the John D. Caputo Archive at the Simon Silverman Phenomenology Center at Duquesne University.]
187 [Reported in William Barrett, "Zen for the West," introduction to *Zen Buddhism: Selected Writings of D. T. Suzuki* (New York: Three Leaves, 2004), xii.]

has its conditions of possibility in a certain attitude of the one who questions it; this attitude is best summarized in the verb 'to let' ['*laisser*']. The three authors doubtless agree with each other less on the resulting theory of being than on this prerequisite. So we will make ours the attitude of 'letting-be,' we will submit ourselves to its rigor, and proceeding from it we will question the world, man, and God. How do the world, man, and God appear if man 'lets them be,' that is, detaches himself from them, and in a way abandons them?

1.1 *Letting, letting-be, releasement* [laisser, laisser-être, délaissement]. To let a thing—what could be more common? We say to the child: leave [*laisse*] the matches. And we say of the anchorite: he has left [*laissé*] the world. In both sentences, the transitive verb *laisser* signifies a rejection. This entirely negative dynamic, however, states only part of the phenomenon that interests us. It expresses the ascetic, moral face of it, that which is the most conspicuous but also the least essential. A more complete experience is reflected in the addition of the infinitive 'to be' ['*être*']. 'Letting-be': this suggests a restoration, the refusal to take hold of something, whatever it may be. Ascetic impoverishment turns into theoretical possession (in the sense of the Greek *theōria*). The negation is denied. The world, man, and God are left to themselves, and also *seen* in their essence. We will examine the ontological (or cosmological), anthropological, and transcendental dimensions of letting-be as well as its result: 'living without why.'

It will turn out, however, that a third step is necessary. The transitive sense of letting-be is abolished along the way. If the world, man, and God are radically left to themselves, who lets whom be? Who acts? Everything is let, but there is no one here who lets. The negation of the negation is thus overcome in its turn. In this regard, we will speak of 'releasement' ['*délaissement*'], both because of the intensive prefix and because of the intransitive character of the substantive. Releasement, *Gelassenheit*, no longer relates back to a thinking or acting subject. This word bespeaks the pure phenomenon of being let [*être laissé*].

1.2 *The Paradigm: The Ten Pictures of the Training of the Bull.* By way of introduction, here is how a Zen tale describes the apprenticeship of releasement. It deals with ten pictures, the originals of which date back to the Song dynasty.[188] They represent the phases of the domestication of the bull. Their order varies slightly in the editions; the one published by Tsushimura[189] seems to us to be the most satisfactory. Over the centuries, the pictures have been accompanied by a brief introduction in prose, and then by a commentary in verse. Other masters have added even more stanzas. Finally, Tsushimura wrote a short treatise for each picture to explain it. The drawings commonly published with these texts date back to an eleventh-century Chinese monk.[190] Here is a brief description of these pictures.

1.2.1 *Searching for the bull.* This picture represents an exhausted and desperate man who seeks the bull, i.e. his soul or Buddha. "Alone, in savage places, lost in the jungle, he seeks, he seeks [..., R.S.] he hears only the cicadas of the evening singing in the maple groves."

1.2.2 *The tracks of the bull.* The seeker has commenced to study diverse philosophical doctrines, he has found the tracks of the truth. But his mind [*esprit*] is still confused, he does not yet know how to distinguish between the good and the bad, the true and the false. "By the water, under the trees, here and there, there are the tracks of the lost bull [..., R.S.]."

1.2.3 *Seeing the bull.* He comprehends the uselessness of knowledge learned from books. He sees the bull: i.e., that the secret is in himself. All his senses are organized in a harmonious order. When the eye is suitably directed, he will notice that this order is nothing other than himself. "The bull is there, entirely alone; nowhere is there a place where it can hide. Its splendid head, decorated with majestic horns, what painter could reproduce it?"

---

[188] Daisetz T. Suzuki, *Essais sur le Bouddhisme Zen*, first series (Paris: Michel, 1972), 429–43. [R.S. uses the French translation in this edition, which has been rendered directly into English. Cf. the English in D. T. Suzuki, *Essays in Zen Buddhism*, first series (London: Rider, 1958).]

[189] Kôichi Tsushimura and Hartmut Buchner, trans., *Der Ochs und sein Hirte: Eine altchinesische Zen-Geschichte* (Pfullingen: Neske, 1958).

[190] Sir Charles Eliot, *Japanese Buddhism*, 3rd ed. (London: Routledge & Kegan Paul, 1964), 413.

1.2.4 *The capture of the bull.* After being lost for a long time in the solitude of the wilderness, he finally found the bull and took hold of it. The rope is stretched between him and the beast; the latter is not yet tamed. It is necessary for him to employ the whip. "With the energy of his entire soul, he has finally taken hold of the bull; but how wild is the animal's will, how ungovernable its power! Sometimes it proudly climbs a plateau, and is there lost in the mist of an impenetrable gorge."

1.2.5 *The grazing of the bull.* A rope is fastened to the nostrils of the bull, it follows docilely. But thoughts are still menaced with confusion, with falsity. As one thought moves, another follows, and then another. It is a question of not relaxing the tension of the rope, of not yielding [*se laisser aller*] to any indulgence. "Once suitably cared for, it will become pure and docile, and even without its chain, without anything to fasten it, it will follow you of its own accord."

1.2.6 *The return on the back of the bull.* The man is sitting on the back of the bull, playing a tune on the flute. Even if someone calls him, he will not turn his head; whatever the seductions, he will never tarry again. "Needless to say, he is now one of those who know."

1.2.7 *The forgetting of the bull.* The bull disappears, the man is left alone. The things are one, the bull is comprehended for what it was, a symbol. "In what serenity does he sit all alone! Though the red sun is already high in the sky, he still seems to be tranquilly asleep, under a thatch roof, his useless whip and rope lying beside him."

1.2.8 *The forgetting of oppositions.*[191] The picture represents a large circle filled with black. It shows nothing more. Bull, man, and nature have disappeared, and with them all oppositions. Only the unity of the circle remains. "Everything is empty, the whip, the rope, the man, the bull: Who has ever embraced with his gaze the immensity of the heavens? On the blazing fire a flake of snow cannot fall; when this state reigns, the spirit [*esprit*] of the ancient master is manifest."

---

191 In certain editions, the eighth and ninth tables are inverted.

1.2.9 *Nature seen in its essence.* A few twigs and flowers now appear. He no longer identifies himself with the transformations, but he observes the changes alone. He himself, from the very first beginning, has never been affected by defilement. Calmly he examines the birth and decline of the things endowed with form. He no longer asserts himself. His serenity is immutable. "Return to the origin, come back to the source! Already this is a false step! It is much better to remain at home, blind and deaf, quite simply and without agitation; sitting in the hut, he takes no notice of external things. See the water flowing—where? No one knows. And the flowers, red and fresh, for whom are they?"

1.2.10 *The return to the city.* A smiling, portly figure carries bags full of excellent things. The man now goes to the market, he goes his way without following the ancient sages. He is entirely free. He joins the wine-bibbers and butchers; he and they are all transformed into Buddhas. "Bare-chested, barefoot, he goes to the marketplace; spattered with mud, with ashes, how largely does he smile. No need for the miraculous power of the gods! For, at his touch, look, the dead trees are in full flower!"

These ten pictures admirably illustrate the progression into releasement. We see that this attitude is not reduced to simple abandonment. It is true that in order to find his Buddha-nature, the man must leave the village, then abandon in turn Buddha, himself, and nature; but his divestment [*dépouillement*] is the prerequisite for his intimate, irrefutable knowledge of what he has 'let.' In the eighth picture, releasement, or the 'who loses gains,' reaches its apogee: all things are entirely discarded, but also entirely present to each other. They are so intimately present to each other that the surface is black. Meister Eckhart will say of this stage that in the ground of the Godhead "the highest angel, the fly, and the soul" (DW 2: 493,9 [Pr. 52, "Beati pauperes spiritu"]) are equal and solely one. This picture makes one understand that everything is left to itself, but without there being any subject that lets it be.

To be sure, the first nine pictures find their meaning in the tenth. The itinerary has been taken with a view to happiness. It would be a misunderstanding, however, to see any intentionality there. Releasement, as the Zen master teaches it, strikes above all at the 'why' of human enterprises. Only when he no longer seeks does the herdsman find.

At the end of this article we will return to this Zen tale. With regard to the eighth picture, the large black circle, Suzuki refers in a note to Meister Eckhart:[192]

> It is interesting to note what a mystical philosopher writes about this subject: "... to be truly poor, man must be as empty of his created will as he was when he was not yet. And I say to you, by the eternal truth: as long as you have the will to fulfill the will of God and have any desire—even for eternity, even for God—you are not truly poor! For he is only a poor man who wants nothing, who knows nothing, who desires nothing."

2. *Releasement according to Meister Eckhart.* As with Zen, Meister Eckhart announces a simple message which, in a certain fashion, comes down to the relationships of man with things. His teaching, formulated in many paradoxes, has nothing of the esoteric or extraordinary. It concerns that which is most ordinary in an existence and that which most men live. It responds to the elementary questions: how will I know myself? How should I live? To this double question, theoretical and practical, Eckhart gives only one response: releasement. To comprehend this totalizing power of releasement will be to comprehend Meister Eckhart. We will try to elucidate successively the three aspects mentioned: ontological, anthropological, and transcendental.

Meister Eckhart is familiar with a great number of words which suggest the complex concept of releasement. The two substantives most frequently employed are *abegescheidenheit* and *gelâzenheit*. The former becomes a technical term in Meister Eckhart and his disciples, and as such has entered the dictionaries today. The equivalent in modern German is *Abgeschiedenheit*. The prefix *ab-* designates a separation (*abetuon*: to do away with something; *abekêre*: turning away, apostasy, etc.). The root, *scheiden* or *gescheiden*, signifies in its transitive form 'to isolate,' 'to cleave,' 'to separate,' and in its intransitive form 'to depart,' 'to die.' Since the modern era,

---

192 Suzuki, *Essais sur le Bouddhisme Zen*, 442 [cf. *Essays in Zen Buddhism*, 375[n1]]; the text of Meister Eckhart is taken from the sermon *Beati pauperes spiritu*, DW 2: 491,7–492,2 [Pr. 52].

this word almost exclusively signifies 'to become deceased.' Georg Trakl has written a celebrated poem entitled "Gesang des Abgeschiedenen." It consists of a song to a deceased friend.

In Meister Eckhart, *abegescheidenheit* translates first of all the Aristotelian *intellectus receptivus* [receptive intellect]. The mind, to know all things, must be empty of all things, *tabula rasa* [a blank slate]. In the School, the comparison with the eye and vision is common: *Quod est susceptivum coloris oportet esse sine colore* [Whatever can receive color must be without color].[193] The mind, which is 'in a certain way all things,' must be perfectly pure, without mixture, in order to know all things. Aristotle called it *nous amigēs*.[194] Eckhart writes: "If the mind knew its pure *abegescheidenheit*, it could not incline toward any thing, but should remain in its pure *abegescheidenheit*" (DW 1: 170,8-10 [Pr. 10, "In diebus suis"]).[195] We see immediately: Eckhart is not content with adapting a vernacular word to a doctrine that had become canonical in his era; on the contrary, translation for him inseparably signifies a reinterpretation. This reinterpretation always takes place in the same direction, from, to put it briefly, the ontological domain into the moral domain. The mind is naturally *abegescheiden*, say the Aristotelians. What you are naturally, you must become in your life, adds Meister Eckhart. *Abegescheidenheit* is not only given [*donnée*], it is ordained [*ordonnée*]. It has been suggested that this use of the Aristotelian philosophy of the intellect is perhaps the most original aspect of Meister Eckhart's work.[196] Meister Eckhart devoted an entire treatise to his concept of

---

193 Thomas Aquinas, [*Sentencia libri De anima*, lib. 2 1. 15 n. 1].
194 Aristotle, *On the Soul*, III, 429, b 23.
195 The Aristotelian context is rendered explicit in the sermon *Homo quidam nobilis*, DW 1: 250,11-251,15 [Pr. 15]. Eckhart first asks: "wie mag das gesin, das abegeschaidenheit des verstentniss sunder form vnd bild in im selber alliu dinc verstat sunder uskeren vnd verwandlung sin selbes?" [how can it be that the detachment of the understanding, without form and image in itself, understands all things without turning outward and transforming itself?] Without entering into the discussion of the simultaneous possession of all ideas—the theory underlying this sentence—this quotation directly concerns the *nous amigēs*. Eckhart also refers to Aristotle: "Nun merket mit flisse, das Aristotiles spricht von dem abegeschaidnen gaisten..." [Now note carefully what Aristotle says of the detached mind...]. The participle *abegescheiden* here literally translates *amigēs*.
196 Bernhard Welte, "Meister Eckart als Aristoteliker," in *Auf der Spur des Ewigen* (Freiburg: Herder, 1965), 197-210.

abegescheidenheit (DW 5: 377–434 [*Vab*]). Let us add that this term is found, like most of Meister Eckhart's concepts, in the poetry of Angelus Silesius, where it takes on a more distinctly ascetic shade.[197]

As for *gelâzenheit*, the root *lâzen* is more immediately comprehensible. As we have said: this attitude consists in regarding objects and events no more in their utility, but rather accepting them in their autonomy. It makes one renounce influences and procures equanimity. This word can also be translated as 'infinite resignation' and as 'serenity.' *Lâzen, lassen*, 'to let,' indicates a break with the habit [*désaccoutumance*] of possessing things, and of possessing oneself. Literally, it should be translated as 'to restore freedom,' 'to untie.' Only secondarily does this word mean 'to abandon,' 'to reject,' or 'to ignore.' He who has learned to 'let be' restores all things to their primitive freedom; he returns all things to themselves. He has unlearned to enslave them to his projects; he has divested himself of all affirmation of self. In the treatise *Rede der underscheidunge, abegescheidenheit* and *gelâzenheit* are employed equivalently (e.g., DW 5: 283,8 [*RdU*]). Often, the verb *lâzen* is nominalized. The transitive use gives rise to Meister Eckhart's most characteristic turns of phrase: "to leave [*laisser*] God," *got lâzen* (DW 2: 25,1 [Pr. 26, "Mulier, venit hora"]), "to leave all things," *alliu dinc lâzen* (DW 2: 81,2 [Pr. 29, "Convescens praecepit eis"]), "to leave the entire world," *alle die werlt lâzen* (DW 2: 241,2 [Pr. 38, "In illo tempore"]), "to leave all creatures," *alle crêatûren lâzen* (DW 2: 319,2 [Pr. 43, "Adolescens, tibi dico"]), "to leave yourself," *dich selben lâzen* (DW 2: 61,5 [Pr. 28, "Ego elegi vos"]). Since such expressions indicate a condition for knowing God, things, the world, creatures, and oneself, the use of the verb 'to abandon,' frequently encountered in translations,[198]

---

[197] "Weil Abgeschiedenheit sich niemand macht gemein, | So muss sie ohne Sucht und eine Jungfrau sein." "Since detachment does not render itself familiar to anyone | it must be without desire and virginal." Angelus Silesius, *Pélerin chérubinique* (*Der cherubinische Wandersmann*). (Paris: Aubier, 1946), 120. [*CW* 2,67: 81.]

[198] This is true of the two current French translations: Maître Eckhart, *Traités et sermons*, trans. Fernand Aubrier and J. Molitor, introd. Maurice de Gandillac (Paris: Aubier, 1942); Maître Eckhart, *Sermons, traités*, trans. Paul Petit (Paris: Gallimard 1942). Madame Jeanne Ancelet-Hustache is a more conscientious translator: Maître Eckhart, *Les Traités* (Paris: Seuil, 1971), and *Sermons I* (Paris: Seuil, 1974). Meister Eckhart, *Selected Treatises and Sermons*, trans. James Clark and John Skinner (London: Faber and Faber, 1958), is a relatively precise translation as to sense, but it completely sacrifices

is, certainly, inexact. We will translate *abegescheidenheit* as 'detachment' and *gelâzenheit* as 'releasement.'

2.1 *Ontological releasement.* "Every being [*Tout étant*] eats God, insofar as he is Being [*Être*]" (*omne ens edit deum, utpote esse*) (LW 2: 276, no. 47 [*In Eccli.*]) Meister Eckhart announces the two fundamental aspects of his ontology: on the one hand, the identity between God and Being, *Esse est Deus* (LW 1: 156, no. 12 [*Prol. gen.*]), on the other hand the analogy of dynamic assimilation of beings to God, *Qui edunt me, adhuc esuriunt* [They who eat me will hunger for more] (Eccles 24:29).[199]

2.1.1 *Esse est Deus.* God is; all that is not God is not. This opposition in Meister Eckhart must be understood most strictly; it is the basis of his ontology. "All creatures are a pure nothingness. I do not say that they are small or anything whatsoever: they are a pure nothingness" (DW 1: 69,8–70,1 [Pr. 4, "Omne datum optimum"]).[200] The dissimilarity between the created and the uncreated is declared to be total: only the uncreated, God, is. 'Creature' designates a being that unceasingly receives itself from elsewhere; it has received existence, life, and intelligence from another. It does not possess itself; the other is its being; it itself is nothingness.

> That which does not possess being is nothingness. Now, no creature has being, because its being depends on the presence of God. Let God turn

---

the similarities of the words: *lâzen* is translated sometimes as 'surrender,' sometimes as 'forsake,' sometimes as 'abandon.'

[199] See the commentary on this verse and its interpretation by Meister Eckhart in Vladimir Lossky, *Théologie négative et connaissance de Dieu chez Maître Eckhart* (Paris: Vrin, 1960), 320–32.

[200] See also article 26 of the Bull of condemnation of Meister Eckhart which literally repeats this phrase: *In Agro Dominico*, March 27, 1329, trans. Heinrich Denifle and Franz Ehrle, in *Archiv für Literatur- und Kirchengeschichte des Mittelalters* 2 (1886); Gabriel Théry, *Édition critique des pièces relatives au procès d'Eckhart contenues dans le manuscrit 33 b de la bibliothèque de Soest*, in *Archives d'Histoire doctrinale et littéraires du Moyen-Age* 1 (1926–1927), 184; finally Franz Pelster, "Ein Gutachten aus dem Eckehart-Prozess in Avignon," in *Aus der Geisteswelt des Mittelalters, Festschrift Martin Grabmann*, ed. Albert Lang et al. (Münster: Aschendorff, 1935), 1112. [LW 5: 225, no. 73 (*Acta*)]

away for an instant from all his creatures, and they will be annihilated. (DW 1: 70,1-4 [Pr. 4, "Omne datum optimum"])

The Aristotelian doctrine of analogy began with the twofold observation that man speaks about being in multiple situations and that the cases in which this word is appropriate are multiple. Analogy is the centerpiece of all metaphysics because it permits one to organize the numerous ways of speaking about being and to show their internal unity. They are not irreducible to each other. Aristotle thus spoke about being with a 'denominative' reference to a primordial sense. Each time we employ the word 'being,' a relation is established, according to Aristotle, to the first of the categories, substance. Later, one will speak of unity of order or analogy of attribution in this respect. This theory will then be extended to the relationship between the Creator and the creature: in the same way as accidents receive being from the substance in which they participate, so does the creature communicate with God. In this type of analogy, one of the two terms is strictly primary. God possesses in plenitude and according to an infinite mode the attributes that the creature appropriates according to a derived and finite mode. This scholastic rationality of creation claims to be in a straight line with the so-called predicative analogy in Aristotle. It permits one to recognize in God the perfections observed in things: in the Creator and in the creature, the perfection is the same. Only its mode of being is not identical. Thomistic ontology permits one to affirm the identity of perfection at the same time as the diversity in appropriation.

It is this last point that Meister Eckhart radically denies. Being is God: there is, properly speaking, no created being. The creature receives being as a loan, *ze borge* (DW 5: 37,5 [*BgT*]). It feeds on God. But the more it eats, i.e. the more it receives of being, the more it hungers. It is not from itself, but entirely from God. "Those who eat me will still hunger." Eckhart comments: *Edunt quia sunt, esuriunt qui ab alio sunt* [They eat because they are; they hunger because they are from another].[201] Even as limited in a particu-

---

201 Here is the whole text: "Notandum etiam quod hanc naturam analogiae quidam male intelligentes et improbantes erraverunt usque hodie. Nos autem secundum veritatem analogiae intelligendo [..., R.S.] dicamus quod ad significandum hanc veritatem analogiae rerum omnium ad ipsum deum dictum est optime: 'qui edunt me, adhuc

lar being [*étant*], being [*l'être*] and all transcendental perfections remain divine perfections—or better: God. Not only is every transcendental, which is convertible with every other, God, but it is so even as realized in a finite being, in *diz und daz*, 'this and that.' The structure of the being of beings is not measured against being which is God but is identified with it. Eckhart thus destroys the old idea of similitude between God and the created. If being is God, there is no similitude through deficiency and limitation, but a pure and simple identity. Beings [*l'étant*], insofar as they are, are God. Concerning anthropological releasement, we will have to examine this theory of identity, and will see in what way it differs from every pantheistic theory. Eckhart certainly does not assert a univocal consubstantiality between God and the creature.[202]

In the same way that 'being is God,' justice is God, and so are goodness, truth, wisdom, etc. The example of justice is most dear to him. "He who comprehends the teaching on justice and the just comprehends all that I say" (DW 1: 105,2–3 [Pr. 6, "Iusti vivent in aeternum"]). What in fact does the qualification 'just' attributed to many persons signify? Justice in the many just persons does not encompass them in the manner of a univocal genus; it is not abstracted from the sum total of the subjects. Nor is it an equivocal concept, designating a purely individual quality, diverse in each

---

esuriunt.' Edunt, quia sunt, esuriunt, quia ab alio sunt." ["Note also that even until today there are some who are in error because they understand the nature of analogy poorly and reject it. According to our understanding of the truth of analogy [...] we say that the text 'They that eat me, shall yet hunger' is perfectly fitted to signify the truth of the analogy of all things to God himself. They eat because they are; they hunger because they are from another." Meister Eckhart, *Teacher and Preacher*, ed. Bernard McGinn (New York: Paulist, 1986), 178–79.] LW 2: 281–82, no. 53 (*In Eccli*).

202 Heinrich Ebeling, *Meister Eckharts Mystik: Studien zu den Gesteskämpfen um die Wende des 13. Jahrhunders* (Stuttgart: Kohlhammer, 1941), 204, defends this position. This is a misunderstanding of Meister Eckhart, evidence of which we see going all the way back to the Avignon trial before the papal court. It is true that in his often paradoxical formulations, Meister Eckhart did not always take care to avoid this misunderstanding. A correct reading of his texts, however, shows that the verdict of pantheism pronounced against him lacks sufficient foundation. See e.g. Hans Hof, *Scintilla animae: Eine Studie zu einem Grundbegriff in Meister Eckharts Philosophie, mit besonderer Berücksichtigung des Verhältnisses der Eckhartschen Philosophie zur neuplatonischen und thomistischen Anschauung* (Lund: Gleerup, 1952), and the response to Ebeling on 133–46.

being and identical only nominally. Justice, as Meister Eckhart comprehends it, is not even a quality: neither abstracted from subjects nor left to their discretion and irreducible multiplicity, it precedes them. It does not perfect any subject, but it annihilates every subject subsisting in itself. "If then the just were many by virtue of a justice that is in each case different, the just would be just in an equivocal manner; or, justice would relate to the just in a univocal way; but here its relationship [to the just, R.S.] is analogical, exemplary, and by primacy" [LW 2: 366–67, no. 44 (*In Sap.*)].[203] 'Analogical' because the just do not possess justice in themselves, 'exemplary' because justice brings about a conformity of all the just to the one justice, and 'by primacy' because justice remains identical in God from whom it comes and in the just. In the same way that, according to Eckhart, light illuminates the luminous medium, but without the latter retaining it, so justice does not become fixed in the just, but remains entirely in God. In this regard, Gilson speaks of imputation,[204] a concept which is probably unsatisfactory;[205] it is accurate, in any case, to insist on the ephemeral character of this gift which occurs *in fluxu et fieri* [in flux and becoming] (LW 2: 627, no. 292 [*In Sap.*]).

It is understandable that Eckhart's accusers found fault with this doctrine of created perfections. In their eyes, he put too much on God's account and too little on that of the creature. In Thomas Aquinas, the creature retained a certain consistency of its own. The word *ens* designated first of all the sensible substance; the being [*l'être*] was created, material; it fell under the experience of the senses. Similarly, justice, goodness, etc. were said by priority of just creatures, good ones. For Eckhart, on the contrary, the qualities of the creature are in truth divine qualities that have become manifest in the world; for him there is strictly no perfection proper to things. The creature in itself is nothingness, just as its justice, its goodness, are nothing-

---

203 *Expositio Libri Sapientiae*, cited by Lossky, *Théologie négative et connaissance de Dieu chez Maître Eckhart*, 370, n. 166.

204 Étienne Gilson, *History of Christian Philosophy in the Middle Ages* (New York: Random House, 1955), 441: "Being is, so to speak, imputed to beings by God without ever becoming their own being, about in the same way as, in Luther's theology, justice will be imputed to the just without ever becoming their own justice."

205 Joseph Koch, "Zur Analogielehre Meister Eckharts," in *Mélanges offerts à Etienne Gilson* (Toronto/Paris: Pontifical Institute of Medieval Studies/Vrin, 1959), 338–42.

ness insofar as they are its own. The Inquisition noted this affirmation of Meister Eckhart: "Goodness is neither created, nor made, nor engendered, but it is only productive, and it engenders the good being [*l'être bon*]."[206] The good man is referred to goodness just as the creature is referred to the Creator. Goodness 'makes' the good man exactly as the Creator 'makes' the world. Goodness is creative like God. It is God. Eckhart says of justice: "The just men take justice so seriously that if God were not just, they would care for God as for a bean" (DW 1: 103,1-2 [Pr. 6, "Iusti vivent in aeternum"]).

Thus the two statements from which we started are clarified: "Being is God," "the creature is nothingness." That the creature is— this is in no way its own doing. It is entirely the doing of God, whom it indicates by its being, just as a wreath of vine leaves indicates at the entrance of a tavern that there is wine (LW 2: 280-81, no. 52 [*In Eccli.*]): without participation, and by an extrinsic relationship.

> God has indeed infused sufficiency and pleasure into creatures, but God alone has kept in himself the root of all sufficiency and the essence of all pleasure. [..., R.S.] The sun indeed illuminates the air and penetrates it with its light, but it does not cast its root there, for when the sun is not there, we have no more light. So God does with creatures. (Pf.: 148,9-19) [DW 2: 294,5-12 (Pr. 41, "Qui sequitur iustitiam")]

The creature receives being as the air receives light from the sun: "in passing, passively, and in becoming."[207] As light is conserved in the

---

[206] "Bonitas nec est creata nec facta nec genita sed tantum generans et generat bonum" [goodness is neither created nor made nor begotten, but only begetting and begets good]. *Rechtfertigungsschrift* §III, 1, art, 1, in Théry, 187 [LW 5: 198, no. 2 (*Acta*)]. Eckhart defends his thesis: "Dico quod verum est absolute et simpliciter" [I say this is absolutely and simply true], ibid., 187 [LW 5: 280, no. 87 (*Acta*)]. The main texts of this debate were collected by Josef Quint in the notes accompanying his publication of the *Book of Divine Consolation, Anmerkungen zu BgT*, DW 5: 62-70.

[207] "Communicat quidem [scil. lumen, R.S.] ipsi medio quasi mutuo et in transitu per modum passionis et transeuntis et fieri, ut sit et dicatur illuminatum, non autem communicat ipsi medio lumen suum per modum radicati et haerentis passibilis qualitatis, ut scilicet lux maneat et haereat et illuminet active, absente corpore luminoso." ["It [the luminous body] does impart something to the medium reciprocally and impermanently, in the manner of a reception, something transitory that happens in it so that it is and is said to be illuminated. It does not impart its light to the medium in the manner of a received quality that is rooted and inherent so that the light would remain

air by the indefectible influx of the sun, so the being of beings is a continuation of God's creative act which confers being. Compared to the Aristotelian-Thomistic tradition, the Eckhartian doctrine is characterized by the fleetingness of borrowed being—evanescent as a ray of sun in the air—as opposed to the permanence, duration, and autonomy of analogous beings according to the analogy of proportionality. Thomas has in view a mode of being of the creature, secondary because diminished, Meister Eckhart a mode of attribution of the divine being, subsequent to God but not diminished. Analogy does not then signify a mode of being, but a mode of presence of the unique being that is God. In such an ontology, the concept of transcendental analogy loses its sense. Only one and the same determination is found in all the analogates: the perfection of the first.[208] Being is numerically and formally one. The transcendental perfections in the inferior analogates never attain a mode of their own; one can call this a "brilliant deception,"[209] or even an "idealist and Nazi anthropological monism" (*sic*);[210] one can also see in it the analogy of a dynamic dependence in which the uncreated possesses everything, and the created nothing, save its insatiable hunger for God. Whichever attitude one prefers, there are three elements that constitute a genuine doctrine of analogy in Meister Eckhart: being as being, as well as all transcendental perfections as such, are formally found in only one of the terms considered, and created beings receive being itself, that is God; in addition to these perfections the creature possesses nothing, is nothingness in itself, and exists only through the manducation of the uncreated *esse*; finally, such a radi-

---

and inhere and actively give light in the absence of the luminous body." Meister Eckhart, *The Essential Sermons, Commentaries, Treatises, and Defense* (New York: Paulist, 1981), 147-48.] LW 3: 59, no. 70 (*In Ioh.*). This theory of the illumination of the air is in significant contradiction with that of Thomas Aquinas for whom the sun is the cause of light, not only *in fieri* [in becoming], but also *in esse* [in being]. *De veritate*, q. 21, a. 4, ad 2m.

208 Joseph Koch, "Zur Analogielehre Meister Eckharts," 347-50, has shown that this doctrine can claim antecedents such as Otto of Freising, Gilbert of Poitiers, and Augustine.

209 M. Galvano della Volpe, *Il misticismo speculativo di Maestro Eckhart nei suoi rapporti storici* (Bologna: Cappelli, 1930): "capziosità geniale."

210 Cornelio Fabro, *Participation et causalité selon S. Thomas d'Aquin* (Louvain: Publications Universitaires de Louvain, 1961), 581.

cal dependence is understandable only in the context of a continual emanation or 'boiling over' ['*ébullition*'] of the perfections going out from the source. This last point vindicates those who see in Eckhart a Neoplatonic essentialist: being, for him, signifies being something. And if by 'being' one designates God, the creature is necessarily nothingness. If 'being' designates the creature, then God will be nothingness. The analogical causality thus entails an exterior and contradictory relation: exterior because it is not really rooted in the created, contradictory because being can only belong to one of the terms. "The analogy of attribution suits the mystics."[211] It forbids, at least, speaking of a hierarchy of degrees of being.[212] With this, it guarantees immediacy between God and man.

The discovery of the nothingness of the creature is the first step in Meister Eckhart's approach. It resembles the first pictures of the Zen tale in its resolution to know about being in general. Like the herdsman, Eckhart discovers traces of what he is looking for in nature: "He who knows nothing but creatures has no need to think of sermons, for every creature is full of God and is a book" (DW 1: 156,7–9 [Pr. 9, "Quasi stella matutina"]). And as in the story of the bull, nature sends the seeker back to himself. It is not the answer. "He who loves the creature loves nothingness and becomes nothingness himself" (LW 2: 354, no. 34 [*In Sap.*]). The moral implication of such an ontology is certainly violent:

> Alas, how many there are who adore a shoe, a bull, or some other creature, and for whom that is the sole concern; what fools they are! As soon as you pray to God for the love of creatures, you are praying for your own damage; for as soon as the creature is a creature, it carries with it bitterness, damage, malaise, and embarrassment. That is why it is nicely done

---

[211] Maruílo Teixeira-Leite Penido, *Le rôle de l'analogie en théologie dogmatique* (Paris: Vrin, 1931), 40.

[212] Pierre Aubenque, *Le problème de l'être chez Aristote* (Paris: Presses Universitaires de France, 1962), 200–201, n. 4, writes: "It is not by chance, but by virtue of the same Platonizing logic, that Meister Eckhart will take up the same univocalizing interpretation of analogy, understood as gradual participation in *Esse*." On the contrary: all of Meister Eckhart's effort goes in the opposite direction. How do these lines of Aubenque agree with the text of Meister Eckhart that we have pointed out in our note on Eckhart in 1.2.10 above?

for the people if they obtain embarrassment and bitterness. Why? They have prayed for it! (DW 2: 25,4-26,2 [Pr. "Mulier, venit hora"])

2.1.2 *Qui edunt me, adhuc esuriunt.* It is necessary for us now to push further the analysis of the dynamism contained in this biblical quotation, which summarizes Eckhartian ontology. In fact, the dynamism in question is nothing other than what we have called 'releasement.' If the creature is nothingness, one should turn away from it, 'leave' it, detach oneself from it. But what does this mean? Does Meister Eckhart teach a pure and simple rejection of the things of the world, a *Weltflucht*? He was a "clergyman appreciated for his administrative qualities,"[213] and escape from the world was not the goal of his preaching. He was even ironic about the reclusive life. He did not think that things merit no attention, but that what in them is worthy of interest is solely being—or God. Every creature must be chalked up to the Creator, and not to itself. The dynamism contained in the metaphor of 'manducation' and ever insatiable hunger can be understood in two ways. Either it signifies one's desire for something that cannot be possessed, or it signifies one's desire for something that can be possessed but cannot ever fill one up. The second solution amounts to saying that God is *bonum honestum* [a genuine good] and not merely *utile* [useful] (as for example a medicine, even a repulsive one) or *delectabile* (i.e. agreeable, even if not good in itself, like alcohol). The second solution is not false; it is insufficient. The hunger of which Meister Eckhart speaks concerns potentiality with regard to being itself. It is thus to be taken in the first sense, as a radical negation, an eternally gaping privation. It is this entitative privation that best expresses the concept of ontological releasement. Deprived of being, the creature is actually released, its actuality is not its own, and it is defined by the consumption of a being [*un être*] which is never appropriated. The condition of finite beings, according to Meister Eckhart, is that of an always unstable begging.

Philosophically, this theory evidently poses some problems. How is being understood in such a privative relationship? Of what exactly are finite beings deprived? Can we still speak of beings? It

---

213 G. Théry, "Le 'Benedictus Deus' de Maître Eckhart," in *Mélanges Joseph de Ghellinck* (Gembloux: Duculot, 1951), 927.

is striking that the German word by which Eckhart translates the *ens commune* [common being] of the scholastics, *wesene*, is rarely employed when he speaks of things. *Unwesene* does not signify the creature's privation of being, but the ground of the Godhead, as we shall see. When Eckhart speaks of the nothingness of the creature, he says *niht*. This word has given rise to the modern German *nicht*. It consists of a negation *n-* and of *iht*. *Iht* signifies 'something,' 'anything whatever.' The creature, according to Eckhart, is not 'a something.' Lossky seems to translate *iht* as 'essence'; the privation would then strike quiddity, the "necessitous essences."[214] This seems to accord poorly with the text we have cited: "Let God turn away for an instant from all his creatures, and they will be annihilated" [DW 1: 70,3–4 (Pr. 4, "Omne datum optimum")]. *Iht* reflects more the complexity of *ousia*, the principle of actuality of existing beings, than it does essence. We are closer to what Martin Heidegger calls *Seiendheit*[215] than to a purely essentialist philosophy. *Niht* is the negation of the fact of being. The creature cannot be represented for itself. It is thought of only as creature, precisely, thus only the relation of begging is thinkable.

The closer one looks, the more one realizes that Meister Eckhart always adopts the most extreme solution; here, the singular being as such, and not merely the *ens commune* or essence, is denied. The terminology is most incisive. With regard to the singular being, Eckhart speaks of *ihtes iht*, 'such an individual being,' 'such a something.' The corresponding negation, *nihtes niht*, is properly translated as 'non-being.' It bespeaks the negation of the fact of being singular as it belongs to a singular being. Beings are not, they do not possess *ihtes iht*. Also it will be correct to speak about a *being* only by keeping in mind this entirely relational foundation of the finite thing vis-à-vis infinite being. This abolition of the beings' own being is a doctrine too widespread among German mystics to be surprising.[216] It is certainly not satisfactory to speak of an "ontology proper

---

214 Lossky, *Théologie négative et connaissance de Dieu chez Maître Eckhart*, 105.
215 Martin Heidegger, *Vorträge und Aufsätze* (Pfullingen: Neske, 1954), 74f. and 240 [cf. GA 7: 72–74, 245]. André Préau translates this word by "beingness" ["étantité"] in Heidegger, *Essais et conférences* (Paris: Gallimard, 1958), 85.
216 In the mystical poetry of the thirteenth and fourteenth centuries, one sometimes encounters the play of oppositions between *iht* and *niht*. Mechthild of Magdeburg

to the spiritual relationship" beyond natural ontology;[217] but perhaps there are experiences of thought to which the traditional conceptual strangleholds suddenly seem inadequate.[218]

It is essential to comprehend this ontological point of departure of the thought of releasement in Meister Eckhart. It would be easy to classify him among the moralists of the *contemptus mundi* [contempt for the world], especially since the Augustinian expression *regio dissimilitudinis* [region of unlikeness] is sometimes found employed in connection with creatures.[219] Nothing could be more erroneous, however. The doctrine of releasement will surely have moral consequences, but these have nothing in common with a desperate discrediting of the visible. Releasement signifies above all what one Canadian commentator has called the "utter outwardness" of the creature in relation to God.[220] Left to itself, the creature is *niht*, nothingness.

The eighth picture of the bull represents nothingness—a large black circle. Everything that can be seen—man, the bull, nature—

---

writes: "Du solt minnen das niht, | Du solt vliehen das iht..." "You shall love the nothingness, | You shall flee from the something..." Cited by Grete Lüers, *Die Sprache der deutschen Mystik des Mittelalters im Werke der Mechthild von Magdeburg* (Munich: Reinhardt, 1926), 293. Angelus Silesius writes: "Mensch, sprichst du, dass dich Ichts von Gottes Lieb' abhält, | So brauchst du doch nicht recht, wie sich's gebührt, der Welt." "Man, do you say that something is holding you back from the love of God? | You do not yet use the world correctly and appropriately." Silesius, *Pélerin chérubinique*, 114. [*CW* 2.34: 76.]

217 "Everything happens as if there were an ontology proper to the spiritual relationship, which has its unity, its certainty, but beyond natural ontology, in such a way that it is antinomic and paradoxical for the latter. This is the 'Who loses gains' of the Gospel." Yves Congar, "Langage des spirituels et langage des théologiens," in *La mystique rhénane* (Paris: Presses Universitaires de France, 1963), 22.

218 A third family of words related to the concept of being should be mentioned, namely *sîn* and *isticheit*. Meister Eckhart applies these latter, constructed from *ist*, it 'is,' principally to God. See e.g. DW 1: 106,1–3 (Pr. 6, "Iusti vivent in aeternum"): "Gotes [..., R.S.] sîn min sîn und gotes isticheit mîn isticheit" [God's being is my being and God's isness my isness].

219 Margot Schmidt, "Regio dissimilitudinis: Ein Grundbegriff mittelhochdeutscher Prosa im Lichte seiner lateinischen Bedeutungsgeschichte," Freiburger Zeitschrift für Philosophie und Theologie 15 (1968): 63–108, has collected thirteen texts by Meister Eckhart on the moral and ontological inadequacy of creatures in relation to God, many of which refer to Augustine, 90.

220 Bernard Muller-Thym, *The Establishment of the University of Being in the Doctrine of Meister Eckhart of Hochheim* (New York: Sheed and Ward, 1939), 113. ["Utter outwardness" is in English in the original."]

has disappeared. In Meister Eckhart, the unity of the visible comes from the fact that it receives its being from God. Perhaps we are not so far from what Zen Buddhism calls 'liberation.' Suzuki writes in this connection: "What is destroyed is the dualism of things, and not their unity. And liberation signifies returning to one's original abode."[221] This original abode is certainly not the same in Christianity and Buddhism. Eckhart does not in fact stop talking about God when he calls the creature *niht*. There is however a striking similarity in the way of thinking about the visible, namely, as beyond the opposition between being and non-being, affirmation and negation. 'The creature is'—here is the proposition that Meister Eckhart aims to deny with such insistence. At the same time, he continues to speak of 'the being of the creature,' in order to add that it 'comes from God.' In other words, with respect to visible things, affirmation and negation lose their meaning simultaneously. In Zen, also, the purified mind which has released the world knows the 'fact of being that' or the 'fact of being such' of things. It knows 'reality in its exact essence.' The condition is the same: to overcome the false dualism between affirmation and negation.

> When the mind is sufficiently trained, it sees that neither negation nor affirmation are applicable to reality, but that truth consists in the knowledge of things as they are, or rather as they become. A really sincere and completely purified mind is the necessary preliminary to the comprehension of reality in its exact essence. As a result, we have *ti yathâ-bhûtam pajânâti* ('he knows *that*, such as it is in reality'), and this was later formulated by the Mahayanists in the doctrine of 'the fact of being that' or 'the fact of being such.'[222]

It is quite instructive to compare the conditions of knowing things as they are in Meister Eckhart and in Zen. For Suzuki, the condition consists in a training of the mind that has become "really sincere and completely purified." Meister Eckhart says of his doctrine of nothingness: "The man who wishes to comprehend this must be entirely detached" (DW 2: 109,1 [Pr. 30, "Praedica verbum"]; the

---

221 Suzuki, *Essais sur le Bouddhisme Zen*, 170 [cf. *Essays in Zen Buddhism*, 143].
222 Ibid. [cf. *Essays in Zen Buddhism*, 143].

word for "detached" is *abegescheiden*). In order to grasp ontological releasement, the mind itself must be released.

2.2 *Anthropological releasement*. Like all created things, man is *niht*, nothingness. But he is not a creature in all his aspects. "There is a certain thing in the soul that is uncreated and uncreatable. If the whole soul were so, it would be uncreated and uncreatable; and this is the intellect" [LW 5: 599 (*Acta*)].[223] We must first examine this teaching of the 'uncreated and uncreatable' intellect; then we will look more precisely at what Meister Eckhart calls the 'ground of the soul' as the place where man is naturally released. In this way we shall see a new sense of *gelâzenheit*.

2.2.1 *The doctrine of the intellect.* The quotation about the "certain thing in the soul" must be surprising. Is the intellect thought of as an entity apart, an incorruptible core in a created and corruptible body? The above formulation is that of the [papal] Bull of condemnation. These lines indeed exude a distinctly Platonizing atmosphere. Is the 'uncreated and uncreatable' intellect so far from the Platonic doctrine of the 'preexisting and immortal' soul? This suspicion must seem all the more justified since Eckhart was brought before the Inquisition by his own Dominican brothers, defenders of the Aristotelian-Thomistic purity in theology. Nevertheless, it is a different issue in Meister Eckhart, and his doctrine of the intellect will prove instead to be more Aristotelian than Platonizing. Let us first listen to his own way of expressing himself.

> I have already said it often: There is a power in the soul that touches neither time nor flesh: it emanates from the spirit and resides in the spirit and is totally spiritual. In this power, God greens and blooms totally, in all the joy and all the honor that he is in himself. There reigns a sovereign joy and a gladness so incomprehensibly great that no one can speak of it fully. For in this power the eternal Father unceasingly engenders his eternal Son, in such a way that this power engenders, in concert, the Son of

---

[223] This is the proposition condemned by the papal Bull. *In Agro Dominico,* op. cit., 639.

the Father, and engenders itself as that same Son, in the identical power of the Father. (DW 1: 32,1-8 [Pr. 2, "Intravit Iesus in quoddam castellum"])

Before the papal court he repeated that God "is received in the intellect" [LW 5: 303 (*Acta*)].[224] Before the tribunal of the bishop of Cologne he had already defended a more abbreviated version of this text [LW 5: 321 (*Acta*)].[225] We are thus dealing with a central element of his thought.

There appears to be a difference, however, between the formulation of the Bull and the text of Meister Eckhart himself. The condemned article is amputated from the part that alone can ensure a just comprehension of it, namely the verbs 'to green and to bloom' and 'to engender,' to which the Cologne proceedings add 'to carry out' and 'to make.' Thus, in his Avignon defense, Meister Eckhart rejects the incriminating article as *stultum*, foolish [LW 5: 572 (*Acta*)].[226] Indeed, as it appears in the Bull, the article treats the intellect as an entity and lends it attributes which belong only to God. The verbs cited, however, change its aspect. That there is a power in the soul whose "operation is identical with that of God," which engenders the Son "in concert" in the soul and in the Father, is something other than a pure and simple identification of the intellect with the 'uncreatable' God. Eckhart speaks of an event. The Curia, on the other hand, thinks in terms of entities. Two families of language confront each other. The ecclesiastical institution of late scholasticism stiffens in a sclerotic, dogmatic terminology. But what is this identity between the intellect and God if it is to be understood as event?

Eckhart compares it to combustion, exercised by fire and undergone by wood:

> Acting and becoming are one. God and I are one in the operation: he acts and I become. Fire transforms into itself everything it reaches: it imposes its nature on it. It is not the fire that changes into wood, but the wood into fire. In the same way, we are transformed into God in order to know him as he is. (DW 1: 114,2-115,2 [Pr. 6, "Iusti vivent in aeternum"])

---

224 *Rechtfertigungsschrift*, § II, art. 13, in Théry, *Édition critique*..., 204.
225 Ibid., § I, 4, art. 5, in Théry, *Édition critique*..., 179.
226 Pelster, "Ein Gutachten aus dem Eckehart-Prozess in Avignon," 1111-12.

As fire assimilates wood, so God assimilates the intellect, so that the latter 'knows' him as he is. This identity is thought on the most traditional model in Aristotelian philosophy: "The thinking and the thought are identical."[227] This model is that of intellection. It had been expressly recognized as valid wherever there is knowledge.[228] Only, Eckhart's predecessors had recoiled from the ultimate consequence of this law of identity in the act of knowing. They had not applied it to the case of the knowledge of God. However, the event-like aspect of this identity has been perfectly recognized in the School: "In that which concerns the intelligibles in act, thought and what it thinks are identical, just as sense and the object of sensation are identical in act."[229] The expression "in act" recurs three times in this sentence of Thomas Aquinas.[230] Extended by Meister Eckhart to the domain of assimilation to God, the identity in the act of knowledge becomes operative identity, 'engendering.' But that this is an authentically Aristotelian piece of his thinking cannot be in doubt.

It is true that Meister Eckhart speaks preferentially in terms of birth [*naissance*] rather than knowledge [*connaissance*]. The event of identity thus comes to affect not thought alone, but also the whole of existence. The intellect that "touches neither time nor flesh" [DW 1: 32,1–2 (Pr. 2, "Intravit Iesus in quoddam castellum")] is the place where God engenders the Word and where he engenders the intellect as Word. Man must be reborn to the Father as the Son of God, the Word. This is the most elevated title of glory with which one can honor the mind; at the same time, this theory of the reciprocal engendering between man and God is no longer confined to the exclusive terrain of a noetic philosophy. Knowledge is a model, but existence is what seeks to unfold itself in identity with God. Not that there is pure and simple coincidence between God and man

---

227 Aristotle, *On the Soul*, III, 4, 430 a 3–4.
228 Thomas Aquinas, *Summa theologiae*, Ia, q. 87, a.1 ad 3m. Thomas comments on a *verbum Philosophi* [saying of the Philosopher], namely that the intellect and the object of intellection are one: "Dicendum quod verbum illud Philosophi universaliter verum est in omni intellectu" [It is to be said that this saying of the Philosopher is universally true in every intellect].
229 [Aquinas, *Sentencia libri De anima*, lib. 3 l. 9 n. 5.]
230 [By "three times," R.S. means the original Latin, not his translation thereof: "Id est si accipiamus intelligibilia actu, idem est intellectus et quod intelligitur, sicut idem est sentiens in actu et quod sentitur in actu."]

in the manner of pantheism. Eckhart always takes care to present this identity as an accomplishment, i.e. as obedience, love, *gewürke* (from the verb *würken*, to make [*faire*]) (DW 1: 114,2-115,2 [Pr. 6, "Iusti vivent in aeternum"]). But the otherness [*l'altérité*] of God appears as derivative and secondary compared to the more original identity between God and man. Distance and difference appear only to reflection; in the act of assent, in existence that believes, they are excluded. Eckhart would say: distance and difference are 'created.' They are thematizable only if identity has been accomplished beforehand. The differences between substances presuppose and indicate identity:

> I have sometimes spoken of a light that is in the soul, uncreated and uncreatable. This light is what I ordinarily treat of in my sermons; it takes hold of God without mediation, uncovered and divested, as he is in himself. This is to be understood according to the actuality of the generation which makes one penetrate into God. (Pf.: 193,16-20) [DW 2: 418,1-4 (Pr. 48, "Ein meister sprichet")]

> God engenders me as himself and engenders himself as me myself, and me as his being and his nature. This is one life alone and one being alone, and one work alone. (DW 1: 109,9-11 [Pr. 6, "Iusti vivent in aeternum"])

This identity is so dear to Meister Eckhart that he does not hesitate to accumulate adjectives against every convention: *ein einic ein ungeschieden* [a single indistinct one] (DW 1: 381,1 [Pr. 22, "Ave gratia plena"]).[231] To the realm of differences and oppositions, these texts prefer that of identity and event. Man is the place where these two realms meet. He is created, there is nothingness in him, but at the same time he carries within him 'an uncreated and uncreatable light.' The salvific action of God can reach him, engender him anew. Moreover, the return to the abode of the Father is inseparably an entirely divine and entirely human work. And it is a work of the whole man, a new birth. It is not solely an act of knowledge.

---

[231] Angelus Silesius will literally repeat this expression: "In Gott wird nichts erkannt: er ist ein einig Ein. | Was man in ihm erkennt, das muss man selber sein." "In God nothing is known: he is a unique One. | What one knows in him, one oneself must be." Silesius, 106 [*CW* 1.285: 68.]

Identity by fire, by knowledge, by engendering: how does the Eckhartian releasement appear in this context? It is this opening, this embrasure, from which one's equanimity can arise, not merely in the face of things, but also before oneself as a participant among the created. Every itch of possession, the enemy of serenity, takes its origin in the creature as creature. To incline towards creatures is to become confounded with them in nothingness. The way of *abegescheidenheit* urges; it is urgent to "leave [*laisser*] nothingness" (DW 1: 170,3-4 [Pr. 10, "In diebus suis"]). He who refuses to do so, even if he believes himself living, is already dead; he annihilates himself. Insofar as there is in man both the created and an uncreated and uncreatable operation, the new birth is also a releasement: to let be the created man in the divinized man. Then the "flower of the intellect"[232] ceases to be only a faculty: the whole being can unfold itself freely—as in the awakening of Zen *satori*, which is "the opening of the flower of the mind," "the removal of a barrier," or "the splendor given to the works of the mind."[233] It signifies "an emptiness of interest and a poverty of purpose"; from this it results that "life feels itself entirely free in its activity."[234]

2.2.2 *The ground of the soul.* In the terminology of Meister Eckhart, as well as that of Zen, the zone so activated in man is sometimes called 'the ground' [*'fond'*]. "The bottom [*le fond*] of a bucket has been punctured," says Suzuki; and he means to speak of "the birth of a new man."[235] In both traditions, too, the 'ground' is understood as "what renders our intellectual operations possible."[236] "Inner knowledge is founded [*se fonde*] in the being of our soul" (Pf.: 39,15-16) [DW 3: 316,5-6 (Pr. 76, "Videte qualem caritatem")]. The ground of the soul is one and simple, beyond the intellect, unknowable to the discursive faculties:

---

232 The expression comes from Proclus, by whom Meister Eckhart had read the *Liber de Causis* at least. William of Moerbeke translates it as "flos intellectus": *De Providentia et Fato*, ed. Cousin (Paris: Minerva, 1864), col. 172, 15.
233 Suzuki, 272. [Cf. *Essays in Zen Buddhism*, 231.]
234 Ibid. [Cf. *Essays in Zen Buddhism*, 231.]
235 Ibid., 271. [Cf. *Essays in Zen Buddhism*, 231.]
236 Ibid., 82. [Cf. *Essays in Zen Buddhism*, 69.]

> It is neither this nor that, and yet it is a certain thing. It is elevated above this and that, higher than the heaven above the earth. [..., R.S.] It is free of all names and divested of all forms, entirely enfranchised and free, as frank and free as God is in himself. It is as totally one and simple as God is one and simple, so that one can in no way plunge one's gaze into it. (DW 1: 39,4–40,4 [Pr. 2, "Intravit Iesus in quoddam castellum"])

The doctrine of the ground of the soul is assuredly the most difficult to grasp in Meister Eckhart. The ground of the soul is distinguished from the intellect in that the latter acts, as we have said. Also, the *gewürke* of the intellect is the essence of the operative identity between God and man. But the ground of the soul does not act. It is not a power. All cognitive powers are made in order to act: those that are turned outward form 'phantasms'; those that are turned inward reflect the soul in itself. But at the root of these activities reigns total immutability. 'Being,' 'image of God,' 'ground' (*grunt*), 'abyss' (*abegrunt, ungrunt*), 'essence of the soul,' 'castle in the soul': all these terms designate the same region eternally at rest in man, where the soul is closer to God than to the powers, i.e. to the created things which the latter grasp. "The intimacy or proximity between God and the soul does not in truth involve any distinction" [LW 5: 249 (*Acta*)].[237]

The operative powers, empirical or intuitive, are opposed to the being of the soul, the *grunt*, like the imprints of the world in us are opposed to the imprint of God. Between the first two powers and the last one, there is a qualitative leap. Yet the concept of soul in Meister Eckhart is not equivocal. The soul does not alienate itself when it turns toward the things of the world or when it reflects itself intuitively in itself. And it certainly does not alienate itself in the ground, where it is of a divine nature. One cannot then speak of a non-identity of the soul thus traversed by the schism between being and acting. There are not two souls; it is not in either of these modes in an 'elsewhere.' The relationship between the active and the passive zone is a relationship of antecedent to consequent. The ground of the soul is "the middle and in some way the center of all the powers" (LW 3: 621, no. 709 [*In Ioh.*]).

---

[237] *Rechtfertigungsschrift*, § I, in Théry, *Edition critique...*, 263.

The antinomy between the *grunt* and the *krefte*, intuitive power and discursive power, allows us to grasp the immutability of the being of the soul. And in a step entirely characteristic of his thought, Meister Eckhart hastens, in all the texts which refer to it, to deny this immutability also. The soul is without ground [*sans fond*], *gruntlôs*, for God operates there, ineffable, *namelôs*. The happiness of man depends on his living entirely from this "ground without ground":

> What then is the 'speaking' of God? It is the work of God. And this work is so noble and so elevated that God alone accomplishes it. Know that all our perfection and all our felicity depend on man passing through and beyond all that is created and temporal, all that *is*. He must advance to the depth that is without ground. (DW 2: 309, 1–5 [Pr. 42, "Adolescens, tibi dico: surge"])

Whatever the exact anthropological scope that we must recognize in this mysterious text, two points seem certain to us. On the one hand, the ground of the soul is a reality. On the other hand, the oppositions (active-passive; God-man) no longer obtain there. Moreover, it must concern something other than speculations. Texts like this one seem to testify about a totally concrete personal experience:

> If you could grasp this with my heart, you would well comprehend what I am saying, for it is true, and the truth itself says it. […, R.S.] So one and simple is this castle, and so highly elevated above every mode and power is this identical unity, that no power or mode can ever look upon it, nor can God himself. In all truth and as true as God lives! God himself will never look into it for an instant and has never looked into it, insofar as he puts on a mode and according to the property of his Persons. […, R.S.] If God should ever cast eyes at it, it will cost him all his divine names. […, R.S.] See, in so far as he is one and simple he penetrates into what I call the castle in the soul, and otherwise he will not penetrate it in any way; it is only thus that he penetrates it and is already in the interior. With this part of itself, the soul is equal to God, and not otherwise. What I say to you here is true; I give you the truth as a witness and my soul as a pledge. (DW 1: 41,5–44,7 [Pr. 2, "Intravit Iesus in quoddam castellum"])

How can we not consider, once again, the Zen experience. It activates the ordinary state of our mind; it does not pass beyond our everyday life. The eighth picture of the training of the bull certainly comes after a long apprenticeship—of "passing through and beyond all that is created and temporal, all that *is*," says Eckhart. But many sayings of the Zen masters suggest that this is nothing extraordinary: "We are here as if we were immersed in water, with head and shoulders in the depths of the great ocean; and yet, in what pitiful fashion we reach out our arms in order to call for water!"[238]

The Eckhartian doctrine of the ground of the soul is the result of a great unitary quest. It is a practical henology—phrases like 'insofar as he is one and simple he penetrates into the soul' simultaneously aim at the overcoming of all dualisms and at a way of life, releasement. In this, it differs from traditional henology, Plotinian for example. Eckhart is not a philosopher, but a preacher whose pressing invitation to live solely off of one's own ineffable ground includes some philosophical implications. He would probably agree well with this expression from a Zen master: "If you desire to see, see directly inside; but when you try to think on it, it is completely missed."[239]

It is reported that the Buddha, after his enlightenment under the Bodhi tree near the city of Gaya and the river Nairanjanā, resolved to keep silent about the truth he had attained.[240] Later, however, like the herdsman in the last picture of the training of the bull, he returned to the world. It remains true, nevertheless, that "he who knows does not speak of it; he who speaks of it does not know."[241] Why is silence preferable? It is because, Suzuki explains, "one must realize the ultimate truth in oneself, by one's own efforts." The content of enlightenment [*l'illumination*] was explained by the Buddha in terms stunningly similar to those of Meister Eckhart: this truth must be "directly perceived (sanditthika) beyond the limits of time (a-kālika), in order to be the object of a personal experience (ehi-

---

238 Suzuki, *Essais sur le Bouddhisme Zen*, 346 [cf. *Essays in Zen Buddhism*, 292-3].
239 Ibid., 359 [cf. *Essays in Zen Buddhism*, 303].
240 Ibid., 57, note: "The wishes I originally had are granted, the Dharma (the Truth) I have attained is too profound to be comprehended. [..., R.S.] All beings are enveloped in avidity, anger, folly, falsehood, arrogance, and flattery [..., R.S.] so it is preferable that I remain silent and enter Nirvāna." This text is taken from the *Sūtra on the Cause and Effect in the Past and Present*. [Cf. *Essays in Zen Buddhism*, 49[n1].]
241 [Cf. Lao-Tzu, *Tao Tê Ching*, 56.]

passika), entirely persuasive (opanayika), and which the wise must each comprehend by accomplishing his own experience."[242]

Meister Eckhart, in turn, seems to have been pressed to speak: "If no one had been present here, I would have preached to this collection box" (Pf.: 181,19-20 [DW 4,2: 774,1-2 (Pr. 109, "Nolite timere eos, qui occidunt corpus")]. But the urgency to keep silent as well as the urgency to communicate come from the same knowledge: that he alone is free who has "left himself all the way to the ground" [*qui s'est "laissé jusqu'au fond"*] (*ze grunde gelâzen*) (DW 2: 415,5 [Pr. 48, "Ein meister sprichet"]).

2.3 *Transcendental releasement*. "Releasement seizes God, but to release God himself is a releasement that few understand."[243]

The ground of the soul does not stand any name, but it is the reality where the antinomy between God and man is overcome. We have seen some anthropological implications of this doctrine of Meister Eckhart. We must now draw out the consequences in respect to his thinking about God. We already know that if God ever wishes to look into the ground of the soul, "it will cost him all his divine names." Indeed, the ineffable ground of man and the ineffable ground of God are one: "Here the ground of God is my ground, and my ground, the ground of God [*Gotes grunt mîn grunt und mîn grunt gotes grunt*, R.S.]" (DW 1: 90,8 [Pr. 5b, "In hoc apparuit"]). "Pure water poured into pure water remains the same," it is said in Zen.[244] We call the region of nameless indistinction referred to in these texts 'transcendental releasement.'

Why 'transcendental'? This adjective, in the Aristotelian tradition as well as in modern philosophy, designates that which surpasses the categories of possible experience in general. But while the former considers transcendental attributes as derived from experience and abstracted from it in the manner of a universal quality, the opposition between transcendental and empirical was accentuated later to the point of confining the one to the understanding as a

---

242 Suzuki, *Essais sur le Bouddhisme Zen*, 72 [cf. *Essays in Zen Buddhism*, 61].
243 "Gelassenheit fäht Gott; Gott aber selbst zu lassen | Ist ein Gelassenheit die wenig Menschen fassen" [Releasement grasps God, but to release God himself | is a releasement that few people grasp]. Silesius, *Pélerin chérubinique*, 124. [*CW* 2.92: 85.]
244 Suzuki, *Essais sur le Bouddhisme Zen*, 149 [cf. *Essays in Zen Buddhism*, 125].

condition of the other. A modern commentator has seen in Meister Eckhart the very principles of the Kantian critical philosophy.[245] We employ the term 'transcendental' to qualify not certain rules of knowledge, but the general a priori condition of all experience, both sensible and intellectual, of the created as well as the uncreated. The identity of the ground of the soul and the ground of God designates this zone of a formless but seminal totality where God, man, and the world are rooted. This zone escapes all representation. Meister Eckhart speaks of it when he says that the soul does not grasp God "insofar as he is good, nor insofar as he is the truth. It penetrates to the ground and continues to search, and it grasps God in his unity and in his solitude [*einoede*, R.S.]; it grasps God in his desert [*wüestunge*, R.S.] and in his own ground" (DW 1: 171,13–15 [Pr. 10, "In diebus suis"]).

Why 'releasement'? We have already exhibited the first signification of this word when speaking of created things. Ontological releasement opens up the difference between the being that is God and beings, thanks to which the latter are maintained, 'let,' in being. A second signification resulted from Meister Eckhart's view of man. Anthropological releasement suggests a return: man must 'leave' the created and live entirely off of that which is uncreated and uncreatable within him. This second signification of the word has an ascetic shade. It is a matter of not possessing things, oneself, the future, etc. ... of not saying: "I am, I am that, I will be, I will not be, I will have a form, I will be without form, I will have a thought, I will be without thought, I will be neither with nor without thought."[246] But more important than this asceticism is the operative identity, the birth of the Word in man. The third signification of the word results from the passage beyond all that can be represented. Eckhart calls this passage the breakthrough (*durchbruch*) beyond God. God then appears as 'let,' as one who has himself been granted from out of the desert or the solitude that precedes him. But to be able to think that which 'lets' God be, one must 'leave' God; one must abandon him.

---

245 Joachim Kopper, *Die Metaphysik Meister Eckharts* (Saarbrücken: West-Ost-Verlag 1955), e.g., 26–28.
246 Suzuki, *Essais sur le Bouddhisme Zen*, 176 [cf. *Essays in Zen Buddhism*, 148–9].

This is why I pray to God to render me quit of God, for my essential being is beyond God, insofar as we grasp God as the principle of creatures. In the being of God, indeed, where God is elevated beyond all being and all difference, I was myself, I willed myself and knew myself; therefore I took it upon myself to create this man that I am. That is why I am cause of myself according to the being [*l'être*] which is eternal, but not according to my becoming which is temporal. That is why I am also uncreated, and according to my uncreated mode, I can never die. Following my uncreated mode, I have existed eternally, I exist at present, and I shall remain eternally. That which I am according to my created being will die and be annihilated, for it is mortal; this is why it must perish with the time. In my [eternal, R.S.] birth all things were also born, and I was the cause of myself and of all things. If I had willed it, neither I nor all things would be. And if I myself were not, neither would God be any longer: that God is God, of that I am a cause. If I were not, God would not be God.—But it is not indispensable to know these things. (DW 2: 502,4–504,2 [Pr. 52, "Beati pauperes spiritu"])

Transcendental releasement, in this text, is described in the terminology of causality. The 'desert,' the 'solitude' above God, is not an active, efficient cause of God, but a passive, ideal one. The expression 'I was cause of myself' is very strong: according to the traditional teaching, only God is *causa sui*. But in my uncreated being, prior to the distinction between Creator and creature, I remain beyond the Creator God. The ground of the soul, identical to the ground of God, is the unique origin of man, of God, and of the world. Origin, in Middle High German, is said in three ways: *ursach, ursprinc, ursprunc*. The first is properly translated as 'primitive thing'; the text above even says only *sach*, thing. Eckhart has in mind the Aristotelian *causa. Ursprinc* and *ursprunc*, on the other hand, translate the Platonic *emanatio*. In the Latin work we also find *ebullitio* (in Middle High German *ûzbruch* or *ûzvluz*), the flow of creatures from out of their cause, which is opposed to the intra-divine *bullitio*.[247] It is the latter which underlies the text we have just read: in the origin beyond the Creator God, 'all things were also born,' i.e. all

---

247 See in this connection the texts cited and the remarks in Lossky, *Théologie négative et connaissance de Dieu chez Maître Eckhart*, 119f.

things 'bubble' in the origin in the state of seeds. As long as there is not yet a created world, or a mortal being to invoke God, God is not 'God.' God appears only as a counterpart to the creature. "That God is God, of that I am a cause"—of that every creature is a cause. Whatever the created being is, as soon as a certain thing is, duality appears between God and this certain thing. Some texts of Zen seem to express a similar thought and accomplish, perhaps, a further step. They speak of the "vast ocean of enlightenment," of the "silence of unity," of "the immense expansion of a calm and translucent ocean," but where at the same time "possibilities of roaring waves" are buried.[248] The symbol of the ocean is characteristic here: life comes out from the sea, but the water still contains it in a formless state. Zen seems to me to go beyond Eckhart in this thought, as for example when it says: "The entire world, heaven and earth, owes its life and its death entirely to this stick."[249] Let a stick be, and there is duality. "A difference of a thumb, and heaven and earth are separated."[250] The origin is then fragmented into a multiplicity of beings, and God appears as He whom men invoke, the partner of the soul, the Savior, the Lord and King, Father, Son, Spirit—as 'not-stick.'

The term most frequently used by Meister Eckhart to speak of the origin anterior to the distinction between Creator and creature is *gôtheit*, Godhead. "God and Godhead are as distinct as heaven and earth" (Pf.: 180,15-16) [DW 4,2: 767,3-768,1 (Pr. 109, "Nolite timere eos, qui occidunt corpus")]. Having reached into the Godhead, the mind no longer has God. *Gôt entwird*, God disappears (Pf.: 180,18) [DW 4,2: 768,3 (Pr. 109, "Nolite timere eos, qui occidunt corpus")]. God acts, while to the Godhead all operation is foreign. The operation is of the order of consequences, *agere sequitur esse* [acting follows being]. In the same way, God 'follows' the Godhead. The desert is not fecund in anything; in the same way the Godhead is arid and creates nothing. In the desert, everything only begins—but God fades away. The desert is the vast solitude; there is no place for two in the desert. The opposition between Creator and creature is abolished. In the desert, there is no use in shouting; there is no one opposite to man to respond to him. Suzuki cites a text of Meister

---

248 Suzuki, *Essais sur le Bouddhisme Zen*, 172 [cf. *Essays in Zen Buddhism*, 145].
249 Ibid., 329 [cf. *Essays in Zen Buddhism*, 278].
250 Ibid., 344 [cf. *Essays in Zen Buddhism*, 290-91].

Eckhart: "It is as if someone, standing in front of a high mountain, were to shout: 'Are you there?' The echo responds: 'Are you there?' If one shouts: 'Come out!' the echo responds: 'Come out!'"[251] In the desert, the wind and the sand sweep away the tracks of the caravans; the footsteps of God are effaced at the same time as those of man and the world.

'Godhead' thus designates the exclusion of every relation in the origin. It is the transcendental condition of the possibility, not only for thinking every difference or otherness, but also for taking the way of releasement. Indeed, this way is like the return to the fatherland. That it solicits us as our greatest possibility of being is already a kind of ontological argument in favor of the Godhead.

> When I was still waiting in the ground, in the bed, in the river and the source of the Godhead, nobody asked me where I wanted to go or what I was doing. There was no one there to interrogate me. But when I came out of it by emanation, all creatures cried out: 'God.' If someone were to ask me, 'Brother Eckhart, when did you come out of the home?,' this would prove that previously I was still in the interior. (Pf.: 181,3–7) [DW 4,2: 771,9–772,3 (Pr. 109, "Nolite timere eos, qui occidunt corpus")]

To think of the origin as Godhead is to refuse to represent it as 'transcendent,' as a hypostasized in-itself of a superior order of things. The 'reflux' into the origin is therefore nothing other than the re-entry into oneself. In traditional terms, the interiority of the 'fatherland' results from a fusion of the Thomistic *reditio completa* [complete return] and the Neoplatonic *epistrophē* [reversion]. The Godhead is the destruction of all metaphysical configurations, exterior or interior to God; the fatherland or the 'home' is within us. Eckhart is here very close to certain formulations of Book Seven of Augustine's *Confessions*.[252]

---

[251] Ibid., 338. [cf. Suzuki, *Essays in Zen Buddhism*, 286–77. Cf. DW 1: 383,1–3 (Pr. 22, "Ave, gratia plena").]

[252] "Intravi et vidi qualicumque oculo animae meae supra eundem oculum animae meae, supra mentem meam lucem inconmutabilem" [I entered and beheld with the eye of my soul—no matter which it was—high above the same eye of my soul, and above my mind, the immutable light]. *Confessions*, VII, 10,16.

"Ignorance is the departure, and Enlightenment the return home."[253] "This sense of returning to or recognizing old acquaintances [*connaissances*] that one experiences at the time of Enlightenment is a familiar fact to students of Zen Buddhism."[254] "To one who is profoundly instructed in this domain, the sense of returning to something familiar really signifies the will installing itself once more in its ancient refuge, after having adventurously wandered more than once."[255] If these sentences must be read in connection with the eighth picture of the training of the bull, then we are allowed to suppose that under entirely different cultural horizons the experience of the mind, when it is pushed to extreme releasement, presents identical fundamental traits. That "the return effaces all the traces of time,"[256] and that it is the work of the will restoring souls "to their original state of freedom"[257]—here are at least two of these fundamental traits. The insistence on the will as the operative faculty for the return is directly linked to the doctrine of releasement. Dispossession is the work of the will. "When this will turns away for an instant from itself and from the created, and returns to its first origin [*in sînen êrsten ursprunc*, R.S.], then the will rediscovers itself in its free way [*in sîner vrîen art*, R.S.] as is suitable, and is free" (DW 1: 94,10–95,3 [Pr. 5b, "In hoc apparuit"]). In contrast to Augustine, Meister Eckhart thinks this return as a 'breakthrough' beyond God into the nameless desert of the Godhead. This theory, which so disquieted the judges of the Inquisition,[258] makes Meister Eckhart today one of the Western thinkers to whom certain Japanese masters turn most willingly. "Eckhart clearly crosses the limits of the customary intellectual world of Christianity and moves into the Zen universe," writes Shizuteru Ueda.[259]

---

253 Suzuki, *Essais sur le Bouddhisme Zen*, 181 [cf. Suzuki, *Essays in Zen Buddhism*, 152.]
254 Ibid., 185 [cf. Suzuki, *Essays in Zen Buddhism*, 156].
255 Ibid., 186 [cf. Suzuki, *Essays in Zen Buddhism*, 157].
256 Ibid., 183 [cf. Suzuki, *Essays in Zen Buddhism*, 155].
257 Ibid., 24 [cf. Suzuki, *Essays in Zen Buddhism*, 24].
258 See the articles 1, 9, 10 of the Bull, *In Agro Dominico*, op. cit. [LW 5: 602,40–603,64 (*Acta*).]
259 Shizuteru Ueda, "Maître Eckhart et le Bouddhisme Zen," trans. Reiner Schürmann, in *La Vie spirituelle* 124, no. 578 (January 1971): 41.

We must now examine the core of this resemblance. We must search for it in a new facet of the doctrine of nothingness in Meister Eckhart. We have seen that 'the creature is a pure nothingness' because it receives its being entirely from God. Here we are concerned with a second sense of 'nothingness': it is the terminus of the breakthrough beyond God. The Godhead is desert, nothingness. So it is by virtue of this new signification of nothingness that Meister Eckhart can seem to move "into the Zen universe." "All things have been drawn out of nothingness; this is why their true origin is nothingness" (DW 1: 94,4-5 [Pr. 5b, "In hoc apparuit"]). Both the departure and the arrival of the way of releasement is: nothingness. Properly speaking, the original boiling, the *ursprunc* (gushing out), is not. The *archē* of all things and of God is without beginning. If the Godhead *were*, being would be the origin. And this latter would be thinkable. But Eckhart thinks the failure of thought before the mystery of an entirely freed man. Original freedom is properly anarchic. Said otherwise, ascetic or moral releasement aims to reproduce in me the freedom I possessed when I was Godhead within the Godhead, or nothingness within the nothingness. In the following two quotations, as is often the case in Eckhart, 'God' must be read as designating the Godhead: "All that is in God is God" (DW 1: 56,8 [Pr. 3, "Nunc scio vere"]).[260] "In God, no creature is more noble than the other" (DW 1: 55,4-5 [Pr. 3, "Nunc scio vere"]). Before my birth into the world, when I was in the depth of God, "the highest angel, the soul, and the fly" were perfectly equal (DW 1: 148,2 [Pr. 9, "Quasi stella matutina"]). In the Godhead, all the seeds of beings are the Godhead. The apprenticeship of releasement thus consists for man in becoming "enfranchised from all images, as free as he was when he was not" (DW 1: 25,1-2 [Pr. 2, "Intravit Iesus in quoddam castellum"]).

In this context, 'nothingness' is still called *niht*, but the most adequate term seems to be *unwesene*. This word designates the darkness, beyond *esse*, with which the ground of the soul is enveloped insofar as it is identical with the ground of God: "The soul acts

---

260 One finds other similar expressions in Meister Eckhart: "In God, there is nothing but God," sermon *Surrexit autem Saulus*, in Pf.: 83,17 [DW 3: 225,11-12 (Pr. 71)]; "what is in the First, is the First," *Quaestiones Parisienses*, LW 5: 37, no. 1; "what is in the One, is the One," *In Ioh.*, no. 66, LW 3: 55.

in *unwesene*, and it follows God who acts in *unwesene*" (DW 1: 151,11–12 [Pr. 9, "Quasi stella matutina"]). *Wesen* bespeaks the totality of what shows itself insofar as it shows itself. But the Godhead does not appear; it is rather the transcendental condition of all that appears. *Unwesene* thus bespeaks the abolition of the positivity of being; the word refers not below but beyond *esse*. It would probably be a reductive interpretation of Meister Eckhart to see that term as a Middle High German translation of the Platonic *hyper-on* [beyond being]. Eckhart expressly says that to call the Godhead a *wesene*, being [*être*], is as correct as to say of the sun that it is black (DW 1: 146,2 [Pr. 9, "Quasi stella matutina"]). God as Person, or as Creator, he says again, is "the fruit of nothingness" (Pf.: 83,4) [DW 3: 224,7 (Pr. 71, "Surrexit autem Saulus")]. Silence alone is appropriate when a man is entirely *gelâzen*, released: original freedom, the 'home,' is to dwell in nothingness (DW 2: 190,1–2 [Pr. 36a, "Stetit Iesus in medio discipulorum"]). Such a man "neither desires, nor has, nor knows, nor loves, nor wills anything."[261]

The nothingness represented by the black circle in the eighth picture of the training of the bull probably corresponds to this transcendental nothingness more than to the ontic nothingness of the thing constituted by borrowed being. Eckhartian releasement points in the direction of a trans-divine 'nudity' where even God is "stripped of his wrapping of goodness or of being, as well as of any name" (DW 1: 152,7–8 [Pr. 9, "Quasi stella matutina"]). "Seizing God in his wardrobe [*in sînem kleithûse*, R.S.]" (DW 1: 183,4 [Pr. 11, "Impletum est"]) and seizing "the castle in the soul," "bared of all forms, divested and free" (DW 1: 44,4; 40,2 [Pr. 2, "Intravit Iesus in quoddam castellum")—both of these advances uncover one and the same nudity, that of perfect detachment or releasement, *blôze abegescheidenheit* (DW 1: 170,9 [Pr. 10, "In diebus suis"]). It is the latter that seems to me to be represented by the Chinese picture in question. But the similarities and dissimilarities between Meister

---

[261] "Wer nichts begehrt, nichts hat, nichts weiss, nichts liebt, nichts will, | Der hat, der weiss, begehrt, und liebt noch immer viel." "Who does not desire, nor have, nor know, nor love, nor want anything / This one yet has, knows, desires, and loves much." Silesius, *Pélerin chérubinique*, 68. [*CW* 1.45: 34.]

Eckhart and Zen will have to be examined for themselves at the end of this article.[262]

2.4 *'Living without why.'* Just as the herdsman, after the experience of the annihilation of the bull, of himself, of nature, and finally of all things, returns to the marketplace "bare-chested, barefoot," in the same way the breakthrough beyond God is translated in Meister Eckhart into a new way of existing in the world. He calls this way of existing "living without why," *sunder warumbe* (DW 2: 289,3 [Pr. 41, Qui sequitur iustitiam"] and elsewhere).

> So when one asks a man: "Why do you eat?"—"In order to have strength."—"Why do you sleep?"—"For the same reason." So it is with all the things that are in time. But someone who would ask a good man: "Why do you love God?"—"I do not know, because of God."—"Why do you love the truth?"—"Because of the truth."—"Why do you love justice?"—"Because of justice."—"Why do you love goodness?"—"Because of goodness."—"Why do you live?"—"My word! I do not know! But I am happy to live." (DW 2: 27,4–10 [Pr. 26 "Mulier venit hora"])

'All the things that are in time' are radically indigent. That which is subject to time and space is not sufficient for itself; its sufficient reason resides in God. The created has 'a why.' People eat and sleep 'for' possessing strength; they act with a 'why.' They seek God 'for' his utility as the richest bestower of good; they act with a 'why.' As long as you live with a 'why,' says Meister Eckhart, you know neither yourself nor God.

> You look for something with God, and you conduct yourself absolutely as if you were transforming God into a candle, in order to use it to find something. And when one has found what one was seeking, one throws away the candle. You act in the same way: what you seek with God is nothingness, whatever it may be. (DW 1: 69,2–5 [Pr. 4, "Omne datum optimum"])

---

262 [R.S's article was initially published in two parts. The first part ends here.]

Why things? Why the world? Why life? Why God? Why myself? The perfectly released man who has experienced the nudity beyond all that bears a name no longer interrogates himself in this way. He has unlearned the search for causes and goals. He no longer seeks, and that is why he has found (Pf.: 177,12) [DW 3: 59,1-2 (Pr. 62, "Got hêt die armen")]: the *archē* and the *telos* which he has experienced are nothingness. He knows: that which is—is. Without why. No longer asking that which is for a reason—this was for him to find the one reason, i.e. the arid solitude of the Godhead where all remains seed. No longer seeking a why among the created—this is thus to find its one why: the uncreated. A perfectly released man would live like a thoroughbred horse, let out at full speed over the spacious expanse of a green meadow: its nature incites it to stretch out in gallops and bounds as much as its forces allow (DW 1: 199,8-11 [Pr. 12, "Qui audit me"]). So with this man. He has found the secret of life. God, man, and the world show themselves to him in the free play of their originary identity. In his action, he is no longer motivated by any external mover. "Those who seek something with their works, those who act for a why, they are serfs and mercenaries" (DW 2: 253,4-5 [Pr. 39, "Iustus in perpetuum vivet"]).

To representational thought, to the theory of substances, this doctrine of the without-why is folly. Metaphysics cannot think of the origin otherwise than as the supreme foundation [*fondement*]. For the metaphysician, no 'cause' beyond God, the cause of the created, can be sought. To speak of an *ursprinc*, a gushing out which is common to God, man, and the world—this is, literally, fabulous. To live without why seems as subversive for mores as the breakthrough beyond God seems insane for dogma. Indicative thought (i.e. the thought of substances) is opposed to imperative thought which opens a path to existence that has become "free as it was when it was not." The first school of thought will only be able to say of a man freed in this way that he "wanted to know more than was necessary, and turned himself away from the truth to turn toward fables" [LW 5: 597,9-11 (*Acta*)].[263]

The true debate concerns an experience of the mind [*esprit*] about which Meister Eckhart testifies in every line, but which his accusers

---

263 Beginning of the Bull, in *Archiv für Literatur…*, 636.

do not share. Eckhart's enterprise is essentially paradoxical: how to speak of the without-why in a language modeled through and through on the sensible substance? Nevertheless, he dares the wager of the speculative mystic: to expose under a rational disguise the fulfilling proximity of the pre-originary origin. That there are holes all over this disguise is still another indication of the fire that consumed him. The struggle for the right concept, when it resorts to the weapon of paradox, is turned into a combat against language—a combat lost in advance for whoever has not relived the radical freedom which is his fatherland.

> When this birth is truly accomplished, no creature will be able to encumber you. [..., R.S.] Moreover, what was formerly a burden for you now favors you. The visage turns itself totally toward this birth. In all that you see and hear, whatever it may be—in all things, you can bring about nothing other than this birth. Indeed, all things become purely and simply God for you. (Pf: 28,32ff.; 29,2-6 [DW 4,1: 488,2-13 (Pr. 103, "Cum factus esset")]

Releasement, the mode of life which results from the 'breakthrough,' can be explicated in terms of emptiness. Man has rid himself of all images, he is empty of representations, and this is why all things are equal to him. But it must be added that God has a *horror vacui* [dread of empty space]: "God can leave nothing empty or unoccupied" (Pf.: 28,16f.) [DW 4,1: 487,4 (Pr. 103, "Cum factus esset")]. This is the sense of detachment as dispossession: to open up a space for God until there is no space left except this one. Then we receive from God 'all that God possesses':

> When God created all creatures, they were so small and so narrow that he could not move in them. Then he created the soul so equal to him and to his image that he could give himself to the soul. What he gives to the soul in what is outside himself, this the soul holds indeed for nothing. God must give himself to me in his ownness, as he belongs to himself, or else nothing is given to me at all and nothing agrees with me. He who wants to receive him totally must have released himself totally and emptied himself. This one receives from God all that he possesses. (DW 1: 71,4-72,2 [Pr. 4, "Omne datum optimum"])

'God must,' *got muoz*. In the breakthrough, the otherness between man and God has been abolished. It results from this that the life 'without why' is a life without invocation. "The humble man need not ask [*bitten*, R.S.] anything [of God, R.S.], but he may well command him [*gebieten*, R.S.]" (DW 1: 246,10-11 [Pr. 15, "Homo quidam nobilis"]). "I will never thank God for loving me, for he cannot do otherwise whether he wills it or not; his nature forces him to do so. I will rather thank him that in his goodness he cannot cease to love me" (Pf.: 231,13-16) [DW 3: 269, 4-7 (Pr. 73, "Dilectus deo et hominibus"]).

'God loves us' would be a relation of exteriority, between subjects capable of love. 'I thank God for loving me' would express the love that one person renders to another person in testimony of reciprocity. 'God loves us'; so speaks 'indicative' theology. 'God must love us' aims to abolish the relation of exteriority. Reciprocity falls away; every relationship between subjects or persons is effaced. We are carried not by the love of God, but by his having-to-love, by his nature. The nature of God is to love; God is love.

The intrinsic necessity that a being [*un être*] obeys lies in its nature. If God carries us in his love, necessarily, then he carries us in his nature or his Godhead. 'God must' is Eckhart's way of evoking the trans-divine origin.[264] 'God must love us': in the love thus lavished, God fades away. 'God' designates someone who loves me because he wills it so. But in his nature, God loves me beyond all willing, and he introduces me where he ceases to be God: in his essential, impersonal unfolding. Then I am loved, necessarily. But 'nobody' is there to love me. To this necessary gift, man will respond with violence: "he may well command him." Detachment forces God toward me, says Meister Eckhart: *daz abegescheidenheit twinge got zuo mir* (Pf.: 484,18f. Cf. DW 5: 402,5 [*Vab*]). 'His nature forces God to love me.' But in his nature, in the Godhead, all is Godhead. The same proposition can then be formulated: '*I* force God to love.' These two propositions say the same origin where the Godhead and I are one, where I am the nature of God. This coercion does not signify an absurd test of strength, a disposition of the human 'subject' with

---

264 Shizuteru Ueda, "Über den Sprachgebrauch Meister Eckharts," in *Glaube, Geist, Geschichte*, Festschrift Ernst Benz, Gerhard Müller and Winfried Zeller (eds.) (Leiden: Brill,1967), 266ff. This study analyzes the expressions according to which 'God must.'

regard to the divine 'subject,' but the contrary: the free unfolding of that which, through the ciphers 'God,' 'I,' has us at its disposal. Necessity on God's part, violence on man's part—the two exalt the same freedom without why.

In concluding this examination of the concept of *gelâzenheit* in Meister Eckhart, it is important to underline one capital fact: Life 'without why' is everyday life. Otherwise said, the released man is distinguished in no way in his comportment from the man with multiple attachments or attributes, *eigenschaften*. On the contrary, he goes back "by the fire and into the stable" (DW 1: 91,4–5 [Pr. 5b, "In hoc apparuit"]). Eckhart makes so great a point of this aspect, which one might call cataphatic, that he does not hesitate to contradict the very letter of the Gospel. Through the meanderings of allegorical exegesis, he comes to the conclusion that not Mary, the contemplative, but Martha, the active, has 'the best part.' "Martha had become so essential that her busyness was no obstacle to her." (Pf.: 53,1f [DW 3: 491,6–7 (Pr. 86, "Intravit Iesus in quoddam castellum etc.")]. Mary, for her part, needs calm and to concentrate at the feet of Jesus. She does not yet find God in all things.

This last trait of Meister Eckhart's teaching brings him even closer to Zen Buddhism. The last picture of the bull signifies exactly that: the acceptance of everyday life, among "the wine-bibbers and the butchers," in its everydayness.

> Before a man studies Zen, the mountains are for him mountains and the waters are waters; when, thanks to the teachings of a good master, he has realized an internal vision of the truth of Zen, the mountains are for him no longer mountains and the waters are no longer waters; but after that, when he actually achieves the sanctuary of repose, once again the mountains are mountains and the waters are waters.[265]

3. *Releasement according to Heidegger.* When *Gelassenheit* is at stake in Martin Heidegger, this word is usually linked to an attitude of thought. Thus, the writing that bears it as a title opposes two modes of thinking, 'calculative' thinking and 'meditative' thinking. This

---

[265] Suzuki, *Essais sur le Bouddhisme Zen*, 25 [Seigen Ishin (C'hing-yüan Wei-hsin) in *Dentō-roku* (*Chin Ch'uan-teng-lu*) or *The Transmission of the Lamp*, cit. in Suzuki, *Essays in Zen Buddhism*, 24.]

opposition has become famous. However, it does not say everything. Even if one does not subscribe to the remark of Heidegger's interlocutor that Eckhart thinks "*Gelassenheit* still within the domain of the will" [GA 77: 109],[266] it remains the case that both the mystical 'Godhead' and the Zen 'satori' designate an event that relates to man. Now, Heidegger uproots the event of releasement from this context. Meister Eckhart points in this direction when he describes the free play, the seminal boiling, in the desert which is beyond being and from which the latter breaks loose like a flame in the night. Being is thus 'let,' given, by the night. But it must be seen that night, the Godhead, signifies for Eckhart the more divine God than God the creator or savior. Seek God 'without why,' he says, then he will be *your* God. "If you are sick and you pray to God in view of health, health is more dear to you than God. Then God is not your God. He is the God of heaven and of earth, but he is not your God" (DW 2: 7,12-8,1-2 [Pr. 25, "Moyses orabat dominum"]). The transcendental concept of releasement in Meister Eckhart thus remains a relational concept: the true relationship to God is the *gelâzenheit* as much of God as of man. God and man are one, nameless, in this identical releasement. In Heidegger, the thought of *Gelassenheit* must be comprehended as a 'step back' from the category of relation and from its extreme case, identity.

The 'satori' also "makes one change one's *attitude* entirely" and constitutes a "re-evaluation of the *relationships* of the individual with the world." At least as it is described by Suzuki, it remains a way for man to situate himself in the relations that shape his world. "It concerns becoming conscious of a new power of the mind, which puts it in a position to judge things from a new point of view."[267] To call this new consciousness 'releasement,' as we have done, is thus to speak again of man, and in view of man. The profundity of *Gelassenheit* in Heidegger seems to us to reside in the fact that he ultimately thinks of it neither as on the basis of man nor above all in view of man. In this respect, his thinking differs radically both from the "old master of reading and living" [GA 13: 42][268] that Meister

---

266 Heidegger, *Gelassenheit* (Pfullingen: Neske, 1959), 35f.
267 Suzuki, *Essais sur le Bouddhisme Zen*, 305-307 [cf. *Essays in Zen Buddhism*, 261].
268 Heidegger, *Der Feldweg* (Frankfurt: Klostermann, 1962), p. 4. This aphorism is found already in a proverb attributed to Meister Eckhart himself: "Wêger wêre ein

Eckhart is for him, and from Suzuki, who expresses, Heidegger says, "what I have been trying to say in all my writings."[269] We see well how this last remark can be referred to the distinction made above between calculative thinking and meditative thinking, and perhaps even, as we shall see, to the distinction between 'letting presence' and 'letting what is present be present.' Nevertheless, the historical dimension, *epochal* releasement—in other words time as the horizon of being—hardly belongs to the essence of satori. We agree with William Barrett, who sees in the unconditional homage rendered by Heidegger to the writings of Suzuki a "slightly exaggerated enthusiasm."[270] Heidegger's point of departure is a reflection on the destiny of Western culture. This point of departure is irreducible to mystical 'breakthrough' and Buddhist 'enlightenment.' Our analysis of *Gelassenheit* in Heidegger must therefore start from a critique of this history, and more precisely of modernity.

3.1 *A released epoch.* The modern epoch is 'released,' *verlassen*,[271] in what shapes its very essence. This is not a thesis, but the fundamental trait of the progressive emancipation of the sciences and technology by which the modern epoch defines itself. We are in the third and last phase announced by Auguste Comte. The sciences and technology have won their autonomy vis-à-vis religion and philosophy. Although diverse and competitive on many points, the sciences have something in common: they establish positive laws from recordable experiences, and this thanks to a thinking of an operational and calculative type. Theory has become entirely positive: according to the Kantian principle, the very verification of theory must be experimental. This is a "challenge" to thought,[272] or even to man, who in the midst of so many 'givens' no longer encounters himself, at least in his essence.[273] Man is for himself 'a given,' but he

---

lebemeister denne tûsent lesemeister" ("a master of living would be of greater help than a thousand masters of reading"), Pf.: 599,19f. [This *Spruch* is not found in DW.]
269 Barrett, "Zen for the West," xi.
270 Ibid. "This remark may be the slightly exaggerated enthusiasm of a man under the impact of a book in which he recognizes some of his own thoughts."
271 [With the German, R.S. indicates that 'relasement' should be taken in the sense of 'abandonment' here.]
272 Heidegger, *Vorträge...*, 22 and 37.
273 Ibid., 35.

does not experience himself as 'given.' He has entered into his own statistics: one factor of calculation among others. The spirit that has become intelligence [GA 40: 49–53][274] summons all things to declare themselves to its inquiries. It demands of all that is a rendering of complete account. Modernity is this conquering rationality. It constitutes the first of the two aspects of "that which, today, *is* all around the globe" [GA 14: 6].[275]

The second aspect of modernity is to be found in its project of a dominating will. The network of calculation, in which the technician captures all the phenomena and the earth itself, is already a submission to action and to transformation. Intelligence is a power, a rough draft of manipulation and killing. The truth that has become exactitude is perverted, *das Un-Wahre schlechthin* [the absolute un-true], because from now on only the will reigns. Its reign promises security. But this security is fashioned outside of the truth, *das Wahre*, which alone 'guards' authentically; everywhere insecurity manifests itself.[276] The human being directs itself in a unilateral manner to the objects at its disposal. Otherwise said, it experiences being as that which stands facing it, as a test of strength: *Gegenstand*. Faced with this world in opposition, the human being asserts itself as subject; it seizes itself as the center of reference of the real. The subject, certain of itself and blindly obsessed with its power, measures everything by the yardstick of its intelligence and its will. The sole type of truth recognized is effectual truth, which 'serves for something.'

This description of modernity may seem excessive. A more elaborate attention to the political aspect of existence would perhaps lead to a less severe view of the contemporary epoch. Heidegger did not attempt this. Eric Weil[277] and Emmanuel Lévinas[278] are among those who advance most resolutely in this direction. The conclusion, however, remains the same as regards the releasement that

---

274 Heidegger, *Einführung in die Metaphysik* (Tübingen: Niemeyer, 1953), 35–38.
275 Heidegger, *Zur Sache des Denkens* (Tübingen: Niemeyer, 1969), 2.
276 Heidegger, *Vorträge…*, 88
277 Eric Weil, *Philosophie Politique* (Paris: Vrin, 1956).
278 Emmanuel Lévinas, *Totalité et infini* (The Hague: Martinus Nijhoff, 1961). Lévinas critiques Heidegger, sometimes violently, for being attached to an experience too limited, namely that of thought. Levinas opposes to it the absolute novelty of the irruption of the Other in front of me, an 'ethical' and, by its character of interpellation, an authentically religious experience.

is our concern. From whatever aspect one considers contemporary man—rebel [*homme révolté*] or hippie, technocrat or maverick—Heidegger's conclusion is difficult to contradict:

> Man is on the point of casting himself over the whole earth and its atmosphere, of usurping and attaching to himself in the form of 'forces' the secret reign of nature, and of subjecting the course of history to the planning and ordering of a planetary government. This same 'rebel' is unable to say, in all simplicity, that which is, to say *what this is*: that a thing *is*. [GA 5: 372][279]

In a critical movement of thought, Heidegger now interrogates the conditions of the possibility of this 'night of the world.' He discovers those conditions in the retreat of something originary, a retreat as old as the history of metaphysics, but one that has become manifest only late in this history. In other words, the West has been released since its beginnings. But this releasement has been manifest, to the ones who know how to see it, for scarcely a century, with the transmutation of all values. Nietzschean nihilism is revealing in that it denounces the metaphysical Other of man as a foundation of human life and thought that is certain, and thus as something at one's disposal. The releasement of the West commences with this question: what is the foundation of all things that 'makes' them be what they are? When it is thought from the side of things (or from the side of man, always therefore from the side of a being), this foundation can be determined functionally. Such a determination proceeds in two steps at least: that which is, because it is manifold, is not a result of itself; that which is, because it receives its unification from man, is by reason of an Other. This Other 'certifies' that which is. The Other which founds is certain. Insecurity, a sign of nihilism, is thus old in the West. Western thought poses the question of the reason of that which is. To demand accounts of the real, to give reasons, to reclaim an ultimate 'why'—here is the characteristic attitude of what Heidegger calls 'metaphysics.' Philosophy in general has arisen from this instinct: to find a certain foundation that anchors all things and reassures the 'restless heart.' It has also found what it looks for: the

---

[279] Heidegger, *Holzwege* (Frankfurt: Klostermann, 1950), 343.

esse, foundation and reason of the *ens*. Only, Heidegger asks: is the ground of things so represented, being in its truth?

Nietzsche had already responded to this question indirectly: there is nothing of being.[280] This is a statement and not an opinion of a gloomy mental lunatic. Nietzsche notices the death of that which made being. Who is *Esse* itself? The one who is dead. What about beings? Will to will. In his writings on modernity, Heidegger's purpose is to read these two responses in their unity. The ungrounding [*l'effondrement*] of *Esse* as the ultimate reason, and the hybris of the projects of the will which has only itself as subject, are the two faces of an identical revendication under which the West has always thought. For a century, that which is seems to have lost its foundations. This loss is the disappearance of something which, in another epoch, appeared self-evident. It is at the moment of the disappearance of reasons that thinking interrogates itself about their destiny: the power of a foundation that they no longer seem to possess—whence did it come? How could that which has for centuries grounded all that is fade away? Are we to say that a piece of the universe has been lost? On this piece, now lost, the universe would have rested until our era; what is this loss that is capable of shaking the rest of the universe? What is lost is more than one 'reason' among others. To ask 'in reason of what' the reasons served as reasons: here is the question of self-inflated reason seeking to explicate the disappearance with the help of what has disappeared. It is the ultimate form of secular oblivion, the oblivion of being. *Esse* as foundation or reason is not being in its truth. The destiny of Western thought is our releasement from being, *unsere Verlassenheit vom Sein* [GA 9: 378].[281]

---

280 Friedrich Nietzsche, *The Will to Power*, ed. Walter Kaufmann, trans. Walter Kaufmann and R. J. Hollingdale (New York: Vintage Books, 1968), 14 (§15): "The most extreme form of nihilism would be the view that *every* belief, every considering-something-true, is necessarily false *because there simply is no true world*"; *The Will to Power*, 4 (§4): "For why has the advent of nihilism become *necessary*? Because the values we have had hitherto thus draw their final consequence; because nihilism represents the ultimate logical conclusion of our great values and ideals." [In this footnote R.S. cites only the German from Friedrich Nietzsche, *Aus dem Nachlass der Achtzigerjahre*, in *Werke in drei Bänden*, ed. Karl Schlechta (Munich: Hanser, 1956), vol. 3., 555, 635, and adds: cf. also 661, 678, 853, 881.]

281 Heidegger, *Was ist Metaphysik?* (Frankfurt: Klostermann, 1960), 19.

Here is the primary meaning of 'releasement' in Heidegger. Philosophy, restless to explain that which is, why it is, its *archē* and its *telos*, has confounded being either with the totality of beings or with the supreme being, God. But it has passed by in silence the question of being itself; being is the unthought of the philosophical tradition. The fading away which terrifies our century and which precipitates it into multiple acts of securing is more than the loss of a piece of the universe: being itself is lacking, *das Sein selbst bleibt aus* [NII: 353]. Traditional philosophy indeed speaks of being 'as being,' but it does so only in order to be able better to think beings (that is, God, the totality of the world, the subject, spirit). It thus remains a thinking of beings; it thinks of being only insofar as it serves its discourse about that which is; being, for it, is an *a priori* [NII: 346]. Being is thought from out of beings and in view of beings. The philosophy of the *a priori* uses being as a pretext in order to 'certify' beings.

The epoch 'released from being' is an era of more than two millennia. But the technological century is the most released of all: the impetus of an authentic questioning, contained in the interrogation of the 'as' ['*en tant que*'], has itself fallen back behind. Perhaps the interrogation 'without why' is possible only at the end of nihilism carried to its ultimate consequences. The breaks of the epoch that goes from Heraclitus to Nietzsche each show in its own way the unique destiny that has come upon the West, that of the releasement from being, *Seinsverlassenheit*. Heraclitus inaugurates, Plato objectifies, Nietzsche completes, and Heidegger thinks this "unique epoch" [NII: 383]. The mystery of being has fragmented into the mystery of man, the mystery of the world, the mystery of God. Only a thinking which poses the question of being for itself—although starting from the one who poses it, still not in view of him or at his service—only this thinking will engage on the way of the mystery which is no longer the way of releasement as forgetfulness but rather of releasement as listening to and as memory. This second aspect, where 'released' is translated not as *verlassen* but as *gelassen*, will once again bring us close to Meister Eckhart.

3.2 *Released beings*. During a seminar held at Le Thor in September 1969, Heidegger distinguished between three meanings of *Gelassenheit*. The first, he said, signals toward that which is, toward beings. The second makes one look less toward the singular being than toward its entry into presence as such. Finally, the third indicates the 'letting' itself which lets that which is present enter into presence. In *Time and Being*, Heidegger had said about this last meaning: "It is important now to think this *letting enter into presence* properly, insofar as presence is released" [GA 14: 9].[282] We will follow these three milestones through the arduous passage of *Gelassenheit*; the third will rejoin under a new mode the historical dimension comprehended in the Heideggerian critique of modernity.

Released beings—this meaning refers to the easier understanding, because it is ontic, of releasement. However, it is not so easy 'to release beings':

> What could be easier, apparently, than to let a being be precisely the being that it is? Or would this task lead us in front of what is the most difficult? So such a purpose, of letting the being be as it is, represents the contrary of that indifference which simply turns its back on the being. We must turn ourselves toward the being, in order concerning it to remember its being; but in this way we must let it repose in itself, in its essential unfolding. [GA 5: 16][283]

In these lines, there is assuredly an attitude of man. 'We,' i.e. humans, must let beings be. Calculation, enslavement of things under the dominating will, any attitude of seizing control over them, must be effaced if beings are to manifest themselves as what they are. It is here that the title of meditative thinking is appropriate. To release beings is to remember them independently of any project about them. There is no doubt that in the contemporary epoch, by reason of the double insanity of intelligence and will, such an attitude is particularly difficult. Meditative thinking, in the technical universe in which we are immersed, consists in saying yes and no at the same time to the products of consumption. We can say yes to their utilization, and nevertheless remain free. We can leave these objects to themselves as something that does not concern us intimately. To refuse to let them take us under their exclusive domination is the contemporary form of detachment. He who releases in this way the

---

282 Heidegger, *Zur Sache*..., 5. "Nun aber gilt es, dieses Anwesenlassen eigens zu denken, insofern Anwesen zugelassen wird." Cf. ibid., 40 [GA 14: 45].
283 Heidegger, *Holzwege*, 20.

technical objects in their totalitarian pretension does not turn his back on them. His 'no' is the condition of the 'yes' to their essential unfolding. Releasement as an attitude of meditative thinking institutes a simple and peaceful relationship with things. The released man lets [*laisse*] them enter into his everyday world and nevertheless leaves [*laisse*] them outside [GA 16: 527].[284]

Releasement of beings and remembrance of their being thus say the same thing. In Heidegger's hardly translatable words: *Besinnung* [mindfulness] is *Gelassenheit* with regard to what alone merits to be questioned, namely being.[285] Epochally released by being, Western thinking must in its turn release beings if it wishes to know what there is in them of being. If it is true that this task leads us "in front of what is the most difficult," it is not simply an affair of speculation. It is difficult to release beings because it is difficult to think of them otherwise than as founded on a supreme *Esse*. Metaphysical speculation seeks the first foundation in the order of being and the last reason in the order of knowing. From this speculation results the attachment to calculation. To release beings signifies nothing less than to renounce a presence at our disposal, a stable reality at hand which allows us to give an account of the real in its totality. But this very renunciation is the condition for the thinking of being. The latter does not represent beings anchored to an immutable order, but thinks of them in their essential unfolding, *Wesen*.

We are doubly justified in invoking a kinship with Meister Eckhart. On the one hand releasement is that attitude of thinking in both thinkers which translates into a comportment detached from the singular being, and which by this remembers what this being is in truth. On the other hand, the being of beings, their truth, is thought of not as a foundation at our disposal, but as *Wesen* in the verbal sense, as coming to light and as dwelling. Heidegger explicitly refers to Meister Eckhart concerning the comprehension of *Wesen*, and he adds that only *das Wesen des Seins*, the manner in which being unfolds itself, deserves to be questioned by the thinking that has disengaged itself from technology [GA 11: 116-7].[286] To release beings is that attitude thanks to which both beings and

---

284 Heidegger, *Gelassenheit*, 25.
285 Heidegger, *Vorträge...*, 68.
286 Heidegger, *Die Technik und die Kehre* (Pfullingen: Neske, 1962), 39.

man who thinks them find their place. The first equivalence of the Middle High German *wesene* indicated by the lexicon is *bleiben*, to remain, to stay, to inhabit; that of the present participle, *wesende*, is *anwesend*, present.[287] Heidegger says that he read many of Meister Eckhart's sermons when he himself was reflecting about being as *Anwesen*. As for man's 'place' that has been rediscovered, a consequence and indication of releasement, it is the subject of the writing entitled *Gelassenheit*. Releasement "gives the perspective of a new native land" [GA 16: 528].[288]

To conclude the discussion of releasement as an attitude before beings, an expression, dear to both Eckhart and Heidegger, admirably sums up this prerequisite to overcoming the oblivion of being: to seek 'without why.' It has been remarked that on this precise point Heidegger is particularly indebted to the mystics.[289] To the supreme being of metaphysics, man addresses himself with all sorts of 'whys.' To it, he can consecrate a place in the city and devote a cult. He can also proclaim it his highest reason for living, that for which the city works and devotes itself—if only as the ideal of gain and accumulation of goods. Being [*L'être*], represented as a supreme being [*étant*], thus enters into the horizon of man. On the other hand, being, as meditative thinking comprehends it, neither founds nor motivates anything. It stands outside the process of deterioration by which the Platonic Good becomes the sum of the modern consumer goods. Being as thought for itself signifies the crumbling of all supports; it poses nothing. It does not pose itself under beings as their base; it supposes nothing. And it does not precede beings as their cause; it presupposes nothing. Being does not pose, nor does it suppose, nor does it presuppose. But beings *are*. To comprehend this is to be able to say: "the rose is without why."[290]

---

287 M. Lexer, *Mittelhochdeutsches Taschenwörterbuch* (Stuttgart: Hirzel, 1966), 315.
288 Heidegger, *Gelassenheit*, 26.
289 Otto Pöggeler, *Der Denkweg Martin Heideggers* (Pfullingen: Neske, 1963), 157.
290 "Die Ros' ist ohn' warum; sie blühet, weil sie blühet | Sie acht' nicht ihrer selbst, fragt nicht, ob man sie siehet" "The rose is without why; it flowers because it flowers | It does not display itself, does not ask if it is seen." [*CW*, 1,289: 69.] See Heidegger's commentary on this verse in *Der Satz vom Grund* (Pfullingen: Neske, 1957), 68-72 [GA 10: 52-60]. The best presentation of the 'without why' is found in Shizuteru Ueda, *Die Gottesgeburt in der Seele und der Durchbruch zur Gottheit. Meister Eckhart und der Zen-Buddhismus* (Gütersloh: Mohn, 1965).

We are dealing here with the domain where the community of thinking between Eckhart and Heidegger is most manifest. Releasement is the condition of the possibility for a comprehension of being in its truth, namely as an unfolding on this side of the relations between subjects and objects. It would be erroneous, however, to pretend that in the rest of his teaching Eckhart is also a 'modern.'[291] He remains a scholastic theologian; but, within the framework that the history of being has assigned to him, this or that thought—*gelâzenheit, wesene, sunder warumbe*—comes to strike down this intellectual heritage,[292] so much so that "the trial of the papal court of Avignon against the theses of the Meister gives the impression of a trial initiated by Being itself against the one who boldly outstripped its destiny."[293]

3.3 *The released present.* The second meaning of releasement signals not toward beings, but toward their entry into presence. Heidegger writes *Anwesen*lassen, whereas later he will write Anwesen*lassen* [GA 14: 45].[294] This second signification, as he explained it in the Thor seminar, insists on presence as presence (and no longer on the present), whereas the latter emphasis insists on that which lets presence, or the letting which lets enter into presence.

*Anwesen*lassen—being is interpreted in the manner of metaphysics. Beings which are present are thought less from out of an attitude of the thinker than from out of what it renders possible: the difference between being and beings. Releasement is linked with the ontological difference; beings are let be, i.e. they are enfranchised,

---

291 Heidegger expressly refuses to make modern philosophy begin with Meister Eckhart. It is Descartes, he says, who inaugurates it; cf. *Die Frage nach dem Ding* (Tübingen: Niemeyer, 1962), 76 [GA 41: 98].
292 For this reason, it seems to us insufficient to try to comprehend Meister Eckhart exclusively from the Platonic, Neoplatonic, Patristic, Aristotelian, and Scholastic intellectual traditions. This criticism is addressed to the most important monographs and studies on Eckhart. Perhaps the reason for this must be sought among the texts usually considered: at least the two publications below are guilty of a clear predilection for the Latin works, to the detriment of the German works: Lossky, *Théologie négative*... ; Koch, "Zur Analogielehre...," 327–350.
293 Bernhard Welte, "La métaphysique de saint Thomas d'Aquin et la pensée de l'histoire de l'être chez Heidegger," *Revue des Sciences Philosophiques et Théologiques* 50 (1966): 614.
294 Heidegger, *Zur Sache*..., 40.

freed in the view of the openness thanks to which they are beings. However, this meaning does not yet say anything about the manner in which the openness, within which the present is present, unfolds.

We know that, first in *Being and Time*—although the expression does not yet appear there—then more explicitly in the publications after the war, Heidegger speaks of the ontological difference in order to break the philosophical polarization between what is thought and the one who is thinking, i.e. truth as adequacy between subject and object. If the Greek word *on* signifies 'being' ['*étant*'] in the double meaning that a being *is* and that it is a *being* that is [GA 5: 344],[295] then the ontological difference refers to an amphibology of the word being [*être*]: it signifies simultaneously that which makes beings be, *Seiendheit*, and also being itself [GA 7: 74].[296] This difference is that which, between being as foundation and being as opening or truth, separates the available at hand from that which no hand has at its disposal, but which on the contrary has us at its disposal. The ontological difference thus bespeaks the duplicity or ambiguity (*Zweideutigkeit*, *Zwiefalt*) [GA 12: 112][297] of being which, in beings, gives itself to be thought as beingness, *Seiendheit*. But far from being added to being, this ambiguity and duplicity is "being itself" [GA 12: 116].[298] The difference does not then propose two things to our representation, so that we compare them according to their respective greatness, and conclude: being is greater. Such an understanding of being *secundum magis et minus* [according to the more and the less] (an understanding which is at the base of the ontological argument) does not think the present from out of presence; it thinks it statically and not as a passage. In Heidegger, the ontological difference signifies that being unfolds as a passage toward beings. Being is itself, and beings are themselves, only in the passage. Being shelters itself in this arrival; it renders itself present by assigning to beings their place. Being lets beings be.

Here, releasement is no longer a determination of existence. It is the fundamental trait of being which unfolds as difference. This unfolding manifests itself above all negatively: being is not a being.

---

295 Heidegger, *Holzwege*, 317.
296 Heidegger, *Vorträge...*, 74f.
297 Heidegger, *Unterwegs zur Sprache* (Pfullingen: Neske, 1959), 118.
298 Ibid., 122.

It is non-being [*non-étant*], nothingness in relation to beings. Being cannot be encountered; only beings can. Being is not present; it is the presence of that which is present. It is in this way that we must understand those formulations with an apparently Eckhartian resonance, such as: "Truth comes from out of nothingness"; "How is it with being? There is nothing with being"; man is "the placeholder of nothingness" [GA 5: 59; 259; 348].[299] No inventory of beings as a whole will ever encounter being. But what is thus radically different from beings lets beings be. Thus beings are present only because nothingness "gives to each being the guarantee [*Gewähr*, R.S.] of being" [GA 9: 306].[300]

How can we not think of Meister Eckhart? For him, the many beings are "the fruit of nothingness" (Pf.: 83,4) [DW 3: 224,7 (Pr. 71, "Surrexit autem Saulus")]; the human soul, when it passes beyond opposable beings, "irrupts into nothingness, away from its created being" (DW 1: 14,3–4 [Pr. 1, "Intravit Iesus in templum"]). The paradigmatic story of the training of the bull, as well as Meister Eckhart's preaching, have amply shown that releasement leads to the experience of nothingness. In the dialogue with the Japanese, the 'guarantee,' *das Gewährende*, finally appears as "the departure from every 'it is'" [GA 12: 145–6].[301] The whole dialogue has releasement for its unspoken theme; the word for departure, *Abschied*, evokes nothingness to such an extent that one should perhaps translate it as 'decease.' *Abgeschiedenheit*, as we have said, signifies firstly death, and only secondarily detachment [GA 12: 64–65].[302] It does seem, then, that Heidegger shares that experience which Zen Buddhism represents by an entirely black picture, and which Meister Eckhart describes in terms of 'desert,' 'solitude,' and 'nothingness.'

The resemblance seems fallacious to us for at least two reasons. On the one hand, in Eckhart, the concept of nothingness is entirely metaphysical. 'The creature is nothingness' and 'the Godhead is nothingness'—even if it is a matter of two totally different meanings of the word (and two different words, *niht* and *unwesene*)—are nevertheless propositions thought from out of the divine *esse*.

---

299 Heidegger, *Holzwege*, 59, 239, 321.
300 Heidegger, [*Nachwort zu:*] *Was ist Metaphysik?*, 46.
301 Heidegger, *Unterwegs...*, 154.
302 Ibid., 68f.

Nothingness in Eckhart always suggests a negation of determination; ultimately, every *eigenschaft*—mode, attachment, property, attribute—is nothingness. *Eigenschaft* darkens serenity because it makes a being such a being, man such a man, God such a divine person. If you take a burning coal in your hands, says Eckhart, what burns you is nothingness, namely the properties of your hand as opposed to the properties of the coal (DW 1: 80, 7–17 [Pr. 5a, "In hoc apparuit"]). Attributive determination is nothingness. From this point of view, *niht* and *unwesene* bespeak the same absence of individuality.[303] The Eckhartian doctrine of nothingness results from its unique purpose: to constitute a divine discourse on God where an ineffable and fulfilling experience is reflected.

On the other hand, Heidegger does not think nothingness as nothingness. He thinks being as the nothingness of beings. Eckhart thinks God as the nothingness of property. Contra both Heidegger and Eckhart, Zen Buddhism points out that satori discovers nothingness *tout court*. In Heidegger, the thought of nothingness serves the comprehension of being; in Eckhart, it serves the comprehension of God; in Buddhism alone, nothingness is felt as such.[304] In a Heidegger-inspired commentary on the pictures of the bull, a participant in the colloquium on "Heidegger and Oriental Thought" believed she could sum up both the teaching of the eighth Zen picture and Heidegger's meditation on 'the thing' (in: *Essais et Conférences* [GA 7: 165-87]) with the lapidary formula "Nothingness (Being)."[305] One can ask whether such syncretism takes seriously the difficulties mentioned in the dialogue with the Japanese: "We Europeans probably inhabit an entirely different house than does a man from East Asia" [GA 12: 85].[306]

Being releases beings; it lets them be. This releasement opens up the ontological difference between the present and its presence, but the latter does not fall under the category of beings which are pres-

---

303 Silesius expresses this same ideal of the abolition of the singular: "Dass du nicht Menschen liebst, das tust du recht und wohl, | Die Menschheit ists, die man im Menschen lieben soll" "That you do not love men, in this you are right: | For it is humanity that one must love in man." Silesius, *Pélerin chérubinique*, 86. [CW 1.163: 51.]
304 Ueda, *Die Gottesgeburt...*, 165.
305 Elisabeth Feist-Hirsch, "Martin Heidegger and the East," Symposium on Heidegger and Eastern Thought, *Philosophy East and West* XX, no. 3 (July 1970): 253.
306 Heidegger, *Unterwegs...*, 90.

ent. It is nothingness. Releasement, when it is no longer comprehended as an attitude of man, signifies the wide abode in which each being receives its place. It signifies an unconditioned openness where beings appear as beings. The word *Anwesen*lassen must be understood in this way.

3.4 *The released presence.* Anwesen*lassen*: the difficulty is not to think of releasement under this last meaning as more remote in some causal *regressus* [regression]. That which releases presence, or which 'gives' presence, is not a source of superior emanation, but rather nothing else than the event of presence itself. Thinking does not then go through "degrees in the sense of a more and more originary origin" [GA 14: 54].[307] It is attentive solely to the letting itself, which lets the entry into presence. The letting is the pure giving. This is not a redoubling of the letting as ontological difference. Thinking no longer questions the present, nor its presence: it rather receives a sign within the ontological difference, thanks to which it turns towards the letting as letting, at work in presence. It is a question for thinking of "following the indication of this sign"; then perhaps it will be given to it "to think being without regard for a foundation of being starting from beings" [GA 14: 5].[308]

We seek to comprehend a sentence from the report of a seminar on *Time and Being*. This sentence is printed in italics: *Nur insofern es das Lassen von Anwesen gibt, ist das Anwesenlassen von Anwesendem möglich.* "The present can be let be present only insofar as there is the letting of presence" [GA 14: 46.][309] It has a strong Kantian resonance: presence and its letting appear as the condition for the possibility of letting something present be present. In other words, the Anwesen*lassen* is the condition of possibility of the *Anwesen*-lassen. On the other hand, the two uses of the verb 'to let' do not have the same meaning. The 'present that is let be present' designates the ontological difference; the second *von* must therefore be used in the sense of the enfranchisement of beings in view of their repose in the place which is let to them within the opening. Also, our translation, with its double recourse to the verb 'to be,' tries to

---

307 Heidegger, *Zur Sache*..., 48.
308 Ibid., 2.
309 Ibid., 40.

reflect the ambiguity of the verb 'to be' itself, an ambiguity which we have seen is the essence of difference. The difficulty in understanding the sentence is thus reduced to the correct comprehension of the words *Lassen von Anwesen*, the 'letting of presence.' Does the verb 'letting' designate the space of the appearance of presence, as it designates above the space of the appearance of present beings? Certainly not, for we have said that it cannot be a question of climbing up through a hierarchy of more and more originary causes. Perhaps the solution resides in the little word *von*. The 'letting *of* presence': should we read an 'objective' or a 'subjective' genitive? Is the presence let, or does it let? If we respond: the presence is let, we strongly risk representing, perhaps in an unacknowledged manner, the 'letting' as an efficient cause, *Bewirken* [GA 14: 56];[310] if we respond: the presence lets, we fall back into the difference between presence and the present, and we are only repeating the first member of the sentence. What matters is to think precisely of being or presence, no longer only on the basis of its difference from beings or the present.

Our examination of Heideggerian releasement started from an analysis of modernity. This appeared to us as the ultimate phase of an older metaphysical history. What matters is to question this history or destiny (*Geschick*). Heidegger says "history of being" [GA 14: 59][311] and thus sees in the ontological difference the secret, unthought source of the way in which beings have been thought. The thought of the *epochē* is thus linked to the thought of the difference, or even to what we have called the released present: "The destiny of being makes its way upon beings, in sudden epochs of truth" [GA 5: 210].[312] It should be noted that this thought of the history of being is distinct from and antecedent to the thought of the released presence. This latter questions precisely: whence come the sudden epochs of truth? Whence comes this characteristic of being to make its historical way upon beings? To interrogate in this way is to comprehend the letting as pure *giving*, as the event of this gift, and as appropriation, *Ereignis*. In other words, this interrogation makes us regress behind the history of being as the history of the

---

310 Ibid., 50.
311 Ibid., 53.
312 Heidegger, *Holzwege*, 193.

unveiling of the difference: behind being as presence and behind time as the horizon of the opening.

There are no epochs of *Ereignis*. But it 'lets' being and time belong to each other. Here is releasement as it appears in the step back behind all ontic considerations. "The destiny of being and the advent of time repose with each other in *Ereignis*" [GA 14: 27].[313] Time and being are "gifts" of *Ereignis* [GA 14: 28].[314] 'To give' is said in German as *geben*. *Es gibt Sein*, there is being [or 'it gives being'], *Es gibt Zeit*, there is time [or 'it gives time']. What is 'it' which gives? Does *Ereignis* give? "It which gives, in '*Es gibt Sein*,' '*Es gibt Zeit*,' attests to itself as the event" [GA 14: 24].[315]

'The released presence': this title now refers to a "fundamental ontology" [GA 14: 39][316] where being is no longer thought on the basis of beings, of the difference, or of its epochal history. Presence manifests an event or an appropriation; being as well as time arrive in that which is proper to them. This event or appropriation releases presence, lets it take place. Our difficulty in the interpretation of the genitive 'the letting *of* presence' proves to be linked to the more general difficulty of representational thought which has imposed its relational procedures on all the European languages. Presence is let, the event lets presence, there is (*Es gibt*) presence: these three sentences say one and the same accomplishment, which abolishes all metaphysics of relations and of causality. It is therefore not surprising that Heidegger is faced with the same difficulty as Meister Eckhart before him: namely that a thinking of accomplishment must still "speak in affirmative sentences" [GA 14: 30]. [317]

It goes without saying that we are far from the *gelâzenheit* of Meister Eckhart. Medieval that he was, the interrogation of being such as we have just retraced it in Heidegger was properly unthinkable for him. But is it not instructive that Heidegger cites Eckhart in contexts where he attempts to think being as an event and not as a static given? Would it be an exaggeration to see in Eckhart one who launched the first attack against the bastion of metaphysical lan-

---

313 Heidegger, *Zur Sache*..., 23.
314 Ibid., 24.
315 Ibid., 20.
316 Ibid., 34.
317 Ibid., 25.

guage? Would he have unlocked some of the primary foundations of the thought which proceeds by the nomination of substances? Through his twofold doctrine of being as accomplishment and of releasement as a condition of its comprehension, Eckhart prepares Heidegger's radically evental ontology, where *Gelassenheit* no longer signifies anything other than the mystery of being itself.

4. *Suzuki and Meister Eckhart.* It remains for us in conclusion to clarify the relationship between Eckhart and Zen Buddhism. We will see from which point of view the pictures of the training of the bull are really paradigmatic. We follow exclusively the parallels between Eckhart and Zen established by Suzuki in *Mysticism, Christian and Buddhist*.[318] There are eight parallels. A few of them seem to us to require some critique.

4.1 *Time.* The first parallel, according to Suzuki, resides in a certain comprehension of time in Eckhart and Zen. The historicity of the facts recorded by the Bible, those of creation and redemption, does not matter to Eckhart. The birth of the Word must be produced in the instant, in the "eternal now" (see for example the sermon *Intravit Iesus* DW 1: 34,2 [Pr. 2]). It is the same in Zen. Through awakening, duration is entirely reduced to the instant. Suzuki concludes from this resemblance that "the God of Meister Eckhart resembles in no way the God of the majority of Christians."[319] It should be replied to Suzuki that, in Eckhart, the atemporal birth of the Word in the soul issues directly from patristic preaching.[320]

4.2 *Isticheit.* Suzuki translates this word as *is-ness*. He writes: "Buddhist enlightenment is nothing more than this experience of *isticheit*."[321] We have seen above that *isticheit*, between *iht* and

---

318 Suzuki, *Mysticism, Christian and Buddhist. The Eastern and Western Way. A Study of the Qualities Meister Eckhart shares with Zen and Shin Buddhism* (New York: Macmillan, 1957). All the citations which follow are found in the seven chapters of the first contribution, 11–33; the citations of our item 4.8 are taken from the third contribution, 61–72.
319 [Suzuki, *Mysticism, Christian and Buddhist*, 5–6.]
320 See Hugo Rahner, "Die Gottesgeburt: Die Lehre der Kirchenväter von der Geburt Christi im Herzen der Gläubigen," in *Symbole der Kirche* (Salzburg: Müller, 1964), 1ff.
321 [Cf. Suzuki, *Mysticism, Christian and Buddhist*, 7.]

wesene, properly designates the nothingness of being of the Godhead.[322] One may doubt here the resemblance. Is not the Buddhist *isness* the fact of being of a thing, nature such as it appears in the ninth picture of the bull? If it is true that Zen Buddhism thinks nothingness as nothingness, does not the *isticheit* of the Godhead, the nothingness of quiddity, speak precisely of God and not of the nothingness at the heart of every finite being? Is it this "theocentric"[323] character of Eckhart's thinking that Suzuki calls, in this same chapter, "mythological accessories"?[324] *Isticheit* of God and *isness* of the thing, both thought of as nothingness, refer in Eckhart and Suzuki to two ultimately opposed experiences: in the one, to God, in the other, to "our ordinary state of mind."[325] It seems difficult to us, then, to conclude with Suzuki: "The Christian experiences are, after all, in no way different from those of Buddhism; terminology is all that divides us."[326]

4.3 *Pantheism.* Both Meister Eckhart and Mahāyāna Buddhism, writes Suzuki, have been unjustly accused of pantheism. We have cleared up this ambiguity as to Eckhart: his comprehension of the identity between God and man is not of the order of substances, but of accomplishment. From this point of view, it would be more exact to speak of panentheism. The Zen experience culminates in the overcoming of all dualisms and in the revelation of that which conditions the many things as well as multiform existence. If the vitality of Zen consists in that it abolishes the oppositions between theism and atheism, transcendence and immanence, etc., and if the *ignorant misinterpreters*[327] of whom Suzuki speaks resort to these false oppositions to pronounce on Zen the verdict of pantheism, then indeed, the experiences of Eckhart on this point were perhaps "singularly Mahāyānistic."[328]

---

322 "Die weselîche isticheit nâch einvaltiger einekeit âne einigen unterscheit" ("essential being according to the simple unity without any difference"), sermon *Intravit Iesus in templum*, DW 1: 19,1–2 [Pr. 1] and elsewhere.
323 Hans Hof, *Scintilla animae. Eine Studie zu einem Grundbegriff Meister Eckharts* (Lund and Bonn: Gleerup and Hanstein, 1952), 16.
324 [Cf. Suzuki, *Mysticism, Christian and Buddhist*, 9.]
325 [Cf. Suzuki, *Essays in Zen Buddhism*, 302.]
326 [Cf. Suzuki, *Mysticism, Christian and Buddhist*, 8.]
327 [Cf. Suzuki, *Mysticism, Christian and Buddhist*, 11.]
328 [Cf. Suzuki, *Mysticism, Christian and Buddhist*, 12.]

4.4 *Detachment and emptiness.* Only the detached man, says Eckhart, comprehends God. We have seen that detachment, for him, signifies the overcoming of all individuality or property (*eigenschaft*). Does this concept resemble Zen emptiness? Suzuki writes: "Whereas Buddhism insists on emptiness in relation to all composed things (*skandha*), and is by this fact metaphysical, Eckhart puts an accent on the psychological significance of pure nothingness, so that God can take possession of the soul without any resistance on the part of the individual."[329] The true stake of this sentence, as it appears to us, is the same as that under the title *isticheit*, namely that the Buddhist concept of emptiness exclusively concerns man's relationship with things, whereas the Eckhartian concept of detachment also aims at theological virtue. Indeed, in Eckhart, God too must abandon all his names and attributes if he wishes to reach the ground of the soul. It is not false, but rather insufficient, to speak of a psychological significance here: the soul can only void itself of all *eigenschaften* because God follows it in this divestment, because it is a matter of one and the same denudation. In other words, the question is knowing whether Suzuki's Buddhism is in any way a thinking about God. He writes: "Eckhart is perfectly in accord with the Buddhist doctrine of *śūnyāta* when he sets out the notion of Godhead as pure nothingness (*ein bloss niht*)."[330] This question refers us to what follows.

4.5 *Tao and Godhead.* 'Tao' literally signifies the way, the route, the passage. The Taoists understand it in the sense of 'truth,' 'ultimate reality,' 'logos.' Lao-Tzu says of the Tao: "It appears anterior to God [..., R.S.]. No name can be given to it. It returns to nothingness. It is called form without form, figure without figure."[331] Suzuki comments, "God is here distinguished from the Godhead, as in Meister Eckhart."[332] If this is so, must Zen be comprehended as more radical in its negations than Chinese Taoism? And would the radicalism in question bear on the categorical refusal in Japanese Zen to speak of God? If yes, what is true of Lao-Tzu cannot be true of Zen: "Lao-Tzu expresses in his classical Chinese way what the medieval Dominican

---

329 [Cf. Suzuki, *Mysticism, Christian and Buddhist*, 14.]
330 [Cf. Suzuki, *Mysticism, Christian and Buddhist*, 16.]
331 [Cf. Lao-Tzu, *Tao Tê Ching*, 4 and 14.]
332 [Cf. Suzuki, *Mysticism, Christian and Buddhist*, 18[n27].]

preacher speaks of in his vernacular German."[333] Elsewhere, Suzuki rightly distinguishes Zen from all religions: "What renders all these religions and philosophies vital and inspiring is the presence in them of what I may call the Zen element."[334] Zen, in itself neither a religion nor a philosophy, would then be found less in the preached content of Meister Eckhart (Godhead or Tao) than in the very fact of his preaching: the sermons, like the blows administered by the Zen masters, exhort one to an experience that is always unique.

4.6 *Learned ignorance.* The Zen masters, says Suzuki, are ignorant people who know, or learned people who are ignorant. It is not difficult to follow Suzuki in this parallel with the Western tradition: 'learned ignorance,' a term of Nicholas of Cusa, but whose roots are found in Eckhart, is the knowledge proper to the man who has unlearned to objectify God in an extrinsic relationship. The dialectic that pushes knowledge and ignorance to their extremes is one of the points of greatest resemblance between Eckhart and Zen. Just think of the apophasis of the eighth picture of the bull and the cataphasis of the tenth, then of the Eckhartian doctrine of the intellect which 'breaks' through God and seizes the Godhead which is *vernünfticheit* (DW 1: 142,7 [Pr. 2], "Quasi stella matutina") and of the Godhead as desert. Knowledge and ignorance cancel each other out: "When a man truly comprehends Bodhidarma, he finds himself sitting for the first time in his home by his fireside."[335] The sixth chapter of Suzuki's text does not then pose a problem.

4.7 *Birth and Nirvāna.* The reciprocity between God and man has been called above a reciprocity of birth: God gives birth in me to his only Son, and I in turn give birth to the only Son in God. Suzuki writes: "How does the painter enter into the spirit of the plant? [..., R.S.] The secret is to become the plant itself. But how can a human being transform himself into a plant? If he wants to paint it, there must be something in him that corresponds to it. [..., R.S.]. He becomes the object that he desires to paint."[336] Is this to say that the

---

333 [Cf. Suzuki, *Mysticism, Christian and Buddhist*, 19.]
334 Suzuki, *Essais sur le Bouddhisme Zen*, 316 [cf. *Essays in Zen Buddhism*, 268].
335 [Cf. Suzuki, *Mysticism, Christian and Buddhist*, 24.]
336 [Cf. Suzuki, *Mysticism, Christian and Buddhist*, 31-2.]

painter is 'reborn' as a plant in the sense that the detached man in Eckhart is reborn as Son of God? Suzuki indeed speaks of identification. "The pulsation of one and the same life animates the painter and his object."[337] As in Eckhart, "the subject is lost in the object,"[338] or rather, these two terms are abolished. If it is true that the Eastern artist "paints the spirit and not the form,"[339] then he captures in the hibiscus "a zero full of infinite possibilities, a void of inexhaustible contents."[340] In other words, the true relation to things (as exemplified in painting) abolishes every relation, and attains nirvāna. "The light as well as the objects are gone; what remains?"[341] A great black circle, nirvāna, new birth.

It seems to us that the resemblance between Eckhart and Zen can be defended here on two conditions. On the one hand, nirvāna must be fundamentally understood not as absence or death, but as an affirmation beyond all opposites. Certain formulas in Suzuki indicate it as a transcendental condition of possibility; nirvāna, he writes, "is that which renders all things possible."[342] We have already suggested that the eighth picture of the bull corresponds to the plenitude of seminal ideas in the Godhead. On the other hand, it is necessary to pass beyond the definition of nirvāna as "a psychic state realized by means of enlightenment."[343] It is indeed quite insufficient to interpret Eckhart's birth of the Word in us as a psychic experience. It is once again Eckhart's theocentrism which here resists syncretism.

4.8 *The castle in the soul and the satori.* We recall the very rich vocabulary applied by Meister Eckhart to the ground of the soul: castle, spark, guard, light, little point. Suzuki writes: "This 'little point' is full of significance, and I am sure that Meister Eckhart had a satori."[344] He defines satori as "opening of a new eye," as "an intuitive look into the nature of things, in contrast to logical or analytical

---

337 [Cf. Suzuki, *Mysticism, Christian and Buddhist*, 32.]
338 [Cf. Suzuki, *Mysticism, Christian and Buddhist*, 32.]
339 [Cf. Suzuki, *Mysticism, Christian and Buddhist*, 31.]
340 [Cf. Suzuki, *Mysticism, Christian and Buddhist*, 28.]
341 [Cf. Suzuki, *Mysticism, Christian and Buddhist*, 30.]
342 [Cf. Suzuki, *Mysticism, Christian and Buddhist*, 28.]
343 Suzuki, *Essais sur le Bouddhisme Zen*, 74. [Cf. *Essays in Zen Buddhism*, 63.]
344 [Cf. Suzuki, *Mysticism, Christian and Buddhist*, 79.]

comprehension."³⁴⁵ Suzuki has well understood Eckhart when he sees in the castle in the soul the dividing line which separates the uncreated and uncreatable region in man from all creatures. But it is still necessary to take all these formulas out of their epistemological context. The castle in the soul is not only a faculty of knowledge; it designates the true identity of man. In certain texts, Suzuki indeed goes beyond the metaphors of the eye and the gaze. How can we not think of the sermon *Jesus entered* [DW 1: 24–45 (Pr. 2, "Intravit Iesus in quoddam castellum")] when Zen invites us to "see into our proper nature"? The following lines cited by Suzuki resemble this sermon on the castle in the soul to the point that one could be mistaken: "Let us look only once into our original Nature, and we shall know the truth, even if we are illiterate and do not know a single word."³⁴⁶

---

345 Suzuki, *Essais sur le Bouddhisme Zen*, 270. [Cf. *Essays in Zen Buddhism*, 32 and 230.]
346 Ibid., 276. [Cf. *Essays in Zen Buddhism*, 235.]

14

Commentary on Professor Caputo's Paper "Mysticism, Metaphysics and Thought"

(1976)

Schürmann presented this English-language commentary on a paper by John D. Caputo at the 1976 meeting of the Heidegger Circle. The complete title of Caputo's text was "Mysticism, Metaphysics and Thought: A Reading of Der Satz vom Grund," which Caputo reworked for his 1978 monograph The Mystical Element in Heidegger's Thought.[347] *In addition to offering valuable insights into the practical a priori, the manifold meaning of being in Eckhart, anarchy, and the civil service of contemporaneous philosophy, Schürmann's commentary can be seen as a supplement to the critique he makes of Caputo in his own 1978 book on Eckhart: "A suggestive comparison with the later Heidegger which pushes, however, the syncretism into questions of detail where it serves neither of the authors considered. [...] Such thematic comparisons tend to forget that the themes of modern philosophy, as Heidegger expressly states, arise with Descartes, not with Meister Eckhart. [...] Generally speaking, Caputo seems to me more reliable on Heidegger than on Eckhart" (WJ, 262, 253n91; not in ME).*[348]

Professor Caputo's project of a topology of three approaches to Being, namely mysticism, metaphysics and 'Seinsdenken' [thinking of being] is quite impressive. It is also awesome. Indeed, where does one stand to undertake such a topology? From which standpoint

---

347 (Athens: Ohio University Press, 1978); rev. ed. (New York: Fordham University Press, 1986), chapters II (minus the appendix) and V. Caputo's paper can be found in *Heidegger Circle Proceedings* 10 (1976): 3–40.
348 See also *WJ* 253n91: "I am ill at ease with parallels between two thinkers so far apart from each other when these parallels become as specific as the following: Heidegger's 'recollection into being' and mysticism at large (Caputo I, p. 483); Heidegger's analogy between Being and thinking, and Eckhart's analogy between God and the thinking within faith (ibid., p. 484); Heidegger's 'Dasein,' and Eckhart's 'ground of the soul' (Caputo II, p. 61); Heidegger's 'Event of appropriation' and Eckhart's 'birth' (ibid., p. 62), etc." R.S. cites John D. Caputo, "Meister Eckhart and the Later Heidegger: The Mystical Element in Heidegger's Thought," in *Journal of the History of Philosophy* 12, no. 4 (October 1974): 479–94, and 13, no. 1 (January 1975); 61–80.

is it possible? It seems to me that the very title 'topology' implies that the ground from which Professor Caputo speaks would have to be the third, the thought of Being. At the same time, though, the general drift of his paraphrase of [Heidegger's] *Der Satz vom Grund* [*The Principle of Reason*] seems to aim at a kind of restoration of metaphysics.

I want to examine the condition at which one can speak of an affinity between mysticism and thought, as Professor Caputo does in his conclusion. I have serious reservations with regard to a point by point comparison between what he calls a mystic and a thinker, more precisely between Meister Eckhart and Heidegger. I have these reservations as long as the condition of such comparisons is not made clear. Professor Caputo's paper addresses itself only implicitly to such conditions. Instead, we are told that both mysticism and thought are non-representational; that for both logical discourse is suspended; that both speak of an event, of releasement, of transcendence, of nothingness, etc.... I think such parallels must be handled very carefully. They must also be handled historically: if it is Meister Eckhart to whom Heidegger is to be compared, one cannot proceed as if the two were contemporaries. Angelus Silesius, too, who after all was only Eckhart's 'versifier,' pertains more to the medieval than to the contemporary world.

Here is my fundamental objection: the sole condition to establish such an affinity between mysticism and thought is of a practical order. Meister Eckhart put it very clearly: "He who wants to understand my teaching of detachment has to be himself perfectly detached" (DW 2: 109,1 [Pr. 30, "Praedica verbum"]). In Caputo's paper this practical a priori recedes, to say the least, behind the search for terminological similarities. To state the same condition otherwise, one can say that to think of Being as releasement one has to be oneself perfectly released. Or again: to understand that Being is "without why," one has to live oneself "without why."

In *Der Satz vom Grund* this requirement to exist in a certain way in order to think a certain thought appears in the context of the "new key" mentioned by Professor Caputo: "The question remains whether and how we, hearing the movements (*Sätze*) of this playing, play along with and join in the playing" (SG 188).[349] The condition to speak of an affinity between mysticism and thought is *whether and how* we join in the 'play.' Now one may object that Heidegger speaks of an attitude in thinking alone, not of a practical a priori. But not only does 'thinking' in the later writings stand for 'Dasein,' also the borderline between thought and practice is hard to draw: "Thinking changes the world," Heidegger says (VA 229).[350] The thinking that must become "hearty" (Gel 27)[351] is a way of existing. Thus I maintain that a mode of *existence*, a way of life, is required to *understand* the kinship between mysticism and thinking. This kinship does not result from a network of detailed comparisons, but from the establishment of the practical a priori in question. Without such a common ground, comparisons remain impressionistic. And the practical a priori allows one at least to pull some strings together in a less impressionistic fashion.

Meister Eckhart's vocabulary of being shows this reciprocity between existence and understanding quite clearly. Eckhart uses three groups of words for 'being.' The word *wesene* (*Wesen*) is the most remarkable because of its semantic broadness. Generally it is used by him to translate in a verbal manner the being of beings (Heidegger would say their beingness) which the Scholastics designated by *ens commune*. But it covers a much wider extent and overlaps with 'essence.' The important stress is on the character of process, which is still preserved today in expressions like "*sein Wesen treiben*," to go about, and "*viel Wesens machen*," to make much ado. "*Er west*" is archaic for "he roams about." In the context of his doctrine of identification between the ground of the mind and the ground of God, Eckhart says that "with no difference we are the same being [*daz selbe wesene*, R.S.]" as God [cf. DW 3: 322,3 (Pr. 76, "Videte qualem caritatem")]. It is clear that Eckhart does not teach substantial identity with God, but a process. This process (*gewürke*) is called either "birth of the Word in the mind" or "breakthrough beyond God." In either case *wesene* designates an accomplishment. In the non-technical usages the middle high German *wesene* also suggests a course of events: it means "way of life," also "household"

---

349 ["SG" = *Der Satz vom Grund.* See now GA 10: 169.]

350 ["VA" = *Vorträge und Aufsätze.* See now GA 7: 234.]

351 ["Gel" = *Gelassenheit.* See now GA 16: 529.]

(*Hauswesen*). In the history of the German language Eckhart adopts this word (*wesene*) at the moment of transition when it does not any longer translate *esse* in all its doctrinal rigor and when it is not yet the modern *Wesen*, which is often a synonym for "human being" (in *Faust II* Mephistopheles arranges for Faust's descent into the Kingdom of Mothers: " ... *Dein Wesen strebe nieder, Versinke stampfend, stampfend steigst du wieder*" [Drive your strivings downward; / to sink you stamp your foot, to rise you stamp again]).[352]

The negation of *wesene* translates the *huper-on* of the neo-Platonists. *Unwesene* is reserved by Meister Eckhart for that essential 'coming forth' which, at the same time, remains 'hidden' ("the concealed desert," "the closet," *Kleidhaus*, the "vast solitude" etc.), that is, for the Godhead beyond God. "The mind acts in *unwesene*, and it follows God who acts in *unwesene*" (DW 1: 151,11–12 [Pr. 9, "Quasi stella matutina"]). In a certain sense *unwesene* could be translated by 'nothingness,' but it points, so to speak, not beneath but beyond being. In the *unwesene* of the Godhead the activity of the ground of the mind and the ground of God is one and the same activity. *Unwesene* as a technical term in Eckhart does not apply to creatures. The *un-* does not negate being, but the cognoscibility of being. And the prefix pushes to the extreme the process-character of being: in the One, the Godhead, the mind's activity and God's activity are one.

The second group of words is totally different; here being is understood as a noun, *iht*. This term is preserved in modern German only in its negation, '*nicht*.' *Iht* means "something," *niht* "nothing." These terms are used particularly in the context of Eckhart's ontology of the sensible substance: "All creatures are mere nothingness [*niht*, R.S.]. I do not say that they are small or anything at all: they are mere nothingness" (DW 1: 69,8–70,1 [Pr. 4, "Omne datum optimum"]). "What does not possess being [*iht*, R.S.] is nothing [*niht*, R.S.]. But no creature has being, for its being depends on the presence of God: were God to withdraw for an instant from all creatures, they would be annihilated [*würden sie ze nihte*, R.S.]" (DW 1: 70, 1–4 [Pr. 4, "Omne datum optimum"]). *Iht* thus designates the sensible substance in its being which is "borrowed" (*ze borge*) from

---

352 [Lines 6303–6304; trans. Stuart Atkins, *Faust I & II* (Princeton, NJ: Princeton University Press, 2014).]

God. *Iht* is the *entitas* of *ens*, or the *ousia* of *on*. It speaks of a being's fact to be. In that sense it is the content that the mind reflects or represents when it apprehends a being as existing in general. When Eckhart says that in truth *iht* is *niht*, when he negates a created substance's fact of being, he states that a thing has indeed no proper being because "being is God" (*esse est Deus*) [LW 1: 156, no. 12 (*Prol. gen.*)]. In the poetry of Mechthild of Magdeburg one finds the same vocabulary: "*Du solt minnen das niht, Du solt vliehen das iht*" (You must love nothingness, you must flee from all something).[353] The *iht* of a substance resides in God, not in itself. This is true both for the individual being of a substance, called *ihtes iht*, and for the common fact to be, *iht*. *Ihtes iht*, "this individual being" or "this something," is not, it is *ein lûter nihtes niht*, sheer nothingness.

> When the mind penetrates into the unmixed light, it falls into its non-being [*nihtes niht*, R.S.], and it is so far removed in this non-being from its created being [*ihtes iht*, R.S.] that its own powers are inefficient to bring it back into its created being. So God places his uncreated being under the mind's non-being [*nihtes niht*, R.S.] and maintains the mind with his being [*ihtes iht*, R.S.]" (DW 1: 14,2–6 [Pr. 1, "Intravit Iesus in templum"]).

The third family of words derives directly from the verb "to be," *sîn*. These are *sîn* and *isticheit*, which is constructed from "is," *ist*, and designates primarily God's being. Eckhart sometimes connects it with *wesene* and calls God the *weselîche isticheit* [DW 1: 19,1 (Pr. 1, "Intravit Iesus in templum")]. *Sîn* and *isticheit* have often the same extension and comprehension: "God's being [*sîn*, R.S.] is my being [*sîn*, R.S.] and God's primordial being [*isticheit*, R.S.] is my primordial being [*isticheit*, R.S.]" (DW 1: 106,1–3 [Pr. 6, "Iusti vivent in aeternum"]). Now it is this concept of *isticheit* that introduces what I called the practical a priori in the understanding of being: "You have to completely founder in your 'yourness' [*in dîner dînesheit*, R.S.] and to dissolve into his 'hisness' [*in sîne sînesheit*, R.S.] so that you understand eternally his being [*isticheit*, R.S.] without any becoming and his nothingness without any name" [DW 3: 443,5–7 (Pr. 83,

---

[353] [Mechthild von Magdeburg, *Das fließende licht der Gottheit* (Berlin: Verlag der Weltreligionen, 2010), 52 ("XXXV. Die wöstin hat zwölf ding").]

"Renouamini spiritu")]. A certain way of life, an attitude or a kind of practice is required to understand being as *isticheit*. What is this practice? Eckhart calls it the elimination of *iht*: "As long as there is any *iht* within the *wesene* of a thing, this thing is not recreated" (Pf.: 88,8–9) [DW 2: 349,4–5 (Pr. 44, "Postquam completi erant dies")]. To think that beings are what they are by their fact-to-be, or by their beingness, *iht*, is to thoroughly misunderstand them. Understanding arises from turning away from *iht*, that is, it arises from detachment. As long as one is attached to the being of things, to their *iht*, one does not know being at all as *wesene*.

Active detachment as the prerequisite for the understanding of being is expressed by Eckhart through the very peculiar adjective *istig*, which is derived from *ist* quite as *isticheit*. But the adjective allows for a comparison: "God is more intimately present [*istiger*, R.S.] to all creatures than the creature is to itself" (DW 1: 106).[354] This text is very striking: the Augustinian *maxime intus* [most inside] is translated by Eckhart through a derivative of the verb to be. *Istig* should therefore be understood as indicating an intensity of being. God appears all the more *istig*, all the more intensely existing, as I myself become detached. The extreme version of this reciprocity between practice and thought is "to abandon God for the sake of God; then God becomes [ours, R.S.] as he is present [*istig*, R.S.] to himself, neither given nor received, but in the presence [*isticheit*, R.S.] that God is in himself" (DW 1: 197,2–5 [Pr. 12, "Qui audit me"]).

Here we have indeed a condition for the thought of being, which is of a practical order. To bring the three technical terms together in one proposition, one would have to say in agreement with Meister Eckhart that the practical annihilation of the self (of *iht*, that is) is the condition for actual identification with the One (identification of human and divine *wesene*), in which alone being can be understood in its verbal character (*isticheit*). The thought of being requires that man exist in a certain way—released, detached, without why.

I should like to suggest now how this same practical a priori is present in Heidegger. Professor Caputo quoted the amazing text

---

354 [R.S. takes this quotation from a fragment provided in DW 1: 97 that is connected with DW 1: 106,1–3 (Pr. 6, "Iusti vivent in aeternum").]

from *Der Satz vom Grund*: "What is unsaid in the saying, and everything depends on it, is that man, in the most concealed depths of his being, first truly is when he is in his own way like the rose—without why. We are not however able to pursue this thought any further here" (SG 7).[355] It is this last sentence that I find amazing. It sounds as if Heidegger recoiled from a consequence of his thinking which he does not want to admit. This consequence is that in order to "think being" man must exist in such a way that in his practice teleology is abolished. Some of the best-known phrases of Heidegger point towards such an *abolition of teleology in practice*, for instance "woodpaths." Let me quote the lines from the opening page of *Holzwege*:

> "Wood" is an old name for forest. In the wood are paths which mostly wind along until they end quite abruptly in an impenetrable thicket. They are called "woodpaths." Each goes its peculiar way, but in the same forest. Often it seems as though one were like the other. Yet it only seems so. Woodcutters and forest rangers are familiar with these paths. They know what it means to be on a woodpath. (Hz 3)[356]

It seems to me that *Seinsdenken* requires that we somehow dismantle the entire machinery of behavior, of goal-directed actions and their evaluation, of inner motivation and outer determination; it requires that we think of action otherwise than as strategy; that we understand it rather the way we try to understand the paths towards being, as *lacking an assignable end*. The type of existence out of which being may become thinkable would then already be misunderstood if it were pressed to produce reasons for its behavior. This type of existence would introduce into human practice what we have already become accustomed to discover in ontology: namely that each path "goes its particular way, but in the same forest. Often it seems as though one were like another. Yet it only seems so." To put the same practical a priori for the thought of being still otherwise: the "life without why" on which "everything depends" cannot be understood in the classic fashion out of *archē* and *telos*. Practical

---

355 [GA 10: 57–58. This is nearly identical to the translation given in Caputo, "Mysticism, Metaphysics and Thought," 13.]
356 [Hz = *Holzwege*. See now GA 5.]

philosophy, the way the West has learned it from the Greeks, has been made impossible by Heidegger. With Heidegger's subversion of the *archē* life all of a sudden appears as literally an-archic. To me, the last line of the passage from *Der Satz vom Grund* quoted above indicates precisely Heidegger's reticence before this practical conclusion. One point at least is sure: to speak of the practice that is required for the thought of being one will not be able to have recourse to the Aristotelian scheme of teleology in action ("Every art and every investigation, every action and pursuit, is thought to aim at some good," beginning of the *Nicomachean Ethics* [1049a1–2]). Practical releasement cannot be defined as purposive activity. The paths on which existence finds itself engaged when it thinks being *out of* and *as* releasement "end in an impenetrable thicket."

Traditionally the normative concept of teleology serves to regulate and eventually legitimize human conduct. It makes acceptable conduct depend on the rational establishment of an end that is thought to be good or desirable if achieved. But what is the understanding of being underlying such constructions? Are striving and performing not basic characteristics of existence only if, prior to any practical theory, being is fixed into casual schemes? Does human action not exhibit a natural proclivity towards ends only upon the condition of a calculative ontological a priori?

In a culture where philosophy has so radically abandoned its task of criticism as to cooperate with the existing system by unending enforcements of its technological rationale, Heidegger's "thought of being" requires an alternative mode to think action. The goalless action that it requires is actually quite subversive—even literally so. It is not beings that call for a ground, but Being as "groundless ground" calls upon existence to let itself be; thus the essence of foundation is reversed. The thought of being is an overthrow (*vertere*) from the foundations (*sub-*). What is a more powerful challenge to the merry-go-round of reason in the calculi that have usurped the title of philosophy, particularly in the Anglo-Saxon world, than to say such a practical No to philosophy's unconditional surrender to technology?

15

The Loss of the Origin in Soto Zen and in Meister Eckhart

(1978, new edition with additions from the 1977 *Lindisfarne Lecture* added by Francesco Guercio)

This text first appeared in a special issue of the journal The Thomist *devoted to Eckhart, an issue that also included an extensive bibliography on the Thuringian master prepared by Schürmann and others.*[357] *Schürmann had already presented the text as a lecture to the Lindisfarne Association, whose meetings were then held at the Church of the Holy Communion in Manhattan. In the lecture, a recording of which has been preserved on magnetic tape, Schürmann offered more details than in the published text about the similarities and differences between Soto Zen and Meister Eckhart and recounted some interesting anecdotes about his study some years earlier with Master Taisen Deshimaru in Lodève, near Montpellier, France. Preceded by the abbreviation L., readers will find in the footnotes the most significant variations in the Lindisfarne Lecture.*

Several[358] Japanese authors who have come into contact with the Western tradition have underlined similarities between key concepts in Zen Buddhism and in Meister Eckhart.[359] Sometimes their state-

---

357 With Thomas F. O'Meara, James Campbell, Philip Stein, and Thomas McGonigle, "An Eckhart Bibliography," *The Thomist: A Speculative Quarterly Review* 42, no. 2 (April): 313–36.

358 [L: ‹ "I looked it up in the *Encyclopedia Britannica* [s.v. "Lindisfarne Gospels"] what I was supposed to understand by the title 'Lindisfarne association,' and I discovered that the Lindisfarne gospels—of which you certainly know more than I do or even of what the *Encyclopedia Britannica* can tell us—that 'they were attributed to the Northumbrian school [...] the Lindisfarne gospels also show the fusion of Irish, classical, and Byzantine elements of manuscript illumination.' So, after having read that, I thought there was a tradition of creative syncretism in your association and that I should encourage this now. [laughter] So, my title is 'The Growth of Knowledge in Meister Eckhart and Soto Zen'; it could also be 'The Loss of the Origin in Soto Zen and in Meister Eckhart.'" ›]

359 See the works by H. Dumoulin, H.-M. Enomiya, W. Heinrich, Dom Le Saux, T. Merton, M. Nambara, K. Nishitani, R. Otto, H. W. Schomerus, D. T. Suzuki, S. Ueda. See also my *Meister Eckhart, Mystic and Philosopher* (Bloomington: Indiana University

ments, for instance Suzuki's, betray a rather superficial acquaintance with the schools of thought that[360] intersect in Eckhart's highly syncretistic teachings. Nevertheless[361] I trust that there are resemblances; that they have to be located very deeply, on an experiential level; indeed that they touch upon the core of Eckhart's mysticism and the core of Zen enlightenment.[362] Such point-by-point comparisons as are sometimes undertaken do not lead very far here. Rather, some hypothesis of interpretation is needed for a re-seizure, at one's own risk, of the matter itself, that is, of the experience to which both Zen and Eckhart testify. Let me call this experience the way of releasement. What I mean by this term will hopefully be clear in the end, although a full appropriation is possible only from a personal standpoint; the point where the interpreter stands in his own quest. The true realm of encounter between such foreign traditions as a far-Eastern Buddhist sect of the twelfth century and our Medieval German late Scholastic is after all my own existence.[363] "The reason why the Buddha so frequently refused to answer metaphysical problems," writes Suzuki,[364] "was partly due to his conviction that the ultimate truth was to be realized in oneself through one's own effort."[365] And in Meister Eckhart: "He who wants to understand [my teaching of detachment, R.S.] has to be himself perfectly detached" (DW 2: 109,1 [Pr. 30, "Praedica verbum"]). "Now I beg you to be exactly as poor

---

Press, 1978), 221–26. The four elements of Eckhart's teaching developed in the present article are exposed more in detail in *ibid.*, 84–121.

360 [L: ‹ "syncretistic themselves" ›]
361 [L: ‹ "my starting point is that" ›]
362 [L: ‹ "So, to dig out this kind of, well, of this unicity of the inspiration between the two, one has somehow to find a hypothesis of interpretation, a starting point. At one's own risk one would have to re-seize the matter itself rather than taking texts here and there. Let me call this experience 'the way of releasement.' I think that the starting point, or the only point, from which one can consider, sort of justifiably, similarities in teachings as far removed as Eastern Zen and Western medieval mysticism... that the only starting point, the only meeting point can be one's own experience, in a sense, or at least an itinerary of experience. And I call this experience 'the way of releasement.'" ›]
363 [L: ‹ "our own experience" ›]
364 [L: ‹ "And Suzuki writes, although he stems rather from the Rinzai school" ›]
365 D. T. Suzuki, *Essays in Zen Buddhism*, First Series (Grove Press: New York 1961), 61. [L: ‹ "So, I quote this to show the locus of comparisons—and 'comparisons' is not the word—rather, the locus of an understanding of the root out of which both Eckhart and this Buddhist would speak." ›]

as I have said, so that you may understand my instruction, for if you do not resemble the truth we are talking about you will never be able to follow me" (DW 2: 487,5-7 [Pr. 52, "Beati pauperes spiritu"]). "Do not worry if you do not understand what I say; indeed, so long as a man does not resemble that truth he will remain unable to grasp my speech" (DW 2: 506,1-2 [Pr. 52, "Beati Pauperes Spiritu"]). Thus there is no other way of responsibly dealing with the convergence noticed by these Japanese authors than to somehow involve oneself in the way of releasement.[366]

The impossibility of escaping one's own lived experience is even more patent in Soto Zen. As is well known, the two major Buddhist sects in Japan are Rinzai and Soto. Rinzai stresses abrupt means to obtain awakening, such as blows delivered by the master, shouts, question-and-answer sessions which a rationalist would qualify as absurd, and *koans*. Still Rinzai has produced an abundant literature, which is not the case with Soto. Indeed Soto simply follows one method, that of "just sitting" quietly in a rigorous posture called *zazen*. In Japanese *za* means to sit and *zen* means meditation. The seated meditation is the beginning, the end, and the essence of Soto, thus enforcing even more the anti-intellectualist slant that characterizes Zen in general. Rinzai and Soto correspond to two different intellectual temperaments,[367] one relying on the concentration of the mind, the other on an intensely felt psychosomatic unity. A Rinzai master may eventually give metaphysical instructions, whereas a Soto master[368] will hardly speak of anything more than the correct way to sit. He will show no interest in finding solutions, and he will be bored with speculations about nothingness.[369] Here are some lines from a sermon entitled "Zazen" by Master Meiho (1277-1350):

> Zen-sitting is the way of perfect tranquility: inwardly not a shadow of perception, outwardly not a shade of difference between phenomena. Identified with yourself you no longer think, nor do you seek enlightenment of the mind or disburdenment of illusions. You are a flying bird with no mind to twitter, a mountain unconscious of the others rising around

---

366 [L: R.S. omits the sentences from "Now I beg you..." to "the way of releasement."]
367 [L: ‹ "tendencies" ›]
368 [L: ‹ "will never give metaphysical instructions" ›]
369 [L: this sentence is omitted by R.S.]

it.[370] Zen-sitting has nothing to do with the doctrine of teaching, practice and elucidation. You do not bother with sutras or ideas. The superior student is neither attached to enlightenment nor to illusion. Taking things as they come, he sits in the proper manner, making no idle distinctions [..., R.S.].[371] All [teachings, R.S.] are comprised in Zen-sitting and emerge from it. Even a moment of sitting will enable you to free yourself from life and death.[372]

As the master-student relationship is the only way to learn Zen, an implicit reference is made throughout this paper to a period of time that I spent with Master Deshimaru from Kyoto, who also lives part of the time in France.[373]

The synthetic concept that I wish to develop as standing at the core of both the experience in *zazen* and of Eckhart's mysticism is the loss of the origin. In a first approach, let me define this concept as the retreat of a metaphysical First,[374] or of an *archē*. By that I designate an ultimate point of reference, for instance Substance in Aristotle, the Christian God in Scholasticism, the Mind in Hegel, etc. I shall thus speak of the anarchic essence of Zen[375] and Eckhartian mysticism. The term "anarchy" has to be understood literally as the absence of a beginning, of an origin in the sense of a first cause. It must also be understood as negating the complement of *archē*, namely *telos*.[376] I claim that the logic of releasement as it is lived in *zazen* and by Eckhart leads to the destruction of origin and goal not only in the understanding of the world but even in human

---

370 [L: this sentence is omitted from the quote by R.S.]
371 [L: this sentence is omitted from the quote by R.S.]
372 In *World of the Buddha: A Reader*, ed. Lucien Stryk (New York: Doubleday Anchor, 1969), 368–69. [R.S. makes some slight modifications.]
373 [L: ‹ "six months in Kyoto, six months in France. And he has a center both in Paris and in Lodève, close to Montpellier" ›]
374 [L: ‹ "the retreat of metaphysical point of reference, an *archē*. *Archē*: a Greek word for principle or origin or first" ›]
375 [L: ‹ "Soto Zen" ›]
376 [L: ‹ "the end. So, absence of *archē* and absence of *telos*. And one could perhaps say—I don't think that is English though—we could speak of [an] anarchic element and [an] ateleocratic [one]—teleocracy, -cracy means 'to reign,' 'to rule,' and 'ateleocratic' the absence of a ruling end, absence of purpose, absence of a goal towards which, I don't know, one individually or world history tends. Absence of beginning and end, of *archē* and *telos*" ›]

action.³⁷⁷ At this point it may suffice, in order to substantiate my *a priori*,³⁷⁸ to remind you of Eckhart's frequent injunction to "live without why" (DW 1: 90,12 etc.),³⁷⁹ that is, without purpose. "Those who seek something with their action, those who act for a why, are bondsmen and hirelings" (DW 2: 253,4–5 [Pr. 39, "Iustus in perpetuum vivet"]).³⁸⁰ "If you ask a genuine man who acts out of his own ground: 'Why are you doing what you do?' he will reply, if his answer is as it should be: 'I do it because I do it'" (DW 1: 92,3–6 [Pr. 5b, "In hoc apparuit"]).³⁸¹ Likewise, a Zen master would simply laugh at questions concerning the beginning and the end of things, the whence and wherefore—for instance of good and evil. Meiho, in the *zazen*-sermon just quoted, also states: "You must guard yourself against the easy conceptions of good and evil."³⁸² He does not mean easy conceptions as opposed to difficult conceptions, but that good and evil are in and of themselves easy conceptions.³⁸³ To make the anarchic intention of his sermon perfectly clear he continues: you should "ask who is above either,"³⁸⁴ that is, above good and evil.³⁸⁵ A human act here is no longer understood out of its origin and its goal, but it is a genuine act precisely in so far only as it lacks both!³⁸⁶ The principle of anarchy may even have political consequences, not the

---

377 [L: ‹ "destruction or abolition of goal both in public and private course of events" ›]
378 [L: ‹ "this *a priori*, that is the practical starting point of absence of origin/absence of end" ›]
379 [L: ‹ "So, the kind of life that one would live, if this abolition or the loss of the origin were experienced as Eckhart and Soto Zen apparently seem to propose to us that it should be experienced, would be a 'life without why,' *Leben ohne Warum*" ›]
380 [L: ‹ "So, how can you continue a 'technological' life, I mean, in any kind of public organization, if those who seek something with their actions, those who act 'for a why,' are bondsmen and hirelings?" ›]
381 [L: ‹ "So, absence of why, absence of purpose, destruction of *telos*, destruction of *archē*" ›]
382 [In *World of the Buddha*, ed. Stryk, 368.]
383 [L: ‹ "He does not mean easy conceptions as opposed to difficult conceptions of good and evil but the easy conceptions which *are* good and evil, that is, good and evil are in and of themselves easy conceptions [laughter]... somehow we have to understand this [R.S. laughs]" ›]
384 [In *World of the Buddha*, ed. Stryk, 368.]
385 [L: ‹ "and then forget about them" ›]
386 [L: ‹ "then it is a genuine human act. So, this is a kind of teaching about human behavior, of practice, of action, that is utterly contradictory to the type of thinking that has made the West and, therefore, conquered the world" ›]

ones recommended by Bakunin and Proudhon,[387] but perhaps in the sense of a replacement of the metaphor of the body[388] in the understanding of the city by the metaphor of play. The metaphor of the body and its members is metaphysical; it refers the different organs in man to the chief organ, the head, and thus allows for an efficacious exercise of authority, as the Roman consul Menenius Agrippa explained to the slaves entrenched on the Aventine Hill. The metaphor of play introduces fluidity into institutions as it deprives corporatisms and established hierarchies of their *archē*.[389] If the way of releasement is anarchic in its essence then the experience of *zazen* as well as of Eckhartian itinerancy is anti-metaphysical.[390] Indeed metaphysics requires a *principium*, a 'principle' to which everything else is referred, and a political philosophy derived from metaphysics requires a *princeps*, a 'prince' or some other supreme authority. *Archē* and *telos* are two modes in which the metaphysical First— Plato's 'Good,' the neo-Platonic 'One' or Scholastic 'Being itself'— appears. I call the loss of the origin the progressive disappearance of this metaphysical First on the path of releasement which is the sole design in Zen-sitting and in Eckhart's preaching.[391] 'Releasement' is the translation of the Middle High German *gelâzenheit*, or the modern *Gelassenheit*. Another way to translate this key concept (derived from *'laxare,'* French *'laisser'*) would be 'letting-be.' I should now

---

387 [L: ‹ "who are called 'anarchists' in the dictionaries" ›]
388 [L: ‹ "which is a very oppressive, repressive metaphor for public action by the metaphor of play. I say, the metaphor of [the] body is oppressive, repressive, in the sense that… well, you may remember the consul Menenius Agrippa in the Roman Empire who succeeded in reconciling the slaves entrenched in a strike on the Aventine hill by telling them precisely the fable of the body and its members: that is, there has to be feet, who have to walk, and there has to be a head, and if there are no feet then the head cannot think either, so, you had better labor and then come back and have the patriarch, the patrician class continue [to] live as it does. So, the metaphor of the body for social life is a hierarchical one and, in that sense, quite oppressive, as I said. Rather the metaphor of play…" ›]
389 [L: ‹ "So, the metaphor of [the] body—and *archē* as well as *princeps* stem from words in Latin and in Greek that relate to 'head'… the guiding *caput*… whereas the metaphor of play introduces fluidity and absence of a *princeps*, which is also the *prince*; so from principles to prince there is only a difference in suffix" ›]
390 [L: ‹ "and that is what I like about it" ›]
391 [L: ‹ "Now, I should like to suggest this progressive loss of origin through four steps,… four steps of a progression towards anarchy, if you wish. And that is what I meant by the title "Growth of knowledge in Soto Zen and in Meister Eckhart." ›]

like to suggest four steps of such progression towards anarchy. They are simply taken from a programmatic declaration by Meister Eckhart himself:

> Whenever I preach I usually speak of detachment and that man must become bereft of himself and of all things; secondly that one should be remodeled into the image of the simple good which is God; thirdly that one should remember the great nobility which God has deposited in the mind in order for man to reach God through it; fourthly of the purity of the divine nature. (DW 2: 528,5–529,1 [Pr. 53, "Misit dominum manum suam"])

I. Detachment

The first of the four steps towards attainment of release is detachment, *Abgeschiedenheit*. It so happens that these four steps of destruction of the origin can very easily be traced in the development of Zen-sitting. I shall first show how detachment is the prerequisite for the seated meditation.[392]

In Zen-sitting everything begins with a violent negation. The masters love to speak of a duel unto death. Either the enemy dies, they say, or I die. This moment of violence to oneself is the beginning of the sitting experience. *Zazen* is a battle-posture for "ego-killing." Quite as in fencing it is the posture that makes you die or live. The position of the chin, the spine, the thumbs, the pelvis: this is the material of which Soto "mysticism," if that word applies, is made. Plus endurance. It is evident that *zazen* originated in the warrior class, the samurai. As in the art of archery the starting posture must be taken with "serene fervor" and deadly seriousness. Again, quite as in fencing, the masters say, a moment of distraction in *zazen* may bring death: in fencing because of the sword, in *zazen* because without satori I am a dead man.

This violent negation is different from an ascetic rejection of the world or of one's desires. Detachment is not more ascetic than any other momentary effort of concentration. It is the exertion of totally

---

392 [L: ‹ "So, my claim that I put before you tonight is that these four steps *in fact* verify... the main moments of experience through Zen-sitting. In Zen-sitting everything too begins with detachment, with the violent negation that is..." ›]

liberating the mind from its images and preoccupations. This is achieved through the perfect seated posture. Not only mental representations have to be chased, or let pass as clouds, but also the very wish for satori, even the very thought of death or of life. The sole object of concentration is the posture. Intellectuals definitely have difficulty with *zazen*. Deshimaru loved to tell how during the Second World War he prevented a Japanese ship loaded with gunpowder from exploding simply by sitting on top of the dynamite for forty-eight hours[393] in *zazen* posture with extreme concentration.

Detachment here means voluntary emptiness: at the outset of *zazen* one has to realize the "twentyfold void," that is, the absence of all preoccupations except for the ferocious determination to sit correctly. If one practices *zazen* for the sake of whatsoever, be it health or enlightenment, it will produce no effect.[394] But medical results and satori may ensue.[395] There are long lists of negations in this tradition: we have to rid ourselves of the things within, any kind of thought, and the things without, any objective quality; we have to rid ourselves even of the quest for emptiness. The will must will not to will. Texts on this matter abound, but I am content here with stating what happens in the seated meditation. There is first of all a violent negation of any object of volition and of conception.

If we now pass to Meister Eckhart we find the same type of violent negation at the beginning of the path of releasement. The word itself that Eckhart uses for detachment expresses the idea of riddance: *abegescheidenheit*, in modern German *Abgeschiedenheit*, is formed from the prefix *ab-* which designates a separation (*abetuon:* to rid oneself of something; *abekêre:* turning away, apostasy) and of the verb *scheiden* or *gescheiden*. In its transitive form, this verb means "to isolate," "to split," "to separate," and in its intransitive form "to depart," "to die." The word *abegescheidenheit*, "detachment" or "renunciation," and related verbs of deliverance evoke, in the

---

393 [L: ‹ "while, around him, fifty other Japanese boats loaded with dynamite were all bombed by the American aircrafts, his was the only boat to reach the harbor. And, because he was sitting for forty-eight hours in *zazen* straight, in extreme concentration on the gunpowder" ›]

394 [L: ‹ "So, that is the 'without why,' huh? This is the paradigm for life. The sitting simply and *not* [to] practice it for any purpose whatsoever, not to achieve mental peace or to get rid of your neurosis or to get a better spine [laughter]" ›]

395 [L: ‹ "but certainly not if you look for them" ›]

allusive thought of Meister Eckhart, a mind that is on the way to dispossessing itself of all exteriority which might spoil its serenity.[396] However, Eckhart's speculative temperament leads him to reflect on the ontological[397] condition of such violent negation[398] of all that can be known or willed. The following lines have in this respect been often misunderstood:[399]

> All creatures are mere nothingness. I do not say that they are small or anything at all: they are mere nothingness. (DW 1: 69,8–70,1 [Pr. 4, "Omne datum optimum"])

What is it that has to be negated at the outset of the way of releasement? All creatures, Eckhart answers.[400] Why is this so? Because, being made, they are already nothing. "Creature" in Eckhart designates a being which incessantly receives itself from elsewhere; it has received existence, life and intelligence from another.[401] It does not possess itself, the other is its being; in itself it is nothing.

---

396 [L: this sentence is omitted.] Angelus Silesius, physician and poet, who died in 1674, was one of those who no doubt have best understood the Eckhartian preaching on detachment. In his *Cherubinic Pilgrim* he adopts even the vocabulary of the Master. He is, so to speak, Meister Eckhart's versifier. *Abgeschiedenheit* [detachment], *Lauterkeit* [purity], *Eigenschaft* [property], *Bildlosigkeit* [imagelessness], *Jungfrauschaft* [virginity]—all the Eckhartian terms are known to him: "Weil Abgeschiedenheit sich niemand macht gemein | So muss sie ohne Sucht und eine Jungfrau sein. [..., R.S.] Vollkommne Lauterkeit is bild-, form-, liebelos, | steht aller Eigenschaft wie Gottes Wesen bloss" "Since detachment makes itself familiar to no one / it has to be without desire and virginal. [...] | Perfect purity has neither figure, nor form, nor love, / it is devoid of all property, as the being of God." Angelus Silesius, *Der cherubinische Wandersmann* (Basel: Schwabe, 1955), p. 41. [*CW* 2.67: 81; 2.70: 82.]
397 [L: ‹ "the more ontological, that is, the question related to the core of metaphysics" ›]
398 [L: ‹ "and, at the end of these four steps, we shall see that he overcomes precisely these metaphysical constructs" ›]
399 [L: ‹ "Now, here come, then, three lines on this initial violence, this initial negation in Meister Eckhart, by which his path of releasement starts, with which everything begins" ›]
400 [L: ‹ "they are all nothingness and, therefore, should be negated and released" ›]
401 [L: ‹ "so, it does not have a being of its own, that is what is meant. Rather, that its being stems from elsewhere. In Eckhart's Christianity, of course, from the Creator God. So, *His* is that being. And to say that (what is it?) that "all creatures are mere nothingness" is not to say that they are without interest or that one should rather beware of them or something like that, not at all. It is simply to say that they do not have any being of their own, that the being that they have is not theirs. Therefore, they are liter-

What does not possess being is nothingness. But no creature has being, for its being depends on the presence of God. Were God to withdraw, for an instant, from all creatures, they would be annihilated. (DW 1: 70,2–4 [Pr. 4, "Omne datum optimum"])

From the condition of creature, Eckhart concludes that the created is nothingness.[402] Sometimes he speaks in images: "As long as the creature is creature, it carries within itself bitterness and harm, wrong and distress" (DW 2: 25,7–8 [Pr. 26, "Mulier, venit hora"]).[403] This is a metaphorical way of stating the nothingness of creaturehood. A short inquiry into Eckhart's vocabulary of being is necessary to understand the concept of nothingness as it appears at the starting point of the way of releasement.

Eckhart uses three groups of words for "being." The word *wesen* is the most remarkable because of its semantic broadness. Generally it is used to translate in a verbal manner the being of beings which the Scholastics designated by *ens commune*. But it covers a much wider extent and overlaps with "essence." *Wesen* is the word for the totality of what shows itself, under the aspect of its appearance. Conversely, *unwesene* is reserved by Meister Eckhart for that appearance which, at the same time, retreats into concealment, that is, into the darkness in which the mind acts in perfect conjunction with God.

> The soul acts in *unwesene,* and it follows God who acts in *unwesene.* (DW 1: 151,11–12 [Pr. 9, "Quasi stella matutina"])

In a certain sense, *unwesene* could be translated by "nothingness"; but as it expresses the abolition of the positivity of being, it points, so to speak, not beneath but beyond being, as the *hyper-on* of the

---

ally called 'creatures' or 'created.' So, the being that they have is not theirs but that is that of their Creator" ›]

402 [L: ‹ "the created in itself is nothing. So, this is a strictly met..., philosophical, if you wish, way of stating that a creature is a creature, that a creature is a thing created, it does not have its being of itself, it does not depose... dispose of its being but, rather, receives it from elsewhere" ›]

403 [L: ‹ "Of course, phrases like these, or images like these, are misleading because they seem to intend this kind of turning away from the world but that is not at all the case, neither in Meister Eckhart's own life—he was an excellent administrator of his order—nor in the intent of what he teaches" ›]

Neoplatonists. In the *unwesene* of the Godhead, the activity of the ground of the soul is identical with the actuality of God. *Unwesene*, then, does not apply to creatures. The opposition between being and nothingness in creatures is expressed in a different terminology. The Middle-High-German word for "nothing" is *niht*. It is composed of the particle of negation *ne-* and of *iht*, "something" or "anything whatsoever." "The creature is nothing." What exactly is it that Eckhart wants to negate in the created? *Iht* is denied; the creature is not "a something." *Iht* designates the existing as such: the creature endowed with a borrowed being, the *entitas* of the *ens* or the *ousia* of the *on*. *Iht* speaks of a being with regard to the fact that it is. It denotes that which qualifies thought to represent to itself a being as a being. *Niht* is the negation of the fact of being. The creature in general cannot be represented as being; its *iht* resides in God, not in itself. The individual being is called *ihtes iht*, "this individual being" or "this something." Here the terminology is most incisive. The corresponding negation, *nihtes niht* is properly translated by "non-being." It expresses the negation of the individual perfection of being. The individual being is not, it does not possess *ihtes iht*.

The opposition between *iht* and *niht* provides the conceptual tool with which Meister Eckhart grasps the domain of the created. "All creatures are *ein lûter niht*": this applies to the created in general. As for *nihtes niht*, it designates that "nothingness" which is the individual creature. Such a creature is *ein lûter nihtes niht*. In all strictness, the individual creature is not. Its being is in God. Its being does not properly belong to itself. This applies to any particular image,[404] to any object or work, and most of all to man himself in so far as he is created:[405] all these inhibit detachment and are *nihtes niht*, nothing (e.g. DW 1: 14,3f. [Pr. 1, "Intravit Iesus in templum"]). The volun-

---

404 [L: ‹ "and at the outset of the path of releasement this applies particularly to images, or any object or work, images that one has in the mind, of which one has to rid oneself, as in Zen-sitting" ›]

405 [L: ‹ "man himself insofar as he is created is nothing, nothing in himself. But you see the possible misunderstandings in phrases like that, that man is nothing in himself, or man is nothing, everything created is nothing ... the misunderstanding is evident if one does not explain, if one does not insist and show clearly that what is meant by nothingness here is that the things created do not have their being, do not have a being which is theirs, but, rather, the being which is that of their Creator" ›]

tary negation at the outset of the way of releasement must not miss a single being.[406]

The third family of words derives more directly from the verb "to be." They are the words *sîn*, to be, and *isticheit*, which is constructed out of *ist*, it "is," and designates primarily God's being. Meister Eckhart sometimes connects it with *wesen* and calls God the *weselîche isticheit* (e.g. DW 1: 19,1f. [Pr. 1, "Intravit Iesus in templum"]). *Wesen*, too, is then mainly found in the context of divine union. Now the union is no longer considered apophatically as a veiling darkness, but cataphatically as an identity in the primordial being. *Isticheit* should be translated by "authentic being." *Sîn* and *isticheit* have often the same extension and comprehension:

> God's being is my being and God's authentic being is my authentic being. (DW 1: 106,1–3 [Pr. 6, "Iusti vivent in aeternum"])[407]

We now understand better Eckhart's enigmatic statement that "the creature is mere nothingness": *iht* comes to a thing as God incessantly lavishes being upon his creature. Let God's prodigality of *iht* cease for an instant, and the universal presence of the cosmos will immediately vanish.

> All creatures are with God and God grants them their appearance together with his presence. (Pf.: 503,15–17 ["Von der übervart der gotheit"])[408]

> Outside of God there is nothing but only nothingness. (DW 1: 358, 2–3 [Pr. 21, "Unus Deus et pater omnium"])

---

406 [L: ‹ "that is, it must throw itself... it must encompass all possible beings: mental, as well as outside and even myself; since only then have I understood what is meant by 'all creatures are pure nothingness'" ›]

407 [L: instead of "authentic" R.S. says "uncreated" in both instances, then adds: ‹ "this is clear then: as a creature, I do not have being. Rather, God's being is my being or my being is God's being, and God's uncreated being is my uncreated being; so, rather, that which supports a creature in its existence, in its enduring existence, is not its own being but that which God bestows incessantly upon it" ›]

408 [Today, this text is not considered authentic and does not appear in DW. Cf. *WJ* 238[n47]; *ME* 145[n3]. L: ‹ "So, they appear insofar as he is present in them. Were he no longer present, they would be as if swallowed in a black hole" ›]

Finally, in some texts 'nothing' takes on a moral meaning; sin is nothing. But by temperament as well as by conviction, Eckhart is not a moralist. These passages are found in his scholarly works, in Latin, and are less significant. Even here, Eckhart proposes a 'metaphysics' rather than a morals of sin.

Both in Soto Zen and in Eckhart detachment thus designates a violent effort upon oneself. That the language of the samurai class is reminiscent of war and that of the class of theologians rather of metaphysical abstraction is perhaps not that important a difference.[409] The profound cleavage that I see at this first stage of the way of releasement is that Eckhart negates attachment for the sake of God:[410] detachment is necessary because of the mode of the divine presence.[411] This mode is called a bestowal *in fluxu et fieri* [in flux and becoming], constant reception. I am not my being, but I receive it; what I am as a creature is nothingness. Here the principle of anarchy, that is, the overcoming of the representation of a metaphysical supreme being which would be the beginning and the end of all that there is, is hardly sensible yet as motivating thought as well as action.[412] But one guesses already that Eckhart's theocentrism, which distinguishes him on this first level from Zen, will perhaps collapse under the implacable logic of releasement which teaches one to let everything be.[413] The boldness of Eckhart's position appears clearly when one has understood that the difference between created and uncreated

---

409 [L: ‹ "Of course, the mental, civilizational differences between Zen and medieval metaphysical speculation are such that from between these two groups one could hardly draw any comparisons; but the root of comparison, the root of the unicity of source lies in a type of experience" ›]
410 [L: ‹ "that is, for the sake of the creator; that was the very reason why he said that 'all creatures are nothingness': they are nothingness because their created being comes to things from their creator. So, in praise of the creator, we say that the creature is nothing in itself. Not so, of course, in Soto Zen, which is not theistic" ›]
411 [L: ‹ "and the Christian representations of [the] creator" ›]
412 [L: ‹ "since the motivation of this negation in Eckhart is, on the contrary, to extoll the creator. So, the *archē*, as creator, is the one who gives me being. Thus, at the outset, we move within a very theistic realm. At the end, this theistic framework will be totally disrupted, also in Meister Eckhart. But one guesses already, although we still move within the representation of a principle, of a first, one guesses already that Eckhart's theocentrism…" ›.]
413 [L: ‹ "So, at the end, God himself will fall under this law to let everything be. God himself will fall under the law of detachment" ›]

introduces identity and otherness into man himself:[414] identity with God in the ground of the mind, and otherness in the faculties or powers of the soul, and in the body.[415] Man is the *locus* of union and disunion. In the 'ground,' man lives in God and God in him; but in his creaturehood, man is of the world. The difference between God and not-God[416] is a cleft that splits man thoroughly. Only out of this cleft can one speak of[417] God, man, and the world. At this point, it should not surprise us any longer that Eckhart actually abolishes the methodological distinction between theology, anthropology and cosmology. All these three sciences would have to develop the same opposition between "in-God" and "with-God" which is entrusted to man alone. He is at the same time the being-there and the being-elsewhere of the origin; he is among all beings the one that is alike-unlike the origin. The discovery of this simultaneous similarity and

---

414 [L: ‹ "that is, man himself is the place of God, since man receives God's presence constantly and, at the same time, he is also nothingness, I mean, he belongs to creatures, so, man is somehow double" ›]

415 [L: ‹ "*der Seelengrund*, the ground of the mind: there we are one with God and otherness from God, that is, separation, total separation, nothing, in this other realm which he calls the body or the faculties of the mind or faculties of the soul" ›]

416 [L: ‹ "lies in man himself. So, the line of partition between God and not-God goes through man himself since in the ground, we are told, man is one with God and then everything else, what is created, is nothing, in his language—which is a little sharp, I must say, and towards the end of the Middle Ages there was this privilege, I mean, this taste for excessive formulations, which is certainly there in Eckhart and brought him into big trouble with the Inquisition" ›]

417 [L: ‹ "of anything whatsoever, of God, man, and the universe. Only out of this cleft, which we are, of this duplicity that we are, can we talk about man. Well, precisely, we will have spoken, will have said the most important [thing] about man when we say that he is both the *place* of God and the *absence* of God. We'll speak of the world and say that the world is nothingness in itself. We'll say of God that he is the one who dwells in the ground of himself. [R.S. is interrupted by an almost inaudible question from the audience, most probably on whether it is to the Christian God he is referring. R.S. replies:] Well, at the outset it is the Christian God, that is the creator of the Christian tradition, but later on his face will change very much. We should keep that in mind and come to that at every single stage because, as the path of releasement progresses, God not only changes in face or in appearance but in the end, as I said, vanishes. So, I said that only out of this cleft between created and uncreated—so, the definition here is 'creator,' alright?—only out of this cleft between what is created and uncreated in man can we speak of man, that is, anthropology, of the world, that is, of cosmology, and of God himself, that is, theology" ›]

dissimilarity to the origin is the result of the first point in Eckhart's programmatic statement mentioned above.[418]

> When the Father engendered all creatures, he brought me forth. I emanated together with all creatures and yet I remain within, in the Father. (DW 1: 376,7–8 [Pr. 22, "Ave, gratia plena"])[419]

Awakening arises from a philosophical meditation on the being of creatures: inclining oneself towards creatures results in being commingled with them in nothingness.[420] Detachment is an urging which demands of man that he "let nothingness be" (DW 1: 170,3–4 [Pr. 10, "In diebus suis"]) and return towards his origin.

II. Remodeling

The second element of teaching announced by Eckhart is "that one should be remodeled into the simple good which is God." This is a step further than detachment. Until now we have spoken of the radical dissimilarity[421] between the created and the Creator; now the man engaged on the way of releasement[422] discovers a similarity between himself and his origin—God as *archē* and *telos* of his road.[423]

---

418 [L: ‹ "So, the first of these four points was 'detachment'" ›]
419 [L: ‹ "So, both I emanated with all creatures when I was created, he says—so, by that I belong to the world and to the realm that he calls of 'nothingness'—and yet I remain within, that is, in the ground of myself as [I] still am of the Father in the Father" ›]
420 [L: ‹ "So, the old teaching in the Neoplatonic school as well as in the Neoplatonic Christian school of Augustine of 'going inwards,' *intus ire, noli foras ire*—don't turn outside but turn inside—has here this particular consequence that in turning inside I discover that core of myself by which I am of the nature, and identical with, the nature of God and identical with God" ›—Cf. Augustine, *De vera religione*, 39, 72.]
421 [L: ‹ "Creatures are nothing, God alone is. And whatever creatures are they simply are because God, so to speak, holds his metaphysical hand underneath them. Now something else appears and God will appear in a different light" ›]
422 [L: ‹ "of letting all things be because they are nothing in themselves" ›]
423 [L: ‹ "and only at the end will these *archē* and *telos* disappear, I said at the beginning" ›]

Releasement appears as assimilation.[424] But again, let us first look at the second step in Zen-sitting.

After the effort of intense negation a remodeling does indeed take place. The tradition describes this as an assimilation to Buddha. The remodeling of the personality through sitting occurs in ten stages:[425]

1) Hell. To the beginner Zen-sitting is literally hell; this is the title some masters give to the sufferings in one's knees, legs, shoulders, spine, etc. The mind is confused, the body feels thoroughly uncomfortable. One feels contracted, anxious, and one counts the minutes left until the end of the session. The face is twisted, all movements betray embarrassment.

2) Avidity. The masters call the second stage that of the deceased who are still hungry for life but cannot satisfy their hunger. They are totally conditioned by desire and avidity. During *zazen* one is eager to obtain enlightenment. The head is pulled slightly forwards as if one were to hit the wall before which the meditation takes place. One is avid for peace,[426] health, mental tranquility and totally preoccupied by these thoughts. The mind is all hunger for acquisition.

3) Sensuality. The next step is called bestiality: like an animal one thinks of eating and drinking, the sexual desire becomes excessive. At the same time, one is often taken over by torpor and drowsiness. The mind sags and easily produces auditory and visual hypnagogic hallucinations. At this stage one sleeps a lot at night, easily half again as long as usual. These hallucinations may simply consist in a feeling of inner expansion. This is the moment when people speak of their unity with the universe, their cosmic soul, their identification with Buddha—in fact, pure imagination.

---

424 [L: ‹ "an assimilation to God: becoming progressively in one's life as one is within the ground of one's mind. And here, again, Eckhart would certainly belong to the tradition of... well, there is the quote from Pindar "become who you are" [Pythian 2, l. 72] taken up by many authors after him for instance, Nietzsche, and Heidegger for that matter. So, what we are within ourselves is one with God but, yet, we have to become what we are on this road called releasement, which here, in this second step—entitled 'remodeling'—appears as an assimilation" ›]

425 [L: ‹ "several stages. So, here, now, I trace very briefly the stages of assimilation throughout Zen-sitting as gathered from several authors of the tradition" ›]

426 [L: ‹ "and thus doesn't have it"›]

4) Battle. This is a state of aggressiveness. One quarrels, tries to win arguments[427] and to make one's superiority felt.[428] When one hears the master's stick hit another adept in the dojo one feels content and thinks: my *zazen* is better. To receive the stick at this point is like a humiliation. One has but one desire; to be the best.[429] And one feels irritated when one becomes aware of one's own irritability, because crankiness does not fit into the picture of perfection.

5) Concern. Things become simplified, but one's mind is very much with daily business. The posture is now good and natural. However it is far from being light, although it is ordinary. Family matters, job problems and the like create unending preoccupations. There occurs a hypertrophy of concrete memory and hence of worries.[430] Details from the past and threats from the future weigh down the posture. According to the Buddhist metaphors, after hell, limbo and animality, this is properly the human condition.

6) Light. This state is compared to that of angels. The Sanskrit term that applies here, *deva*, is from the same Indo-European root as *dies*, day, but also *deus*, god. The idea is that of radiance. The posture becomes so pleasant that one falls into narcissism. To practice *zazen* is pure joy, and many take these agreeable feelings for satori. But in genuine satori no extraordinary kind of feeling prevails.

7) Dogmatism. At this stage one feels totally at home in Zen, not only physically as in the previous moment, but also intellectually. One has the correct answers about releasement and dispossession, one understands the meaning of emptiness, and one is ready to dispense instruction to whoever wants to listen. One has studied the scriptures and again one feels enlightened. But this is merely intellectual enlightenment. One lives among ideas.

8) Immobility. It now seems superfluous to practice *zazen* with others. One retreats into solitude and meditates alone for long periods. The consequence is a physical stiffness and mental rigidity. One thinks one has outgrown the masters and refuses to accept their correction. By excessive self-reliance the mind grows hard. There is

---

427 [L: ‹ "who is the better master" ›]
428 [L: ‹ "how well one sits" ›]
429 [L: ‹ "in the classroom" ›]
430 [L: ‹ "Quite as apparently in analysis: all of a sudden memories release and all comes up in an extraordinary amount and disorder" ›]

no compassion in such a human being. His personality has become immobile; he does not progress unless he opens himself up to others.

9) Compassion. Along the roads in Japan one can see statues of Bodhisattva: Buddha is not locked up in temples but belongs to all, hence the location of these statues in public places. Likewise at this penultimate state one belongs to all. One has somehow become a living Buddha. All attachments are gone. The posture is perfect. One does not desire enlightenment, yet one communicates a sense of it. One is able to practice Zen-sitting at any place, even in the middle of city crowds.

10) Nothingness. One Japanese name for Buddha is '*hotoke*,' which means to untie, release, set free, disentangle, divest, lay bare, become nothing. This is the state of complete awakening. Whether one sits in the Zen posture or whether one does not sit makes no difference any longer. I shall briefly refer to this state again a little later.

It is important to see that these stages do not necessarily follow one after the other. In one single session one may pass from a beginner's state to a much more advanced one. One may go through several states and then regress again very quickly. The ideal is, as Master Dōgen put it, to keep our hands open so that all the desert's sand may pass through them; if we close our hands we shall retain only a few grains of sand. Such is the goal of the remodeling of the personality in Soto Zen. The process of assimilation makes one become like Buddha.[431]

Meister Eckhart does not hesitate to say[432] that the process of assimilation makes us become like God. "One should be remodeled into the image of the simple good which is God." A simile frequently used by him in this regard is that of fire: when a burning straw is brought close to a tree-trunk, the wood, at first, refuses to catch fire. The dissimilarity is too great. But an ember buried in the ashes and smoldering overnight will not long resist the flame; crackling will soon fill the fireplace.[433] Likewise man is assimilated to God.

---

431 [L: ‹ "at least, that's what we are told" ›]
432 [L: ‹ "something quite similar, namely that detachment makes us become like God. Later on he will say more than that" ›]
433 [L: ‹ "So, there's an assimilation, and here in the metaphor of heat. If you put a match here [R.S. presumably gestures to or touches something], I don't think you will

The technical term here is *gelîcheit* which means both similarity and equanimity.[434]

> God's endeavor is to give himself to us entirely. Just as fire seeks to draw the wood into itself and itself into the wood, it first finds the wood unlike itself. It takes a little time. Fire begins by warming it, then heating it, and then it smokes and crackles because the two are so unlike each other. The hotter the wood becomes, the more still and quiet it grows. The more it is likened to the fire, the more peaceful it is, until it becomes entirely flame. That the wood be transformed into fire, all dissimilarity must be chased out of it. (DW 1: 180,7-13)[435]

Quite as in Zen, the strategy of releasement leads from dissimilarity to similarity, and from similarity to union. The comparison with the fire which, by assimilation, attracts the ignitable to the perfection of the ignited, suggests a slow growth too: in order for the blaze to absorb the wood, "it takes a little time."[436] The wood is reborn as the "son" of the blaze, by *gelîcheit*. When the absorption is completed, the wood will be the perfect image of the fire:

> Nothing is so much alike and unlike at the same time [..., R.S.] as God and the creature. What is there indeed so unlike and like each other as these whose unlikeness is their likeness, whose indistinction is distinction itself? [..., R.S.] Being distinct by indistinction, they resemble by dissimilarity. The more they are unlike, the more they are alike. (LW 2: 112,7-12 [*In Exod.*])

---

all go up in flames, although one day with Deshimaru in Lodève there was a strong smell of fire—or something on the second floor—there was a strong smell of fire, stronger and stronger, and smoke coming out of the windows and, apparently, something was going on underneath. And, of course, we panicked, more or less, and said, 'Let's get out!'—he said, 'No! You sit!' [R.S. ends up laughing; laughter in the audience]" ›]
434 [L: ‹ "which means at the same time *Gleichheit, Gleichmut*, that is 'serenity,' and *gelîcheit, gleich*, that is, 'similarity': similarity and equanimity" ›]
435 [L: ‹ "So, all dissimilarity, that is all which at the beginning of this road appeared as nothingness and God's being in us... this must be chased out so as to accelerate or to bring to completion the process of assimilation" ›]
436 [L: ‹ "Likeness is more than equality, likeness is a progression" ›]

The like and the unlike are resolved by flames and incandescences. Assimilation spreads the simplicity of that to which we are likened.

Gelîcheit means more than equality. It gathers two beings under the same becoming, such as fire and wood in combustion, while equality is non-dialectical and exhausts itself in comparisons. Between the child and the father there is a likeness based on common ancestry and destiny. Between the father and his business associate, there is equality—for instance before the law. Equality refers only to the present. Similarity and assimilation, on the other hand, point upstream: *gelîcheit* recalls the source or the beginning; it also points downstream: it intimates the assimilation, that is, the goal or end of the transformation.[437] Assimilation is like an exodus; it is properly the transition from the origin as *archē* to the origin as *telos*.

In some sermons, Eckhart expands his theory of assimilation into a theology of the image of God: "outside of likeness, one cannot speak of an image" (DW 1: 265,4–5 [Pr. 16b, "Quasi vas auri solidum"]).

> An image is not of itself, nor is it for itself. It has its origin in that of which it is the image. To that it belongs properly with all that it is. It does not belong to what is foreign to this origin, nor does it owe anything to this. An image receives its being immediately from that of which it is an image. It has one being with it and it is the same being. (DW 1: 270,2–6 [Pr. 16b, "Quasi vas auri solidum"])

Eckhart's speculation on the being of images echoes patristic ponderings on the same subject. Imagine a man standing before a mirror. Properly speaking, where does the image that absorbs his attention reside?[438] Does its being inhere in the body from which it emanates, or rather in the reflection which he contemplates? "The image is in me, of me, towards me," answers Eckhart (DW 1: 154,3

---

437 [L: ‹ "the goal of the road" ›]
438 [L: ‹ "These Fathers of the Church, both Greek and Latin, as well as Eckhart after them, they would ask: properly speaking, where does the being of... where does the image reside? In me, standing in front of the mirror, or in the mirror? Answer: entirely in me, and it is only in the mirror because I'm standing there, quite obvious, but nevertheless is less obvious when we speak... when we apply this theory of the image of God to the relation between creator and created" ›]

[Pr. 9, "Quasi stella matutina"]). Were I to move back a step, the image would no longer exist.[439]

> Every image has two properties. The first is that it receives its being immediately from that of which it is an image, without interference of the will. Its outgoing is indeed natural, and it thrusts itself out of nature like a branch from the tree. When an image is cast on a mirror, our face will be reflected in it whether it likes it or not. [..., R.S.] The second property of the image lies in its resemblance. (DW 1: 265,9–266,3; 269,1 [Pr. 16b, "Quasi vas auri solidum"])

The first point accords with the conclusion on created being: the image has no proper being, being comes to it from another, it does not exist originarily. The image exists only in its "outgoing" (*ûzganc*). The second point explains from where it extracts its being: it is nothing else but that very dependence we call reflection. Eckhart applies these considerations to the relationship between man and God. Man, as an image of God, remains "with" him of whom he is the image, distinct from him and not "in" him.[440] Man as an image emanating from God stays at the periphery of the origin.[441] A first application of the principle of anarchy occurs when Eckhart states that man must become *ungelîch*, unlike anything created, and totally *entgelîchet*, no longer resembling any being, so as to be perfectly like God.

These remarks on mirroring and on the being of an image are one model used by Eckhart to explain his theory of similarity and assimilation. According to another model, that of the human word, he will say that man should be an "adverb," *bîwort*, to the Word or Verb[442] of God.

---

439 [L: ‹ "likewise in the relation between God and man: the image is entirely in God and I am but the reflection of it. Were God to withdraw, to step aside, so to speak, the being of... the image that I am would vanish away. So, the image, or... to say that man is the image of God, is but one way to say that he is nothing but *dependence* on God, that that is all his being. And without this first being, without the origin here, he would wither away as the state of Marx did" ›]
440 [L: ‹ "So, as an image of God, I am *with* him, but in the ground of myself I am *in* God" ›]
441 [L: ‹ "and has to assimilate himself still further" ›]
442 [L: ‹ "capitalized, which is Christ. We should become an adverb to the Verb—to the *Logos*, to the *Verbum*, to the Word which is the Son of God" ›]

I have in mind the little word *quasi* which means "like"; children in school call it an adverb. This is what I intend in all my sermons. The most appropriate things that one can say of God are "Word" and "Truth." God called himself a "Word." Saint John says: 'In the beginning was the Word,' meaning by this that we should be an adverb to this same Verb. (DW 1: 154,7–155,3 [Pr. 9, "Quasi stella matutina"])[443]

A detached human being is destined to become an ad-Verb.[444] Eckhart's thought proceeds along the following lines. A man speaks. Through the numerous words of his discourse, it is possible that one single utterance makes itself heard and stands out to whoever knows how to listen.[445] To the hearer, words may then seem suddenly so transparent that he is able to declare: "Now I know exactly what you mean." From the flow of many statements,[446] he is able to assimilate the single intention that they all purport. We speak of what someone "means," although he pronounces perhaps many sentences and periphrases. The numerous words "mean" one single utterance. A single thought or sense makes itself understood in all the vocables. We do not only follow word after word, but we "get

---

443 "Ein einziges Wort hilft mir, schreibts Gott mir einmal ein, | So werd' ich stets ein Lamm mit Gott gezeichnet sein" "One single word can help me, if God one day inscribes it in me, | I shall be for always a lamb marked with the seal of God." Angelus Silesius, *Der cherubinische Wandersmann*, p. 114. [*CW* 2.37: 77.] This single word is God's Word.
444 [L: ‹ "totally *pointing towards* the Word of God" ›]
445 [L: ‹ "But this is not a word that could be written down, rather, it is such that when you open a text by him, for instance [William] Blake, you say 'this can only be Blake,' without even looking at the drawings. Or, the Gospels can be read as *one* word, or Meister Eckahrt's sermons, for that matter" ›]
446 [L: ‹ "many statements in a conversation, or many statements handed down to us through the tradition from an author, we will be able to assimilate *one* single intention, *one* single word that is *meant* throughout all his pronouncements and sentences and paraphrases. The numerous words that mean one single word, one single utterance. And it is this word in which—and it is, of course, not for an author, I mean in which it stands as an image for what a man is in his life, or writings, or discourse—this *single* word that, we are told, should become 'adverb' to the Verb: one could call this, if you wish, 'a word of existence,' that is that by which, in which an existence, a human existence, has its core, its knot, its center. So, *that* should become 'adverb' to the Verb, to the Verb that is God, a word [an] author [is] assimilated to, to [the] Word of God" ›]

the idea," we comprehend one single utterance which is necessarily broken up into many words.

It may also happen that this single utterance appears as the focus where the sheaves of thought and feeling converge. It is around this type of utterance that biographers build their reports. Such a focus is a Word of existence: a forever unpronounceable single Word in which a life is comprehended. From the struggles of a man an utterance emerges which shows and conceals itself as the impetus behind the many expressions coming from him and transmitted to us. The gospels can be read in this way and so can the sermons of Meister Eckhart.

This *wort*, Word of existence, has to become a *bîwort*, adverb for the Verb. God has not begotten man "like" his image, but he has made him "in" or towards his image: *ad imaginem*, ad-Verb. The assimilation always remains to be perfected. The secret of the mind, understood as an image, is *ad:* it is unlike all things, yet like God. Eckhart draws perhaps too radical a distinction between the human mind as an image of God and creation in general; conversely, he does not distinguish the mind enough from the divine Persons. Like the Son and the Spirit, the mind is defined by its *ad* which establishes it near to God. Just as Christ is with the Father, the detached man should be with Christ, in turn engendering the unique Word which he becomes himself. Then the assimilation will be perfect. In a sermon on Justice, Eckhart illustrates this teaching by the proximity of Eve to Adam:

> The just live eternally "with God," directly with God, neither below nor above. They accomplish all their works with God, and God accomplishes his own with them. Saint John says: 'The Word was with God.' It was totally alike and next to him, neither below nor above but alike. When God created man, he drew woman from the rib of man, so that woman was alike to man. He made her neither from the head nor from the feet, so that she would be neither above nor below man, but that she would be equal to him. Likewise the just mind is to be equal with God and next to him: exactly alike, neither inferior nor superior to him. (DW 1: 106,4–107,4 [Pr. 6, "Iusti vivent in aeternum"])

The word is with God (*bî gote*), Eve was with Adam,[447] the just man is with Justice: likewise the man devoid of all created images is with God and is the image of God.

From likeness[448] springs praise:

> What praises God? It is likeness. Thus everything in the soul which is like God praises God. What in any way is unlike God does not praise God. In the same way an image praises the artist who has imprinted upon it all the art that he has in his heart, thus making it entirely like himself. This similarity of the image praises its master without words. (DW 1: 318,4–8 [Pr. 19, "Sta in porta"])[449]

Eckhart's way of expressing man's remodeling into similarity with the divine is certainly more abstract than the itinerary of Zen-sitting. The concreteness of *zazen* stems from the importance, extraordinary for a Westerner, that Soto masters attribute to the body and its development. Also Eckhart's theory of assimilation is far more theocentric than Zen. Despite these two reservations[450]—and the more we discover now the anarchic element in Eckhart the more they will both collapse—it should be clear at this point that the logic of the way of releasement in *zazen* and in Eckhart is to deliver what is most originary in man through the unlearning of possession and attachment. The ultimate attachment that has to be let go is the idea of origin[451] in the sense of cause and end, of project and goal. This

---

447 [L: ‹ "as Eve is with Adam—a little 'sexist' here [laughter in the audience]—the just man is with Justice—always pointing towards the source" ›]
448 [L: ‹ "only from such likeness, only from such assimilation, from such being-with" ›]
449 [L: ‹ "So, the same can be said here about a work of art. You go into the Metropolitan Museum and you see from far away that good old friend Donatello, or whoever, and you say well, if you are among old friends there, saying that you are recognizing them from afar. So, you understand what Meister Eckhart would call—I'm paraphrasing Meister Eckhart here—a Word of existence which immediately recalls that which Donatello, or whoever else, uttered in history and with which we associate his works. So, the work of art praises its master quite as the master praises the word to which he should be related: as an adverb to Verb. What counts here, beyond the speculation about adverb—which is only a metaphor after all—is Eckhart's way of expressing man's remodeling into similarity..." ›]
450 [L: ‹ "that is, that we, in our Western tradition, in Eckhart's tradition, are more intellectualist and more theocentric" ›.]
451 [L: ‹ "origin itself, and of God" ›]

fundamental renewal of the human being through the apprenticeship of releasement has now to be explained in terms of its consequence, the loss of the origin.

III. Nobility

The third thesis in Eckhart's preaching requires "that one should remember the great nobility which God has deposited in the mind in order for man to reach God through it." Eckhart has dedicated an entire treatise, *The Nobleman* (DW 5: 109–119 [*VeM*]), to this concept. "Nobility" is a technical term in his writings which designates the capacity of the ground of the mind to unite itself to the ground of God.[452] It is roughly equivalent to Augustine's "*capax Dei.*" Man's nobility lies in his natural indistinction from God: "Where there is distinction you will find neither the One nor being nor God nor rest nor happiness nor satisfaction. Be One, then you find God" (DW 5: 115,7–9 [*VeM*]).[453] The unity that is naturally given[454] remains at the same time a task to be achieved: one must become "One with the One, One from One, One in One; and in One, One—eternally" (DW 5: 119,6–7 [*VeM*]). Here the difference between the originative and the originated has vanished.[455] But again, let us first look at Zen-sitting.

Zen can be qualified in general as a quest for identity, and this in a twofold sense. On the one hand it is a quest for the self.[456] The following words are engraved on the meditation stick: "We must see our true self, we must look into the truth of our mind." On the other

---

452 [L: ‹ "in Meister Eckhart... which is in fact a reappropriation of Saint Augustine's—if you aren't familiar with this tradition—Saint Augustine's expression 'man is *capax dei*,' that is, the mind is capable of receiving God. So, nobility here means this capacity that the mind has to receive God. It designates the capacity of the ground of the mind to unite itself to the ground of God" ›]
453 [L: ‹ "If you are interested in the sources of this teaching, this could literally be a quote from Plotinus: 'Be One, then you find God'" ›]
454 [L: ‹ "*Gabe* is an *Aufgabe*: the unity that is naturally given with God has to be yet achieved as a task" ›]
455 [L: ‹ "the difference in saying: 'Thou shalt become one,' the difference between origin and originated, has totally disappeared. So, this is a state of identity. And there Eckhart ceases to be theocentric at all. And here I think we leave the schemes of thought of the inherited Christian metaphysics of the West" ›]
456 [L: ‹ "identity with oneself, self-identity" ›]

hand *zazen* as a quest for identity is also a quest for identification, namely with Buddha—and thus a loss of identity. It is the practice of sitting in the mind's impersonal center. In his chapter *On Life and Death* Master Dōgen, the founder of Soto Zen in the thirteenth century, wrote: "If we release our body and our spirit, if we forget our self and if we abandon ourselves to the power of Buddha, mental activity becomes useless; we are ready to separate ourselves from life or death, we awake, we become Buddha."[457] The key to *zazen* lies in the realization that self-identity and identification with Buddha are one and the same, and that they arise from the perfect posture. Man's nobility, according to Zen, is to become Buddha and thus to become himself. Now this is nothing extraordinary; there is not the slightest trace of extasis in Soto Zen.[458] Rather the enlightenment is the awareness of our most ordinary self, the space we live in when our mind is open rather than constricted; when it is no longer inhibited by self-erected obstacles. It is no surprise that *zazen* is useful for accelerating psychoanalytic treatment, as it removes in ourselves all that obstructs total presence to whatever there is. Zen is the uninvolved attention to things as they are rather than as they should or used to be. As Suzuki puts it: "Zen is our ordinary mindedness; that is to say there is in Zen nothing supernatural or unusual or highly speculative that transcends our everyday life. When you feel sleepy, you retire; when you are hungry, you eat."[459]

I do not claim any doctrinal identity between releasement in *zazen* and in Eckhart's sermons. However, it should be patent by now that releasement exhibits the same structure in either case: it is an existential itinerary, its essence is the unlearning of possession, its starting point is an effort of the will, its consequence—and this is the point I want to make now—is an identification with the origin[460] by which the distinction between originative and originated[461] is abolished. The essential feature of the origin is to show itself as a cause: efficient or formal cause when it appears as *archē*, final cause when it appears as *telos*. The principle of anarchy which determines

---

457 Quoted by Taisen Deshimaru, *Vrai Zen* (Paris: Le Courrier du Livre, 1969), 71.
458 [L: ‹ "It's rather something very concrete" ›]
459 Suzuki, *Essays in Zen Buddhism*, 302.
460 [L: ‹ "a union, more than likeness—a union, a oneness, an identity" ›]
461 [L: ‹ "between origin and originated, creator and creature" ›]

the way of releasement both in Zen and in Meister Eckhart consists in the destruction of causality as an appropriate category[462] for the understanding of being. It is important to see that the progressive loss of the origin in either case is a matter of practice.[463] By temperament Zen insists more on the destruction of causality as the "why" and "wherefore" in daily life whereas Eckhart is a metaphysician. Again, I do not claim that the concept of the origin designates the same reality in Zen and in Eckhart. It obviously does not since[464] already the representation of a highest being is totally alien to Buddhism. But I do claim that in the progress of releasement the idea of an ultimate—be it a principle of life, or a supreme cause, or even an ethical reason for behavior—becomes meaningless. Before carrying this idea of anarchy still further, let us look at Eckhart's theory of identity as the concept of nobility suggests it.[465] Indeed, resemblance with God is not enough. To be an image of God is not enough:[466]

> Scripture says that we have to become like God. "Like," the word is bad and deceptive. If I liken myself to someone else, and if I find someone who is like me, then this man behaves as if he were I, although he is not and deceives people about it. Many things look like gold, but since they are not, they lie. In the same way all things pretend to be like God; but they are lying, since they are not like him. [..., R.S.] God can no more suffer likeness than he can suffer not being God. Likeness is something that does not occur in God; what does occur in the Godhead and in eternity is oneness. But likeness is not oneness [*gelîcheit enist niht ein*, R.S.]. Whenever I am one with something, I am not like it. There is nothing alien in oneness. In eternity there is only oneness, but not likeness. (DW 1: 215,10–216,1; 216,3–7 [Pr. 13, "Vidi supra montem Syon"])

---

462 [L: ‹ "as the prime vehicle for the understanding of being, of things, or of events" ›]
463 [L: ‹ "not of speculation" ›]
464 [L: ‹ "the origin in Meister Eckhart is the Christian creator, transformed and re-amalgamated through Neoplatonic currents and others, the Chaldean oracles which have given so much food for thought in Plotinus and other Neoplatonic thinkers. So, certainly, the origin that is lost, so to speak, is not the same but it is the loss of such a first cause or point of reference which is comparable" ›]
465 [L: ‹ "So, in Eckhart there is this theory of identity between the ground of the soul and the ground of God, or the ground of mind and the ground of God" ›]
466 [L: ‹ "assimilation is not enough, to be an image of God is not enough, to be adverb is not enough" ›]

How are we to understand this oneness or identity with God? Eckhart never speaks[467] or thinks of substantial identity, rather he calls this an identity "*ein im gewürke,*"[468] identity in operation.

We may think of what happens in music, when the hearer is "all ears."[469] If he does not know how to reproduce inwardly, simultaneously, identically, that[470] which his ears hear, if by distraction or incapacity he omits to accompany in himself the sounds that the senses perceive, then he does not know how to listen. Properly speaking, perfect listening implies that the distinction between the soloist, on one side, and the listener, on the other, is no longer true.[471] Through the unique event of the song which enraptures us, one identical being accomplishes itself. Thus the fundamental determination of existence is "operative identity" or, in homage to Aristotle, "energetic identity."[472] According to Eckhart, human existence seeks to fulfill itself in identity. This trait appears particularly in the most decisive acts of life: in the foundation of a family or of a community, in a dialogue that actualizes what I called earlier two "words of existence," or again in the acceptance of destiny. These events always unite those whom they affect, but one has to be very released, *gelassen*, to respond properly to what destiny sends. Eckhart suggests an example to explain this: consider what happens in conversation. Through your words a clearance of understanding opens up which points towards the word of existence murmured in all that you say or do. But the event of such an opening is the work of neither you nor me. The "we" is not the achievement of the "I"

---

467 [L: ‹ "—and there again has been misunderstood—of substantial identity, that is, he does not even operate with such notions as 'substance,' as pantheists after him would, and I think of Spinoza, or as the people on the Inquisition tribunals would; that is *not* what he has in mind: it is not [in] a *substantialist* unity that we are the same… —although he does use the word *substantia* but it then means other things—" ›]

468 [L: ‹ "*Einheit im Gewirke,*" one in operation, in process, in becoming" ›]

469 [L: ‹ "which happens very rarely" ›]

470 [L: ‹ "the beautiful piece of music that he hears, then he doesn't hear it! If, by distraction or by lack of culture, he is unable to enter into the sonata that he hears, then he doesn't hear it!" ›]

471 [L: ‹ "that I am 'one in operation' with the soloist and so *will I?* perform with him" ›]

472 In Aristotle *energeia* signifies neither "agent" nor "effect," but action inasmuch as it produces the effect, operation in progress. Aristotle, *De Anima*, III, 7, 431 a 5, trans. R. D. Hicks (Amsterdam: Hakkert, 1965), 139 f.

or of the "you," rather it comes to be of its own accord. When it occurs there "is" nothing else besides itself. In such moments two existences are determined as identical: identical in the *gewürke,* that is, in the event. When applied to the realm of deification this scheme shows man living no longer "with" God but "in" him:

> God is not found in distinction. When the soul reaches the original image [of which it is a reflection, R.S.] and finds itself alone in it, then it finds God. Finding itself and finding God is one single process, outside of time. As far as it penetrates into him, it is identical with God [..., R.S.] not included, nor united, but more: identical. (Pf.: 85,36–86,1; 86,3–4) [DW 2: 341,4–9 (Pr. 44, "Postquam completi erant dies")]

> Identical is the event as God begets me as himself and begets himself as me.[473] He begets me as his essential being and as his nature. There is one life and one essential being and one work there. (DW 1: 109,9–10 [Pr. 6, "Iusti vivent in aeternum"])

> The ground of the soul and the ground of God are one single essential being. (Pf.: 467,15 ["Daz ist swester Katrei"])[474]

Eckhart wants to insist so much on this energetic identity[475] between God and man that he does not hesitate to accumulate adjectives against all customary usage: *ein einic ein ungescheiden* (DW 1: 381,1 [Pr. 22, "Ave, gratia plena"]), one unique unity without difference. The true nobility of the ground of the soul lies in that a released man becomes the *locus* where the energetic identity of God, of himself and of the world produces itself. The universe is genuinely "universe," that is, turned towards the One, only in a released man. Eckhart repeats as a kind of axiom:

---

473 [L: ‹ "Here this identity of *gewürke,* of operation is expressed—as ever so often in Meister Eckhart—in the vocabulary of 'giving birth,' of 'procreation.' And Eckhart is best known, after all, for his doctrine of the birth of the Word in the mind, the birth of Christ in the soul" ›]

474 [Today, this text is not considered authentic and does not appear in DW. Cf. *WJ* 240[n92] / *ME* 173[n4]. L: ‹ "and 'essential being' is *wesen,* which is a verb and therefore refers to a *process* rather than to a state or substantial state or so" ›]

475 [L: ‹ "identity by process" ›]

All that is in God is God; (DW 1: 56,8 [Pr. 3, "Nunc scio vere"])

In God, no creature is more noble than the other; (DW 1: 55,4–5 [Pr. 3, "Nunc scio vere"])[476]

In God, there is nothing but God; (Pf.:: 83,17) [DW 3: 225,11–12: (Pr. 71, "Surrexit autem Saulus de terra")]

What is in the first, is the first; (LW 5: 37,8–9 [*Qu. Par.* 1])

What is in the One is the One. (LW 3: 55,2–3 [*In Ioh.*])

These propositions can be read with reference to the theory of the preexistence of all things in God,[477] or the theory of the divine ideas.[478] But to be content with such a Neoplatonist reading of Meister Eckhart would mean[479] to auscultate the letter of his sermons, unmindful of releasement, which remains the existential condition for the understanding of Eckhart's ontology. He always comes back to this necessity of abandoning both human and divine *eigenschaft* (property, selfhood, individuality):[480]

---

476 [L: ‹ "nobility is that the ground of the mind is divine" ›]
477 [L: ‹ "inherited from Plato" ›]
478 [L: ‹ "that is, that all things have the mode of pre-existing in God, a model, an archetype, a paradigm from which they are then created and of which they are a copy, so to speak" ›]
479 [L: ‹ "to be forgetful of releasement. — The most beautiful, the most admirable work that has been written ever on Meister Eckhart is this extraordinary book by Lossky, Vladimir Lossky in French: *Théologie négative et connaissance de Dieu chez Maître Eckhart*, Negative theology and knowledge of God in Meister Eckhart. It is an absolute masterpiece *but* he, with his enormous culture of the patristic tradition as well as Neoplatonic tradition, ties Meister Eckhart back to the past traditions, that is, Neoplatonic and Greek Fathers of the Church and Latin Fathers of the Church. Now, I say that to do so, certainly, one can find nearly for every sentence a paradigm in the earlier traditions but then one is forgetful of the very core, of the 'mobile,' if you wish, of Meister Eckhart, which is this progressive unlearning of possession, and releasement. In that insight, Meister Eckhart anticipates later doctrines rather than reproduces former ones" ›]
480 [L: ‹ "*eigenschaft* means property, as well as attachment, selfhood, individuality. So, both God and man have to abandon their property, selfhood, or identity. And now, we have quite another concept of God, namely, the ground of God and the ground of mind are one only insofar as God abandons his properties, which are: to be creator, or

I wondered recently if I should accept or desire anything from God. I shall consider this carefully, for if I accepted something from God, I would be inferior to God like a serf, and he, in giving, would be like a lord. But in eternal life, such should not be our relation. (DW 1: 112,6–9 [Pr. 6, "Iusti vivent in aeternum"])

Eternal life means that man may live again, here and now, out of his ground,[481] and that releasement may accomplish itself, so that God, man, and the world play out their identity.[482] Man's nobility makes him be the *locus* of the unity of God, man, and the world.[483] Such identity is already in me,[484] not in germ, but in totality, exactly in the same way as God is in me: not according to his effigy, but in totality.

The difficulty in reading Meister Eckhart arises because such a bold[485] cataphatism is mixed, as we shall see, with a no less bold apophatism. Classing Meister Eckhart exclusively among the[486] defenders of either the first or the second of these intellectual attitudes results in missing the very core of his thought. On this mat-

---

to be Father, Spirit, and Son, etc., all the Christian determinations. So, in order to be one with the soul, or in his true nature he is one with the mind but, as such, beyond the trinitary formulations, the creationist formulations, and others" ›]

481 [L: ‹ "So, that is the eternal life that he [Meister Eckhart] speaks of, since he says that the ground of the mind is eternal and... in the now moment it is eternal, so that eternal doesn't mean everlasting, or something, eternal life means that releasement may accomplish itself" ›]

482 "Dies alles ist ein Spiel, das sich die Gottheit macht, | Sie hat die Kreatur um ihret willn erdacht" "All this is a play that the Godhead gives itself | It has conceived the creature for its own sake." Angelus Silesius, *Der cherubinische Wandersmann*, p. 45. [*CW* 2,198: 100.] "Der Mensch hat eher nicht vollkomme Seligkeit, | Bis dass die Einheit hat verschluckt die Anderheit" "Man has no perfect happiness | Until unity has swallowed up otherness." *Ibid.*, p. 55. [*CW* 4.10: 152.]

483 [L: ‹ "the universe" ›]

484 [L: ‹ "in me, in the ground of the mind" ›]

485 [L: ‹ "such bold affirmation, affirming that we are one with God, identical—what the scholars call 'cataphatism'—is mixed with a no less bold apophatism—that is, negations, that, in fact, we cannot know anything about God—and here we say that we know everything since we are *one*. Later on, we will say we don't know anything at all, but not only about God, even about ourselves; we are not able to know anything. So, wait for the apophatic movement and then I'm going to shut up! [laughter in the audience]" ›]

486 [L: ‹ "affirmative tradition—what was called *theologia affirmativa* in the Middle Ages; cataphatism, for those who like Greek—would be to reduce the violence of the path of releasement and, thus, miss the very core of his [Meister Eckhart's] thought" ›]

ter, it is doubtlessly prudent to speak of the "dialectic" of Meister Eckhart.[487] The loss of the origin now appears more clearly: if God were to be represented as a lord, "and I, inferior to God, like a serf," then the classic metaphysical titles such as prime analogate, supreme being, first cause, etc., would apply.[488] But, Eckhart continues, "such should not be our relation." What, then, should be our relation? Pure identity, not difference. It is perhaps this anarchic element that the officers of the Inquisition sensed in Eckhart. They were obviously unable to grasp his teaching,[489] and they certainly did not share the slightest bit of Eckhart's spiritual experience. Eckhart was perfectly right when he accused them of "short and imbecilic intelligence"[490]—so much so that the Bull of condemnation had to resort to literal distortions.[491] But these judges probably had an instinct that sensed what I call the principle of anarchy in Eckhart. Perhaps they even sensed that this principle is indeed harmful, for instance for institutions. Which institution can do without some kind of First, be it an authority or an ideal?[492] Likewise the hidden anarchy may be the reason for the unforeseeable and provocative behaviour of some Zen masters. Man's nobility tolerates neither lord nor master above him. A contemporary Marxist concludes from this that "Eckhart has claimed, at least in theory, the treasures alienated in heaven as man's own goods."[493] Without making him into a theoretician of the medieval peasant upheavals, however, one can say at least that Eckhart's type of thought does away with the very

---

487 Cf. Maurice de Gandillac, "La 'dialectique' de Maître Eckhart," in *La Mystique rhénane* (Paris: Presses Universitaires de France 1963), 59–94.
488 [L: ‹ "but all these classical metaphysical titles for God—*Father* is one of them—are certainly one of dependence: 'I am as a serf and He is like a Lord'" ›]
489 [L: ‹ "anything of his teaching at all" ›]
490 [L: laughter in the audience.] Gabriel Théry, "Édition critique des pièces relatives au procès d'Eckhart," *Archives d'Histoire doctrinale et littéraire du Moyen Age*, I (1926/27): 205 [LW 5: 344, (*Acta*)]; see similar epithets *ibid.* 196 and 248.
491 [L: ‹ "which is proved now. I mean, they falsified lest they *didn't?*' know how to condemn him" ›]
492 [L: ‹ "whatever they be: the authority can be a human being, or the authority of a common conviction or something" ›]
493 Ernst Bloch, *Atheismus im Christentum* (Frankfurt a.M.: Suhrkamp, 1968), 94 [citing Hegel, *Die Positivität der christlichen Religion*, 1800]. Cf. H. Ley, *Geschichte der Aufklärung und des Atheismus*, I (Berlin: Deutscher Verlag der Wissenschaften, 1966), 357–444.

representation of a hierarchy[494]—certainly in the ontological sense and perhaps in the social sense. I should say that the thrust of his argument is never "indicative," pointing towards degrees of being, but "imperative,"[495] pointing towards degrees of existential development. Indicative thought[496] treats of substances, and by stressing their independence and sufficiency in being,[497] it assigns to man his place within the universal order.[498] Such a thought is unable to grasp Eckhart's teaching of identity[499] and identification. Imperative thought, on the other hand, addresses the hearer in his way of being;[500] it is protreptic. There is thus an ontological meaning to the literary form chosen by Meister Eckhart, preaching. It is not accidental that he was a preacher, quite as it is not accidental that language in Zen Buddhism takes the form of oral instruction or conversation. Such language urges our freedom to commit itself upon a path that remains unthinkable to representational metaphysics. As we shall now see, this path does not stop with the identity with God. It actually leads beyond God.

IV. Pure Nature

The fourth thesis in Eckhart's program was "the purity of the divine nature." God's nature is often called the Godhead. "God and Godhead," Eckhart says, "are as distinct as heaven and earth" (Pf.: 180,15-16) [DW 4,2: 767,3-768,1 (Pr. 109, "Nolite timere eos, qui occidunt corpus")].[501] It is in the name of the strictness of release-

---

494 [L: ‹ "at this point of identity: no longer master or serf, no longer first or derived, no longer cause or effect" ›]
495 [L: ‹ "saying 'thou shalt become one!' ›]
496 [L: ‹ "is that of, well—if you wish—the Inquisition or, the metaphysical traditions before and after Meister Eckhart" ›]
497 [L: ‹ "a substance full, rounded, given" ›]
498 [L: ‹ "showing where he belongs: a little lower than angels, a little higher than the tigers and cats [laughter in the audience]" ›]
499 [L: ‹ "if it remains within, what I call, this indicative framework" ›]
500 [L: ‹ "and it was not by chance that Eckhart was a preacher: his teaching is thoroughly hortatory, if you wish, or protreptic, from *trepein*, 'to turn,' 'turning around,' that is aiming at a conversion, if you will" ›]
501 [L: ‹ "So, we are to understand a level—if you wish, but, perhaps, it will be the abolishment of all kinds of levels, I mean of any kind of superposition of levels—the

ment that[502] Eckhart criticizes the pretension of the supreme being to the rank of the origin. The supreme being still has a "why," namely all other beings.[503] The God entirely deprived of a "why" is pure nothingness. As I quoted earlier, "God acts in nothingness" (*unwesene*). It is perhaps here that the parallel with Zen Buddhism is most obvious. Perfect releasement leads into pure nothingness. The Zen student, Dōgen says, "passes entirely beyond the stage of the infinity of consciousness and attains and abides in the stage of nothingness."[504] Let me simply render here some notes taken at Deshimaru's *mondos* (sessions of questions and answers) on this last step of the way of releasement.

Nothingness means forgetfulness: of things and of oneself, and even of *zazen*. Nothingness also lies beyond the opposition between being and non-being. Nothingness does not mean absence of truth, nor even absence of error; rather the mind lets errors be what they are and is indifferent to truth.[505] Nothingness is neither sacred nor profane, it has no religious connotation. The sense of the holy is incompatible with pure nothingness. Nothingness means total privation of forms as well as fullness of forms[506] at the same time, that is, all things are one in nothingness. The genuine Zen experience is the discovery of nothingness at the very heart of all that is present. It is also the discovery of the seed from which all thinking and knowledge arises. But no thought and no knowledge can reach it, as no thought can reach us in our unborn condition. Another word for nothingness is thus birthlessness. One master reportedly told his disciples: "If you can tell me what pure nothingness is you get thirty blows with the stick; and if you cannot tell me what it is you will also

---

distinction between God and Godhead: Godhead is the nature of God, without a name, without a history, certainly not a history of the Jewish-Christian tradition where God is with his people, etc., rather God and Godhead are as distinct as heaven and earth" ›]

502 [L: ‹ "even God has to be abandoned" ›]

503 [L: ‹ "to speak of 'creator' is to refer him to all other beings of whom he is the source, the cause" ›]

504 [Cf. *World of the Buddha*, 235.]

505 [L: ‹ "the mind lets both truth and error be what they are and is indifferent to both truth and error" ›]

506 [L: ‹ "so, of nothingness, in the Soto tradition, apparently you can only speak in affirming opposites always: truth and error, emptiness of forms, fullness of forms, and then passing beyond these" ›]

get thirty blows."[507] Does Zen Buddhism think the absolute nothingness which in the Western tradition has remained unthinkable?[508] One may doubt this, for the experience of nothingness here leads man back "among the drunkards and the beggars":[509] "Carrying a gourd he goes out into the market; leaning against a stick he comes home. He is found in company of wine-bibbers and butchers; he and they are all converted into Buddhas."[510]

If we lose sight of the *practical* core of Zen we get irreversibly lost in abstract considerations of ontological and moral meanings of nothingness: that is, forms of negating being or forms of negating purpose in action. The same is true with Meister Eckhart:[511] outside the practice of releasement his statements about man's return into the pure nature of God[512] receive a monistic ring which[513] would make them sound either atheistic, as in Nietzsche's view,[514] or idealistic as in Hegel's.[515] In other words, active releasement is the practical *a priori* for any correct understanding of both Zen and Eckhart.

---

507 [This seems to be R.S.'s variation on a koan by Tokusan.]

508 [L: ‹ "I do not know that; well, if Zen Buddhism really thinks absolute nothingness, I certainly have the impression that the Western tradition never has thought *absolute* nothingness but nothingness under certain guises, saying, for instance, God is nothingness then he is not *absolute* nothingness. One may doubt that Zen Buddhism also thinks absolute nothingness, for the experience of nothingness..." ›]

509 [L: ‹ "we are told. This is from the famous Ten Oxherding Pictures, which trace this kind of progression in a more detailed way; in the last picture you see Buddha with a bag on his shoulder and" ›]

510 Suzuki, *Essays in Zen Buddhism*, 376.

511 [L: ‹ "if we lose sight of this central interest in releasement that is practical" ›]

512 [L: ‹ "into the pure Godhead" ›]

513 [L: ‹ "they do not have; that is pantheistic—if you wish—which they certainly do not have. But these negations of God, and saying one should pass beyond God, break through God, he [Meister Eckhart] says, were liked by some people and disliked, of course, by others; Nietzsche, for instance, praises them as 'genuinely atheistic' in the *Gay Science*; and Hegel says they are 'genuinely idealistic' [laughter in the audience]" ›]

514 Friedrich Nietzsche, *The Gay Science*, §292, trans. W. Kaufmann (New York: Vintage Books 1974), p. 235.

515 Franz Von Baader remarks in his diary (*Sämtliche Werke*, ed. F. Hoffmann (Leipzig: H. Bethmann, 1851–1860), vol. XV, p. 159: "Very often, at Berlin, I was in the company of Hegel. One day I read him some texts of Meister Eckhart, an author of whom he knew only the name. He was so delighted that he gave before me an entire course devoted to Meister Eckhart. At the end he also confided to me: 'Here we have found at last what we were seeking,'" quoted by I. Degenhardt, *Studien zum Wandel des Eckhart-Bildes* (Leiden: Brill, 1967), 114.

The principle of anarchy which governs the way of releasement is probably best expressed in those passages where Eckhart states that the pure nature of God is without a why,[516] *sunder warumbe*, and that he who wants to penetrate into this pure nature must himself live without why (e.g. DW 1: 90,12 [Pr. 5b, "In hoc apparuit"]).[517] Whoever has abandoned himself entirely and "lets" himself live without an *archē* and a why is not motivated by any exterior inducement, not even God:

> Why do you love God?—I do not know, because of God.—Why do you love the truth?—Because of the truth.—Why do you love justice?—Because of justice.—Why do you love goodness?—Because of goodness.—Why do you live?—My word! I do not know! But I am happy to live. (DW 2: 27,7–10 [Pr. 26, "Mulier, venit hora"])

God is, man lives, things subsist and perish—all this without a why. Eckhart expressed this in multiple ways. His meditation on the why points beyond God as an origin. God, man, and the world are considered in their anarchic emanation (*ûzbruch*, Ausbruch or *ûzvluz*, Ausfluss) where they "bubble forth"[518] from the pure nature, the Godhead, without a why.

---

516 [L: ‹ "and I said, at the beginning, that that is the goal of his life, of his understanding of life: live without why, *sunder warumbe, ohne Warum*" ›]

517 "Die Ros' ist ohn' warum, sie blühet [weil sie blühet], | Sie acht't nicht ihrer selbst, fragt nicht ob man sie siehet" "The rose is without why, it flowers because it flowers | It pays no heed to itself, asks not if it is seen." A. Silesius, *Der cherubinische Wandersmann*, p. 35. [CW 1,289: 69.] Martin Heidegger comments on this verse by claiming the authority of Meister Eckhart: *Der Satz vom Grund* (Pfullingen: Neske, 1957), pp. 68-72. [GA 10: 53.]

518 Eckhart does call the Godhead "origin," *ursprunc*, it is true, but in the very literal sense of "primitive (*ur*-) springing" (from the verb *springen*, to spring). Another Middle-High-German form, today obsolete, was *ursprinc*, effervescence, efflorescence. The idea is always that of a kind of eruption. In Eckhart's Latin works the equivalent expressions are *bullitio* and *ebullitio*. The first of these terms refers to the boiling within the Godhead before God, man and the world emanate; it refers to the Life before life, in which I already was before I came to be. The second, *ebullitio*, indicates the boiling-over of the archetypes from the Godhead, that is, the emanation of all created things from their primitive ground. "'Life' means a kind of seething in which a thing ferments and first pours itself into itself, all that it is into all that it is, before spilling over and pouring itself outside" (LW 2: 22,3–6 [*In Exod.*]). "Die Gottheit ist ein Brunn, aus ihr kommt alles her, | Und läuft auch wieder hin, darum ist sie auch ein Meer" "The God-

What is the sense of a quest which seeks to transcend even God as the origin of all that there is?[519] The metaphysician will object that beyond God, the highest being, no origin can be thought of. But are the new birth and releasement thinkable as long as the excellence of God is in this way objectified? If God is represented as the duplicate beyond or within man,[520] that is, as the Perfect above our imperfection,[521] the divine birth can only be represented by sacrificing either identity to difference[522] (God as the partner of the soul, Pietism), or difference to identity (God as the oceanic substance which swallows up the soul, Pantheism). Meister Eckhart, however, maintains both identity and difference.[523] He attempts to think the origin prior to the manifestation of[524] the threefold. To do so, he turns towards man as that being who needs only to come back to himself for the question of[525] the origin to be raised. There is no other path than that of releasement which can overcome the representation of God as the highest being. A person will be released only when he ceases devoting and dedicating himself with attachment to enterprises big or small, good or evil. Let God be, stop seeking him, abandon God, and then you will find him. Only he who does not

---

head is a well, everything comes from it, | and everything runs again unto it: hence it is also a sea." Angelus Silesius, *Der cherubinische Wandersmann*, p. 52. [CW 3.168: 137.] "Wenn ich in Gott vergeh, so komm ich wieder hin, | Wo ich in Ewigkeit vor mir gewesen bin" "When I lose myself in God, I return | to where I have been from all eternity, before me." *Ibid.*, p. 72. [CW 5.332: 235.]

519 [L: ‹ "that is the thought difficult to receive for Western mentality: why break through—a *Durchbruch*, he speaks of—why break through beyond any representable God—representable as 'other,' as 'Creator,' as 'Savior' or whatever. For a metaphysician this is utter nonsense" ›]

520 [L: ‹ "greater, of course, even that greater than which nothing can be thought—that is Anselm [of Canterbury's] formulation [*Proslogion*, 2]. So, he is the greatest duplicate of man" ›]

521 [L: ‹ "I think releasement still does not reach its goal..." ›]

522 [L: ‹ "and then we have the theism—God up there and the soul here, in Pietism, for instance" ›]

523 [L: ‹ "but locates them *within* God, so that God is identical and different with himself, and so is man: in the distinction between God and Godhead and in the distinction between the ground of the mind and the mind" ›]

524 [L: ‹ "God, man, and the universe. So, Godhead seems to be the *archē* without *archē*, that is, the origin without... the *non*-origin *beyond* God, man, and the universe." ›]

525 [L: ‹ "this anarchic origin" ›]

seek will find.[526] There is no higher attestation[527] of God than this diffidence.

Leaving things, leaving God, living without a why: these teachings of Meister Eckhart surely sound subversive. Indeed they are literally a subversion, an overthrow (*vertere*) from the foundation (*sub-*).[528] Why the world? Why God?[529] Why man? Why identity?[530] They are, Meister Eckhart answers, without a "why." For traditional metaphysics the thought of a threefold interplay of God, man and the world which enacts itself for no reason is sheer folly. But Eckhart charges that the intellectual quest for unshakable[531] foundations keeps itself aloof from any genuine[532] disclosure as it is attached to the "why," to the *raison d'être* of things.[533] One imagines what happens to the scholastic constructions when unexpectedly a preacher comes along who unveils the nothingness of foundations;[534] the scholastic mind is seized with dizziness. The God whom this other way of thinking annihilates in his function[535] of foundation is perhaps indeed the God of western Christianity. If you seek God for the sake of a foundation, Eckhart says, if you look for God even for the sake of God himself, then:

> you behave as though you transformed God into a candle in order to find something with it; and when one has found what one looks for, one throws away the candle. (DW 1: 69,2–4 [Pr. 4, "Omne datum optimum"])

---

526 In Angelus Silesius, *Gelassenheit* receives the same meaning: "Gelassenheit fäht Gott; Gott aber selbst zu lassen | Ist ein' Gelassenheit, die wenig Menschen fassen" "Releasement grasps God, but to release God himself | is a releasement that few people grasp." *Der cherubinische Wandersmann*, 42. [*CW* 2,92: 85.]

527 [L: ‹ "to this anarchic origin than the diffidence of saying 'only he who does not seek will find'" ›]

528 [L: ‹ "turning around, turning up from the foundations" ›]

529 [L: ‹ "why creation? why life? [...] why I, myself?" ›]

530 [L: ‹ "cannot be answered" ›]

531 [L: ‹ "unshakable ground, for a first" ›]

532 [L: ‹ "genuine releasement" ›]

533 [L: ‹ "to a purpose of things, and *that* he [Meister Eckhart] wants to break beyond because, seeking and looking for such a purpose, such a why, such goals, we are not totally detached, nor totally released" ›]

534 [L: ‹ "of the *fundamentum inconcussum*, the unshakable ground" ›]

535 [L: recording stops here abruptly.]

Meister Eckhart only draws the ultimate consequence of letting-be. What is, let it be. Everything could as well not be, but since it is, let it be. God, man, and the world could not be, but since they are, let them be. But the mind is invited to move beyond them.[536]

As the *archē*, the origin as wherefrom (represented by the words "since they are"), is without a why, so, too, the *telos*, the origin as whereto (represented by the words "let them be"), is without a why. For Eckhart, such thought leads man into the desert, which is prior to God, man, and the world.

> I have spoken of a power in the mind. In its first manifestation, it does not apprehend God. It does not apprehend him in so far as he is good, nor in so far as he is the truth. It penetrates into the ground, it pursues and burrows, and it apprehends God in his oneness and in his desert (*einoede*); it apprehends God in his wilderness (*wüstunge*) and in his own ground. (DW 1: 171,12–15 [Pr. 10, "In diebus suis"])

The desert is not fertile in anything: likewise the Godhead is arid, it does not create anything. In the desert everything begins only: but God disappears. The desert is the vast solitude, there is no place for two in the desert. The opposition between a Creator and a creature vanishes. In the desert entreaties are of no avail, there is no opposite of man towards whom he might raise his hands. In the desert, the wind and the sand wipe out the traces of the caravans; the steps of God disappear together with those of man and the world.

The desert is full of seeds but they do not sprout there. The Godhead is a house, Eckhart says, full of people but from which no one as of yet has gone out. Let the dwellers go out into the street and they will be hailed: "God," "Eckhart"…

> God becomes; where all creatures enunciate God, there God becomes. When I still stood in the ground, the soil, the river and the source of the

---

536 "Wo ist mein Aufenthalt? Wo ich und du nicht stehen. | Wo ist mein letztes End', in welches ich soll gehen? | Da wo man keines findt. Wo soll ich dann nun hin? | Ich muss noch über Gott in eine Wüste ziehn" "Where is my stay? Where you and I are not. | Where is the last end to which I should tend? | Where one finds none. Where then shall I go? | I must move still higher than God, into a desert." Angelus Silesius, *Der cherubinische Wandersmann*, 61. [CW 1.7: 28.]

Godhead, no one asked me where I was going or what I was doing. There was no one there to question me. But when I went out by dehiscence, all creatures cried out: "God." If someone were to ask me: "Brother Eckhart, when did you leave home?" this would indicate that I must previously have been inside. It is thus that all creatures speak of God. And why do they not speak of the Godhead? Everything that is in the Godhead is one, and of this nothing can be said. (Pf.:: 181,1–10) [DW 4,2: 771,9–772,4 (Pr. 109, "Nolite timere eos, qui occidunt corpus")]

Whoever speaks of God intends to speak of his most sublime counterpart, that is, of a being opposable to other beings. He invokes him as the one who saves, the one who judges..., always as the Other. But to speak of the Godhead is to think of a pre-originary origin, prior to all opposition; it is to think of God's "pure nature," his "concealed intimacy," his "abysmal," "limpid," "hidden, anarchic essence." As in Zen, properly speaking the pre-originary origin is not. The purity of the divine nature is sheer nothingness. Indeed, if the anarchic origin were to be, its being would make it opposable to other beings. If the sermon "*Beati Pauperes Spiritu*" still calls the negated *archē* "first cause" this only indicates Eckhart's embarrassment in being unable to express a non-metaphysical thought in a metaphysically fixed language:

> When I still stood in my first cause, I had no God, I was cause of myself [..., R.S.] But when by free will I went out and received my created being, then I had a God. Indeed, before there were creatures, God was not yet God, but he was what he was. (DW 2: 492,3–4; 492,7–9 [Pr. 52, "Beati pauperes spiritu"])

He was what he was: the anarchic origin is radically unknowable. The expression "I was cause of myself" is very strong: according to the traditional teaching God alone is *causa sui*. Here it is applied to man. Let me conclude by continuing the quote from this famous sermon which suggests perfectly the ultimate stage of the loss of the origin on the way of releasement:

> This is why I pray to God to rid me of God, for my essential being [*mîn wesenlich wesen*, R.S.] is above God in so far as we comprehend God as the principle of creatures. Indeed, in God's own being, where God is

raised above all being and all distinctions, I was myself, I willed myself, and knew myself to create this man [that I am, R.S.]. Therefore I am cause of myself according to my being which is eternal, but not according to my becoming which is temporal. Therefore also I am unborn, and according to my unborn being I can never die. According to my unborn being I have always been, am now and shall eternally remain. What I am by my [temporal, R.S.] birth is to die and be annihilated, for it is mortal; therefore with time it must pass away. In my [eternal, R.S.] birth all things were born, and I was cause of myself as well as of all things. If I had willed it, neither I nor any things would be. And if I myself were not, God would not be either: that God is God, of this I am a cause. If I were not, God would not be God. There is, however, no need to understand this. [DW 2: 502,4–504,2 (Pr. 52, "Beati pauperes spiritu")]

16

The Law of Nature and Pure Nature: Thought-Experience in Meister Eckhart

(1984/1986–1987)

Schürmann first presented this text in German at the Kyoto Philosophy Symposium in 1984. His own English translation, which serves as the basis for our edition below, was published three years later. In contrast to chapter 15, here Schürmann views the gap between Eckhart and Zen to be unbridgeable, owing to a lingering intellectualist theocentrism. This chapter overlaps in part with the material on Eckhart in Schürmann's posthumous magnum opus Broken Hegemonies, *although in the latter work Schürmann will praise Eckhart precisely for what he faults him for in this essay. Rather than failing to cross over into the pure nature of the Godhead (and hence to approximate Zen), Eckhart accepts that both it and natural law are simultaneously legislative; for the late Schürmann, Eckhart becomes a paradigmatic thinker of the tragic 'double bind.'*

"Die kleinste Kluft ist am letzten zu überbrücken."
("The narrowest cleft is the last to be bridged.")
Friedrich Nietzsche[537]

In an encounter between Eastern and Western thought, the European tradition of natural law must appear as an entirely foreign body to the Asian counterpart, who lacks any equivalent of it. In the tradition of so-called classical natural law, from Cicero approximately to Duns Scotus, philosophers sought to derive the general foundations of our knowledge of right and wrong from the order of nature, both external and internal. They also sought to deduce from these principles certain contents, even propositions of law.

As in many instances of the tradition he received, Meister Eckhart's concept of nature, too, stands out as a borderline concept. On the one hand, Eckhart repeats arguments, common in the School,

---

537 Friedrich Nietzsche, *Also sprach Zarathustra*, Zweiter Teil, "Das Nachtlied." Trans. Walter Kaufmann. *Thus Spake Zarathustra* (New York: Penguin, 1978), 106.

which straightforwardly presuppose the representation of nature as a pregiven order. In this scholastic strategy in his doctrine, external nature appears as a hierarchical system of beings, and inner, i.e., human, nature appears as a hierarchical system of powers of the soul. These two orders correspond to each other. They prescribe for man goals which 'naturally' steer his actions and which he has therefore an obligation to pursue.

On the other hand—and this concern outweighs and eventually cancels the scholastic—Eckhart is interested in understanding nature not as pregiven hierarchy but as an event, not as a text but as *texere* [intertwining], not as an organized whole (*natura*) but as a happening (*nasci*: 'to be born,' the verb from which derives the noun 'nature'). What amounts linguistically to a step back from the nominal to the verbal form implies in fact no less than the decline of the classical natural law constructs altogether (to be restored on a totally different basis only in the 17th century). In his thought-experience leading to that step back as well as to that decline, Eckhart approximates experiences that speak through certain texts of Zen Buddhism. For example, his doctrine of 'divine darkness' and 'wasteland' points in this direction; they call to mind the concept of *śūnyāta* which is often translated as 'emptiness.' Buddhist connotations may also be seen in the contrast he draws between the creaturely given properties and the task to detach oneself from them, which reminds one of the dialectic of self-nature (*Jisho*) and non-self-nature (*Mu-jisho*). Moreover, the experience that all things originate in the soul may have its counterpart in the experience of the 'middle' (*chu*). The all-important 'return to the world,' due to which active Martha is said to have chosen the better part over contemplative Mary, has a genuine Zen ring insofar as in Zen all activity is to be carried out with selflessness (*anātman*). These various points of resemblance form a counter-strategy to his scholastic strategy. However, they bring Eckhart only into the vicinity of Zen. The 'narrowest cleft' of which Nietzsche says that it is the last to be bridged separates Zen from even his most radical teachings.

It is difficult to describe this vicinity because our Western languages are generally 'metaphysical': we are able to understand experiences only to the extent that we grasp them conceptually (a redundant phrase, 'grasping conceptually,' since in Latin as well as in German the word 'concept' means 'what has been grasped'). As to the language of Zen, it is so intent on freezing all grasping and conceptualizing that it prefers risking endless paradoxes. Eckhart's verbs, as opposed to noun forms (he is not only the *Lese-und Lebemeister* [GA 13: 89], the master in reading and living but also a master in speaking) are meant to dissolve objectifications just as Zen paradoxes are. Still, Meister Eckhart remains a thinker. If at its core Zen Buddhism is "nonthinking," as Shizuteru Ueda says,[538] a complete harmony cannot be expected from a comparison with even the most daring thinkers of the Western tradition. Things look a little different when Zen is held to be "the basic fact in each philosophy and religion," as Daisetz Teitaro Suzuki believes, who declares categorically: "The light and life of all these religions and philosophies originate from that which I like to call their Zen-element."[539] But even so large a notion of Zen does not entail that in the speculative tradition this element should also be apprehended speculatively. The opposite is the case: the Zen-element would lie each time in the thought-*experience* upon which a given traditional conceptual system draws in order to sustain itself. Ueda's minimalistic and Suzuki's maximalistic interpretations of the East-West dialogue agree in that both require every instance of discursive thinking to be measured against an experience which itself escapes discursive representation. This requirement already accounted for the blunders of the various church commissions that were appointed to judge Eckhart's orthodoxy in the beginning of the 14th century. It should prevent us today from seeking contact points between Eckhart's sermons and Zen from the bird's-eye view of the 'history of ideas.' In what follows, Eckhart's displacement of the concept of nature will be examined as to the thought-experience from which it arises and which makes that displacement necessary.

To put it briefly, his thought-experience declares itself in the twofold sense in which he speaks of 'pure nature.' In Eckhart's scholastic thought strategy, this concept translates the Latin *essentia*, whatness or essence. In this sense, pure nature is always the nature

---

538 Shizuteru Ueda, "Das Erwachen im Zen-Buddhismus als Wortereignis," in Walter Strolz and Shizuteru Ueda (eds.), *Offenbarung als Heilserfahrung im Christentum, Hinduismus und Buddhismus* (Freiburg: Herder, 1982), 232.
539 Daisetz Teitaro Suzuki, *Essays in Zen Buddhism, First Series* (New York: Grove Press, 1961), 268.

of something. It names the genus or the species that sets a standard for the individual, which must correspond to that standard if it is to become what it is. In Eckhart's counter-strategy to such standard-setting arguments, however, the concept of pure nature recalls the Latin *actualitas*, the actual being of anything given insofar as it simply is. As such, pure nature cannot set standards any more. Its double meaning points to an experience of thinking in which it becomes impossible to conceive natural standards for our actions.

I. Pure Nature as a Standard

a) In-dwelling and Positing

"*In suo quisque est gradu firmiter collocatus*" [Each is firmly placed in its rank].[540]

Eckhart's understanding of nature sets out along familiar lines. Through his differentiation between 'in-dwelling' (*einsitzen*) and 'positing' (*setzen*) Eckhart repeats what has been construed since Augustine as intradivine *lex aeterna* [eternal law], and its external effect, *lex naturalis* [natural law]. The creator is the ordering principle insofar as he dwells in himself (*er sitzt in sich ein*); and he orders the whole creation by positing it. The order of nature consists in the interplay of this double positing. "God has no name but is a place and the positing of all things and the natural place of all things created. Where it is highest and purest, heaven has nothing spatial. Yet in its downfall, in its effect, it is the place and the positing of all things corporeal under him" (DW 2: 200,5-8 [Pr. 36b, "Ez was âbent des tages"]).[541] More succinctly stated: "Whatever is higher orders and posits all that is lower" (DW 2: 178,4-5 [Pr. 35, "Si consurrexistis cum Christo"]). And: "Within the order of nature, the higher dominates the lower and rules it naturally, and the lower obeys the higher and subjects itself naturally to it" (DW 2: 122,4-6 [Pr. 31, "Ecce ego mitto angelum meum"]). Such dominance and

---

540 Cicero, *De Republica*, Book I, 45.
541 [R.S. adds: "All quoted translations are revised by me."]

ruling is what Eckhart means by positing. God posits all things into their place and rank. He 'is the positing itself' and therefore is not in turn confined to spatial bounds. What appears as 'nature' here is that domain in which everything existent has been posited and ordered through 'downfall,' that is, through descending causality. Considered in itself—i.e., not in its relationship to the world—in-dwelling does not belong to positing, and God does not belong to the world. Only from a certain point of view, namely from that of causality, is God or 'heaven' part of nature, but not where he is "highest and purest."

God's own nature, which Eckhart also calls his 'Godhead' (*Gottheit*), will turn out to be just what is highest and purest. That, however, is something entirely different from nature in the sense of indwelling and positing or, as Eckhart expresses it in more obviously Neo-Platonic terms, from nature in the sense of God's resting within himself and his proceeding outward.

Whatever needs to be posited or must proceed outward in order to exist, is of a spatial kind and has its place. If one wishes to speak of a natural law according to Meister Eckhart one can only mean the order spread out in-between God's indwelling and the posited world. The German word for 'law' (*Gesetz*) contains this double meaning inasmuch as the prefix '*ge-*' indicates, on the one hand, a collocative form and, on the other, a past participle. What is *gesetzt* is both 'together' and 'put' thus. Eckhart calls 'downfall' such positing via the descending causality, in which God's indwelling becomes effective outside and beneath him.

In his indwelling God touches and sustains all posited creatures. Without his indwelling they would be annihilated. He lends them their being which is therefore not theirs. Due to that ontological poverty, no living being can hand down his own being to his offspring. Creatures receive their being on "loan" or "lease" (DW 5: 37,5 [*BgT*]). Indeed, whatever is posited belongs to him who posited it: "What is my own I owe no one. If I owe it to someone, it is not mine; it belongs to him who gave it to me" (DW 2: 108,2–4 [Pr. 20, "Praedica verbum"]). God's positing is always new: "No creature owns its being, for this depends on God's presence. If God turned away from his creatures for only a moment, they would be annihilated" [DW 1: 70,1–4 (Pr. 4, "Omne datum optimum")]. Eckhart formulated this doctrine of *creatio continua* [continuous creation] concisely in saying that God gives his creatures their being "*in fluxu et fieri*" (LW 2: 627, no. 292 [*In Sap.*]), in a continuous influx (*Zufliessen*) and becoming. If God's indwelling 'sustains' the posited creatures, the inevitable conclusion is that this indwelling designates the very being of which Eckhart says that it is God: "*esse est deus*," being is God [LW 1: 156, no. 12 (*Prol. gen.*)]. Thus the natural order is constantly posited anew in its being, which is not its own, and not only God's, but God. Such is the first aspect of the natural law as Eckhart describes it here. Without God's indwelling, nature would vanish into nothing.

The expression 'indwelling' (*Einsitzen*) can be taken as a remote translation of the Plotinian-Dionysian expression *aut-hypostaton*, 'self-possession.' If one remains content with this first aspect of the way Eckhart views the natural order, other aspects are bound to get lost. 'Dwelling' and 'positing' designate secondly an action—one and the same action. Only insofar as God is a dwelling in himself can he also 'give' his being (in contrast to the parents who must 'withhold' their borrowed being from their children so that these can be themselves). The one act of indwelling-positing amounts therefore to a sharing. Only an agent who possesses himself completely can also give himself fully.

Third, indwelling-positing induces "a highest and a lowest" in all creatures. What is the factor that sets apart the high from the low? "According to the nobility of its nature, the more each creature dwells in itself, the more it is capable of manifesting itself outwardly" [DW 1: 225,8–10 (Pr. 13a, "Sant Johannes sach")]. High is what comes closer to self-possession, low is what imitates it in a weaker way. In this way, [... says][542] Eckhart, a "golden chain" comes about in which "the highest [creature, R.S.] sets its foot on the head of the one below it" (DW 1: 211,10–212,3 [Pr. 13, "Vidi supra montem Syon"]). Each posited being, inasmuch as it possesses itself according to its place or rank, resembles the one that completely dwells in himself. However, the less it can communicate itself, the more remotely it resembles the self-possessing and self-manifesting origin. The act of indwelling-positing connotes therefore an order of participation.

---

542 [The English text was improperly typeset here and has been corrected in accordance with the German edition.]

Fourth and last, one must distinguish with Eckhart between original and non-original exteriorization (*Entäusserung*). It is divine or god-like to manifest oneself 'outwardly'; it is undivine or unlike God to look 'outside' oneself for what one lacks. In each rank, what stands higher in the chain of beings will be "rich in itself," "*per se dives*" [LW 2: 265, no. 38 (*In Eccl.*)], simply because it approaches more closely the unity of self-possession and of manifestation. As the distance from the origin increases, the dependence upon something alien increases also, along with need and desire.

The chain is broken only once, namely, after the first link: "God moves all things, while he himself remains unmoved" (DW 1: 224,12 [Pr. 13a, "Sant Johannes sach"]). This break means that the highest being also *in*habits all others: it must both occupy its place at the summit of the pyramid of nature and provide the space for all places in this pyramid. This systematic difficulty permeates theistic metaphysics since Plotinus and Augustine. Even Kant was to address it, viz. in the dynamic antinomies of pure reason.

* * *

To be sure, Zen Buddhism does not deny a pregiven order of nature. The masters even insistently urge their students not to violate it. However, at least of Japanese Buddhism, it would be difficult to say that it assigns this order the role of an ultimate representation. It is [not][543] conceived such that an obligation can be derived from it. The natural order does not provide rules or standards for human action. The Japanese word for nature consists of two signs, one of which means 'self,' and the other 'thusness.' Natural is whatever "is as it is": the mountain, high, and the valley, low. This order can also be called divine: "The Buddha is present in mountain and water" (*The Mountain-Water Sutra*[544]). It is true that the mountain and the water reveal their pure naturalness, their thusness (*tathāta*), only to a trained, quiescent eye. In Koan literature dogmatic questions are often answered in a blatantly paradoxical way, with a short description of nature. "A monk spoke to Tairyu: 'In the end the human

---

543 [Added in accordance with the German text: "Sie wird nicht so verstanden, daß man von ihr ein Sollen ableiten kann."]
544 [By Dōgen.]

body will decay. What is the incorruptible *dharma* body?' Tairyu answered: 'Flowers cover the hill like brocade, the valley is lying in deep shadow.'"[545] Instead of the requested information concerning death and immortality this master points to the hills and valleys: they themselves are the indestructible Dharma body. Dharma, then, must indeed be understood as the law of nature. It is the interdependency of all things, their mutual inclusion in becoming. Nishitani calls it "mutual penetration" (*egoteki*). In it "mountains and rivers, by being mountains and rivers, are not mountains and rivers; just as the self, by being self, is not self; and [in this alone, R.S.] mountains and rivers are real mountains and rivers, and the self is the real self such as it actually is."[546] In order to experience nature as pure being-as-it-is, the mind has to situate itself in such a way that the "thusness" can be apprehended as such. This situation is one of negation: as the mind turns to pure thusness, the mountain ceases to be a mountain, the valley ceases to be a valley. They are experienced as sustained by emptiness. Only in the mediation through this experience of *śūnyāta* is the mountain purely mountain, the river purely river, the valley purely valley, the self purely self. The mediating step through emptiness allows one to think of nature as thusness, but it does not allow one to construe the law of nature, Dharma, as the standard for ethical norms, let alone to derive obligations from it.

In certain currents of Confucianism it has been attempted to justify existing forms of society by deriving them from the pregiven natural order. Nothing of the kind happens in Zen Buddhism, with the exception perhaps of the first of three stages in learning, as described, for example, by Master Seigen Ishin: "Before a person studies Zen, for him mountains are mountains and water is water; when under a good teacher he gains insight into the truth of Zen, the mountains for him cease to be mountains, the waters cease to be waters; but later, when he truly reaches the state of rest, the mountains again become mountains and the waters again become

---

545 "Hekiganroku," in *Two Zen Classics*, ed. and trans. Katsuki Sekida (New York: John Weatherhill, 1977), 358.
546 Keiji Nishitani, *Was ist Religion?* (Frankfurt: Insel, 1982), 262. [Cf. Keiji Nishitani, *Religion and Nothingness*, trans. Jan Van Bragt (Berkeley: University of California Press, 1982), 166.]

waters."[547] The first stage is sustained by an interest in explanation. What is 'high' and what is 'low'? This question is put to nature, to man, and to society, just as it is asked in the Western metaphysical tradition, parts of which, as I have shown, Meister Eckhart appropriates unquestioningly. The mediating step through the thought of emptiness makes that interest vanish. An 'insight' occurs and the explanatory interest proves to be a disease of thinking. In the last stage, nature is again the issue, but in such a way that it can now be said: "In mountain and water, the Buddha is present." Nature manifests itself as unity, also called Buddha-nature. In it all otherness, such as between things and self, between high and low, has disappeared.

The following sermon by Butsugen may help clarify how the natural law is understood as simple, unique thusness:

> A while ago, the monk who was waiting on me said to me that it was raining too heavily and that the assembly would not be able to hear me. Oh, brethren, do you hear me now? I say: when the rain pours violently it is the best moment for all of you to listen. Most people would be able to say that the rain itself is the great sermon. Is that correct? I say: no, it is not! The pouring of the rain is the sermon *you* are giving. Do you understand? As soon as this insight comes to you, there is not much left for you to understand.[548]

The falling of the rain shows how things are connected to each other, for example, according to the law of gravity. Most people can read such phenomena, the book of nature, and are able to discover in it certain regularities. But the insight consists in seeing through the illusion of an otherness between self and rain. Thus when the falling of the rain becomes the sermon "which *you* give," then, nature becomes an event, a *nasci* or a birth from the original emptiness.

---

547 D. T. Suzuki, *Essays in Zen Buddhism*, 24, mod.
548 D. T. Suzuki, *What is Zen?* (New York: Harper & Row, 1972), 5, mod.

b) Alchemy of Forces

"Est quidam vera lex, recta ratio, naturae congruens… " [549]

Natural law in the strict sense, i.e., as obligatory for man, requires a reflection on the correspondence between nature outside us and within us. In Eckhart, this is done through a reflection on the powers of the soul. Since the beginning of classical natural theory in Stoic philosophy, this turn to the well-ordered soul has been the systematic point of departure. Cicero says: "There is one true law," namely "right reason, which coincides with nature." This law demands that reason rule over instincts. Eckhart, too, speaks of "right nature" (DW 1: 170,7 [Pr. 10, "In diebus suis"]), and one feels as if one were reading a Stoic of the middle period—or Cicero himself—warning against the illusion of the older Stoics who had thought one could achieve complete *apatheia* or impassivity of the senses: "Now, some simple-minded people believe they are able to reach the point where the presence of things stimulating their senses no longer means anything to them. But they won't succeed." Even the Roman pleasure in the struggle against pleasure surfaces in Eckhart: "We should be able to reach the stage where a well-ordered, godlike will renounces all natural pleasures […, RS] Look, then struggle would turn into sheer pleasure" (DW 3: 491,18–19 and 491,20–492,1–3 [Pr. 86, "Intravit Iesus in quoddam castellum etc."]). From the order of higher and lower spiritual powers, he even derives *apatheia* which is more of the spirit than of man: "The passions of the senses and the lower powers do not concern the spirit" (DW 5: 271,7–8 [*RdU*]). Finally, the 'right intention' (*rechte Meinung*) of man—apparently Eckhart's translation of *recta ratio*—gets inscribed into the eternal law according to which the world emanates from God, remains sustained by him, and aims back at him: "The beginning of this intendedness is God, he is the one who carries it out, and […, R.S.] it terminates in divine nature" (DW 1: 164,11–13 [Pr. 10, "In diebus suis"]). Thus the correspondence between the order outside us, or eternal law in the large sense, and the order within us, or natural law in the strict sense, remains in the high Middle Ages an unquestioned piece of

---

549 Cicero, *De Republica*, Book III, 22

doctrine. In its pre-Christian formulation this meant that the *imperium* of reason over the senses is rooted in God's *imperium* over the world. The moral natural law (*Gesetz*) is rooted in God's positing (*setzen*) of the world.

However, Eckhart takes some liberty with these transmitted thoughts. Impassiveness turns into non-attachment (*Abgeschiedenheit*). This, his main concern, speaks through the very order of nature. The *lex aeterna* demands non-attachment inasmuch as all species and genera tend to return to their 'pure nature.' This is now to be understood as the receptivity for species and genus-forms, abstracted from individuals. Thus the pure nature of grain consists in its susceptibility to yield oats, wheat, rye, barley; the pure nature of metal in its susceptibility to receive the forms iron, copper, etc.; the pure nature of animal in that it is open to the forms of anything capable of procreation. *Lex natura* instructs us to free ourselves of all forms and to come to resemble again the nature of our species: "Humanity in itself is dearer to me than this human being I am carrying" (DW 2: 18,4–5 [Pr. 25, "Moyses orabat dominum"]).

What is the aim when form returns or is 'driven back' into its pure nature? "I have said repeatedly that the soul cannot be cleansed if it is not driven back into its primordial purity in which God created it, just as copper cannot be turned into gold even when it is burnt twice or thrice without being driven back into its primordial nature" (DW 2: 599,1–4 [Pr. 57 " Vidi civitatem sanctam Ierusalem novam"]). Here, 'primordial nature' appears as a means, not as the end of a process. The goal of alchemical processes is gold. What goal does man pursue in cleansing himself through non-attachment? Just as in alchemistic purification, he aims at what stands highest in its genus and to which everything else in that genus is subordinated. The goal he pursues is God the Father. "That of which the Son is the image, the soul too shall become the image. When it is so led up into God, retained and contained in him, all creatures become subject to it" (DW 1: 399,2–4 [Pr. 23, "Jêsus hiez sîne jüngern ûfgân"]). The alchemist liquefies metals into fluids in order to produce the noblest of all metals; likewise, according to Eckhart's trinitary thought-model, the powers of the soul must be purified back until they reach God's pure nature and must thereby be ordered anew. The two strategies of the soul's breakthrough beyond the divine persons and of the birth of the Son in the soul lead to the same thoroughly traditional imperative of the well-ordered life of the soul. "With all its might, the soul must break through to the divine order" (DW 2: 121,2 [Pr. 31, "Ecce ego mitto angelum meum"]). Divine order consists in that from God's pure nature his triune nature springs forth: power (*potentia*, Father), wisdom (*sapientia*, Son), and love (*caritas*, Spirit): "What is God's order? Wisdom springs forth from divine power, and love, that is the fire, springs forth from both; for wisdom or truth, power and love/fire are on the periphery of the essence (*Wesen*) which exceeds everything, pure and without nature" (DW 1: 119,6–120,1 [Pr. 31, "Ecce ego mitto angelum meum"]). 'Exceeding essence' (*überschwebendes Wesen*) is Eckhart's translation of the Neo-Platonic *hyper-on*, divine being inasmuch as it transcends any conceptual grasp. He also calls it 'unnatured nature' in contrast to God's threefold or 'natured nature' (see DW 2: 120, Remark 1). God's inner order then, consists in that his *natura non naturata* [non-natured nature] releases out of itself his threefold *natura naturata* [natured nature]. According to the image of the circle to which Eckhart alludes, this means that God's pure nature orders his threefold nature the way the center of a circle orders each point on its circumference. "This then is the divine order. Wherever God encounters in the soul a resemblance with this order, there the Father gives birth to his Son" (DW 2: 120,4–5 [Pr. 31, "Ecce ego mitto angelum meum"]).

The details of this resemblance between the economy of the soul's powers and the divine economy cannot be pursued here. Just to mention the best known among these factors: in man, too, there is an "unnatured" core, his pure or formless nature. Eckhart calls it the spark of the soul. In the thought strategy in which he follows the natural law doctrine, this spark of pure nature functions as the ordering principle for intuitive and discursive reason as well as for the will or love. The sensual powers in man must be subordinated to the triad thus derived from the representation of the Trinity.

Here again, there may be good reasons to speak of a parallel. Buddhism acknowledges, to be sure, something akin to a hierarchical self in which the 'lower' levels must learn to obey the 'higher' ones. Perhaps the Zen path can even be summarized as that small step from the 'I' which is active to the 'Self' which lets everything be. If so, then there, too, one has to speak of a natural law which enjoins man to order his life. But this order consists in something entirely different from reason subjugating the senses. What is to be wrestled with is not the flesh but rather Karma, our reality, as it originates from causal chains that cannot be disentangled. These relationships unavoidably link every human being to all other living beings. They define therefore a law that integrates him in all three domains of Dharma. These domains are: (a) drives and appetites, (b) thing-like data in their countless forms and shapes, and (c) structureless gods and ideas.[550] Understood in this widest sense—in the singular, not the plural, form, i.e., not as designating elements of existence—Dharma is a law of being and a norm for man. But in its highest sense, as Buddha's body of truth, it is a "golden haired lion,"[551] something that can be contemplated only in silent wonder. The Buddhist learning process which most closely corresponds to the classic Western task of ordering one's soul, consists in fully assuming the consequences of one's own actions, that is, one's Karma. Both servitude to it and liberation from it appear most clearly in Keiji Nishitani's interpretation of Karma as the temporal nature of our being which we carry to term as a self-incurred bondage. In classical natural law-theory each spiritual power is bonded to its so-called formal object but can also liberate itself from its attachment to the world by turning away from it, going inward and upward. Nishitani describes Karma in a similar manner: "The unceasing newness of time shows simultaneously two aspects: on one hand, the aspect of creativity, of freedom and infinite possibility, on the other, the aspect of infinite burden, of inescapable necessity."[552] But since the Karma bonds are inescapable without being morally binding and as the Dharma law is obligating without imposing an order, any similarities between *lex natura* and the Buddhist natural law remain purely external. It is true that, both in Eckhart and Zen, these sets of laws, albeit essentially unlike each other, take on merely provisional roles. In Japanese this is called *ke* (appearance, illusion). In both contexts, systems of norms are made possible only by virtue of a more primordial event (in Japanese, *shoki*). Therefore such systems cannot pretend to be ultimately obligating. Eckhart declares the hierarchical

---

550 *Bi-yän-lu: Niederschrift von der smaragdenen Felswand* (*Writing from the Emerald Rock*), ed. by Wilhelm Gundert, 2 vols. (München: Hanser, 1960), vol. 1, 92.
551 *Bi-yän-lu*, 129.
552 Keiji Nishitani, *Was ist Religion?*, 337. [Cf. *Religion and Nothingness*, 220.]

order of nature, since it is created, to amount to mere nothingness.[553] Thus the *ordo* concept loses for him its hegemonic role.

II. Against Nature as Standard

Meister Eckhart's logic of non-attachment leads him beyond all mensurating representations, beyond all ideas of one being or one structure of beings capable of setting ultimate standards. This becomes evident in the two terms for which, it would seem, he is on the contrary most indebted to Christian Neoplatonic metaphysics: 'origin' (*Ursprung*) which he understands literally as a springing forth (*Entspringen*; middle high German *urspringen*) and 'swinging up/imaging back into God' (*Ein- oder Zurückbilden in Gott*). *Prohodos* (Latin, *exitus*) 'process or procession'—Eckhart also says 'emanation' (*Ausfluss*)—is the metaphysical model for the concept of origin; *prohodos* is the coming forth of everything created from God. 'Imaging back' (*Rückbildung*) comes from the opposite group of metaphysical concepts: *epistrophē* (Latin, *reditus*), 'return' or 'regress'; Eckhart says also 'swinging up' (*Aufschwung*), the going back of spiritual creatures to God. What displacement does Eckhart's concept of nature undergo when he understands process and return in terms of the coming-forth from pure nature and of the imaging-back into it?

a) Pure Nature as Origin

Eckhart, we have seen, also calls the whatness of a being—soul of an angel, God—its 'pure nature.' Species-nature or specific nature is 'pure' inasmuch as it remains free of all the supplementary and accidental determinations of a particular carrier. That is, however, not the only sense in which he speaks of 'pure nature.' The phrase is also used without any reference to a substratum, in an absolute sense, without designating the nature *of* anything. Thus he calls the hierarchy of all beings "the undefiled, pure nature." The point is that in it all differences between species disappear: "outside this pure

---

553 [The English text was improperly typeset here and has been corrected by adding R.S.'s own sentence in accordance with the German edition.]

nature even an angel is no more knowledgeable than this piece of wood" (DW 1: 212,1 and 212,6–213,1 [Pr. 13, "Vidi supra montem Syon"]). Eckhart's thought-model is clearly the doctrine of the pure act of being taught by his predecessor, Thomas Aquinas. Thomas held that the pure act is limited according to the rank of a thing. Thus an angel adds less matter and therefore less potency, less passive possibility, to the pure act than does a piece of wood. The actuality of being however, remains the same throughout all things, whether or not they are endowed with a soul or intellect. Eckhart now speaks of pure nature where Aquinas spoke of pure act. Just as with Thomas the *actus essendi* [act of being] as such is not susceptible of a more or a less or of a hierarchy, so the differences of natural species disappear, according to Eckhart, as soon as nature is contemplated in its 'purity.' He translates *esse* with the middle high German verb *wesen*, 'essencing' or 'being.'

By that he means—in total accord with Aquinas—the "simplicity and purity of being" (*Einfältigkeit und Bloßheit des Wesens*). Thomas, however, would not have added the following: "Turn away from all things and hold on to yourself as pure being" (DW 2: 266,1–2 [Pr. 39, "Iustus in perpetuum vivet"]). Pure nature in its absolute sense means pure actuality, the very essence of event, and so does 'being' (*Wesen*) when taken in its verbal form.

As he reduces pure nature to pure actuality, Eckhart announces the transmutation to which he subjects his understanding of nature: 'nature' now designates an event. Hence his phrase, repeated like a formula, "*wesen und nature*" (see, for example, DW 1: 109,10; 165,1; 193,9; 194,5; 199,7; 200,2; etc. [Pr. 6, "Iusti vivent in aeternum"; Pr. 10, "In diebus suis"; Pr. 12, "Qui audit me"]). This juxtaposition of being and nature is easily misunderstood if it is separated from active non-attachment. Non-attachment consists in unlearning one's hold on things as they are endowed with accidental properties; its goal is to conform with the necessary, and, in that sense, 'pure' nature, unrestricted by any kind of potentiality. He articulates conceptually his idea of nature as event. Yet his thinking remains obscure as long as that event is not taken to be non-attachment itself. Historically, Eckhart's two theses on being, which have earned him much controversy ever since his days, both bear out that non-attachment is the practical condition for theoretical thought: "Being (*das Wesen*) is God, *esse est deus*" (LW 1: 156, no. 12 [*Prol. gen.*]), and its consequence: "All creatures are sheer nothing" (DW 1: 69,8 [Pr. 4, "Omne datum optimum"]). Only by virtue of such a polar opposition between *esse* and *nihil* can nature as the hierarchy of all species lose its nomothetic function—a consequence that was not lost on the inquisitors. The hierarchical ladder of things posited by God, insofar as it is created, is nothing for Eckhart. Whatever owes its being to a maker, has no being of its own and is nothing in that sense. As a consequence, nature, constituted like a hierarchy of entities, ceases to provide the framework within which standards, rules, or norms can be legitimated. Only the event of turning away from things, from their classes and ranks of nobility, is of ultimate value to someone non-attached. The priorities among things have become meaningless. For the Latin tradition of natural law, it was the eternal order of essences that provided the unquestionable context from which to derive binding representations and statements. Eckhart now demotes this order to the rank of mere 'properties' (*Eigenschaften*) which one must learn to let be. Alone in such letting-be can nature be experienced 'purely,' being be proven pure actuality, and the whole metaphysics of substances be treated as provisional thinking.

Only on the condition of letting-be can the union of a man devoid of properties with a God equally devoid of properties be thought. Whoever remains is independent of both form and accident, that is, who remains free, is unattached to any form and chance occurrence, that is, whoever keeps himself free is necessarily of one and the same pure nature with God. In his doctrine of non-attachment, according to which formless God and formless man become "one being and one nature" [cf. DW 3: 322,8 (Pr. 76, "Videte qualem caritatem dedit nobis pater")], Eckhart does not present two entities, man and God, in order to compare their natures only to find God's nature greater than man's, and then to perform an abstraction from which the 'naturally' unequal somehow emerge as equal in spite of the distance between the uncreated and the created. Eckhart does not deny that God is greater than man; but he denies that thinking that analyzes substances and the eternal law connecting their essences learns anything essential about God. The double meaning of the old German word *Wesen* (being)—both a noun and a verb— renders Eckhart's intention in a nutshell. Non-attachment then amounts to renouncing thinking in nouns, abandoning substantial-ism and attempting a thinking in verbs. Contrary to contemporary German usage, in Eckhart *Wesen* does not mean 'essence.' He does not speculate about the nature of a thing belonging to this or that species or genus, but attempts another, a different thinking. This thought stands unattached to anything representable.

The Zen masters, as well, teach that the theory of substances and their whatness does not offer the experience of anything original or *essential*. This appears from a poem attributed to the Third Patriarch:

> The obstinate loses the right measure,
> inevitably turns the wrong way.
> Let go, and It will give itself!
> It never leaves, It never stands still.[554]

The doctrine of natural law would be nothing without the representation of a measure that always stands fixed. For example, the strength of the Stoic who does not pay more attention to the instincts than they deserve due to their rank, lies in his obstinate adherence to that pregiven order of high and low. He holds fast to that unchanging *imperium* of reason over all instincts. But the Patriarch teaches that the true measure reveals itself only to him who lets go and ceases to hold fast. Letting-go or letting-be thus seems to be the encompassing attitude required for a life in agreement with the right measure. In this it is similar to non-attachment.

The kinship with Eckhart may, however, go further and Sengtsang may be viewing the attitude of letting-go as more than the practical precondition for understanding the right measure. "It," the measure, he says, never leaves and never stands fixed. What can this mean if not that the right measure is always new yet not different each time? The always new and always different would be accidental; and the never new and never different would be the order of essences. The Patriarch seems to have in view neither the accidental and its contingency, nor substance and its permanence. What then is always new and yet never different? Only letting-go as such. It is ever anew a matter of 'letting-go' all representations of a supreme standard. If this be what the poem is meant to say, then its third

---

554 *Bi-yän-lu*, vol. 2, 85.

line must be understood as a tautology. Letting-go is nothing other than the self-giving of the measure. It is the measure itself. But that had turned out to be the very sense of non-attachment. According to Meister Eckhart, *Abgeschiedenheit* is not only the practical precondition for experiencing nature as 'pure'; it is nature itself understood as event.

In the same text that contains the quatrain, more is said of the 'measure.' "The polar star remains immovable. It stands still, without stain. So it offers itself eye to eye. There is nothing more to it." The polar star serves as the traveler's guide. From whatever region it is viewed, it stands there, unmoved. But there is nothing more to it, outside its being that mark or measure. The master who gives the instruction, explains it thus: "In the three domains there are no entities. How can one look there for a spirit? The four great elements (earth, water, fire, wind) are basically void."[555] In other words, if, in addition to that measure-giving—or behind it, or at its 'basis'—one were to look for that entity or even some spirit that sets the measure, 'one would have turned the wrong way.' Therefore this master praises one of his disciples who simply turns a somersault in front of him and then walks out. No entities, no essences, but merely the letting-go of entities, essences, elements, spirits: this is the right standard.

From the hierarchy of substances or essences it may be possible to derive a naturally obligatory order; not so from the event of non-attachment. In the step back from whatness to pureness (*Bloßheit*) the very possibility of a natural law in the classical sense breaks down.

a) Pure Nature as "Imaging Back"

The word-pair 'image-imaging back' (*Bild-Einbilden*) occurs with many meanings in Eckhart's sermons. Here too the semantic shift from the noun to the verb form is decisive for the problem of nature as ultimate representation and hence of natural law.

What Eckhart says of the noun 'image' sounds highly paradoxical: "Thus God has all images in him, yet not like the soul or any other

---

[555] *Bi-yän-lu*, 84.

creature but as God: in him there is nothing new and no image at all" (DW 2: 600,13-14 [Pr. 57, "Vidi civitatem sanctam Ierusalem novam"]). God has all images and no image. Eckhart distinguishes two modes of 'having-in-oneself': 'like the soul or any other creature' and 'as God.' In the soul, there is place for novelty. It can acquire new images. Such acquisition is the work of the intellect. That is why someone non-attached is said to keep himself free of "all those images he has ever comprehended" (DW 1: 12,2 [Pr. 1, "Intravit Iesus in templum"]). The soul gathers images (*Bilder*) by forming thoughts and opinions, by making up and cultivating representations, by mirroring this and that in itself. Man shapes (*bildet*) himself by constantly absorbing something new into his soul and bringing it into ever sharper focus.

God, by contrast, possesses images but is not shaped by them. He owns them without perceiving and shaping, without mirroring *(abbilden)* or forming *(bilden)* them. In him there is "nothing new and no image." He has "all images in him," not as copies *(Abbilder)* but as archetypes. In the soul all images have a mode of being. Archetypes are modeless: "In God the images of all things are identical but they are images of things non-identical. The highest angel, the soul and the mosquito have the same archetype in God" (DW 1: 148,1-3 [Pr. 9, "Quasi stella matutina"]). They are God himself: "What is in God, is God" (DW 1: 56,8 [Pr.3, "Nunc scio vere"]). When Eckhart states of God both that he has all images in him and that there are no images in him, one can easily see how the noun *Bild* translates the Greek '*eidos.*' He sides with Plato in describing God as the 'idea of all ideas' (see Plato's *Phaedrus*), and not with Aristotle. 'Image' does not translate the formative principle in an individual substance, knowable through abstraction.

He translates, however, the Greek term in yet a third sense: "A carpenter building a house has first preformed its image in himself" (DW 2: 397, 2-3 [Pr. 47, "Spiritus domini replevit orbem terrarum"]). Eckhart speaks here of the image, neither ideal nor abstracted, which must accompany every production. When a house is being built according to plan its idea must remain identical throughout the process of construction. The image of the house exists, then, first in the imagination of the architect, then in the master plan; it directs each step in the building process and finally stands there, realized in wood and stone, visible to everyone. In this instance, Eckhart means by *bilde* neither archetype nor copy, nor concept, but rather something like a blueprint-image.

If we assume with Heidegger that the experience of producing is the basic experience of Western metaphysics and that Aristotle's *Physics* has remained, for that reason, its "foundational book,"[556] it is not difficult to tell which has been the first and normative meaning of 'ground' or 'foundation' (*Grund*): it is the image in the sense of an artifact's aspect (*eidos*) as it guides its fabrication throughout the various production stages. The principle of sufficient reason *(Satz vom Grund)*, although formulated only much later in history, has obtained then, yet unformulated but still systematically first, ever since Aristotle analyzed motion as the key phenomenon in all being. Since the beginning of metaphysics, being as such falls within the domain of validity ruled by the principle of sufficient reason: nothing is made without a preconceived eidetic blueprint. Every becoming is guided by an 'image.' We have understood the end to which a case of becoming leads when we have understood that reason. 'End' in Greek is *telos*. The en-telechy of each being is its blueprint or its goal-image (*Leit- oder Zielbild*).

To the image understood as entelechy and as sufficient reason, Meister Eckhart contrasts another understanding of reason and thus of image. He follows a counter-strategy which already surfaced in the context of 'pure' nature and of the verb form 'essencing.' He actually states of God's 'pure' nature: "Here, God's foundation is mine and my ground is God's ground" (DW 1: 90,8 [Pr. 5b "In hoc apparuit"]). But if God's ground is my ground then it is not God's, and if my ground is God's ground, it is obviously not mine: just as previously 'pure' nature could be neither God's nor mine, here the otherness among substances is being traced back to a more originary oneness. As if to stress that in simple or pure nature the one ground cannot serve as an eidetic blueprint for any being, Eckhart at once rules out any teleological construct of this oneness as a misconception: "You must produce your works solely from this innermost ground—without any why" (DW 1: 90,11–12 [Pr. 5b "In hoc apparuit"]). Without why: that is to say, without the goal or end

---

556 Martin Heidegger, *The Essence of Reasons*, trans. Terrence Malick (Evanston, IL: Northwestern University Press, 1969), 111 and *Wegmarken* (Frankfurt: Klostermann, 1967), 312. [GA 9: 242]

that my being aims at, according to Aristotle and Thomas, by virtue of its form.

Quite as before, Eckhart pursues this counter-strategy against the prestige of teleology by means of a verb: 'imaging'; thus he states "one must be imaged back into the simple good which is God" [DW 2: 528,6-7 (Pr. 53, "Misit dominus manus suam")]. 'Imaging-back,' then, implies again that in its process anyone who keeps himself non-attached both loses all images and retrieves them all in their fullness. He loses all images as representations to which one can cling; he retrieves all images as archetypes of the persons of the Trinity as well as of all things created. He finds himself "imaged-back into the godhead, the first image without image" (DW 2: 456,12-13 [Pr. 50, "Eratis enim aliquando tenebrae"]). Renouncing representations, he gains archetypes, since in the godhead, "all that lies a thousand miles away from me is as close to me as the place on which I am now standing; there is fullness there and completeness of the whole godhead, there is oneness" (DW 2: 86,7-87,1 [Pr. 29, "Convescens praecepit eis"]).

He who lives 'without why,' without any representation of a *telos* deemed natural, succeeds at imaging himself back into the one ground, into oneness. This ground or oneness, however, cannot be flatly equated with God. Therefore Eckhart must differentiate between God and godhead; "God and godhead are as far apart as heaven and earth" [DW 4,2: 767,3-768,1 (Pr. 109, "Nolite timere eos, qui occidunt corpus")].[557] The origin is a groundless ground, an abyss; and since it yields no sufficient why, no eidetic blueprint for making and acting, it is essentially indeterminate. "No image reveals the godhead for us" (DW 3: 323,3 [Pr. 76, "Videte qualem caritatem dedit nobis pater"]). Therefore he also calls it a wasteland or desert (DW 1: 171,14-15 [Pr. 10, "In diebus suis"]). Thus Eckhart opposes imaging-back, godhead, and groundless ground to image, why and sufficient reason.

Nature as whatness corresponds to image, why and sufficient reason; while pure nature corresponds to imaging-back, godhead, and groundless ground. "The soul must be imaged-back into the primor-

---

557 Meister Eckehart, *Deutsche Predigten und Traktate*, ed. Josef Quint (Munich: Hanser, 1963), 272.

dial purity" (DW 1: 56,1 [Pr. 3, "Nunc scio vere"]): into indeterminate purity, but not into any eidetic nature. In the context of imaging-back, nature therefore appears as "groundless nature" (DW 3: 113,3 [Pr. 66, "Euge serve bone et fidelis"]). Groundless ground and pure nature mean one and the same thing.

The oneness of the soul's and of God's ground pertains to the same order. This oneness, understood as a verb (*einen*), brings us closer to imaging-back. "When the soul gives up all attachment to images and alone beholds the single One, then the pure being of the soul passively (*leidend*) encounters the pure, formless being of divine oneness" (DW 3: 437,13–438,1 [Pr. 83, "Renouamini spiritu"]). What Eckhart here calls passivity *(Erleiden)* lies at the core of his doctrine of imaging-back. It indicates once again the process-character of being which renders nature, as an ultimate representation, inoperative.

During the years of his most intense preaching, Meister Eckhart was the Prior of the Dominican monastery in Strasbourg. Just before that time, some particularly realistic stained-glass windows had been installed in the nave of the cathedral for the instruction of the common folk. What happens, now, when someone asks (about these paintings): "These are Karl the Bald and Ludwig the German during the oath-giving at Strassburg?" Eckhart answers: "The image is not 'of' itself nor is it 'for' itself" (DW 1: 269,2–3 [Pr. 16b, "Quasi vas auri solidum"]). Whoever is struck by the colors and the new painting technique has not understood it as *image*. It is not 'of' itself, i.e., it does not exist out of its own pictorial resource but out of Karl's or Ludwig's whom it represents. Nor is it there 'for itself,' i.e., for its own sake, but for the sake of the beholder. Eckhart expresses this non-being of the *image*, which is but a consequence of his thesis about the non-being of all creatures, by pointing again to nature: the object is reflected in a natural way and reaches the beholder naturally. Here, 'natural' means: without mediation, without any effort of the will. "The image receives its essence immediately from that whose image it is, over and above the will, for it issues naturally and breaks out from nature just as a branch from a tree" (DW 1: 265,9–266,1 [Pr. 16b, "Quasi vas auri solidum"]). In a faithful portrait a face presents itself as immediately as a branch grows out of a trunk. In the terms of the metaphysics of *wesen*—the verb 'being,' not the noun 'essence'—this means that the image 'is' neither glass nor color; its being is *showing*. This does not mean that Eckhart intended to deny the existence of substances such as glass and color in the painting. But he denies that a theory of substances allows one to understand at all the process of iconographic cognition, for it deprives the metaphysician of ways to thematize the event 'this is Karl' as such. Hence Eckhart's strategy against the theory of substances. The same concern underlies his reference to passivity or suffering—to *pathein* and pathos—hence his 'pathetics' of non-attachment. Being is always to be understood as happening. A picture such as the stained glass window has no being of its own, it bears or suffers the being of Karl the Bald and Ludwig the German. As a picture it is but a copy, it is entirely the coming-to-presence of what it represents.

This understanding of being as event also shows in which direction the opposition between image and imaging-back is meant to point. The soul as rendered one with the imageless godhead becomes a pure reference (*Verweis*), a pure 'with' (*ad*) turned towards the godhead. It becomes a pure "adverb" (*Beiwort*) (DW 1: 154,7–155,3 [Pr. 9, "Quasi stella matutina"]).[558] But the soul can only be so "turned towards God" (John 1:1) if it keeps itself actually non-attached to any image as representation, just as I recognize the image of a face only in actual beholding. In the activity of seeing or hearing, the *means* and thereby the substances in their otherness, fail us. With the imperative of 'imaging-back into God' Eckhart makes the Aristotelian tradition his own, according to which, in actual understanding, the otherness of substances is annihilated. The soul's 'imaging-back into primeval purity' thus points to the direction of pure *energeia*. This, in pure nature, is of one and the same actuality with God. In that direction of thinking, it becomes impossible to maintain nature as a system of hierarchical orders. Ultimacy belongs solely to the event adumbrated by such expressions as imaging-back, breaking-through, and being born (*nasci*, whence *natura*). With the injunction to image oneself back into an originary purity, Eckhart may come the closest to Zen Buddhism. Such a comparison touches, however, upon the most difficult issue

---

558 [R.S.'s English text reads: DW 1:164,12–14. Reference has been corrected in accordance with the German edition.]

in the Japanese-European dialogue. That issue is expressed in the Sanskrit concept of emptiness (*śūnyāta*). It seems that the Eastern party is more willing than its Western counterpart to recognize that issue behind Eckhart's metaphors of 'purity,' 'wasteland,' 'desert,' 'unrepresentable origin.' The theistic concerns of the Christian commentators usually set barriers to a simpler thought-experiment. Precisely from the viewpoint of classical natural law theories one can only agree with Nishitani when he writes that in non-attachment alone—"as understood by Eckhart or the Buddhistic *śūnyāta*"—"submission to the power of the law is at the same time emancipation from it." Nishitani quotes Eckhart's Augustinian phrase according to which "God's ground in me is closer to my own self than I can be" [cf., e.g., DW 3: 142,2 (Pr. 68, "Scitote, quia prope est regnum dei")]. The 'suprapersonal aspect' in Eckhart's concept of God, he adds, points to emptiness, especially "when Eckhart speaks of absolute nothing in order to designate the *Wesen* of the personal God."[559] Thus purity (*Lauterkeit* or *Bloßheit*) and emptiness share at least a few traits. Both name an absolute nothing, not the relative one which Nishitani identifies with the *nihil* in 'nihilism'; both point to an event designated by a verb (*Wesen*); in both the natural order with its laws remains something provisional, without ultimate binding power; in both, a concrete liberation or emancipation occurs; and, in the pursuit of each of them, one eventually returns to a 'ground' which, even though it is the original fullness of natural forms, provides no sufficient reason, since, as 'pure,' it cannot be thought of as *a* being.

In spite of the obvious affinity with Eckhart's description of the godhead's original purity and of man's imaging-back into it, the "narrowest cleft" becomes apparent, too, that which separates him from Zen and of which Nietzsche says that it is last to be overcome. All Meister Eckhart's fervor is devoted to theism. He wants it nude, in its most extreme dispossession. For all their radicalism, his metaphors remain for him ways and means to transfer (*meta-pherein*) ourselves into God. It is an open question for me if the same holds for the Zen metaphors. A Koji (independent scholar) "awakened to the great insight," that is to *satori*, and composed the following

---

[559] Keiji Nishitani, *Was ist Religion*, 161ff. [Cf. *Religion and Nothingness*, 90.]

poem in which concepts of opposites such as 'all-one,' 'learning-non-willing,' and 'Buddha-emptiness' are used equivalently:

> The great All congregates in One.
> The individual learns to be without will.
> This is the practice ground of the exalted Buddha.
> The heart is empty; the home-coming is accomplished.[560]

III. The Far East

The Neo-Platonic thought-model of emanation and return allows one, by way of a conclusion, to describe in greater detail the "narrowest cleft" that separates Meister Eckhart from Zen. Shizuteru Ueda writes: "Motion out of oneself is extreme self-negation and motion back into oneself is the most immediate self-affirmation."[561] It is noteworthy that in Zen, (1) the dialectic of going-out and coming-back, *exitus* and *reditus*, is placed solely within the human realm; (2) negation precedes affirmation; (3) apophasis belongs to going-out and kataphasis to return; (4) the twofold motion has a goal: the self. The objective of Zen dialectic is to free the self from itself so that it can give itself over to the non-self and thus truly find its way back to itself. These four points place Meister Eckhart near the Zen masters but they also point to a distance that remains hard to bridge—the distance between Eastern thought and Western monotheism.

1) In Zen, going-out and return are theoretical denotations for what is called, from a practical viewpoint, 'the great death': the turning away from the self-enclosed 'I-am-I' and from its consequences such as ignorance (delusion), hatred and greed. To be sure, for Eckhart, flowing-out and breaking-through have an eminently practical meaning too, but the praxis he has in view—non-attach-

---

560 *Bi-yän-lu*, vol. 2, 176.

561 Shizuteru Ueda, "Die Bewegung nach oben und die Bewegung nach unten: Zen Buddhismus im Vergleich mit Meister Eckhart," in Adolf Portmann and Rudolf Ritsema (eds.), *Eranos Jahrbuch* 1981 (Frankfurt: Insel 1982), 237. [Cf. trans., "Ascent and Descent: Zen in Comparison with Meister Eckhart (I)," in *The Eastern Buddhist* XVI, no. 1 (1983): 62].

ment—has no sense other than uniting one with God. This becomes clear precisely in the moral interpretation of the flowing-out and breaking-through. Non-attachment remains meaningless unless one treads its path unto God's pure *actualitas* (*bloßes wesen und bloße nature*). For the non-attached, says Eckhart, the beginning and end of all striving is God; likewise "the fulfillment of striving is God himself and it is pure divine nature" (DW 1: 164,12–14 [Pr. 10, "In diebus suis"]). In such contexts, and against the scholastic background, 'pure nature' and 'God himself' designate the same thing since only in God does actuality exclude any potentiality, or, as Eckhart says: pure nature excludes any species nature and any receptivity for properties. As was shown, the metaphysics of emanating and returning gets displaced toward the processes of 'originating' (*Ursprung*) and 'imaging-back' (*Einbilden*). Such a displacement in no way amounts to abandoning the theistic arena. On the contrary, Eckhart seeks to speak of God in a less representational way than metaphysics would allow.

2) The dialectic of negation and affirmation stands in a different context for Eckhart and is structured differently than in Zen. Eckhart's concept of flowing-out may be a translation of the Plotinian *prohodos* or the Biblical creation but in both cases it means an affirmation, which is God's affirmation of the sensible world. Not before German Idealism did the second term of the triad 'indwelling—flowing-out—breaking-through,' which is the positing of the other, take on the character of a negation. Only after the turn toward speculative subjectivism can the old triad be rephrased as 'position—negation—superelevation.' Eckhart does not at all understand the second term as God's self-negation, be it only because this would contradict the so-called 'analogy of attribution.' If in Zen there is no affirmation without negation, no 'downward path' without an 'upward path,' this may give, in Eckhart's view, an acceptable description of a lifetime's task—a description, nevertheless, that leaves the sense of the task unnamed. Moreover, if the first term of the triad, in-dwelling, is understood as self-closure (*Selbstverschlossenheit*)—Eckhart calls it "property"—then the ethical triad 'property—denial—affirmation' perverts the theistic model 'indwelling—flowing-out—breaking-through.' As Zen Buddhism does, Meister Eckhart regards this reversion as the root of all human evil. But for him it would remain incomprehensible as perversion if we

did not already know basically the archetypal model and did not measure our own actions on it. In Neo-Platonic terminology, the gap which opens here between Eckhart and Zen can be described as the disregard in Zen for a first model. If the copy (*Abbild*), *eidōlon*, is a distortion of the first model (*Urbild*), *eidos*, then Buddhism remains mute before the origin of beings so distorted, prior to their distortion. Eckhart, on the other hand, traced that origin beyond any being. His first model can therefore be called hyper-eidetic.

3) In the realm of knowledge, the Zen teachers and Meister Eckhart seem to agree in preferring the negation, apophasis, over all affirmation, kataphasis. As for Zen, the impossibility of purely cognitive illumination is exemplified by each Koan in its very paradoxical style. Eckhart held what his own masters taught concerning God: *scitur melius nesciendo* [he is better known in unknowing] (Augustine) and *de deo non possumus scire quid sit* [of God we cannot know what he is] (Thomas).[562] Eckhart's kataphatic statements—for example, about the higher and lower ranks of certain powers of the soul—follow from the doctrine of flowing-out, as his apophatic statements, from that of breaking-through. In Zen Buddhism the situation is reversed. Apophasis belongs to the going-out and the kataphasis to the return. Motion outward from the self, as its own negation, is here apophatic. The self loses itself, it does not recognize itself anymore. It finds and recognizes itself again only when it has absorbed into itself both nature and its fellow-humans, and has returned into itself. Here, too, the cleft between Eckhart and the East seems to be wider than what their unanimous praise of unknowability might have led one to believe. Already for Plotinus the pure *energeia* of the 'One' and, for Thomas, God as *actus purus* were unknowable. We can know and name substances and their relationships but not pure processes. Eckhart's 'detachment' and the 'great Death' of Zen are such processes. In German, the words suggest this identity of processes, since the unattached (*die Abgeschiedenen*) are the dead. Still, the reversion of apophasis and kataphasis in the Buddhistic understanding of going-out and returning shows that in *satori* my true nature and with it all things are 'immediately' retrieved—not only instantaneously but also without

---

562 [Cf. Augustine, *De Ordine*, 16.44 and Thomas, *S.Th.* I^a 1,7 ad 1.]

any mediating agency. If, according to Eckhart, negation and not affirmation defines the return, then my nature and the world can only be retrieved in the godhead. Both internal and external nature are mine in God's nature. Eckhart's sermons desubstantialize the original triad, 'God—I—World,' yet they do not turn it into a passage from I to world to self.

4) The goal of Zen dialectic lies, however, in just this return to the self. It loses itself in the upward path, and retrieves itself in the downward path. All exercise in negation and affirmation—be it in sitting, in dialogue or in service—are constantly aimed at the self. The exercises serve the purpose of separating the self from illusory substantiality and to dissolve it into a process. So the Zen student is able to retrieve his "face before he was born,"[563] just as Eckhart states of non-attachment that it sets man "as free as he was when he was not yet" (DW 1: 25,2 [Pr. 2, "Intravit Iesus in quoddam castellum"]). But for Eckhart such freedom or 'virginity' serves the purpose of receiving God in oneself and of giving birth again to his world in God's nature. Gaining oneself without gaining God amounts, for Meister Eckhart, only to losing oneself. It would mean taking the condition, i.e., the task to kill all properties and 'modalities,' for the conditioned, i.e., our birth in the godhead that is free of all property and modality—and thus to miss the unconditioned, the godhead.

In the four points mentioned, both the Zen tradition and Meister Eckhart go beyond metaphysics. It is non- or rather trans-metaphysical to think being as event. All concepts of nature are thereby made invalid that represent it as posited order. Moreover, it is non- or trans- metaphysical to assign to thought the singular as its content: the individual self in its awakening (Zen) or in its breakthrough into the godhead (Eckhart). The singular, as Aristotle had discovered, stands outside the reach of concepts. Eckhart's ministry, as a preacher already, indicates that his concern is with the singular. As to Zen, in the book *Hekiganroku* it is written: "Joshu asks Tose: 'What happens when a person of the great Death comes back to life?' Tose answered: 'You shall not go out in the night; wait for daylight and come.'" This means according to Katsuki Sekida's inter-

---

563 D. T. Suzuki, *Essays in Zen Buddhism*, 47.

pretation: "During the night thieves are out; you shall not go around stealthily. Come to me when you have reached Enlightenment."[564] Great Death and enlightenment happen each time to the singular and for this singular, or they do not happen at all.

As much as Zen and Eckhart resemble each other in these transgressions of the limits set by representational thought, it is clear that Eckhart, in the transition from laws of nature to pure nature, puts into question the metaphysics of *order* only to gain access to a more radically theistic thinking.

---

564 *Two Zen Classics*, 259 and 261.

17

Introduction to Lecture Course on Meister Eckhart

(1993)

Schürmann's final semester of teaching at the New School was devoted to Meister Eckhart (and to Heidegger's Being and Time*). Since the typescript for Schürmann's lecture course on Eckhart overlaps significantly with the material on Eckhart in* Broken Hegemonies, *where Eckhart is viewed as a thinker and lover of the tragic double bind, here we include only the course's introduction. The course description reads: "The aim of this course is, on the one hand, a reconstruction of the main philosophical issues in Meister Eckhart and on the other, an interpretation of what may be termed his ultimacy claim."*

My purpose in this seminar is twofold. On the one hand, we shall attempt a reconstruction of Meister Eckhart's thinking. This is a difficult matter. He wrote complex Latin treatises and commentaries, the most systematic of which—the *Opus Tripartitum*—remains incomplete. In these Latin works, Eckhart speaks primarily as a late Scholastic. He lived probably from 1260 to 1327: at a time when Neoplatonist, Arabic and neo-Aristotelian topics mix in an extraordinarily learned and over-determined filigree. This is the time of the great cathedrals, and philosophical speculation 'takes off' as it were more than ever. At the same time he was a preacher. He preached in medieval German, and in the history of the German language he figures as one of the great molders of the language, comparable to Luther two centuries later. In his German sermons he speaks much more freely, and it is through the transcripts of these sermons that the innovative force of his thinking has stayed alive. (These transcripts were written down—how, we do not know—by the highly educated nuns to whom he spoke, many of them widows from the great crusades). In his Latin and German works, the topics are essentially the same. But in the German texts his formulations are more daring. Boldness of thought and of phrasing is indeed what characterizes his teaching throughout. It brought him before the Inquisition, and he died shortly before the papal bull[565] that condemned some of his utterances appeared.

On the other hand, I wish to propose an interpretation in this seminar. Philosophers are professionals of what one may term ultimacy claims. Now Eckhart fulfills that job description of the philosopher in a rather strange way. He constantly speaks as an advocate of a highly stratified universe, obviously indebted in this to Neoplatonist constructs—as well as to a feudal view of the world which it would never occur to him to put into question (he was a knight of the von Hochheim lineage). Universals are more real than individuals, and universals come in a graded order. According to this argumentative strategy, philosophy is what it has been primarily in the West: advocacy of order.

Yet there is another conceptual strategy that he pursues throughout his Latin as well as German texts. This strategy brings together the cluster of concepts for which he is actually known. He speaks of "the birth of the Word in the Soul," of man's "breakthrough beyond God," of "detachment" and "releasement," of the "ground of the soul" as "identical with the ground of God"... The organizing concept—but it is not a concept, rather a description—in this other strategy is 'detachment,' in modern German *Abgeschiedenheit*. The birth of the Word in the soul, the breakthrough, etc. all designate aspects of detachment.

No hierarchy here any more, but a deliberate and vehement gesture to erase hierarchies. "I recently wondered whether I should accept or desire anything from God. I want to consider this carefully, for by accepting anything from God I would be under him as a servant, and he in giving would be like a master. But it should not be thus with us in eternal life" (DW 1: 112,6-9 [Pr. 6, "Iusti vivent in aeternum"]; W II, 136, text condemned by the papal bull).[566] "Detachment forces God towards me" (Pf.: 484) [DW 5: 402,5 (*Vab*)]. "I pray God to rid me of God, for my essential being is above God insofar as we comprehend God as the principle of creatures" (DW 2: 502,6-7 [Pr. 52, "Beati pauperes spiritu"]; W II, 274). This erasure of nature as order is stated perhaps most forcefully in the Latin works: "That alone

---

565 [Titled *In agro dominico*.]
566 ['W' refers to the three-volume translation of Eckhart by Maurice O'C. Walshe titled *Sermons and Treatises* (London: Watkins, 1979–1987).]

properly lives which is without a principle" (*Hoc enim proprie vivit quod est sine principio*, LW 3: 16, no. 19 [*In Ioh.*]). God is 'principle' with regard to organized nature. He is its beginning and its end. On the other hand, to speak of breakthrough, detachment, living without a principle... opposes to the advocacy of order a line of argumentation of which it is not clear that it is comparable with order.

For pre-moderns, order depends mostly on the representation of ends. Nature is well ordered inasmuch as every agent in it pursues its natural end, that is, what it is made for, its 'why.' Now Eckhart conceives this dialogue about the why, hence about teleology: "'Why do you love God?—'I do not know, because of God.'—'Why do you love truth?'—'Because of truth.'—'Why do you love justice?'—'Because of justice.'—'Why do you love goodness?'—'Because of goodness.'—'Why do you live?'—'My word! I do not know! But I am happy to live'" (DW 2: 27,7-10 [Pr. 26, "Mulier, venit hora"]; W II, 97). Or again: "Those who seek anything with their works, those who act for any why, are thralls and hirelings" (DW 2, 253,4-5 [Pr. 39, "Iustus in perpetuum vivet"]; W II, 97). This thematic discrepancy between a rigid teleological natural order and the repeated gesture of erasing it makes for conceptual incongruity. It is what I wish to pursue in my remarks this semester.

* * *

Neo-Aristotelian 'Being,' Arabic 'Intellect,' Neoplatonist 'Oneness'

I hope that the part of reconstruction can be taken care of primarily by students' reports. I could then devote most of my own presentation to the conceptual incongruity in question. Not that this is somehow a marginal issue. As I have tried to suggest, the conflict between the two argumentative lines goes to the heart of the matter in Meister Eckhart. It may well be the 'very issue' at stake in all of his diverse works. Also, in tracing that discrepancy between natural order and—to make it brief—detachment, all of Eckhart's main themes are of course involved. I therefore suggest that at least some of the seminar reports be historically oriented. The historical connections are not something that I plan to pursue, although they are indispensable to understand Eckhart. It would be very helpful if some of you gave presentations showing Eckhart's philosophical debt to Aristotle, to the Neoplatonists in general and Augustine in particular, to the Arabs. It would also be very welcome to have some reports about the 'history of efficacy'[567] of Eckhart's thought, that is, of what has become of it in the later history of philosophy.

For now I wish to draw your attention to three thematic strains in his writings: Neo-Aristotelian 'being,' Arabic 'Intellect,' and Neoplatonist 'oneness.' I want to point out briefly how Eckhart makes these received teachings his own, and how he displaces their meaning towards the thematic cluster of 'detachment.'

Neo-Aristotelian 'being.' In a well-known Latin text, "Parisian Questions" (LW 1: 156, no. 12 (*Prol. gen.*), trans. Armand Maurer, p. 85),[568] he writes "Being is God," *esse est deus*. Eckhart belongs to the Dominican School of Thomas Aquinas, and he stands in constant debate with Aquinas' neo-Aristotelianism. In Cologne he may even still have studied with Aquinas' teacher, Albert the Great who died in 1280 at the age of 87. Now Aquinas had said "God is being itself," *ipsum esse*. This had allowed him to hold that all things take part in God's being, hence the doctrine of the analogy of being. The important point is that in Aquinas' teaching of participation, things created make being *their own*. Now when Eckhart says 'being is God,' being no longer belongs to things. Rather—and we will see this of course in detail—they 'borrow' being from God, which remains God's. "All creatures have no being, for their being depends on God's presence. If God turned away for an instant from all creatures, they would perish" (DW 1: 70, 2–4 [Pr. 4, "Omne datum optimum"]; W I, 284). And in the Latin works: "nulla creatura habet esse" [no creature has being] [LW 5: 225, no. 73 (*Acta*)]. There is no longer an analogy by participation, but an analogy of total appropriation—'analogy of attribution.' You see at least that when one says 'being is God,' it is one whenever it occurs, and it is divine;

---

567 [I.e., *Wirkungsgeschichte*, often rendered less literally as 'reception history.']
568 [*Parisian Questions and Prologues* (Toronto: Pontifical Institute of Mediaeval Studies, 1974), modified. The citation is actually of Eckhart's general prologue to the *Opus tripartitum*.]

whereas when one says 'God is being,' God's being is construed as pure being, while all things created add something to being, namely their own limited way to be.

The point is that with this reversal of formulation, we have already a thought of identity. If being is God, then whenever we encounter *it*, we encounter *him*. One may call this 'mysticism,' but it is certainly not 'pantheism' since all assertions of identity in Meister Eckhart—this is something we will come back to constantly—depend on a certain way of life. His assertions of identity, such as 'being is God,' are not speculative assertions about nature, but practical assertions about a way of living. Which entails that this concept of being is different from the neo-Aristotelians': God, too, has to 'do' something. "If God is ever to catch a glimpse of it, it will cost him all his divine names and personal properties: all these he must leave outside should he even look in there" (DW 1: 43,3-5 [Pr. 2, "Intravit Iesus in quoddam castellum"]; W I, 77). That is, God has to give up his being as 'creator,' as 'Father, Son, Spirit,' as 'Savior,' etc. ... This assertion of identity in being thus indicates how Eckhart transmutes a metaphysics of analogy by participation into something entirely different. I will stress throughout that there is another way of thinking—a way other than metaphysical—that comes to the fore in Eckhart.

Arabic 'intellect.' Eckhart teaches furthermore that God is pure intellect.

> There exists nothing that is purer than God and more exclusively intellect than he. This is why God is unique. Also, since he is intellect or understanding, that is, pure understanding without admixture of any other being, this one God through his understanding calls all things into being. This is so because in him being is intellect. As much as a thing possesses intelligence, so much it possesses God. Indeed, God is present nowhere and never except in the intellect. (LW 4 : 267-70, nos. 301-304 [S. XXIX, "Deus unus est"])

At first sight, this is not difficult to understand. Eckhart speaks of the old doctrine of divine ideas. God calls all things into being inasmuch as he possesses in his intellect their ideas or forms. But then, and this is the interesting slippage here, among things created God is said to be present only in their intellect. Again, all speculation about nature is cut out. It is human intellect that is the locus of God. How so? The background here is the Aristotelian doctrine of the subsisting intellect as transformed by the medieval Arabs. Al-Farabi, Avicenna (Ibn-Sina), and Averroes (Ibn-Rushd), all three hold that the active intellect moves the world and that it is one in all thinking beings—in all men. As moving the world, it contains the forms of all things moved; as one in all minds, it accounts for their capability to know God.

Eckhart, now, goes one step further, leaving actually this intellectualism behind. "I declare that it is not my opinion that God understands because he exists, but rather that he exists because he understands. God is intellect and understanding, and his understanding itself is the ground of his existence" (LW 5: 40, no. 4 [*Qu. Par.* 1]; Maurer, p. 45). Eckhart here takes his distance from 'ontology' and tries to think purely of a process. He finds the model for this in Aristotle's treatise *On the Soul*, bk. III [430a3–4]: "In the act of knowledge, the knower and the known are one." We shall have to come back to this identity through *energeia*.

Neoplatonist 'Oneness.' The last strain of thought transmuted and de-metaphysicized by Eckhart that I wish to point out is Neoplatonist. In the high middle ages, Neoplatonism meant most of the time Pseudo-Dionysius Areopagita. His 'negative theology' is entirely a speculation about hierarchy. "The Hierarchy is a holy order, [it requires, R.S.] a knowing and an acting by which [our mind, R.S.] assimilates to the divine nature. Through the light granted from God, [the mind, R.S.] is raised in due proportion to the imitation of God" (*Celestial Hierarchy*, III, 1). The divine nature is oneness. Here oneness is the essential feature of a certain being (in Plotinus oneness is not the predicate of any being). A technical term in Dionysius is super-eminence. God is super-eminently good, true, one... Eckhart makes that hierarchical view his own:

> Now we speak of the soul's order. A pagan master says the soul's supereminent natural light is so pure and so clear and so elevated that it touches the angelic nature. It is so faithful [to the angels' nature, R.S.] and so faithless and hostile to the lower powers that it will not flow into these or illuminate the soul [in them, R.S.] unless these lower powers be subordinate

to the higher powers and the higher powers, to the highest truth. (DW 2: 121,3-122,4 [Pr. 31, "Ecce ego mitto angelum meum"]; W II, 33)

This highest truth is God's oneness.

The slippage away from the representations of hierarchy and order occurs as Eckhart displaces oneness towards a process that unites man and God. "Acting and becoming are one. God and I are one in this work: he acts and I become. [..., R.S.] Thus we are changed into God so that we may know him as he is" (DW 1: 114,2-115,2 [Pr. 6, "Iusti vivent in aeternum"]; W II, 137). Into this transmutation of oneness belong all of Eckhart's perplexing formulations of identity. "Identical is the event as God begets me as himself and begets himself as me. He begets me as his being and his nature. There is one life and one being and one work there" (DW 1: 109,9-11 [Pr. 6, "Iusti vivent in aeternum"]; W II, 135).

I have pointed out three displacements whereby Eckhart leaves—such will be my claim—metaphysics understood as a system of order. One of these displacements sets out from the neo-Aristotelian doctrine of being, the other from the Arabic doctrine of agent intellect, and the third from the Neoplatonist doctrine of the one. Each time the displacement leads toward a certain identity. But this is not an identity according to a logic of things. Eckhart is not saying that the entity 'soul' is identical with the entity 'God.' With Eckhart we will have to try to think differently than according to the logic of things. We will have to try to think according to his logic of detachment.

I should like to conclude with a quote from his Defense before the Inquisition. He may be taking back some of the sharpness of what I called his displacements, but he is explicit about where he wants to lead his listeners. The beginning of these lines contain an allusion to Pseudo-Dionysius' treatise *The Divine Names*.

> In the nakedness of his essence which is above every name, [God, R.S.] penetrates and falls into the naked essence of the mind which is itself also without a proper name [..., R.S.]. He gives to the mind his divine and deiform being. [..., R.S.] This is something moral. Man is to renounce everything and to bare himself [..., R.S.], to love God without mode and without any property entailing mode. (LW 5: 347-48, no. 122 [*Acta*])

Eckhart first gives one more description of non-entitative identity. Then he adds: "This is something moral." It is with the term 'moral' that he takes back some of the force of his other statements. Still it is clear that he is speaking of detachment: man is to renounce everything, bare himself, let-be all mode and property.

Appendix 1

The Word of God

(1964, trans. from the French by Ian Alexander Moore)

This paper was handwritten by Schürmann during his second year of studies at the Dominican school of theology Le Saulchoir. It was submitted to Father Dominique Dubarle for his course in fundamental theology on Spinoza's Theologico-Political Treatise. *It is dated February 1, 1964. The paper examines several stages in the development of the meaning of the Hebrew phrase* dabar ha-shem *('word of God') in the Old Testament, emphasizing its dual nature as received from above and as human, and its dual function as doctrine (the Ten Commandments) and as an unsettling event.*

To show with the help of fundamental givens in the exegesis of the Old Testament that the notion of the *Word of God* neither amounts to being simply the communication of knowledge received from on high nor is reducible to a simple human word.

Setting Out the Problem

To be sure, a study on the biblical notion of the Word of God should be centered on Him who is himself the Word [*Parole*], the *Verbum* [*Verbe*], the second Person of the Trinity. Through our acquaintance with the revelation of the New Testament, we know that it was He who lay under every manifestation of the divine, prior to or outside of explicit faith in Christ.

However, a consideration of only the manifestation of the Word in the Old Testament is itself rich in significance (as a *preparation* and an *example*) for the situation of Christ, who both came "directly from on high" and was "simply human."

As an elaboration of "fundamental givens in the exegesis of the Old Testament," our work will be comprised first of an

I. analytic part

where will attempt to indicate a few things about the

1. phrase [*mot*] "Word of God"

and

2. its history within the Old Testament.

Then, in a

II. synthetic part,

we will try to draw out

1. the full meaning of the phrase

and to show how

2. the prophet is the one charged with the Word, who in a simple human word expresses in a deeply upsetting manner "knowledge received directly from on high."

I. Analytic Part

Lacking in-depth exegetical knowledge, here we will have to content ourselves with only a few indications, poorly supported by too few biblical references.

1. *The word for "Word"* is almost always רָבָד, *dabar*, or one of its derived forms. Sometimes, it is true, it is situated on the borders of the *teaching* given by the priests; one then finds other roots.

At the origin of רָבָד (which the Septuagint translates either by *logos* or *rhēma, rhēmata*), there is the idea of '*being behind*,' of a *background* or *underside*. The verb then means '*to bring forth what was behind*,' 'to express what is in the heart,' or as S. Jacob says: 'actualize' ['*passage à l'acte*'].

It immediately appears that the two Greek terms render very poorly the profoundly *dynamic* meaning of Hebrew. We will have to come back to this.

2. *The chronology* not of the redactions but of the *history of Israel* shows that the word רָבָד has undergone an *evolution*. We will consider only that long period between the legislation at Sinai and the time of the great prophets, and we will distinguish three phases in this evolution:

a) Moses 'brings forth' the will of God that had been hidden up until then: the "Ten Commandments [*Paroles*]," *devarim*, will regulate life, indeed for the entire history of the People of God. There is thus an element of *constancy* here, of perpetual validity of the Word thanks to which *an event* acquires a meaning that will be valid for all times: Moses's encounter with Jahweh becomes normative for the personal life of all Jews of all times. This historical event is, to be sure, dynamic, upsetting to the highest degree, but we must not forget that the expression *dabar* is aimed at the *Law* much more than at the prophet and his action that reveals this Law. We can therefore summarize this first step by saying that the term *dabar*, *in the Decalogue*, first has *the meaning of constancy, of a norm, and much less of a deeply upsetting event*. The Greek translation by *logos* seems to be the most justified in this legislative context.

b) With Samuel, the word *dabar* expresses a more *personal* and *event-like* reality: God calls out "Samuel! Samuel!" (1 Sam 3:4) to give him a very precise historical mission: "You are to tell him [Eli] ..." (v. 13). It is a mission that applies to a specific moment in history and to a limited number of Jews: Eli and his family. The dimension "outside of time," which characterized the "commandments [*paroles*]" of the Torah, is absorbed here by the very "incarnated" dimension of a specific, effective word, to be addressed to a few determined faithful.

We summarize: *in the call of Samuel*, the *dabar* found an *event-like significance unknown in the Decalogue*, but which, although rich in consequences for *all* the people of Israel, *is valid initially for only a few beings*.

A further remark: the "effective word" was of primary importance for *all the peoples of the East*. What distinguishes the *dabar* of Jahweh from that of the other gods is Samuel's awareness of being called out to by a *personal God*, the God who has already spoken to Abraham, Isaac and Jacob, to Moses...

We will not return to this point. This awareness holds for all subsequent prophets; it is best expressed by this verse from the Song of David (2 Samuel 23:2):

> "The Spirit of Yahweh speaks through me,
> his word is on my tongue."

The one who is inspired is aware of being only *the instrument of someone else*. This digression brings us back to the very heart of the decisive stage in the evolution of the *dabar*:

c) *The Prophets*. If, in Samuel, the word was addressed only to one family, the great prophets feel they are *sent to all the people of Israel*. Just like Samuel, they speak by means of an effective word that brings about an event (or *ought* to bring it about: to obey the *dabar* is salvation; not to obey, perdition), but this event has *national dimensions*.

Sometimes, the order given by the prophet is even addressed to infidels: "'Up!' he said 'Go to Nineveh, the great city, and preach to them as I told you to'" (Jonah 3:2). It is thus by having faith in this word that one is saved, despite one's belonging to another people.

What is important in this final stage of our analytical research is the emphasis placed on *the public character of the preaching*, which, in the prophets, is added to *the word that provokes a salutary event* such as we had already encountered in Samuel.

We are at the end of our first part. The outcome reveals three phases of *dabar*:

– word once uttered by Moses, having perpetual value for all the people
– word uttered by Samuel against a family and asking for a specific event
– word uttered before an entire people, also asking for a specific event.

II. Synthetic Part

The goal of our research will now be to show from the givens already elaborated how the word of God in the Old Testament designates "the communication of knowledge received directly from on high" all the while being a "human word." We will limit our considerations to the last stage we have analyzed, namely, that of *prophetism*.

1. The full meaning of the word *dabar*.

It designates both a *meaning* that the man of God gives *to human and historical realities* and the exhortation *in human words* to conform to this "divine" view of things.

a) *The prophet is a giver of meaning.*

God, addressing his people through the prophet, wants them to *understand* their *destiny*. Because of the intimacy that unites him to Jahweh, the prophet *is acquainted with* this plan of God. He thus speaks to men to *make explicit* what they may already know *implicitly* through their faith.

The prophet 'knows' in the first place *the values of the current state of things*: he demands conversion, return, and penance. It is a knowledge which he gets from God whether by his lucid *view* of the situation in which he lives and that God shows him in its truth, whether by *vision, hearing*, or also by *prayer*. The prophet *says what he knows*, and he cannot help saying it; cf. Jeremiah who groans under the weight of his vocation, because the people are not always ready to receive this knowledge, this *meaning* of the state of things in which they live.

The prophet then 'knows' the *things to come*. It is in this sense that we usually speak of a 'prophet': he is acquainted with the destiny of Israel, as well as of other peoples, and he tries to express this knowledge of imminent threats and dangers. Here again, his preaching is often met with nothing but contempt and unconcern.

b) The prophet says more than just a human word.

If earlier we insisted on the *notional* character of the *dabar* by which the prophet preaches the true meaning of things, this preaching, as we have already said, is nevertheless also the preaching of an *effective, dynamic* word. Here we find the deepest meanings of '*dabar,*' which neither *logos* nor *rhēma*, nor even *rhēmata*, renders (the latter word nevertheless comes closest, insofar as it expresses the series of events that constitute the "history" of salvation).

The *dabar* is deeply upsetting because—whether through *gesture, language,* or *image*—it is linked to the truth of God: the "If you do not change your life…" repeated by all the prophets is an exhortation to conform to the salvation thus revealed. (Although the word "*revelation*" is improperly used in the context of visions and oracles, their sequence constitutes the *Revelation* of God throughout *history*.)

The full meaning of the word *dabar* thus includes both *the notional communication of the truth of God's plan* and a *preaching that derives its dynamism and effectiveness from this divine truth itself.*

2. A second synthesis: the person of the prophet.

Here, we will content ourselves with a simple summary of the elements already indicated that make up the 'prophetic attitude.' We mean that the one who is officially *charged with the dabar* re-lives within himself the two aspects that we have discovered in the Word: listening to the revelation of divine truths and announcing it to men through a preaching rich in event-like meaning.

May this remark serve as a *conclusion*: the eternal Word will perfectly contain in its incarnated person what the prophet lives while groaning and with his Ah! Ah! Ah! (Jeremiah 1:6). The Old Testament *dabar*, from Moses to the great prophets, was fundamentally only an *announcement* and preparatory *example* of the Word made flesh: Jesus Christ.

Appendix 2

The Unknown God, Early Draft

(1966, trans. from the German by Ian Alexander Moore)

This is a significantly different earlier version of chapter 4.

"God, what a time we're living in!" We treat the word 'God' in a way we would never allow ourselves to do with the names of our friends and family members. It would never at all occur to us to include someone who is close to us, our mother for example, in these never-thought-through phrases so as to lend them more weight. Too highly do we respect those whom we are fond of to grumble thoughtlessly about the times in their name. For, we know too well that behind this or that first name there is a heart that waits for words of affection and not careless repetition.[569]

When we have God so constantly on our lips, without thinking anything by it—should this perhaps be because we aren't at all acquainted with him? What do we know about God? Certainly, over the years, we have heard and learned a lot about him. But what, then, of him have we experienced?—just as, for example, I can have experienced, in interacting with another person, that he has precisely the same freedom, which I otherwise took for granted for myself, to do and to leave undone [*lassen*] what he wants; that he is not at all something like an admiration machine, before which I need only move into the right light to achieve the pre-calculated success; rather, I truly am dealing with a free human being. All of a sudden I may have felt that this other person has the power to refuse to trust me, to love something other than what brings me joy; indeed, that I will never grasp how it comes about that he can think so differently than I can, that he is so *free* to accept me as his friend or to refuse to grant me his thou [*sein Du*].—Such an experience, in which I encounter this-one-here with complete immediacy as the free, independent other is the experience of a mystery. "Truly,

---

[569] ['thoughtless circumlocution' (*gedankenloses Herumreden*) is crossed out in the typescript.]

I will never completely understand you"—this is how we express ourselves when the unfamiliar and different breaks forth from the vicinity of the familiar. The unknown, the unknowable, flashes up among the features that we know. From now on, we will be careful not to treat this person as though we had him[570] at our disposal at every step and turn. In his freedom, his mystery has confronted us.

Has God ever confronted us in the mystery of his freedom? Have we ever experienced him in his inability to be compelled, how it breaks forth here and there from a countenance among people? Then God would have become godly for us again, would no longer be the dullest word with which we decorate our empty phrases.— Let us examine for once how we actually speak about God. If God is to become meaningful for me in his divinity or Godhead [*Gottheit*], then each of the words that I use must possess a completely special weight of reality. Let us, for once, subject one or another of these words, with which we could answer the question "what do you know of God?," to closer scrutiny.

First of all, there is the word 'good.' Yes, God is good: in his goodness he created the world, sent us his son as the redeemer, and ultimately offered me salvation [*das Heil*]. We live in a time when Christians seem to rediscover the so often quoted sentence of the Gospel, "in so far as you did this to one of the least of these brothers of mine, you did it to me" [Matthew 25:40], in an entirely new way: the goodness that I show [*walten lassen*] to the poor and suffering is fundamentally already a piece of the infinite goodness of God himself. There are not two ways of being good, of which the one would belong to God and the other would be 'purely human'—just as there are not two types of love. Within my narrow limits, I succeed at being good by virtue of the limitless goodness of God, and I am able to love by virtue of the all-encompassing love of God.—Once we try to appreciate what we are actually thinking when we assert that God is 'good,' we are first confronted with the need to put ourselves into his hands: he is worth our trust, since he has stood by us so far and will continue to stand by us. But are we really building upon God when we think in this manner? Perhaps the word that Meister Eckhart called out from his pulpit to the faithful also applies to us:

---

570 ['his doing and leaving undone' (*sein Tun und Lassen*) is crossed out.]

"Some people say: 'I have ten *malter* of grain and just as much wine this year; I firmly trust in God!' Quite right, I say, you have complete trust—in the grain and wine!" We may succeed in experiencing God anew in the mystery of his freedom if we say: no, God is not good!— his goodness is of such an unprecedented kind that our word 'good' is as appropriate as it is unfit to describe this goodness.

We call someone 'good' who lifts us up, consoles us, who speaks to us with his heart. "You're a good person," we say, because we have received something, and we are right to do so. But we have received everything from God, we have received even ourselves, indeed everyday we receive him in all the unexpected ways he invents to bestow himself on us. What is the point of the word 'goodness' when applied to God, since, after all, we receive more than 'a good' and since, after all, he does not just 'do good' by us? God does nothing good, he does what is godly. And his godliness is so highly elevated beyond the meaning we typically confer on our words that we would do better to be silent before God and to worship him in stillness and simplicity. Even after the coming of Christ, we should still speak of the 'unknown God,' whose true goodness is inexpressible. Every tongue should therefore be silent before the mystery of God, since all our words, rather than striking his core, fall short of it. We burn to someday imbibe his goodness in an eternal gaze and eternal wonderment. Only then will we really know it. Today, however, we prefer to say, so that God for us may again become God, that his goodness is even better than our word 'good' is able to say.

Additionally, we could say "God is spirit" in response to the question, "what do you know of God?" Our faith experiences that these words are correct. Indeed, in contrast to the Marxist hope in an earthly wellbeing, we await, on the basis of the promise of felicity made to us, the eternal love exchange of our resurrected and therefore spiritualized body with God, "whom no man has seen" [1 Timothy 6:16]. How do we come close to this God of our hope? Here, too, the time in which we live helps us to make a significant new discovery, when its thinkers tell us that the earth came from a primitive original state, that individuation and complexification are the law of its evolution, and that it is moving toward a spiritualization at the end of which there could be something like an 'Omega

Point'[571] of God-worldly, personal unity. At the end of the development, the entire universe will have transformed into the spirit of the father and of the son. In this way, we learn to think of God no longer as opposition to the material realm, thus to juxtapose God and his own 'spiritual world' with our 'earthly world'; we experience better that there is no opposition to God in the realm of the created. Nevertheless—and in spite of all the appeal that this great thought of Teilhard de Chardin has—in order for God to appear again to our faith in his devotion-worthy Godhead, we should not attempt to think of him as opposition to or as the developmental goal of matter, nor should we at all conceive of God as 'this or that'[572] in contradistinction to this or that piece of matter. Hence: as long as 'spirit' is still somehow imprisoned for us in the conceptual pair 'spirit/matter,' we should dare to utter the following sentence: no, God is not spirit... he is, rather, the incomprehensible that has created and holds embraced all matter and everything spiritual. In a world in which God can no longer function as a stopgap in the fields that are still white for the sciences (for these 'gaps' are becoming narrower and narrower), it is crucial that the God who is misunderstood as an always ready-to-hand ultimate explanation would again become the God of faith who always offers himself, that God for us would again become God. And faith understands the word 'spirit' ['*Geist*'] differently than we usually do (for example from the perspective of the 'humanities' ['*Geisteswissenschaften*']). Our everyday thinking represents things to us. But precisely that which we are capable of representing to ourselves is not God. God is rather the one who alone deserves our marveling silence and at whom we arrive only when we have cast aside all representational thinking from our faith. When we encounter him in his Godhead, God will appear to us as always 'more unknown.' We have thoughtlessly applied too many representations to God and have grown accustomed to an image of God of which we will have to admit one day (for example, when the

---

[571] [A phrase from Pierre Teilhard de Chardin's *The Phenomenon of Man* (first published in 1955). In R.S.'s second year of philosophical studies at Le Saulchoir, he took a course on this book.]

[572] [An Eckhartian phrase, frequently referenced by R.S. See, for example, *WJ*, 61, 176, 194 / *ME*, 105, 276, 301.]

thought of death calls into question all familiar modes of representation) that he is no longer at all able to redeem us.

Only when we negate all the titles that we so casually impose on God, such as 'goodness,' 'spirit,' and much else; when God all of a sudden appears as unknown to us and we believe we cannot get beyond the mystery of his freedom, only then is our heart ready to receive the message of the incarnate one. Yet we ought to, and must, bear witness to him in human words; the greatest thing we can say now of God is that he has encountered us in his son Jesus Christ. Only when we have had the experience, through the grace of his son, of how terrifyingly real God is may we also use the words of this son and say: "God alone is good" (cf. Luke 18:19) and "God is spirit" (John 4:24). The familiar God of phraseology becomes the unknown God of mystery; only the latter can speak and attribute [*zusprechen*] to us the undeniable word which is his son.

Appendix 3

Evaluation by Claude Geffré

(1967, trans. from the French by Karl von der Luft)

In this document from January 21, 1967, the theologian Claude Geffré, O.P., at the time rector of Le Saulchoir, evaluates Schürmann's essay "The Philosophical Presuppositions of Meister Eckhart's Christology" (see chapter 7, above).

Fr. Reiner Schürmann

I very sincerely admire the coherent and vigorous way in which you[573] have sought to bring Meister Eckhart's fundamental intuition about the identity between the ground [*fond*] of the soul and the ground of God together with his relative indifference regarding the Incarnation as the historical birth of Christ. My acquaintance with M. Eckhart is unfortunately too elementary to be capable of making a competent judgment on the entirety of your work. But I nevertheless have a very good impression.

The intuition of M. Eckhart is nicely captured in a few pages. The creature is nothing insofar as it is distinct from God; it coincides with the Divinity itself insofar as it returns to its original source, beyond the distinction between God and the created. You are right to interpret this return to original unity in terms of *birth*, and to do so in a Trinitarian context. One thus understands why M. Eckhart has little interest in the historical birth of the Son in history. He seeks less the intelligibility of the Incarnation as an historical event than that of the new birth of the spiritual creature as son of God.

I have also noted certain very pertinent remarks in the third part concerning the philosophical presuppositions of his Christology, above all regarding the ontological difference. It is indeed his conception of the relations between being [*l'être*] and beings [*l'étant*] in the spiritual creature that allows him to identify the "ground of the soul" with the "ground of God."

---

573 [Geffré and R.S. use familiar pronouns with each other.]

These few pages thus manifest an already very profound knowledge of the great Thuringian doctor, at once so fascinating and so obscure. I must say, however, that you seem less successful when you attempt to situate M. Eckhart historically in relation to his precursors. I have noted certain assertions which are much too decided, and which a better acquaintance with the history of ideas at the end of the Middle Ages will compel you to nuance.

It seems to me, for example, that the Christology of M.E. is faithful to [the Council of] Chalcedon and to St. Thomas regarding the relationship between Person and nature in Christ. But it is true that he has an entirely different conception of *esse* (in his essentialist perspective, the hypostatic Union is an informing of the humanity of Christ through the divine Being...) and that he uses the non-assumption of the person in Christ as the foundation for a mysticism of "detachment" in every creature.

You critique those who place M.E. in the lineage of the late Neoplatonists and you think that he no longer belongs to the intellectual world of the Middle Ages, either because of his original conception of time or because of his rejection of analogy and [his rejection] of a representation of a hierarchical cosmos.

All this would require many nuances. If you read the work of *Lossky*,[574] you will notice that M.E.'s conception of the moment is typically Platonist. You will also notice that one must never separate in him a mysticism of union with God by identity from a real participation of the created effects in the first Cause which allows for true analogical predication. "Platonist participation completes the efficient causality of Aristotle in the German theologian's doctrine of creation, in order to remedy the foreignness of created effects, which for Eckhart would be equivalent to a reduction to nothingness" (Lossky, p. 82 [of *Théologie négative et connaissance de Dieu*]). "Creation *ex nihilo* gives rise to a relationship of analogy between all created beings [*êtres*] and God" (ibid. p. 287).

To speak of Eckhart as "an intellectualist mystic of profoundly Aristotelian inspiration" seems to me full of equivocations... The genius of M. Eckhart is irreducible to any of his predecessors, but his

---

574 [Vladimir Lossky, *Théologie négative et connaissance de Dieu chez Maître Eckhart* (Paris: Vrin, 1960).]

quest for the Ineffable fits in well with the movement of the return of the soul to God as identified with the One, which is characteristic of the natural mysticism of Neoplatonism.

I hope that you pursue so penetrating a reading of the work of Meister Eckhart, but by imposing on yourself the asceticism of a rigorous attention to the *history* of the doctrines before delivering yourself up to hypotheses or seductive comparisons.

Fr. Claude Geffré

Appendix 4

Letters from Bernhard Welte

(1967–1971, trans. from the German by Ian Alexander Moore)

Bernhard Welte (1906–1983) was a priest and professor of Christian philosophy of religion in Freiburg. Schürmann studied with him during his sojourns in Freiburg in 1965–1966 and in 1968.

11 February 1967

Dear Mr. Schürmann!

I still have to thank you[575] very cordially for your lovely letter from 29 December and for the text of your Eckhart-study that you included.[576] Your greetings delighted me and I return them cordially; you are far from forgotten in Freiburg.

I have looked through your study a bit, especially the last five pages. As a whole, it seems to me to be very fine work, and I am glad that you have let yourself engage with the thought of Meister Eckhart so intensely. At the level of detail, however, I would make more careful distinctions. On pp. 12 and 13,[577] you speak, for example, of the difference between constituting and constituted being. There is, of course, this difference in Meister Eckhart. But it is much more significant that he places weight on the unity of the occurrence of constituting more than placing value on the twoness of the constituting and the constituted.

And then it seemed to me that, in conjunction with this, you were too inclined to equate, on the one hand, the relation of the divine

---

575 [Welte uses formal pronouns with R.S.]
576 ["The Philosophical Presuppositions of Meister Eckhart's Christology," chapter 7, above. Although two letters from R.S. to Welte (29 December 1966 and 15 December 1967) are mentioned in the latter's letters, we were unable to locate any letters from R.S. to Welte. Nor, aside from the four we translate here, do there seem to be any other extant letters from Welte to R.S.]
577 [In the subsection of "The Philosophical Presuppositions" titled "The Ontological Difference."]

origin constituting all beings to beings as a whole with, on the other, the latter's relation to the human intellect. Certainly, these relations are aligned in Meister Eckhart, but what is at issue for him with *intellectus* is something peculiar and quite special. In this it is similar to Thomas's doctrine of *participatio*. There, too, the being of all beings is occasionally interpreted as *participatio*. But, in a superior sense, *intellectus* is also *participatio* in Thomas.

For this reason, I would not separate so succinctly between the thought of *participatio* as it appears in Thomas and the thought of unity as it appears in Meister Eckhart. Yet I would hesitate to understand the latter thought as that of a univocal unity. In any case, I cannot recall this expression in the texts of the Meister, nor do I believe it is appropriate.

Therefore, I would probably also distinguish between analogy and identity in a more nuanced way. If one follows the justification for the thought of analogy in the texts of Thomas Aquinas, one will soon see that this thought is not so far removed from those contexts in which Meister Eckhart speaks of identity. In a context that is seen to be similar, Meister Eckhart only emphasizes something different.

This much only to give you a few indications for further work and thinking. I send you my best regards and wish you a beautiful light for all your paths!

Please give my regards to all my dear acquaintances in Saulchoir who wish to remember me, especially *Père* Geffré!

Cordially,
Your
B. Welte
(Prof. Dr. B. Welte)

* * *

24 January 1968

Dear Brother Schürmann,

It is high time that I reply to your lovely letter from 15 December. Meanwhile, you have been ordained a deacon; I am delighted by this and I wish you good progress on the path you have begun.

I am especially interested in what you write about your work on Meister Eckhart. The thought of symbolic difference[578] seems to be very fruitful; you were presumably inspired by Ricœur.[579] I believe that the matter can in fact be interpreted in this way in the Meister's sense. I am also glad to see that you have a gentle and careful language regarding these things. This is a good sign, for then the thought can hardly not be good.

The relation between the Thomist doctrine of being and that of Meister Eckhart must be considered carefully. I am, in any case, not entirely sure whether one may characterize Thomas's thought so simply as static and intellectualist. Certainly, there are strong static elements in it, in accordance with an older tradition that Thomas occasionally reinforces. But it is not the only thing that is at work in Thomas. Here, there is much to be learned in particular from the works of Chenu.[580] Thomas, too, has plenty of elements from the Augustinian and Dionysian traditions. If he is static in the sense of the prevailing metaphysics, then this is not in the sense of a closed stasis. In many passages, he is quite loose and open. Of course, it would be necessary to investigate this more precisely. An investigation into the role of *reditio in seipsum* ["Return to oneself"] would not be a bad point of departure for this.

---

578 [I.e., for the initial project for his dissertation, titled "God and Man, His Symbol: An Interpretation of Meister Eckhart." See our afterword, below, for more details.]

579 [See, for example, Paul Ricœur, *The Symbolism of Evil*, trans. Emerson Buchanan (New York: Harper and Row, 1967), and *Freud and Philosophy: An Essay on Interpretation*, trans. Denis Savage (New Haven: Yale University Press, 1970).]

580 [Marie-Dominique Chenu was a Dominican theologian deeply involved with Le Saulchoir. See his book on the institution: *Une école de théologie: Le Saulchoir* (Kainlez-Tournai: Le Saulchoir, 1937). For his work on Thomas, see, for example, *Toward Understanding Saint Thomas*, trans. Albert M. Landry and Dominic Hughes (Chicago: Regnery, 1964), and *Aquinas and His Role in Theology*, trans. Paul Philibert (Collegeville: Liturgical Press, 2002).]

As regards the intellectualist element in Thomas, it must, all the same, be remarked that *intellectus* in Thomas means something different from what we are in general inclined to understand by intellect. Rousselot was indeed the first to take note of this in his old and still fine book *L'Intellectualisme de Saint Thomas*.[581] And as regards Meister Eckhart, there are enough passages in his work to show that he takes on and shares the specific spirit-intellectualism [*Geist-Intellektualismus*] of Thomas, together with its vitality as it was already thought beforehand by the latter.

These are only a few pointers with which I would like to respond to your messages in a stimulating and suggestive, but delighted manner. Just keep working efficiently and you will certainly achieve something good and interesting, and also something useful in service of the faith and of the church.

This much for today, with best, cordial wishes from Freiburg,
Your
B. Welte

* * *

---

581 [Paris: Alcan, 1908. In English as Pierre Rousselot, *Intelligence: Sense of Being, Faculty of God*, trans. Andrew Tallon (Madison, WI: Marquette University Press, 1998).]

19 December 1968

Dear Brother Schürmann!

At last I have been able to read through the largest part of your work, namely the entire first and second chapters of the first part.[582] A long, solitary train ride proved helpful. I must however admit that I have not yet been able to look more closely at the third chapter and the entire second part. But I do not want to make you wait any longer for a reply and thus will tell you what I can say at the moment about your train of thought.

What made a particular impression on me is your interpretation of the symbol as the identity of the non-identical, and this in clear contrast to metaphor, analogy, and image. And then the ontological extension of your thoughts on the symbol in the second chapter, in which language in its symbolic character and then the existence of the human in its symbolic structure are first shown, so that everything converges finally into a comprehensive symbol-ontology.

This is in any case an original thought; it is, in my estimation, very worthy of being voiced and put up for public discussion. It is also a thought that, it seems to me, is thoroughly coherent in itself and step by step comes together into a cohesive whole.

The development of your thought also bears witness to your rich literacy in the domains of past and present philosophy and poetry and hagiography. In connection with this wealth of learning, however, I found your style unusually verbose, at least for a German reader. Perhaps this has to do with the literary form that suits you. On the other hand, I would, in view of this and in the interest of a further clarification and precision of your thought, advise you to undertake the following experiment. Could you not attempt to concentrate the entire essential content of your work in a text of ten pages? I believe this would be completely possible if you were cautious about expressing textually only your genuine theses and the essential justifications for them and left everything else to the side. I suspect that the genuine structure of your thought, including any

---

582 [See the table of contents and discussion of R.S.'s "God and Man, His Symbol" in our afterword, below.]

weak spots in the development, would become much clearer to you. And for an attentive reader who is well disposed toward you but also critical, it would alleviate the burden immensely. Would you not like to undertake such an experiment?

As regards your interpretation of Meister Eckhart's thought, I repeat that I have not yet read this portion of your work and probably won't be able to read it in the coming weeks. But you already presented me with the essentials earlier. And therefore I will repeat my reservations about this plan. Essentially, these are based on two considerations. First, your thought of a symbolic ontology is, as I said, so self-contained, so impressive, and in many respects also so surprising that it does not need to be supplemented, as it were, with reference to Meister Eckhart. I fear that this would not be an organic appendix for the reader. And that would be a shame.

My other reservation concerns Meister Eckhart. I see several essential difficulties in the application of your very impressive thoughts on the symbol to Meister Eckhart's formulations of identity. The symbol, as you interpret it, is a being [*ein Seiendes*], insofar as we observe it as such and, so to speak, as an external formation [*Gebilde*]. Language and existence also become symbols by being observed and interpreted by thinking. What is at issue in Meister Eckhart, however, is something entirely different. Not observation and interpretation, but rather a path of experience. His formulations of identity, at least the most decisive of them, describe entirely precise and concrete experiences, toward which the Meister again and again offers the path of detachment [*Abgeschiedenheit*]. As I have on occasion already emphasized, the intellectual vocabulary of these phenomenologically precise descriptions of experience goes back to the corresponding formulations in Thomas Aquinas's Aristotle-commentaries.[583] Those formulations, however, are descriptions of particular fundamental experiences of seeing or of knowing that become possible on the basis of the fact that we see and that we know and thus actually take the paths of these human modes of comportment and do not merely observe them from without. This seems to me to be a fundamental difference; even if it must be admitted that there is

---

583 [See especially Bernhard Welte, "Meister Eckhart als Aristoteliker," *Philosophisches Jahrbuch* 69, no. 1 (1961): 64–74.]

an interplay here. But, on account of this difference, I would always have reservations about characterizing the Meister's formulations of identity as formulations of a symbolic identity. I fear that this would not be able to lead the reader down the path that the Meister recommends, but rather distance the reader from that path.

This is more or less what I am able to write to you at the moment about your work. Please take my openness as a sign of my friendly interest in you and in your work. I would like to help you as far as I am able; your cause [*Sache*] is, I believe, worth every effort to be helpful.

That's all for today. I add many good and cordial greetings. May your ways and days be blessed, may the light of the Christmas Christ quicken your spirit and heart.

Cordially,
Your
B. Welte
(Prof. Dr. B. Welte)

* * *

Undated [presumably 1971]

Dear Father Schürmann!

Many thanks for the Meister Eckhart-Issue of *La Vie spirituelle*.[584] I really enjoyed rummaging around in it. Recently, I had a very good conversation with Mr. Ueda, who is living in Germany at present. I also paid particular attention to the Marxist contribution; previously, I had not been familiar with this sort of consideration of Meister Eckhart. And, of course, I also looked at your own contribution: it is very beautiful, especially with its lights and reflections from around the world.

The booklet has once again confirmed that I should perhaps one day publish my own Eckhart-studies as a book.[585] For I believe I still have a lot to say about this based on my longstanding preoccupation with Thomas and Albert and Eckhart. But for now I'm still working on other things.

I take the small book as a sign that you are well and feel good, which is also a joy for me. Here, too, we are well. All of your acquaintances send their regards with mine.

With cordial, good wishes and greetings,
Your
B. Welte

---

584 [Vol. 124, no. 578 (January 1971), edited by R.S., and including essays by R.S. ("Maître Eckhart, expert en itinérance," see chapter 10, above); S. Ueda ("Maître Eckhart et le bouddhisme zen," which is R.S.'s translation of the end of Ueda's *Die Gottesgeburt in der Seele und der Durchbruch zur Gottheit*; see chapter 11, above for R.S.'s review of the latter), and A. M. Haas ("Maître Eckhart dans l'idéologie marxist"), among others.]

585 [The book would appear in 1979 as *Meister Eckhart: Gedanken zu seinen Gedanken* (Freiburg: Herder).]

Sources for the Chapters

1. "The Reredos (1965)." Untitled in the original French. Diaphanes private files. Unpublished.

2. "To Live According to the Gospel (1966)." Untitled in the original French. Diaphanes private files. Unpublished.

3. "Letter to Heidegger, and Schürmann's Report of His Meeting with Heidegger (1966)." *Graduate Faculty Philosophy Journal* 19, no. 2 (1997): 67–71.

4. "The Unknown God (1966)." Translation of "Der unbekannte Gott." *Der Christliche Sonntag*, no. 22 (May 29, 1966): 174–75.

5. "A Spiritual Dimension of Technology? (1966)." Translation of "Geistliche Dimension der Technik?" *Der Christliche Sonntag*, no. 29 (July 17, 1966): 229–30.

6. "Easter on Christmas: A Sermon on Love and Death (1966)." Translation of "4e dimanche d'Avent." Diaphanes private files. Unpublished.

7. "The Philosophical Presuppositions of Meister Eckhart's Christology (1967)." Translation of "Les présupposés philosophiques de la Christologie de Maître Eckhart." Reiner Schürmann papers, NA.0006.01, The New School Archives and Special Collections, The New School, New York City, USA, Box 3, Folder: 41–42.

8. "The Phenomenon of the Question in Theology (1967)." Translation of "Le phénomène de la question en théologie." Reiner Schürmann papers, NA.0006.01, The New School Archives and Special Collections, The New School, New York City, USA, Box 3, Folder: 41–42.

9. "Peregrine Identity (1969)." Translation of the epigraphs, introduction, and conclusion of "Identité pérégrinale: Le concept de détachement dans les sermons allemands de Maître Eckhart." Bibliothèque du Saulchoir, call number 326 B 312, and Dominikanerkonvent St. Josef Düsseldorf, call number N-006-00219. The latter copy is available online: https://digital.dombibliothek-koeln.de/ddbkhd/content/titleinfo/523718.

10. "Meister Eckhart: Expert in Itinerancy (1971)." Translation of "Maître Eckhart, expert en itinérance." *La Vie spirituelle* 124, no. 578 (January, 1971): 20–32.

11. "Book Reviews about Eckhart (1968–1974)." Translations of: 1. "[Review of] B. Weiss, *Die Heilsgeschichte bei Meister Eckhart*." *Revue des Sciences philosophiques et théologiques* 52, no. 4 (October 1968): 798–800. 2. "[Review of] I. Degenhardt, *Studien zum Wandel des Eckhartbildes*." *Revue des Sciences philosophiques et théologiques* 53, no. 1 (January 1969): 176–77. 3. Introduction to Ueda Shizuteru, "Maître Eckhart et le bouddhisme zen." *La Vie spirituelle* 124, no. 578 (January 1971): 33–42. 4–5. "Indications bibliographiques." *La Vie spirituelle* 124, no. 578 (January 1971): 90–93. 6. "[Review of] Masumi Shibata, *Les maîtres du zen au Japon*." *La Vie spirituelle* 124, no. 578 (January 1971): 122–24. 7. "[Review of] Maître Eckhart, *Les traités*. Trad. et introduction de J. Ancelet-Hustache." *La Vie spirituelle* 124, no. 582 (May 1971). 8. "[Review of] Maître Eckhart, *Sermons*, I (1–30)." *La Vie spirituelle* 128, no. 605 (November–December 1974): 936.

12. "To Find, at Last, The Origin (1973)." Translation of "Trouver enfin l'origine." *La Vie spirituelle* 127, no. 596 (May–June, 1973): 388–96.

13. "Three Thinkers of Releasement: Meister Eckhart, Heidegger, Suzuki (1974–1975)." Translation of "Trois penseurs du délaissement: Maître Eckhart, Heidegger, Suzuki. Part One," and "Trois penseurs du délaissement: Maître Eckhart, Heidegger, Suzuki. Part Two." *Journal of the History of Philosophy* 12, no. 4 (October, 1974): 455–77; 13, no. 1 (January, 1975): 43–60.

14. "Commentary on Professor Caputo's Paper 'Mysticism, Metaphysics and Thought'" (1976). *Heidegger Circle Proceedings* 10 (1976): 41–49.

15. "The Loss of the Origin in Soto Zen and Meister Eckhart (1978)." *The Thomist* 42, no. 2 (April): 281–312. / "Lecture delivered by Reiner Schürmann at Lindisfarne Association" (1977), audiotape archived at the Boyce Centennial Library of The Southern Baptist Theological Seminary, Louisville, KY, USA.

16. "The Law of Nature and Pure Nature: Thought-Experience in Meister Eckhart (1984/1986-1987)." *Krisis* 5-6 (1986–1987): 148–69. / "Naturgesetz und blosse Natur: Über eine Denkerfahrung bei dem Meister Eckhart." *Zen Buddhism Today* 2 (1984): 127–49.

17. "Introduction to a Lecture Course on Meister Eckhart (1993)." "Meister Eckhart" Lecture Notes in Reiner Schürmann papers, NA.0006.01, The New School Archives and Special Collections, The New School, New York City, USA, Series IV: 3–11.

18. Appendix 1: "The Word of God (1964)." Untitled in the original French. Reiner Schürmann papers, NA.0006.01, The New School Archives and Special Collections, The New School, New York City, USA, Box 1, Folder 35: 1–15.

19. Appendix 2: "The Unknown God, Early Draft (1966)." Translation of "Der unbekannte Gott." Diaphanes private files. Unpublished.

20. Appendix 3: "Evaluation by Claude Geffré (1967)." Reiner Schürmann papers, NA.0006.01, The New School Archives and Special Collections, The New School, New York City, USA, Box 3, Folder: 41–42.

21. Appendix 4: "Letters from Bernhard Welte (1967–1971)." Letters to Reiner Schürmann, in Reiner Schürmann papers, NA.0006.01, Box 1, Folder 4; Box 3, Folder 41–42.

Editors' Afterword

Francesco Guercio and Ian Alexander Moore

Today, many readers of Reiner Schürmann (1941-1993), the New School philosopher of 'ontological anarchy' and the 'tragic double bind,' are vaguely aware that he was, for a time, a priest. They may also know that, in the 1960s, he studied at the French Dominican school of theology Le Saulchoir, an intellectual and practical vanguard both of the *nouvelle théologie* that sought to return to the true sources of the mystery of living faith beneath the layers upon layers of antimodern neo-scholasticism, and of the radical worker-priest movement, which had aligned itself with the proletariat in an effort "to share in the living conditions of millions of oppressed people and to show solidarity with their fights," as one manifesto from 1954 put it.[1] Few, however, have had the opportunity to engage with Schürmann's writings during that fervent period, as these *theologische Jugendschriften* (to recall the title of a collection of writings from Hegel's youth) were unpublished until now, printed in unexpected places, or later reworked by their author in such a way as to obscure their more theologically oriented beginnings. (The last can be most clearly seen in Schürmann's prizewinning 1976 novel *Origins*, where there is no talk of religion or of his time at Le Saulchoir as paths he pursued to come to terms with the complicity of his forebears in National Socialism; in an interview from the following year, Schürmann even neglects to mention his theological training, calling himself a former student of philosophy and international relations instead.[2] And yet, as we will discuss in §11, below,

---

1 Quoted in Ulrich Engel, "'Vital Opposition': Marie-Dominique Chenu O.P.—Fundamental Categories of His Theology Reflected in the Conflict Surrounding the French Worker-Priest Movement," *Angelicum* 90 (2013): 961-76 (971). For more on the 'new theology' at Le Saulchoir, see Jürgen Mettepenningen, *Nouvelle Théologie–New Theology: Inheritor of Modernism, Precursor of Vatican II* (London: T & T Clark, 2010).

2 Reiner Schürmann, *Les origines: Récit*, new edition (Toulouse: Presses Universitaires du Mirail, 2003) / *Origins*, trans. Elizabeth Preston (in collaboration with the author) (Zurich: Diaphanes, 2016). French interview with Victor Malka for the radio program "Écoute, Israël" ("Hear, O Israel!") of France Culture, September 4, 1977, transcript

Schürmann saw fit to publish a short first version of *Origins* in 1973 in a Dominican journal on spiritual life edited by his former teacher at Le Saulchoir [see chapter 12 in this volume].)

This English-language volume makes some of the most important writings from Schürmann's early period available for the first time in any language.[3] Here, readers can see how Schürmann began to develop many of the ideas for which he would later be known, such as 'releasement,' 'life without why,' 'an-archy,' and the 'double bind,' while he was living and studying—unorthodoxically, by his own admission—within the tradition of the Catholic Church and "the schemes of thought of the inherited Christian metaphysics of the West."[4] The publication of these early writings allows readers

---

located in the Reiner Schürmann papers, NA.0006.01, The New School Archives and Special Collections, The New School, New York City, USA, Box 1, Folders 10–11, p. 3.

3 These mostly unknown texts come from a variety of places: files preserved by Schürmann's family (chapters 1, 2, 6; appendix 2); a German-language Christian weekly (chapters 4–5); the Reiner Schürmann papers at The New School for Social Research (chapters 7–8, 17; appendices 1, 3–4); the Bibliothèque du Saulchoir and the Dominikanerkonvent St. Josef Düsseldorf (chapter 9); a French-language, Dominican journal (chapters 10, 12; portions of chapter 11); and the proceedings of the American Heidegger Circle (chapter 14). The still-unpublished original French of chapters 1 and 8 is forthcoming in a French-language collection of Schürmann's writings edited by Vincent Blanchet, Émeline Durand, and Ian Alexander Moore for Vrin press.

While other texts by Schürmann from his early period and beyond fit into the scope of the present volume, they either overlap too much with material we decided to include or have been reserved for other volumes in the "Reiner Schürmann Selected Writings and Lecture Notes" series published by Diaphanes Press. The following texts, for example, will appear in *The One: Writings on Henology and Neoplatonism*: "Die Erkennbarkeit des 'Einen' aus Exitus und Reditus" (1966), "Neoplatonic Henology as an Overcoming of Metaphysics" (1983), and "The One: Substance or Function?" (1982/2002). A volume on Schürmann's engagement with Heidegger will include: "Über den Wechselbezug, bei Heidegger, von Wahrheit und Freiheit" (1964), "Le sentiment d'angoisse comme constitutif de l'existence authentique: Une étude du 'Concept d'Angoisse' de Kierkegaard et de 'L'Être et le Temps' de Heidegger" (1965), "Heidegger and Meister Eckhart on Releasement" (1973), and "Heidegger and the Mystical Tradition" (1972–1975/2020). Schürmann's 1964 paper "Sur le fondement de l'impossibilité dans le système critique de Kant, de la preuve ontologique de l'existence de Dieu" will appear as an appendix to material by Schürmann on Kant and, before then, in Italian translation in *La discordanza: Scritti scelti di Reiner Schürmann*, ed. Francesco Guercio (Vicenza: Neri Pozza, 2023). Finally, Schürmann's article on Eckhart for the *Encyclopedia Britannica* is available for free online: https://www.britannica.com/biography/Meister-Eckhart.

4 In this volume, 249[n455].

not only to ponder the weight that Schürmann's theological training had, both philosophically and existentially, on him but also to consider the stakes of his own public distancing from—if not deliberate omission of—those years he spent within that very tradition for his thinking as a whole. The volume also includes related writings from subsequent decades, giving readers the chance to appreciate how Schürmann's thinking on God, the medieval Dominican philosopher Meister Eckhart, Zen Buddhism, and Heidegger (who is frequently in the background of Schürmann's texts, even when he is not mentioned by name) developed over the course of Schürmann's career.

It would be a fruitful exercise to trace some of Schürmann's late concepts back to the theological milieu in which they emerged. One might, for example, read the tragic double bind in light of Schürmann's initial stress on "peregrine difference,"[5] or even see the fissured "referential semiology"[6] of *Broken Hegemonies* through the lens of his early desire for the utter "abolition of language."[7] While we will occasionally signal such points of convergence in this afterword, our main focus will be on analyzing Schürmann's writings in this volume—especially the earlier, lesser-known ones—and situating them in the context of their development. Proceeding more or less chronologically and in parallel with the chapters of the volume, we will also show how the different 'ways of releasement' not only shaped the lifework of Reiner Schürmann but shed light on his philosophy as a whole (however much he may have wished to keep some of those ways in the dark or leave them behind).[8]

---

5 In this volume, 112.

6 Reiner Schürmann, *Des Hégémonies brisées*, 2nd ed. (Zurich: Diaphanes, 2017), 20 / *Broken Hegemonies*, trans. Reginald Lilly (Bloomington: Indiana University Press, 2003), 11. In Schürmann's 1966 sermon "Easter on Christmas" (chapter 6 in this volume), for example, words are already viewed as fissured, and that fissure is traced back to death.

7 In this volume, 152.

8 One may wonder about the legitimacy of publishing writings that their author did not bring out or have the chance to revise while alive. It is an age-old, complex debate we cannot address in detail here, though we do take it up more extensively in a forthcoming monograph, tentatively titled *Life without Why: Reiner Schürmann and the Imperative of Releasement*. Further, we take it to be significant and encouraging, if not sufficiently justifying, for our editorial work that, throughout all his travels, Schürmann never made the decision to destroy his early writings but, instead, considered them worth preserving and, in some cases, returning to later in life. We believe, at any rate, that publishing these early materials will help readers to better understand

First, however, a few words on the term 'releasement' and its history are in order.

§1. The Manifold Meaning of Releasement

I've consulted the sages in Israel, I've spoken with Hannah Arendt, whom I love enormously, even ferociously in a certain way. And my book [i.e., *Origins*] is like a quest for a word, for an explanation. Something that I'll be able to put in my head to know why I belong to this history. It's a quest for a spiritual attitude that the Germans have for seven centuries named with a term [i.e., *Gelassenheit*] that means serenity [*sérénité*]. I had written a first book on Meister Eckhart, who coined this term, and I'd like people to see that the two books and a third one that I'm writing now [i.e., the book that would become *Heidegger on Being and Acting*] speak about this subject, about this serenity.[9]
—Reiner Schürmann, 1976

The word *Gelassenheit*, which, as Schürmann indicates in the epigraph, Eckhart coined in its Middle High German form *gelâzenheit* in the thirteenth century as a synonym of *abegescheidenheit* ('detachment,' 'cutting away'; *Abgeschiedenheit* in Modern German), today has the sense of serenity or calm composure.[10] However, for Eckhart, as for Heidegger, the various senses of the word are closer to its root *lâzen* ('to let'; *lassen* in Modern German). It means not just letting go, but also being let and letting be. To capture these various senses, we typically follow Schürmann in translating *Gelassenheit* with the English 'releasement' (*délaissement* in Schürmann's French). In Schürmann's Heidegger-inspired interpretation of Eckhart, releasement signals not merely a state wherein action ('I release') and

---

Schürmann's path of thinking and will be of benefit to whoever undertakes to follow it after him.
9 Schürmann, French interview with Victor Malka, op. cit., p. 2. Here and below, all translations for which an English edition is not supplied are our own.
10 Meister Eckhart. *Die deutschen und lateinischen Werke* (= DW and LW, followed by volume, page, and line or section numbers), herausgegeben im Auftrag der Deutschen Forschungsgemeinschaft (Stuttgart: Kohlhammer, 1936–), DW 5: 283,8.

passion ('I am released') have been completed, but, fundamentally, a way of being that is more akin to the middle voice: the deepest aspect of my being (what Eckhart calls the spark or citadel of the soul and Heidegger calls Dasein or mortality) and the deepest aspect of being itself are both implicated in the selfsame *event* of releasement. In Schürmann's words:

> If the world, man, and God are radically left [*laissé*] to themselves, who lets [*laisse*] whom be? Who acts? Everything is let, but there is no one here who lets. The negation of the negation is thus overcome in its turn. In this regard, we will speak of 'releasement' ['*délaissement*'], both because of the intensive prefix and because of the intransitive character of the substantive. Releasement, *Gelassenheit*, no longer relates back to a thinking or acting subject. This word bespeaks the pure phenomenon of being let [*être laissé*].[11]

Schürmann also renders *Gelassenheit* with 'letting-be' (*laisser-être*) and occasionally, as in the epigraph above, with 'serenity' (*sérénité*), although he doubtless always has the Eckhartian tradition of releasement in mind, as he does when he uses the related concept of 'detachment' (*Abgeschiedenheit, détachement*) or, as he would later render it in "The Law of Nature and Pure Nature" (chapter 16 in this volume), 'non-attachment.'

Previous work on Schürmann has shown how *Gelassenheit* and its cognates appear in a variety of sometimes overlapping, sometimes fleeting ways in his corpus, in both secular and specifically Christian contexts (sometimes these contexts overlap, too).[12] Secularly (if not always atheistically), Schürmann uses it to refer to:

1. a call to detachment or letting go;
2. a description of the wandering, event-like identity of the essence of God and the human, of the origin and the human, or of being and the human;
3. seeing the divine or the origin in all things;

---

[11] In this volume, 156.
[12] Ian Alexander Moore, "On the Manifold Meaning of Letting-Be in Reiner Schürmann," *Journal of Continental Philosophy* 2, no. 1 (2021): 105–130. Some of the material in this section and below reproduces and expands on passages from this article.

4. letting things be as they are in their singularity;
5. a way of living 'originarily,' 'an-archically,' or 'without why' (which Schürmann gets initially from Eckhart and later develops with respect to Nietzsche, Zen, and Heidegger);
6. the meaning of being itself;
7. existential conversion;
8. a strategic, militant means of radical enlightenment (which Schürmann links to Kant's *Ausgang* from self-incurred tutelage, translating the German as 'release');
9. and acceptance of the tragic, inescapable double bind of life.

In a specifically Christian way, Schürmann uses it to refer to:

10. imitation of Christ's *kenōsis* or 'self-emptying' on the Cross;
11. active charity;
12. letting oneself be taken by the possibility of eternal life (which Schürmann allows as a possibility toward the end of his life).

This list is likely not exhaustive, as other nuanced referents of *Gelassenheit* could perhaps be retrieved and identified in Schürmann's writings. It attempts, nonetheless, to provide a sense of the diverse range of meanings the term takes on for him during his lifetime. We will encounter many of these ways of releasement in what follows. Our aim, however, is less to examine them on their own terms than to trace Schürmann's pursuit of them in the context of his writings on God, Eckhart, Zen, and (less directly) Heidegger, to which we now turn.

§2. Eckhart and the The(i)ological Difference

[T]he key theme of current theology is the dilemma of the Bible itself, which, on the one hand, forbids us any image of God and, on the other hand, announces to us the personal God.
—Claude Geffré[13]

[N]one of the great thinkers of the Middle Ages went as far or were as bold as Eckhart. [...] He gives word to an experience, a thought, that is not only thought, but lived. [...] What is at issue for him can be understood only through a sort of assimilation [to the divine], or it will not be understood at all.
—Bernhard Welte[14]

Schürmann's lifelong engagement with Meister Eckhart began in earnest in Fall 1965 during a sojourn in Freiburg, Germany, where he had gone to study abroad with the professor of Christian philosophy of religion Bernhard Welte (1906–1983). Welte, a Catholic priest heavily influenced by Heidegger, taught a course on Eckhart that Schürmann would later identify as having "inspired my work."[15] It left Schürmann philosophically and existentially captivated by the mystical thought of the Meister. In a one-page text dated November 11, 1965 (chapter 1 in this volume), which is more a manifesto or confession than an academic study, Schürmann tries to come to terms with incompatibilities between Eckhart's mystical teaching of the divinity or 'Godhead' (*Gottheit*) beyond the representable and relatable God (*Gott*), on the one hand, and the doctrines of the Christian faith, on the other. "The reredos before which I sacrifice," Schürmann begins, "has two panels."[16] On the first wing is

---
13 Geffré, "Le problème théologique de l'objectivité de Dieu," in *Procès de l'objectivité de Dieu: Les présupposés philosophiques de la crise de l'objectivité de Dieu* (Paris: Cerf, 1969), 241–76 (242).
14 Bernhard Welte, "Gedanke des Meisters Eckhart," Universitätsarchiv Freiburg, Germany, call number E 8/226, pp. 1, 6.
15 Letter from Schürmann to Caputo, November 11, 1972, in the John D. Caputo Archive at the Simon Silverman Phenomenology Center at Duquesne University. A transcript of an audio recording of a later version of the course survives in Welte's *Nachlass*. See the previous footnote.
16 In this volume, 9.

the abyssal, predicate-less Godhead, with which an aspect of the human soul is always implicitly, albeit rarely explicitly, united. Language must fall silent in the face of such divinity. Unknowable, this Godhead can nevertheless be experienced. In the spirit of theological universalism, Schürmann suggests that this experience lies at the basis of teachings as varied as Daoism, Buddhism, and Heideggerian phenomenology. It is noteworthy that, at the age of twenty-four, Schürmann is already referring to both Eckhart and Heidegger, the two thinkers who would remain closest to him for the remainder of his life. He also cites the Anglican bishop John Robinson, whose best-selling *Honest to God* (1963) popularized the labors of the Protestant theologians Paul Tillich, Dietrich Bonhoeffer, and Rudolf Bultmann and acted as a "bombshell that blew the roof off the church."[17] Schürmann writes in this early French text:

> Meister Eckhart says that the soul is above God, and God's messenger, the bishop Robinson, would like God finally to be once again 'without God' ['*sans Dieu*,' an allusion to the title of the French translation of Robinson's book, *Dieu sans Dieu*]. Heidegger, too, has been seized by that which is radically unknowable [*inconnaissable*]. I understand these authors, for the same gift has been given to all. And why should we be surprised that there are profound resemblances between the experience of the 'Tao,' of the Buddhist 'Emptiness,' of the thinker's *Es gibt Sein*, etc., if it is the same divine that gives itself [*le même divin qui se donne*]?[18]

The other wing of this metaphorical reredos, however, bears the image of an addressable, relatable God:

> I know that God loves me, loves all men, and that he speaks to each human being, in a language intimate and wholly personal; that he is there at the heart of all human experience, and with all the more love as the latter becomes sin. Saint Dominic said 'my Mercy, [what will become of sinners?]' and I say it with him.[19]

---

17 Lloyd Geering, "Theology Before and After Bishop Robinson's *Honest to God*," *Journal for the Study of Religion* 31, no. 1 (2018): 224–36 (224).
18 In this volume, 9.
19 In this volume, 10.

It is important, Schürmann continues, to heed God's call, although he also recognizes alternative paths to divine presence. In any case, trust in Christ's power to decide on opening up his dialogical relationship is key, at least according to this side of reredos:

> We should be able to feel, touch, and embrace this dialogue that men, so secretly, have with their Savior; this would be the most beautiful path for knowing [*connaître*] Jesus Christ. I believe, however, that this experience of extension [*prolongement*] (of man to the Son of man), which is rather an experience of presence, is also undergone [*se fait*] in unusual ways, where the Catholic Church would scream in fear. It is not we who decide the 'how' of this dialogue, but Jesus Christ who knows, better than we do, the human dough and the ways of kneading it.[20]

In the final paragraph, however, Schürmann finds a different way of responding to his dilemma. He looks, not to the wings, as it were, but to the center of the hinge that joins them. Applying Heidegger's idea of the ontological difference between being and entities to what might be called a 'the(i)ological difference' between the unnameable Godhead or Divine (*to theion*) of the first wing and the loving father or savior God (*ho theos*) of the second, Schürmann writes:

> The return, the approach of progressive elimination, stops at a paradox. The philosophers call it the ontological difference: God 'gives' being [*Dieu 'donne' l'être*], and at the same time he has wanted us to be able to know him [*le connaître*] as something 'ontic.' Each human event is mysterious, but the source of the mystery is precisely this 'rift [*faille*] in God.' And the rift is a solid rock: with God's help, I will be able to build there a life that has *meaning* [*y construire une vie qui ait un* sens].[21]

Anyone familiar with Schürmann's later thought might be surprised by this final sentence. Is Schürmann, *the* twentieth-century philosopher of 'life without why,' really positing a solid foundation on which to make his life meaningful? Not exactly. Although

---

20 Ibid.
21 Ibid.

Schürmann will eventually distance himself from foundationalism in all its guises—and, moreover, from Christianity—it is not as though the rock of this early text were the rock of faith, i.e., the *petros* of Peter on whom Jesus was to build his church (Matthew 16:18; see also Deuteronomy 32:15 and Matthew 7:24). Schürmann's rock is not merely broken; oxymoronically, it is *itself* the break, the *faille* or 'fault' that, in French as in English, has both seismological and axiological connotations. Intentions aside, this seemingly infelicitous, architecturally unsound figure anticipates Schürmann's later principle of anarchy and double bind (see §14, below), as well as his final efforts to "establish" himself "expressly on the fissured ground."[22] It also demonstrates Schürmann's youthful struggle with Eckhart and Heidegger, with the teachings of the Church, and with what he would soon call 'the unknown God.'

§3. The Inkling of the 'Thou'

A "Christian philosophy" is a piece of wooden iron and a misunderstanding.
—Martin Heidegger[23]

Viel hat von Morgen an,
Seit ein Gespräch wir sind und hören voneinander,
Erfahren der Mensch; bald sind wir aber Gesang.
Much has from the morning on,
Since we are conversation and listen to each other,
the human experienced; soon though we will be song.
—Friedrich Hölderlin[24]

On January 16, 1966, at the behest of Welte, Schürmann wrote to Heidegger requesting a visit. In the letter (in chapter 3 in this volume), the young friar relates that he had interrupted his studies at Le Saulchoir to go to Freiburg "in order to begin doctoral work on 'the unknown God in the thought of Meister Eckhart' under Professor

---

22 Schürmann, *Des Hégémonies brisées*, 646 / *Broken Hegemonies*, 560.
23 Martin Heidegger, *Gesamtausgabe*, 102 vols. (Frankfurt: Klostermann, 1975–), vol. 40, pp. 8–9. Henceforth "GA," followed by volume and page number.
24 "Friedensfeier," cited in Heidegger, GA 12: 121, and in this volume, 77.

Welte's guidance."[25] Schürmann posed two questions, both of which display an impressive knowledge of Eckhart and of the notoriously difficult later Heidegger. The first question concerned the relevance of Eckhart's ontology for contemporary—which is to say, by unspoken implication, Heidegger's own—thought:

> did [Eckhart] perhaps think being as self-sending, as only eventfully experienceable? Meister Eckhart's 'sole thought' is aimed at the unification of the 'separated soul' with God. Insofar as the soul lets all things be, it breaks through to the ground where the Godhead continually creates all things, and which in this breakthrough also becomes my ground. The unity is a unity of the "fabric" in which God operates and I become— become son, that is. Being is thus thought as course of experience, and not represented as ontic 'standing reserve' ['*Bestand*']. Closer to the soul than any created thing, the "unknown God" is experienced in the event of words [*Zuspruch*, also 'consolation,' 'exhortation'], beyond this and that [*jenseits von allem Dies und Das*], and, for that reason, it always remains a 'nil of all things.' Might not Meister Eckhart's thinking help us along in a meditation directed at being which always withholds itself and, in this very withholding, addresses itself to us?[26]

Schürmann's first question, or rather set of questions, is, admittedly, laden with Heideggerian jargon, which, however frustrating it may be to the uninitiated, can nevertheless help us to appreciate the context in which Schürmann was reading and would continue to read Eckhart. Note, first, that Schürmann is *not* asking whether Eckhart ranks among the "great thinkers," each of whom, in Heidegger's interpretation of Western philosophy, ultimately has just "one thought."[27] Schürmann takes this for granted, and he knows Heidegger would agree.[28] Instead, Schürmann is asking, as Welte recently had in a lecture at Le Saulchoir,[29] whether Eckhart's sole

---

25 In this volume, 13–14.
26 In this volume, 14.
27 GA 8: 53.
28 See GA 10: 56.
29 Bernhard Welte, "La métaphysique de Saint Thomas d'Aquin et la pensée de l'histoire de l'être chez Heidegger," *Revue des Sciences philosophiques et théologiques* 50, no. 4 (October 1966): 601–614. Later published in German as "Rückblick auf die

thought of becoming one with God—or better: with the Godhead at the source of the Trinity—escapes the 'ontotheology' of substance metaphysics, that is to say, the representation of being either as *a* being or in terms of being*s*. Is Eckhart's Godhead, in other words, something like Heidegger's non-metaphysical, self-concealing being (*Sein*), which Heidegger occasionally marks by using the obsolete spelling *Seyn* ('beyng'), by crossing the word out, or by using the term *Seiendheit* or 'beingness' when being pertains strictly to the being *of* beings? The ground of the soul and the ground of God are implicitly already one ground, but we must explicitly own up to this (*er-eignen*) through a process of separation or detachment (*Abgeschiedenheit*) from all things. We must—and here Schürmann again uses one of Eckhart's most important terms for Heidegger—*let* them be (*sein lassen*). What we then discover is not a static unity, but what Eckhart calls, in Middle High German, *einheit in disem gewürke* or 'operative identity,' which Schürmann is doubtless referring to with the term that is translated as 'fabric' in the last block quotation (cf. modern German *Gewirke*).[30] (Unfortunately, the original German of the letter, with the exception of the words we have interpolated, has not been published and could not be located.[31]) Is, as Schürmann seems to hint at, this energetic unification with God something like Heidegger's 'event of appropriation' (*Ereignis*)? And isn't there something essentially concealed and mysterious about it,

---

Metaphysik: Thomas von Aquin und Heideggers Gedanke von der Seinsgeschichte," *Wort und Wahrheit* 12 (1967): 747–57.

30 DW 1: 114,4–5 (Pr. 6, "Iusti vivent in aeternum"). Cf., in this volume, 14[n10].

31 Jean-Marie Vaysse did, however, consult the original German for his translation of the letter into French. Where the English has 'fabric,' Vaysse, more closely in accord with our conjecture, has *effectué*: "L'unité est une unité de ce qui est effectué, dans lequel Dieu agit et où je deviens." Reiner Schürmann, "Lettre de R. Schürmann à Heidegger du 16 janvier 1966," trans. J-M Vaysse, in *Autour de Reiner Schürmann*, ed. Jean-Marie Vaysse (Hildesheim: Olms, 2009), 153. Further, in "Meister Eckhart als Aristoteliker," *Philosophisches Jahrbuch* 69, no. 1 (1961): 64–74, which seems to be one of Schürmann's sources, Welte also cites the passage from Eckhart, translating it into modern German as "Gott und ich, wir sind eins in diesem Gewirke, er wirket und ich werde." Welte even speaks, as Schürmann soon will, of an "energetic identity [*energetischen Identität*] of what is nevertheless ontically distinct" (72). "The identity," Welte explains further, "is an authentic one, but it is an identity of happening [*Geschehens*], of *energeia*, or, as Meister Eckhart says, of operation [*Gewirkes*]" (73). For Schürman's earliest use of the phrase, see in this volume, 46.

just as, for Heidegger, *lēthe* or 'concealment' insuperably subtends each and every disclosure of truth (*alētheia*, 'un-concealment')?

In a report of his meeting with Heidegger on March 11, 1966 (also in chapter 3 in this volume), which he wrote in French in the form of a letter to his mentor at Le Saulchoir, the hermeneutic theologian Claude Geffré, Schürmann does not relate what Heidegger said about Eckhart. However, Schürmann's later recollections of this meeting (or possibly of similar meetings) suggest that Heidegger answered these questions largely in the affirmative. Heidegger even divulged to Schürmann that he had read Eckhart's German sermons at precisely the time in which he had been trying to understand being as *Anwesen* or 'presencing.'[32] While every scholar of Heidegger's thought should ponder this claim, we are interested less in the significance of the encounter between Schürmann and Heidegger for understanding the latter's *Denkweg* than in its significance for Schürmann's own path of thought and for his understanding of what it means for thought to be on a path.

Referring, in particular, to Heidegger's later work on language, Schürmann emphasizes the primacy of existential experience, which had also been crucial for Welte. Schürmann means, not the German *Erlebnis*, which in Heidegger's (and Hans-Georg Gadamer's) later parlance refers pejoratively to subjective, inner life, but the German *Erfahrung*, which suggests both journeying (*Fahren*) and danger (*Gefahr*). Thinking is not an abstract affair. It requires the risky engagement of the whole human. As Schürmann would explain in a later, more introspective writing (chapter 12 in this volume):

> Letting be [*Laisser être*]: this opens a path. An initiation, perhaps, but not a threshold crossed once and for all. Dare dispossession, with an animal patience. These words say it well: peregrination, peril, experience. Our essential peregrination, the experience of ourselves, remains perilous.[33]

---

32 Some of these reports are reproduced and discussed in Ian Alexander Moore, *Eckhart, Heidegger, and the Imperative of Releasement* (Albany: State University of New York Press, 2019), 185–186, 219–20[n5], and 225–26[n24].
33 In this volume, 152.

Or, as Heidegger had already put it in the introduction to "The Essence of Language":

> The three lectures that follow [...] are intended to bring us face to face with a possibility of undergoing an experience [*eine Erfahrung zu machen*] with language. To undergo an experience with something—be it a thing, a person, or a god—means that this something befalls [*widerfährt*] us, strikes us, comes over us, overwhelms and transforms us [...] To undergo an experience with language, then, means to let [*lassen*] ourselves be properly concerned by the claim [*Anspruch*] of language by entering into and submitting to it.[34]

But Schürmann is also prefiguring his later work on the practical *a priori* and on anarchic idoloclasty. In his 1981 doctoral dissertation on Heidegger, for example, he will describe what is ethically and politically at stake in the semantic complex 'experience–peregrination–peril,' suggesting, however, that there may come a time in which we cross the threshold once and for all:

> the experience (*Erfahrung*) of the "destiny that unfolds our essence"—of destinal peregrination (*Fahren*)—is perilous (*Gefahr*). Concretely, this peril means that, in order to fully enter into an economy that is "without why" and "released" [*"délaissée"*], it is first of all necessary to precipitate the decline of everything in public life that stands in the way of the without-why and of letting-be [*laisser-être*].[35]

---

[34] GA 12: 149 / *On the Way to Language*, trans. Peter D. Hertz (San Francisco: Harper & Row, 1971), 57.

[35] Reiner Schürmann, "Politique et déconstruction: Heidegger et les fondements de la philosophie pratique," Thèse pour le Doctorat d'Etat ès Lettres et Sciences Humaines (Université de Paris-Sorbonne), 630 (loosely translating GA 8: 169). This quotation cannot be found in the published version of the dissertation: Reiner Schürmann, *Le Principe d'anarchie: Heidegger et la question de l'agir*, new edition (Bienne: Diaphanes, 2013) / *Heidegger on Being and Acting: From Principles to Anarchy*, trans. Christine-Marie Gros in collaboration with the author (Bloomington: Indiana University Press, 1987). Interestingly, the corresponding passage in an earlier, English-language article (Reiner Schürmann, "The Ontological Difference and Political Philosophy," *Philosophy and Phenomenological Research* 40 [1979]: 99–122 [115]) is less radical: "quite as the severalness of Being uproots rational certainty, so the peregrine essence of Being uproots practical security. The words seem to suggest this: the experience (*Erfahrung*) of such peregrination (*Fahren*) is full of peril (*Gefahr*). The groundwork for an alternative

In any case, already for the early Schürmann, in order to properly understand being, we must first experience it, and for this it is necessary that we submit to journeying out beyond ourselves—or better, given the jargon of the time, beyond our 'inauthentic' selves—in search of being. Once we have consented to do so, we will come back to ourselves—to our 'authentic' selves—and learn that being itself is a kind of journey, giving or 'sending itself destinally' (*sich schickend*) in different epochal arrangements throughout history (*Geschichte*). Or, in Eckhart's terms, in order to properly understand the Godhead, we must detach or release ourselves from all things. When we do so, we will understand that the deepest meaning of the Godhead is a detachment or releasement 'without why,' and we, too, will be able to live a life of joyful wandering without why.

Schürmann's second set of questions in his letter to Heidegger asks about the utility of ancient words—especially biblical words—for addressing and assenting to the mission of being:

> can the wondering silence in the face of the gift of being not recollect certain words that were first brought forth in a stutter and later 'sublated' on account of their inadequacy? And can it not consent to the event thanks to an inkling remaining from them? I have in mind above all this one word, 'thou.' The mystery of the gift could be experienced as mystery of the 'thou,' without thinking's having to fall into representation (for example, the repetition of a source of being [which is] revealed to it), while it remains within the boundaries set to it as thinking. Even in breaking through all of God's titles (such as 'the good' or 'truth'), there still subsists for Meister Eckhart the inkling of the 'thou.' Might not the proposition 'being is given' (*'Es gibt Sein'*) [literally, 'It gives being'] be expressed in the form 'thou givest being' (*'Du gibst Sein'*) without injury to the mystery?[36]

If Heidegger, as is well known, draws on countless terms from classical Greece in his attempts to rethink being, he largely avoids their

---

to organizational political philosophy will have to be so multifarious as to allow for an ever new response to the calling advent by which Being destabilizes familiar patterns of thinking and acting."

36   In this volume, 14–15.

counterparts in the Hebrew Bible and their specific senses in the New Testament. Even when he does consider the latter, it is often to dismiss them as derivative and philosophically irrelevant.[37] Yet what, Schürmann asks, of the way in which God is addressed? What, to put it in German, of the *Du*? This informal pronoun has a variety of referents, but most relevant for our purposes is its application to God, whom Martin Buber had called *das ewige Du*, "the eternal thou," of which "every singularized [*geeinzelte*] thou is a glimpse."[38] Can we not say 'thou' to the mysterious gift of being, without abandoning the domain of thought for faith or turning this gift into an object of representation or into an ultimate foundation? After all, even in the breakthrough to the Godhead, when all traditional attributes have fallen to the wayside, Eckhart is still, according to the early Schürmann, able to call on a 'thou.' Can the thinker—and it is as a thinker that Schürmann writes to Heidegger, however much it was his "secret hope" that he "would manage to make him speak about God"[39]—can the thinker not do the same for what gives being?

Heidegger's reply during their meeting contains one of his most important (and neglected) commentaries on faith and extra-philosophical experience, albeit not in his *ipsissima verba*. Heidegger initially responds in terms that will be familiar to readers of his lecture "Time and Being." Being is not the same as entities, and that which gives being—the 'It' in the phrase *Es gibt Sein*, 'It gives being'—is not the same as being or as the being of those entities. For example, the being of a table, however one might interpret it (as substance, as creature of God, as object, as resource), is different from the table one uses to write on. But that which enables being to be thought of in various ways is *itself* different from these ways. Hence we have (1) entities, (2) the being or beingness of those entities, and (3) the 'It' (or what Heidegger also calls beyng or the event of appropriation) that grants (2).

How does the 'thou' relate to this schema? Heidegger explains that the 'thou' is not, as Schürmann had asked (and hoped), coex-

---

37 See, for example, Heidegger's remarks on the tongues of Pentecost in "The Essence of Language" (GA 12: 191–92), or his comments on the opening of John's Gospel (GA 12: 12).
38 Martin Buber, *Ich und Du* (Stuttgart: Reclam, 1983), 71, cited in this volume, 26.
39 In this volume, 16.

tensive with the 'It' that gives being. And yet, the 'thou' is not wholly unrelated to this schema either, as one might have expected Heidegger to say based on a famous remark he had made in 1953: "Within thinking, nothing can be accomplished that would prepare for or have a say in what occurs in faith and grace. If I were so addressed by faith, I would close up shop."[40] This is because the experience of the 'thou' is *not*—contrary to Schürmann's expectations, perhaps—an experience of faith, "although," Heidegger admits, "what is usually designated by 'experience of faith' naturally touches upon it very closely."[41] The experience of the 'thou' is an experience that surpasses philosophical articulation, but one for which thinking nevertheless *prepares*. Beyond entities, beyond beingness, and even beyond the 'It,' the 'thou' is, as it were, the unthinkable *fourth* dimension toward which Heidegger says, remarkably, that his thought had always been heading. The thou, and not being, would thus be, as it were, the "one star"[42] he never stopped following. In Schürmann's account of Heidegger's explanation:

> the gift of being opens up within *Dasein* the possibility of receiving and of saying 'thou.' […] [W]hen the possibility of saying 'thou' to more and to something other than a human being is realized, it is not this 'es' that is addressed by the 'thou,' but rather something beyond it. However, for that, a privileged experience is required which man can never obtain by his own doing, but which only this 'thou' can grant. The experience is no longer one of thought alone, but of all of oneself (those are still [Heidegger's] own words). In this sense, philosophy does not speak about that experience. It does, however, open the paths on which such an experience may become real. In Heidegger's view, Hölderlin certainly had that experience. […] Heidegger understands his entire philosophy as a preparation for this experience of Something Else [*un Autre-Chose*] of which philoso-

---

40 In Hermann Noack, "Gespräch mit Martin Heidegger," *Anstöße: Berichte aus der Arbeit der Evangelischen Akademie Hofgeismar* 1, no. 2 (1954): 30–37 (33).
41 In this volume, 17. Despite this proximity, it should be stressed that Heidegger would still view faith as altogether outside the schema of entities/beingness/It/thou. Faith and the experience of the "thou" are, in other words, incommensurable, and it would be as erroneous to rank them as it would be to equate them.
42 GA 13: 76.

phy itself can no longer speak. [...] [P]hilosophy's role is to open the way by which an unutterable experience may be given, but such an experience would no longer belong to philosophy; it would be the privilege of the one to whom it is granted.[43]

If we have dwelt so long on this exchange, it is not merely on account of its relevance for Heidegger scholarship (even if one might reasonably doubt whether Schürmann misunderstood Heidegger here; for, to our knowledge, Heidegger never speaks about thinking as preparing for an experience of a thou, however significant the last god, the other beginning, and the wholly other may be in his writings.) More importantly, for the present study, we have focused on this exchange because of its impact on Schürmann's own trajectory. Schürmann, in fact, never ceased to wonder about the limits of an 'effable' translation of an ineffable experience, even if the type and content of such experience would change drastically over his career. Furthermore, after his meeting with Heidegger, he would no longer, in any of his extant writings, seek to discern a 'thou' in the gift of *being*, even if he was not yet ready to give up on this possibility in person.[44] Schürmann's one-time confrère Jean-Miguel Garrigues, O.P., for example, provides evidence of Schürmann's personal openness in his recollection of Schürmann's awe-inspiring performance during a nine-day retreat at the medieval Castle of La Chaux in Bourgogne, where nineteen French- and German-speaking Dominicans had gathered in September 1967 to discuss, of all things, Heidegger's essay "Nietzsche's Word: God Is

---

43 In this volume, 18.
44 Indeed, if the sermon Schürmann delivered during the season of Advent in 1966 is indicative of his own beliefs, he was not yet ready to give up on the 'thou' as savior and "vanquisher of death." For Schürmann the preacher, Eckhart's message of eternal birth was, in other words, "insufficient," as was the imitation of Christ on Good Friday. One must also look to Jesus's resurrection on Easter. Schürmann explains: "Christmas is no match for the reality of death," for "when the certainty of death comes to verify our existence, only the following affirmation will enable it to resist the ordeal: God saves." In this volume, 39. This is perhaps the most surprising claim from the later lover of tragic wisdom who sought, in the wake of Nietzsche, to stay true to the earth. And yet it was a claim to which Schürmann would again become receptive in his final years, albeit privately. See Moore, "On the Manifold Meaning of Letting-Be in Reiner Schürmann," 126–29.

Dead." Garrigues recalls: "[Schürmann's] knowledge of Heidegger's thought, more developed than that of most of us, his perfect German-French bilingualism, his personal brilliance and charm made him the real animator of this meeting." Schürmann's interpretation of Heidegger nevertheless struck Garrigues as peculiar:

> [Schürmann] already had a very personal reading of Heidegger, in a Gnostic sense of Eckhartian inspiration that I doubt conformed to the thought of the master from Freiburg im Breisgau. In particular, I was not very convinced that his preoccupation with 'Du sagen' (in Martin Buber's sense), of 'saying Thou' [*'dire Tu'*] to Heideggerian 'Sein,' made sense [*ait un sens*] in the latter's thought.[45]

In any event, there is no doubt that Heidegger complicated Schürmann's understanding of the addressability of the unknown God.

For instance, in the conclusion of a presentation on Proclus for one of Welte's seminars in July 1966, Schürmann makes plain that it is impossible to say 'thou' to the Neoplatonic One (at least in Proclus's version of it): "The 'One,' even if it can be determined to be 'uncreated' and 'eternal' [...], is nevertheless not an addressable god [*anrufbarer Gott*]; rather, it is a metaphysical principle with which a person can become one. Perhaps his philosophical-religious syncretism blocked Proclus from saying thou [*das Dusagen*] to an addressable god."[46] As for saying 'thou' to the unknown God, the complications that Heidegger introduced are most apparent in what can best be described as a sort of eponymous sermon on this figure (chapter 4 in this volume).

---

45 Email to Ian Moore dated July 15, 2021. Schürmann's protocol of the first session of the retreat is available in Schürmann et al., "Interprétation par M. Heidegger du mot de Nietzsche 'Dieu est mort': Rencontre philosophique, 1er–10 septembre 1967, La Chaux," Bibliothèque du Saulchoir, call number 198 B 14.

46 Schürmann, "Die Erkennbarkeit des 'Einen' aus Exitus und Reditus," Universitätsarchiv Freiburg, Germany, call number E 8/189, and Reiner Schürmann papers, NA.0006.01, The New School Archives and Special Collections, The New School, New York City, USA, Box 2, Folder 25, p. 13.

§4. The Unknown God

Was GOtt ist weiß man nicht: Er ist nicht Licht / nicht Geist /
Nicht Wonnigkeit / nicht Eins / nicht was man Gottheit heist:
Nicht Weißheit / nicht Verstand / nicht Liebe / Wille / Gütte:
Kein Ding / kein Unding auch / kein Wesen / kein Gemütte:
Er ist was ich / und du / und keine Creatur /
Eh wir geworden sind was Er ist / nie erfuhr.
What God is no one knows: He is not light, not spirit,
Not bliss, not one, not what is called the Godhead:
Not wisdom, not reason, not love or will or goodness:
No thing, nor non-thing, not an essence or a mind:
He is what I and you (no creature),
Did not experience, ere we became that which He is.
—Angelus Silesius, "Der unerkandte GOtt"[47]

Even if Schürmann never delivered it as a sermon, and even if he himself decided to publish it in May 1966 as an article in the popular Christian weekly *Der christliche Sonntag* (*The Christian Sunday*) (now published under the title *Christ in der Gegenwart* [*The Christian in the Present*]),[48] this text, titled "Der unbekannte Gott" ("The Unknown God"), attempts to provide an answer to the questions concerning the addressability and knowability of God. It nevertheless also corroborates Schürmann's growing distance from the discipline of theology, which he will soon, in the spirit of Heidegger, denigrate as derivative. Heidegger had, after all, explained during their meeting that, as Schürmann recounts:

> it would properly amount to theology to say that man can only say 'thou' to what in a granting gives itself in the '*es*' because he also harbors his origin within it. For, according to Heidegger's argumentation, to consider man as always in relation to a 'thou' would, to put it coarsely, make

---

47 Angelus Silesius, *Cherubinischer Wandersmann: Kritische Ausgabe*, ed. Louise Gnädinger (Stuttgart: Reclam, 1984), 4.21: 154.
48 Two markedly different drafts survive in Schürmann's papers. The earlier version (misleadingly labeled "II") does not, unlike the later version ("I") that served as the basis for the publication, contain a final section on God as a 'thou.' The earlier version is available in translation in Appendix 2 in this volume.

prayer an obligation for everyone. Indeed, if every man always already had a personal relation to this 'thou' which lies in mystery, one would be able to reproach those not respecting this 'thou,' with living in contradiction to their being. That is precisely what dogmatism does.[49]

Schürmann's quasi-homily corresponds thematically and linguistically to much of his thought around this time, when Trinitarian theology was beginning to lose its hold on him. Schürmann would soon write to Geffré from Israel that he was "becoming more of a monotheist [as opposed to a Trinitarian], [as well as more of] a disciple of Eckhart and Heidegger, someone who hopes for the experience of God, than a Christian preacher speculating on the essence of Christ."[50]

Why a sermon? Schürmann's text is a gloss, albeit an implicit one, on St. Paul's defense of the *known* God at the ancient Athenian Areopagus. Whereas, according to Paul, those who worship at the "altar inscribed: To An Unknown God" (*Agnōstos theos*) are themselves ignorant (*agnoountes*) of the omniscient, all-creating God and his filial redeemer (Acts 17:23),[51] those who complacently think they know God via such attributes as 'good,' 'spirit,' and personal addressability (i.e., as a 'thou') are, according to Schürmann, not only ignorant in the worst, least literal sense of the word but are in grave danger. Indeed their very salvation is on the line. In tacit opposition to Paul, whom he never addresses by name, Schürmann contends that "[e]ven after the coming of Christ, we should still speak of the 'unknown God'":

> For, only when we negate all the titles—'goodness,' 'spirit,' 'thou'—that we so casually impose on God; when God confronts us as an unknown God and we believe we cannot get beyond the mystery of his freedom, only then is our heart ready to receive the message of the incarnate one. Otherwise we will remain stuck to an image of God of which we will have

---

49 In this volume, 18.
50 Letter to Geffré, written sometime during Sukkot (September 28–October 5) 1966 (quoted in Moore, "On the Manifold Meaning of Letting-Be in Reiner Schürmann," 122).
51 Here and (with the exception of the Lord's prayer) below, we cite from *The Jerusalem Bible* (Garden City, NY: Doubleday, 1966), which is the English translation of the French Bible that Schürmann used during his time at Le Saulchoir.

to admit one day (for example, when the thought of death calls into question all familiar modes of representation) that his countenance no longer at all has the radiant power to redeem us.[52]

Like Eckhart and Heidegger, Schürmann's discourse is hortatory. Schürmann writes to encourage, even to scandalize, his audience. He wants his readers to negate their commonplace representations of 'God' and to turn toward the mysterious Godhead, toward what he oxymoronically calls, echoing Eckhart, the "known-unknown God" (*bekannten-unbekannten Gott*).[53] In Eckhart's words, which themselves invoke those of Pseudo-Dionysius (whom, incidentally, Eckhart, like most in his day, believed to have been the very Dionysius converted by Paul at the Areopagus [Acts 17:33]):

> Dionysius exhorted his pupil Timothy in this sense saying, 'Dear son Timothy, [...] with untroubled mind soar above yourself and all your powers, above ratiocination and reasoning, above works, above all modes and existence, into the secret still darkness, that you may come to the knowledge [*bekantnisse*] of the unknown super-divine God [*unbekanten übergoteten gotes*].'[54]

Paradoxically, arriving at such 'knowledge' does not eliminate the essentially unknown character of the Godhead. Eckhart can, at times, accordingly prioritize un-knowing and non-knowledge. For example, answering potential queries from his congregation in two other Middle High German sermons, he preaches:

> Is *that* the best thing for me to do—to raise my mind to an unknowing knowledge [*unbekantez bekantnisse*] that can't really exist? [...] Am I supposed to be in total darkness? / Certainly. You cannot do better than to place yourself in darkness and in unknowing [*unwizzen*].[55]

---

52 In this volume, 27.
53 Ibid.
54 DW 4: 359,146–360,149 (Pr. 101, "Dum medium silentium tenerent omnia") / *The Complete Mystical Works of Meister Eckhart*, trans. Maurice O'C. Walshe, rev. Bernard McGinn (New York: Crossroad, 2009), 34.
55 DW 4: 478,41–44 (Pr. 103, "Cum factus esset Iesus annorum duodecim") / *The Complete Mystical Works of Meister Eckhart*, 56.

What is the final end? It is the hidden darkness of the eternal Godhead, which is unknown [*unbekant*] and never has been known and never shall be known. God abides there unknown in Himself, and the light of the eternal Father has ever shone in there, and the darkness does not comprehend the light.[56]

A similar tension between knowledge and non-knowledge, between affirmation and negation, will pervade Schürmann's unknown God essay. Here, too, we find prefigurations of Schürmann's later notion of the double bind.

Following a conversational introduction to the essay, wherein Schürmann asks whether we have ever experienced God in a godly way—in the way, for example, we occasionally experience the enigmatic freedom of another person—Schürmann proceeds to elucidate three well-known biblical verses in which traditional predicates are ascribed to God. Or rather, Schürmann does not so much *elucidate*, that is, shed light on, these verses as seek to return them to the obscurity from which they first emerged in language, to a darkness that the light of the representable God cannot reach. Again like Eckhart and Heidegger, Schürmann cares little for the context of his source-text.[57] Experience is all.

First, Luke 18:19: "no one is good but God alone." "Is God good?," Schürmann asks in response. On the one hand, no, God is not good, at least not insofar as we associate God's goodness with reliability or utility, that is, with his goodness *for* us. In this sense, God is 'no good,' as one says of something that has no use value. Schürmann can therefore have recourse to Eckhart:

> Perhaps the word that Meister Eckhart called out from his pulpit to the faithful also applies to us: "Some people say: 'I have ten *malter* of grain and just as much wine this year; I firmly trust in God!' Quite right, I say,

---

[56] DW 1:389,6–10 (Pr. 22, "Ave gratia plena") / *The Complete Mystical Works of Meister Eckhart*, 283. Eckhart refers back to this passage in DW 2: 476,12–477,1 (Pr. 51, "Hoc dicit dominus: honora patrem tuum"). Cf. John 1:5.

[57] For Eckhart's hermeneutic disregard of context, see Bernard McGinn, *The Mystical Thought of Meister Eckhart: The Man from Whom God Hid Nothing* (New York: Crossroad, 2001), 27. For Heidegger's, see Ian Alexander Moore, *Dialogue on the Threshold: Heidegger and Trakl* (Albany: State University of New York Press, 2022), especially chapter 2.

you have complete trust—in the grain and wine!" We may succeed in experiencing God anew in the mystery of his freedom if we say: no, God is not good![58]

On the other hand, yes, God is good, but this would have to be a goodness beyond everything we are familiar with as good. It would have to be a goodness that is no different from godliness. If God's being and action are inseparable, then he "does nothing good [*tut nichts Gutes*]; he does what is godly [*er tut Göttliches*]," as Schürmann phrases it.[59] (Schürmann does not spell this out, but if, as he says, it is true that "There are not two ways of being good, of which the one would belong to God and the other would be 'purely human,'" then our goodness would also have to be understood as godly.[60] This reading would align with Eckhart's treatment of the just, good, and true person as no different—to the extent that they are just, good, and true—from justice, goodness, and truth themselves, hence as no different from God himself.) Before the mystery of such an unknown God, whose goodness cannot be separated from his godliness, Schürmann, at this point in his argument, advocates both silent worship and excessive predication, both the *via negationis* and the *via eminentiae* of Pseudo-Dionysius and his successors.

Second, John 4:24: "God is a Spirit." "Is God spirit?," Schürmann asks in response. Inasmuch as God is thought to be incorporeal, it might make sense to call him spiritual, but Schürmann is wary of the dualism—bordering on the Gnostic heresy he likely wants to fend off—that this could lead to: God or spirit would be *opposed* to everything material. And yet it is not as though God were located elsewhere. God, at least the God of the end times, does not admit of the spirit/matter opposition. While one might expect Schürmann to appeal to Paul's First Epistle to the Corinthians at this point (15:28: "And when everything is subjected to him, then the Son himself will be subject in his turn to the One who subjected all things to him, so that God may be all in all"), he instead, in an earlier draft version, refers to Teilhard de Chardin's idea of a reconciliation between mind

---

58 In this volume, 23.
59 Ibid.
60 In this volume, 22.

and matter in the Omega Point. But, in a next step, Schürmann distances himself even from Teilhard:

> in order for God to appear again to our faith in his devotion-worthy Godhead [*Gottheit*—one of Eckhart's favorite words—] we should not attempt to think of him as opposition to or as the developmental goal of matter, nor should we at all conceive of God as 'this or that' [*'dies und das'*—one of Eckhart's favorite execrations—] in contradistinction to this or that piece of matter.[61]

Rather, we must move beyond all "representational thinking" (*vorstellendes Denken*—a favorite phrase of Heidegger's—) including that of God as *Geist*, "so that God for us may again become God," that is to say, the mysterious, unknown God—the "true God worshiped in *all* religions."[62] Hence, the unnameable, mystical, 'monotheistic' God (to recall Schürmann's aforementioned letter to Geffré). Only by releasing ourselves *from* the fetters of the represented God—i.e., by leaving him behind—and releasing ourselves *for* his abyssal Godhead—i.e., by letting the latter hold sway—will we be ready, Schürmann adds, to receive the Word. Apophatic detachment thus becomes the *sine qua non* of authentic Christian life. Centuries earlier, after declaring, in negative theological fashion, that "God is not good," Eckhart too had preached a divine spiritlessness:

> God is not loveworthy, He is above all love and loveworthiness.
> —'Then how should I love God?'
> —You should love God nonspiritually [*nichgeistliche*]: that is to say the soul should be de-spirited [*nichgeistig*], stripped of spiritual dress. For as long as the soul is in spirit form, she has images; as long as she has images, she has means; as long as she has means, she has not unity or simplicity, and as long as she has not simplicity she has never rightly loved God, for true love lies in simplicity. Therefore your soul should be de-spirited of all spirit, she should be spiritless [*geisteloz*], for if you love God as He is God, as He is spirit, as He is person and as He is image—all that must go!

---

61 In this volume, 314.
62 In this volume, 25; emphasis added.

—'Well, how should I love Him *then?*'
—You should love Him as He is: a non-God, a non-spirit [*Ein nit-geist*], a non-person, a non-image; rather, as He is a sheer pure limpid One, detached [*gesvndert*] from all duality.
And in that One may we eternally sink from nothingness to nothingness.[63]

Third, Matthew 6:9, the opening of the Lord's Prayer: "Our Father, who art in heaven," or in the German of Schürmann's youth: "Vater unser, der *Du* bist im Himmel," "Our Father, *thou* who art in heaven." "Is God a 'thou'?," Schürmann asks in response. His initial answer smacks more of Martin Buber than Meister Eckhart, despite Schürmann's earlier claim that a trace of the 'thou' remains even after the Eckhartian breakthrough to the Godhead. The 'thou,' Schürmann says at this point in his career, is the best way to escape idolatry. When you say 'thou' to someone, you open yourself to the mystery of an encounter. Of course, by itself, the pronoun 'thou' refers to no one in particular; yet, in context, by calling on the each-time-singular addressee of the utterance in which it is proffered, it calls them out as the counterpart of an always singular address. Saying 'thou,' you are not addressing an 'it'; you are always addressing *someone, a* someone who is included and then held in a dual, dialogical relationship and who, by the very fact of 'being there' in such a relationship, can eventually transform you. This is, however, just a preview of the radical transformation afforded by 'the eternal thou' (Buber's phrase, which Schürmann fails to credit)—a thou that alone can provide rest and that alone makes possible encounters with other people, i.e., with other 'thou's. "Every singularized [*geeinzelte*] thou," writes Schürmann,

> is a glimpse [*Durchblick*] of the eternal thou. Whoever begins to say thou will not find rest until he succeeds in addressing [*anzusprechen*] the godly thou and corresponding [*entsprechen*] to it. An all-encompassing ability-to-say-thou [*ein allumfassendes Du-sagen-Können*] is given to being human, and that means he is able and called on [*aufgerufen*] to say thou to the all-encompassing.[64]

---

63 DW 3: 441,6 and 447,11–448,9 (Pr. 83, "Renouamini spiritu") / *The Complete Mystical Works of Meister Eckhart*, 463–65.
64 In this volume, 26.

It is worth lingering on this passage and following Schürmann's argument closely, for what he is depicting here is a doctrine of the 'thou' as no less than a token of God's infinite love for us and of our freedom as evidence of this love. Our all-encompassing ability to say 'thou' is also a call to say 'thou' to the all-encompassing, in which alone we will find rest. The reason for this restlessness is that no singularized 'thou' can ever exhaust the human capacity to say 'thou'; only the 'godly thou' can. In Schürmann's words: "every beloved being commit[s] the injustice of not being God: it can never completely satisfy and fulfill our power to say thou."[65]

What is implied here is that, with the capacity to say 'thou,' the human being is nonetheless given the freedom by God *not* to find rest in addressing the 'eternal thou' and, instead, to keep saying 'thou' only—restlessly—to singularized 'thou's. In other words, by being able to address God as 'thou' and to correspond to it, the human being is, at the same time, able *not* to address God and *not* to correspond to God's "eternal pledge"[66] [*Zusage*] of 'being there' as an addressable God, one who is 'knowable' by means of such addressability. For, Schürmann adds significantly, "[t]he God to whom I say thou is the God *whom I know.*"[67]

Just a year earlier, in "The Reredos," Schürmann had said that God "has wanted us to be able to know him [*le connaître*] as something 'ontic.'"[68] In "The Unknown God," Schürmann instead suggests that it is out of his love for the human being that God bestows himself as 'addressable' and 'knowable' through our saying 'thou' to him—i.e., in a linguistic, dialogical relationship.

And yet, Schürmann continues, God is more than his relation to us or to the world. He does not need the world, and he does not need us. Saying 'thou' to God reduces him to a "'God-for-me.'"[69] It reduces God to being there as an addressee of our call, as well as an addresser of the pledge to be there, then, now, and always, as such an addressee. It thereby ends up locking him up in the dual or 'thou'-bound anthropomorphic relation thus established.

---

65 Ibid.
66 In this volume, 27.
67 Ibid.; emphasis added.
68 In this volume, 10.
69 In this volume, 27.

However, we can only know the 'God-for-me' and not God in and for himself. God makes himself addressable as a 'thou' only to leave us free to correspond to his pledge to be God-for-us. Yet, Schürmann adds, it is only by saying "'I-for-God'" that God "becomes godly again."[70] Here, the 'thou' becomes the cipher of any relation to an addressable God (*anrufbarer Gott*), and all our 'I's, in their absolute ontological dependency, are 'I's-for-God, since the only real 'I'—as 'I-for-I'—is God in his absolute ontological independence.

Between 'I' and 'thou' there opens up a chasm, a space of addressability and knowability in which the 'call' can resound and the ability to say 'thou' can (and can *not*) be actualized, a distance that Schürmann will later refer to as 'peregrine difference.' Although the 'eternal thou' makes dialogical love for any 'thou' possible, it does not exhaust the mystery of God. Prior to any encounter, even prior to any "God whom I can encounter," God *is there*.[71] That is why even the 'thou' is ultimately inadequate. We may therefore "dare the sentence: no, God is not a 'thou.'"[72]

Incidentally, if we recall Schürmann's report of his visit to Heidegger, we will notice that the Freiburg philosopher was not wrong in pointing out the subtle 'theological' danger in the young friar's desire to address "what in a granting gives itself in the '*es*'" (of the *Es gibt Sein*) as a 'thou.'[73] (Already in "The Reredos," Schürmann had clearly stated that no one and nothing but God "'gives' being."[74]) Yet, Heidegger perhaps was mistaken in considering the capacity to say 'thou' to the all-encompassing to be an obligation to prayer: we could certainly—and, as he feared, dogmatically—"reproach those not respecting this 'thou'" for failing to actualize their capacity to say thou to it; however, the possibility that is afforded to them to *not* actualize that very *Dusagen*-capacity to the 'eternal thou' would not amount —as Heidegger had dreaded—to "living in contradiction to their being,"[75] but rather—as is implied in Schürmann's argument—

---

70 Ibid., mod.
71 Ibid.
72 Ibid.
73 In this volume, 17.
74 In this volume, 10.
75 In this volume, 18.

to enacting the human freedom to only love singularized 'thou's as it is bestowed on us by the all-encompassing.

In the concluding paragraph of the essay, however, Schürmann seems to present an alternative method to the one pursued heretofore. Rather than linguistic detachment—from titles for God such as 'good,' 'spirit,' and even 'thou'—he proposes the imitation of Christ:

> The paradox of the known-unknown God can be resolved [*aufgehoben*] only in a living form. For us, this means that we can overcome it only by daily imitation of Christ [*Nachleben Christi*, more literally 'living after or in accordance with Christ']. [...] The greatest thing we can say now is that we have experienced God in the crucified one.[76]

But then, in the final sentence of this dense, precocious paper, Schürmann again returns to the primacy of "the unknown God of mystery," since "only the latter can *zusprechen* to us the one true word, which is his son."[77] Note that the term *zusprechen* not only connotes speaking (*Sprechen*) and consolation (*Zuspruch*), but typically means 'to attribute.' Thus, by the end of the essay, it is not those who believe in the name of Jesus—or those calling God 'good' or 'spirit,' or, even, calling on him by calling out 'thou'—who have "power to become children of God" (John 1:12); it is rather those who *experience the unknown God*.

In Spring 1966, Schürmann is not yet ready to proclaim publicly, with Eckhart, that each of us is at bottom already coequal with the Son, or even more radically, that each of us is at bottom already of "a single oneness" (*ein einic ein*)[78] with the very Godhead beyond Father and Son. But, remarkably—and heretically—Schürmann does seem to believe, as we suggested earlier in the discussion of God qua spirit, that the specificity of Christian life is a *consequence* of the universally accessible experience of the Eckhartian Godhead. Christ, in other words, is not the only way to God (cf. John 14:6). Rather, the unknown God is the only way to Christ. To return to the earlier metaphor of the reredos, it is as though Schürmann were saying: the only way to gaze properly on the Christian panel—the

---

76 In this volume, 28.
77 Ibid.
78 DW 1: 381,1 (Pr. 22, "Ave, gratia plena").

known God addressed as the 'thou' that 'bestoweth *our* freedom'—is to have first turned our eyes to the other panel—the unknown God, who knows himself "in the knowledge of himself" though is unknown to us "in the mystery of *his* freedom."[79] In lieu of a rifted rock, Schürmann gives us stepping stones.

This picture of Christianity, in which one is able to discern the light of Christ only after having gotten lost in the "darkness of the eternal concealment"[80] of the Godhead, is not the final one that the early Schürmann paints, however.

§5. Of Faith, Theology, Philosophy, and Mysticism

God is better known by not knowing.
Love, and do what you want.
—Augustine of Hippo[81]

In three other texts composed in 1966 and 1967, Schürmann more clearly articulates his understanding of the specificity of Christian faith vis-à-vis theology, philosophy, and mysticism. The first (chapter 2 in this volume), which survives only in the form of an excerpt of a letter dated February 16, 1966, is a diatribe against the 'two-nature/one-person' doctrine of the Council of Chalcedon. The second (chapter 5), titled "A Spiritual Dimension of Technology?," is a letter to the editor of *Der christliche Sonntag* written in July 1966 in response to an article published in the magazine the week before on Christian *Gelassenheit*. The third (chapter 8) is a thirty-eight-page typescript that Schürmann wrote for a course on theological methodology. It dates from Easter 1967 and is titled "The Phenomenon of the Question in Theology." We will discuss each of these texts in turn.

First, we should note that Schürmann was disturbed by the Church's unstinting adherence to the main teaching of the Council of Chalcedon (451 CE), which understood Jesus Christ as two natures in one person. It is not that Schürmann was a Nestorian ('two persons: one human, one divine') or a Monophysite ('one divine person'). The

---
79 DW 1: 150, 7 (Pr. 9, "Quasi stella matutina"); in this volume, 22; emphasis added.
80 DW 1: 382,4–5.
81 Augustine, *De Ordine*, 2: 16.44; *In Epistolam Ioannis ad Parthos*, 7.8.

problem was rather the outdated, abstract philosophical language for Christ's incarnation. Like so many of the faithful, Schürmann aims, as Francis of Assisi had attempted seven centuries before him, to "live according to the Gospel free from the complications of language and misunderstandings about God."[82] But he does not believe that one can separate practice from theory here; for, the latter is a part of life, too, and its metaphysical-historical sclerosis threatens the possibility of a living faith today. What is needed is a new language in theology, a language not just for "the unknown God [*le Dieu inconnu*]," but for "a Son who is also unknown [*un Fils aussi inconnu*]."[83] Indeed, in Schürmann's view, the times have changed so much that "to repeat over and over again that Jesus Christ was 'man and God' can be no more intelligent than to cry out all afternoon: 'great is the Artemis of the Ephesians'!"[84]

Schürmann does not flesh out the new language in this short excerpt from February 1966, but a few of his theological references suggest its skeleton would be largely Heideggerian. He cites Bultmann, the Protestant theologian of demythologization, who drew on Heidegger's early philosophy to try to uncover the existential core of Christianity behind its mythical and supernatural garb. Schürmann mentions Geffré, who drew on Heidegger's later thought to call for a new *Kehre* or 'turn' in theology.[85] And he tells the unnamed addressee of this letter to ask Geffré about Welte's work on Chalcedon. In this work, Welte drew not just on transcendental Thomism, but also on Heideggerian concepts, both early and late, to articulate a notion of Christ's incarnation as dynamic and event-like (*ereignishaft*). Welte speaks of a "theological difference" (*theologische Differenz*) between the timeless, Greek categories of Chalcedon and the eventual and relational (*Beim-anderen-sein*) descriptions of Jesus in the Gospel. Theology today must work out this difference, and to do so it must, in Welte's words, "move beyond Chalcedon."[86] Schürmann couldn't agree more:

---

82 In this volume, 11.
83 Ibid.
84 Ibid., citing Acts 19:28.
85 Geffré, "Le problème théologique de l'objectivité de Dieu," 255.
86 Bernhard Welte, "Zur Christologie von Chalcedon," in *Auf der Spur des Ewigen* (Freiburg: Herder, 1965), 429–58 (457). For Welte's work on Chalcedon and his Christology more broadly, see Godzieba, *Bernhard Welte's Fundamental Theological Approach to Christology* (New York: Lang, 1994), especially chapter 2.

> Instead of speaking incessantly of the divinity of Christ, we would do better to try to broaden this phrase in the sense of an immediacy within the event, of Christ to God. [...] To speak [with the bishops of Chalcedon] of a 'hypostatic' union has become, to say the least, a limited language.[87]

This text on Chalcedon displays not only Schürmann's growing contempt for entrenched theology, but also his openness to revitalize it for the times. Revitalization means more here than being up to date. It means finding words for an age and a faith that have begun to slip free from the grip of Western metaphysics.

By the search for *language*, we do not mean to suggest that Schürmann was unconcerned with the contemporaneous plight of his fellow humans. Far from it. In his 1966 text on technology, Schürmann alludes to an offshoot of the worker-priest movement, referring to "a group of French Dominicans" active in "'profane' work" not merely to proselytize, but also for the betterment of the world. In the wake of this trend, he argues that the "spirituality of our time can only be a 'spirituality of the profane,'" which is to say that theology should try to locate a spiritual dimension in even the most widespread, seemingly most secular phenomenon of the epoch: technology.[88]

Creation once groaned for redemption (Romans 8:22–23). Today, however, 'creation' amounts to little else than human fabrication, and 'redemption' to little else than good social policy. These words may mean more to the Christian, but the surplus is stored only in the private sphere. The believer feels torn between two contradictory worlds. And yet, careful attention to the phenomenon of technology reveals that it follows the same pattern as Holy Week: abandoning theories that prove insufficient ('death') and adopting new ones in the hope of greater accuracy ('resurrection'). Christianity and technology are therefore not structurally opposed to one another, even if there is a crucial difference in the way they relate to the object of their quest. From the perspective of technology, salvation is always

---

87 In this volume, 12.
88 In this volume, 30. For more details on the spirituality of the profane and the *prêtres au travail*, see Yann Raison du Cleuziou, "De la contemplation à la contestation: Socio-histoire de la politisation des dominicains de la Province de France (1954–1969)," section II, http://www.afsp.msh-paris.fr/congres2007/ateliers/textes/at17raisonducleuziou.pdf.

pending. We can never heal ourselves, because nothing we do is ever enough. This becomes all the more evident the more we progress. Our inability to heal ourselves becomes patent in technology. Hence, Schürmann contends that the technological age may be even more fit than ages past to open us up to receive the only one who can bring salvation.

Schürmann next claims that everyone is working for the kingdom of God. The profane and the religious spheres are implicitly one. Only, most people—Christians or not—fail to recognize this, whether from an unbelieving rejection of the paschal mystery or from a believing rejection of its enactment in the day-to-day affairs of technological life. Our shortcomings come from a lack of love, that is, of that in which the unity of the profane and religious consists. Provocatively, Schürmann maintains that love works bidirectionally: we love others by loving Christ, and we love Christ by loving others. "There is but *one* love," Schürmann declares; "in it, we create a better world with every effort, and it also drives us to encounter Christ in faith. It is impossible to love Christ without loving others and impossible to love others without coming closer to Christ *in the same movement.*"[89] In more recognizably political terms, this means that Christians "must actively participate in the process of transformation in the world,"[90] not instrumentally in order to love Christ, but *as* the single love *of* the singular, infra-rational Christ (in both senses of the genitive). In the words of Marx, they too must stop "only interpret[ing] the world" and instead work "to change it."[91] The spiritual dimension of technology should manifest itself immanently, not as a truth imposed from without.

Schürmann concludes with an unsourced quotation, presumably from one of the Dominican worker-priests he mentioned at the outset of the text. The quotation powerfully demonstrates the soteriologically universalist, politically leftist, and thoroughly undogmatic orientation of the milieu of which Schürmann saw himself a part:

---

89 In this volume, 35.
90 In this volume, 36.
91 Eleventh Thesis on Feuerbach, cited in Schürmann, *Reading Marx: On Transcendental Materialism*, ed. Malte Fabian Rauch and Nicolas Schneider (Zurich: Diaphanes, 2021), 18, where, however, he develops it in terms of an "ontology of practice."

It seems to me that the one who has found *agapē*—that is, who loves as Christ loved—is already saved. I think it is more important for love to grow—even covertly—than for Christ to be proclaimed to a community into which he himself has not already been carried by way of a love lived practically. Whoever feeds the hungry and washes the feet of his brother belongs to God, whether he knows him or not.[92]

Schürmann's sympathy for the primacy of the profane practice of love can be seen as the other side of his sympathy for the unknown God. Both are singular, both without why, both "completely heretical."[93]

These 'heretical' ideas would soon work their way into Schürmann's academic work at Le Saulchoir, much to the chagrin of some of his professors. The final text we want to consider in this section is the only extant student paper from Schürmann's specifically theological training at the institution.[94] Schürmann's first three years of study were devoted to philosophy, and his fourth year was spent in Freiburg. His fifth year, 1966–1967, in which he wrote "The Phenomenon of the Question in Theology," included general courses on dogma, morality, exegesis, doctrinal history, canon law, spiritual theology, and liturgy.

---

92 In this volume, 36.
93 Schürmann used the last phrase in acknowledgement of how his ideas on Chalcedon (and thus indirectly on the unknown God) would sound to the addressee of "To Live According to the Gospel," in this volume, 12. Marie-Joseph Le Guillou, professor of oriental theology at Le Saulchoir, denounced the spirituality of the profane as heretical the following year. Interestingly, Le Guillou chose the same example as did Schürmann and the unnamed worker-priest: "Ultimately, economics would no longer allow any affirmation of theology; the practical consequences are no less serious than the speculative consequences, since they lead to a veritable heretical reversal [*inversion hérétique*] of the link between the love of God and the love of neighbor: active love of neighbor would be the sole attitude through which our love for God could be manifested, as though our charity for God should remain *always implicit* in the love of man; or, the spirituality of the profane [*spiritualité du profane*] *as profane* becomes the very trace of the action of God the Savior in the world." Le Guillou, "Réflexions sur la nature et l'unité de la théologie," in *Mélanges offerts à M.-D. Chenu* (Paris: Vrin, 1967), 370.
94 An earlier paper, submitted in February 1964 for a course on Spinoza's *Theologico-Political Treatise*, was technically a part of Schürmann's philosophical training, despite its Biblical-exegetical scope. This paper, titled "La Parole de Dieu," looks at how the Hebrew phrase *dabar ha-shem*—'word of God'—develops in the Old Testament, stressing its significance as an unsettling event. See, in this volume, appendix 1.

Schürmann's paper on theological methodology begins with a preface by his confrère Philippe Nouveau. Nouveau speaks of Schürmann as a guide leading his readers to the authors he discusses but also beyond them to what Schürmann declared earlier was the key concept of his worldview: the mystery. But Nouveau says Schürmann does so as a self-avowed philosopher, not a theologian—a philosopher who, furthermore, prepares for something in the face of which philosophy must fall silent:

> He [Schürmann] calls himself a philosopher and not a theologian. But do these polemics of the bottoms of the valleys still matter on the summits? We prefer, in silence, to listen to his song from across the river and to watch the sea with him as the evening sun sets upon it.[95]

Schürmann begins "The Phenomenon of the Question in Theology" with the suspicion that theology is capable of posing questions only on the basis of certain givens or presuppositions—"revealed truths"—that themselves cannot fundamentally be questioned, at least not if the theologian wishes to remain within the "community of believers."[96] Theology, as theology, cannot pose "the question of all,"[97] i.e., the question of being. Only philosophy has this power. The phenomenon of *the* question does not manifest itself to the theologian. The title of Schürmann's paper, "The Phenomenon of the Question in Theology," is therefore a contradiction in terms.

Such, at least, is the worry, which Schürmann develops by way of an analysis of Proclus's *Elements of Theology*, Heidegger's lectures on Nietzsche, a couple of passages from Aquinas and Eckhart, and *Lumen gentium* (the dogmatic constitution of Vatican II). Schürmann does not exactly allay this worry when it comes to theology proper, but he does, in the conclusion of his essay, allow for faithful philosophy or philosophical faith as a way of life. This way of life would combine Heidegger's insight into the unique question of being and Kierkegaard's insight that faith is always a matter of becoming faithful. In contrast to theology—which, as Schürmann writes earlier in reference to Aquinas's *Summa theologiae*, "treats

---

95 In this volume, 57.
96 In this volume, 59.
97 Ibid.

not of the singular [...] but of principles: God and the theologian know all things by their principles!'"[98]—the singular life of faith knows the singular God, even as it holds onto the question of all:

> The believer [*L'homme croyant*] lives as much off the divine light in himself as off his questioning of being. Existence that believes [*L'existence croyante*] always implies an intrinsic relation to the existence that does not believe: the two are merged in a single adventure that is thus the adventure with God, of Paul or of John. If the theologian knows God and all things according to their principles, the believer knows God in the singularity of his own life as a believer [*en la singularité de sa propre vie de croyant*].[99]

Schürmann seems to be trying to articulate the relation between philosophy as the search for the 'it' that 'gives being' and the experience of the 'thou' for which, as Heidegger had said to him during their conversation (although without saying more), philosophy can do no more than prepare. In "The Phenomenon of the Question in Theology," Schürmann recapitulates Heidegger's claim as follows:

> Being and time say the Same. In a rare privileged experience, the Same (in Heidegger's eyes, Hölderlin was one of those to whom this grace—*Huld*— was granted) lets itself be experienced [*se laisse éprouver*] in the life of a man. The gift of the Same opens up in being-there [*l'être-là*, i.e., Dasein] the field where a 'thou' can be received and can be said [*se dire*]. 'Thou' is thus not fused (one would need to say: Thou art not thyself fused—how difficult it is to escape representation!) with being or with what gives being. Being is not itself that which gives being, it is given. When the 'thou' comes about, granting itself [*s'accordant*] from elsewhere than a being-with-beings [*un étant-avec*], it comes neither from being nor from that which gives being: Thou art not that which gives being. Thou only canst grant the light in which this experience comes about. When thou grantest it, philosophy ceases: the ineffable experience is unthinkable, is addressed not merely to thought (and as Heidegger has confessed, here is his profound intention ever since the publication of *Sein und Zeit*): the

---

98 In this volume, 81.
99 In this volume, 92.

thinking of being must prepare for this experience, but it does not manufacture or capitalize on it [*ne la monnaie pas*]. In a world dominated by the sciences, technology, and art as merchandise, the thinking of being is a preparation for this experience of Something Else [*un Autre-Chose*] of which philosophy itself can no longer speak.[100]

Only, Schürmann goes further than Heidegger was willing to. Schürmann speaks not only of the 'it' and not only of the 'thou' as Hölderlin, for example, experienced it, but also, beyond Heidegger, of the "very closely"[101] related experience of faith and, in passing, of the mystical experience for which *faith* can do no more than prepare.

Whereas the questions of faith and philosophy remain questions in the life of the believer, they "would," Schürmann writes, "be abolished" in the life of the mystic.[102] As the 'thou' was to Heidegger's *Es gibt Sein*, so is mysticism to Schürmann's understanding of faith. Schürmann describes this privileged mystical experience as contrasted with philosophical faith in the conclusion of his 1967 paper:

"The phenomenon of the question in the life of the believer" overcomes this suspicion [about the incompatibility of theology and philosophy] provisionally; the leap into the concreteness of faith is not a leap outside of the lingering abode [*demeure*] that the question of being is for man. But when the provisional shall cease before the power of glory, every question

---

100 In this volume, 79. Schürmann again returns to his conversation with Heidegger in a text dating presumably from the late 1960s/early 1970s. We translate the relevant passage here, for the record: "Heidegger invites us to ask ourselves about this gift, by leaving enigmatic [*laissant dans l'énigme*] 'that' which gives. / Whoever experiences this gift will recover a lingering abode [*une demeure*]. [...] The man [...] who knows how to hear again, who corresponds to the calling [*l'interpellation*] of the gift, will either fall silent, or else will dance and sing. Hölderlin, in Heidegger's eyes, is one of those to whom this experience was granted [*accordée*]. Thinking, the thinking which Heidegger wants to teach us, stops at the threshold of a call. It opens the way where such a call by the Mystery can be heard. / Heidegger understands his whole philosophy as a preparation [...] for this experience of an Elsewhere [*un Ailleurs*] where philosophy cannot lead." Schürmann, "La 'crise de l'occident,' dans la pensée de M. Heidegger," Reiner Schürmann papers, NA.0006.01, The New School Archives and Special Collections, The New School, New York City, USA, Box 1, Folder 25, pp. 8–9.
101 In this volume, 17.
102 In this volume, 92.

and every anxiety shall be struck dumb in the silence of the one who willed them the better to be loved, and this silence shall live off of song and laughter.[103]

Schürmann's analysis, especially of theology, is, to be sure, insufficiently precise, for which his teachers Kleiber and Bernard Quelquejeu did not hesitate to criticize him in their evaluations.[104] To cite just two examples: it is unclear why the tension between philosophy and theology as a science or discipline is overcome in the life of faith, even if it is the case that the life of faith does not abandon the question of being. Additionally, even for Heidegger, it is not always the case that theology is necessarily subordinate to philosophy. For instance, in a late seminar with a group of Marburg theologians, Heidegger granted the legitimacy of this analogy of proportion

theology : God :: philosophy : being

but with the caveat that, while the first pair is in the same ratio with the second, they are incommensurable.[105]

Whatever the validity of these critiques, this early essay on the phenomenon of the question in theology displays Schürmann's developing interests in singularity, in mysticism, and in ways of thinking and being outside of principles. Over the next few years, he will take Eckhart—whom he will call an "expert in itinerancy"[106]—to be the best guide to pursue these interests. Indeed, in a 1968 book review (in chapter 11 in this volume), Schürmann ties his fate to his future work on Eckhart:

---

103 In this volume, 93.
104 These evaluations are available in the Reiner Schürmann papers, NA.0006.01, The New School Archives and Special Collections, The New School, New York City, USA, Box 3, Folder 41-42.
105 Reference and discussion in Jean-Yves Lacoste, "Preface to the 'Quadrige' Edition of Heidegger et la question de Dieu," trans. Stephanie Rumpza, *Journal for Continental Philosophy of Religion* 2 (2020): 159-74 (167).
106 In this volume, 104, and title of chapter 10. Readers should not be misled by Schürmann's definition of Eckhart as an 'expert.' For Schürmann, Eckhart is indeed the one who experienced (*experiri*, in Latin)—i.e., wandered through the perils of—releasement and learned unlearning to become perfectly *abgeschieden* and *gelassen*. Only an *expert* can guide through the *experience* of releasement.

[The author, Bardo Weiss,] absorbs Meister Eckhart's system with the help of a system borrowed from modern manuals of dogmatic theology; he is content to signal the points of intersection between the two "grids," without "thinking," in the strict sense, their meaning. [... W]e await a study on this hermeneutical difference itself—it is our destiny.[107]

§6. Toward *Wandering Joy*

For what we name detachment, know, Oh son, that is Union itself.
—Bhagavad-Gita[108]

At Easter Time in 1969, Schürmann submitted his thèse du lectorat to the faculty of Le Saulchoir, thus completing his years as a student of philosophy and theology and obtaining the right to teach in the Dominican Order.[109] His thesis was titled *Identité pérégrinale: Le concept de détachement dans les sermons allemands de Maître Eckhart* (*Peregrine Identity: The Concept of Detachment in Meister Eckhart's German Sermons*).[110] Two years later, Schürmann would defend a significantly different, much longer version of his text as a dissertation at the Sorbonne, which he then published in 1972 with minor revisions under the title *Maître Eckhart ou la joie errante* (*Meister Eckhart; or, Wandering Joy*) and again in English in 1978 as *Meister Eckhart: Mystic and Philosopher*.[111] When Lindisfarne Books

---

107 In this volume, 138.
108 Cited in this volume, 96.
109 Some of the material in the following five sections appeared earlier in Francesco Guercio and Ian Alexander Moore, "The Call of the Origin: On Christology, Conversion, and Peregrine Identity in Reiner Schürmann's Early Work on Meister Eckhart," *Medieval Mystical Theology* 32, no. 1 (2023): 2–17.
110 Bound copies of Schürmann's typescript can be found in the Bibliothèque du Saulchoir, call number 326 B 312, and the Dominikanerkonvent St. Josef Düsseldorf, call number N-006-00219. The latter copy is available online: https://digital.dombibliothek-koeln.de/ddbkhd/content/titleinfo/523718.
111 Schürmann, "Identité pérégrinale: Sermons allemands de Maître Eckhart," Thèse pour le Doctorat du Troisième Cycle présentée à l'Université de Paris IV–La Sorbonne, June 1971, Bibliothèque du Saulchoir, call number 439 C 194. *Maître Eckhart ou la joie errante: Sermons allemands traduits et commentés* (Paris: Planète, Denoël, 1972). *Meister Eckhart: Mystic and Philosopher. Translations with Commentary* (Bloomington: Indiana University Press, 1978).

republished the English version in 2001, this time under the title *Wandering Joy: Meister Eckhart's Mystical Philosophy*, the leading Anglophone scholar of Christian mysticism Bernard McGinn described it as "[o]ne of the most penetrating and original studies of the great fourteenth-century Dominican. It is a boon for all students of Eckhart to have this ground-breaking book available."[112] Eckhart scholar Richard Woods, for his part, found Schürmann's text to be "deep and insightful" and noted that it had "established the philosophical and theological relevance of Eckhart's thought for a generation of students."[113] And more recently, Alex Dubilet has emphasized how *Wandering Joy* "bring[s] to the front the theoretical freshness, inventiveness, and excitement that can be recovered in Eckhart's thought—a speculative engagement that exceeds the boundaries of the interest of the historian."[114]

What scholars have not been able to appreciate, however, is the significant changes Schürmann's path-breaking study underwent over a five-year span from its first formulation in the 1967 essay "The Philosophical Presuppositions of Meister Eckhart's Christology" (chapter 7 in this volume); through its 1969 submission as a thesis at Le Saulchoir (selections available in chapter 9) and its 1971 article-length summary under the title "Meister Eckhart, Expert in Itinerancy" (chapter 10); to its book-length publication in 1972. Four topics are particularly noteworthy in this regard: the specifically Christological dimension of Eckhart's doctrine of the begetting of the Son in the ground of the soul and in the selfsame ground of God (§7); Schürmann's description of a logic of conversion in Eckhart and St. Francis (§8); Schürmann's attempt at a hermeneutics of the symbol (§9); and the practical outcomes of the ontological difference among being, beingness, and beings as it is inflected by what Schürmann calls wandering or 'peregrine' difference (§10). These crucial points, which, to greater and lesser extents, will later find their way into shorter essays but are not addressed extensively, if at all, in *Maître Eckhart ou la joie errante*, reveal not only the philosophical and theo-

---

112 Bernard McGinn, blurb for Schürmann, *Wandering Joy*.
113 Richard J. Woods, O.P., *Meister Eckhart: Master of Mystics* (London: Continuum, 2011), xii, and blurb for Schürmann, *Wandering Joy*.
114 Alex Dubilet, "[Review of] Flasch, Kurt. Meister Eckhart," *The Medieval Review* (2016), https://scholarworks.iu.edu/journals/index.php/tmr/article/view/22473/29445.

logical preoccupations behind Schürmann's "surge of interest"[115] in reading the Thuringian Master, but also the existential stakes of an authentically detached and released exegesis of Eckhart's preaching of *Abgeschiedenheit* and *Gelassenheit*. For the young Schürmann, the four points are intertwined. We untangle them here so as to shed light on the most considerable shifts between Schürmann's early interpretation of Eckhart's message, especially in *Peregrine Identity*, and his interpretation of it in *Maître Eckhart ou la joie errante*. (Later, we will have occasion to see how Schürmann's interpretation continues to develop in writings after *Maître Eckhart ou la joie errante*.)

§7. Overcoming Christology?

> It is to be noted that God the Word has taken on human nature and not a human person.
> —Meister Eckhart[116]

The first change we want to highlight between the early writings and *Maître Eckhart ou la joie errante* concerns the status of Christianity in Eckhart's writings. Eckhart was no doubt a man of faith. But do not his teachings, for example of the oneness of the Godhead and the spark of the soul at the source of the Trinity, testify to experiences shared by other traditions? And if so, can they not be translated, without loss or betrayal, into non-Christian discourses, such as that of Zen Buddhism or even that of Heidegger's philosophy? Based on *Maître Eckhart ou la joie errante*, one might well conclude in the affirmative. In that text from 1972, there is only one relevant passage on the specifically Christian dimension of Eckhart's work, a passage that Schürmann nevertheless subtly, but tellingly, amended for the 1978 English edition. Here, to begin, is a literal translation of the French original from 1972:

> There is a great temptation to confuse the overcoming of the Son with the overcoming of Christianity altogether. Hegelians, Marxists, and Buddhists

---

115 In this volume, 100.
116 Cited in this volume, 49.

have succumbed to this. Judged by the yardstick of a dogmatic account of the history of salvation, the thought of Eckhart can indeed hardly appear Christian [*peut effectivement paraître peu chrétienne*]. But the logic of detachment reflects the logic of the way of the cross [*Mais la logique du détachement répand un reflet du chemin de la croix*].[117]

In the final sentence of the quotation as it is found in the 1978 English version, a qualifier is introduced, the grammatical mood shifts, and the assertion becomes tentative:

> But it may well be that the logic of detachment somehow reflects the logic of the way of the cross.[118]

Indeed, in the interim, Schürmann expressed himself more directly (albeit not in print). In a paper on "Heidegger and the Mystical Tradition," written in the years leading up to his decision to leave the priesthood in 1975 but never published during his lifetime, Schürmann relegates Eckhart's Christian terminology to mere "cultural conditions":

> Meister Eckhart's vocabulary is Christian. The attitude of Releasement reflects itself in a movement between man and God. I consider, though, that this is due to cultural conditions: the experience itself is not religious.[119]

Or as he said in a 1977 lecture when discussing union with the Godhead:

> The unity that is naturally given remains at the same time a task to be achieved: one must become "One with the One, One from One, One in One; and in One, One—eternally" (DW V, p. 119, 6f.). Here the difference

---

117 Schürmann, *Maître Eckhart ou la joie errante*, 257. Here and below, we give the pagination for the 2005 paperback (Paris: Payot & Rivages).
118 Schürmann, *Wandering Joy*, 162; emphases added. Here and below, we refer to the 2001 republication of the English.
119 Reiner Schürmann, "Heidegger and the Mystical Tradition," ed. Francesco Guercio, *Journal of Continental Philosophy* 1, no. 2 (2020): 284–303 (288). This paper was written while Schürmann was teaching at Duquesne University (1972–1975). Cf. Reiner Schürmann, "Heidegger and Meister Eckhart on Releasement," *Research in Phenomenology* 3 (1973): 95–119 (95–96).

between the originative and the originated has vanished. [...] Eckhart ceases to be theocentric at all. And here I think we leave the schemes of thought of the inherited Christian metaphysics of the West.[120]

It would seem, then, that there is nothing specifically Christian at the core of Eckhart's thinking or, at least, nothing specifically Christian that should be taken for granted.

Yet this conclusion is the result of a progressive 'de-theologization' of Eckhart's imperative of releasement and a progressive universalization of his appeal to live without why. In the late 1960s, Schürmann was instead more confident—albeit not certain—about the Christian core of Eckhart's teaching and preaching. For example, in the 1967 essay specifically dedicated to "The Philosophical Presuppositions of Meister Eckhart's Christology," Schürmann had not yet dared to call the Eckhart's Christianity into question. Eckhart was, to be sure, "less interested in reflecting on Christ's ontological constitution" or in "the intelligibility of the historical God-Man" than in the "filiation" of the Son in the soul—which does not take place in historical time, but, rather, unfolds in the essential *nunc* or the *nullum tempus* of eternity.[121] And Eckhart's utter disregard for the historical Jesus and his focus on what Schürmann, in this early essay, labels an "existential turn" in Christology were likely already signaling to the young friar the unorthodoxy of his fellow Dominican: to "exist as a Christian" means nothing more than to "detach myself from my person in the moment and [to] give birth in myself to the Son of God."[122] Yet, according to the very early Schürmann, there was "nothing heretical" about Eckhart's answer to the radical question "How is Jesus Christ present in my life?"[123] On the contrary, even though Eckhart considered human 'nature,' and not the human 'person,' to be the "locus of divine filiation,"[124]

---

120 In this volume, 249n455. See §13, below, for Schürmann's later retraction of this claim and contention that Eckhart's theocentrism is instead unyielding and marks a narrow yet unbridgeable difference from Zen.
121 In this volume, 51.
122 In this volume, 53.
123 In this volume, 52.
124 In this volume, 50. Schürmann's mentor Claude Geffré did not, in contrast, find this aspect of Eckhart's teaching to be as radical as Schürmann had assumed. See Geffré's evaluation in appendix 3 in this volume.

what he was proposing with his preaching was nothing less than "a path to existence that is an 'imitation of Jesus,' a *kenōsis* of the Christian."[125] Hence, in 1967, Schürmann can judge that Eckhart's thought "is 'Christian.'"[126]

In his 1969 thesis, Schürmann continues to take the question seriously as to whether Christianity is an inextricable element of Eckhart's teaching and preaching, although his interest in the Meister is becoming even more Heideggerian. We must, to be sure, release ourselves from all attachments so as to be able to own up to and live out our oneness with the detachment or releasement of the Godhead. This is, as Schürmann had already said in 1967, the "intuition of Meister Eckhart."[127] But now, in 1969, Schürmann sees the Eckhartian "spirit of letting-be" as diametrically opposed to the domineering, "Promethean attitude" of our age,[128] just as Heidegger sees *Gelassenheit* as diametrically opposed to technological *Gestell*.

There are two things in Eckhart that, when properly understood, make Schürmann lean toward attributing an essentially Christian dimension to his work. The first, as we already suggested, pertains to Christ's *kenōsis* or 'self-emptying' on the Cross as recounted in Paul's Epistle to the Philippians (2:7–8). Although, as Schürmann continues to note, Eckhart was not particularly interested in the historical Christ, Eckhart's "destruction of theology as a science of God" was not aimed at overcoming Christology altogether but rather at distilling, through detachment and letting be, its essentially practical meaning: *imitatio Christi*.[129] Schürmann ventures to state that "for Eckhart, theology, the *logos* about God, is nothing other than precisely the preaching of detachment or of conversion," and even that, for the Meister, "theology does not exist independently of the preaching of conversion."[130] The 'imitation of Christ' is the only way to experience God without the reified 'God'; it is the only way to experience the divinity or Godhead without yielding to the temptation of begging for entitative moorage. For, as Schürmann declares,

---

125 In this volume, 51.
126 Ibid.
127 In this volume, 42.
128 In this volume, 106.
129 In this volume, 119.
130 Ibid.

only the person who sets out on the way of detachment and thus undergoes the ordeal or "test of fire" that is the abandonment of "all supports to faith"—even the support of God himself—shall "follow Jesus Christ on the way of the Cross."[131]

Christ's self-emptying cannot, however, be dissociated from his love for humankind. Imitating him thus means being "united in [...] love [*agapēn*]," as Paul writes in the second chapter of his epistle just before presenting the *kenōsis* hymn (v. 2). This is the second aspect of Eckhart's Christianity that Schürmann stresses in the 1969 thesis, invoking the superiority of Martha over Mary in Eckhart's eighty-sixth sermon ("Intravit Iesus in quoddam castellum etc.") and recalling his earlier remarks in "A Spiritual Dimension of Technology?" Conceding now that Eckhart's daring mystical speculation and fervent imperative preaching might have led him to trespass the limits of Christian doctrine, Schürmann nevertheless argues in his favor by affirming that "if there is *hybris* in the work of Meister Eckhart, it is at least good to the extent that it leads to a mercy that acts among men."[132]

These two aspects bring Schürmann to conclude that "Eckhart's thinking, in spite of the reservations that we have articulated and that should not be minimized, is profoundly Christian in inspiration [*d'inspiration profondément chrétienne*]."[133] Yet it is unclear how literally we are meant to take the word 'inspiration' here. Does Schürmann mean that Eckhart was motivated by (but may well have moved on from) Christianity, as 'inspiration' is often casually spoken of today? Or does he mean that Eckhart's preaching of the love of detachment was pneumatically animated by the very breath of the Holy Spirit? Whatever Schürmann may have answered later in life,[134] it would be peripheral, if not inappropriate, for him to give a definitive answer here, if indeed his aim in turning to Eckhart was a

---

131 Ibid.
132 In this volume, 122.
133 In this volume, 121.
134 Not only, as mentioned, does Schürmann 'de-theologize' Eckhart just a few years later; he also de-theologizes the term *kenōsis*, using it for the emptying out of the *archē*—the ultimate normative authority—and of epochal history—the history of Being—as governed by it. Schürmann, *Des Hégémonies brisées*, 10, 592, 691, 700 / *Broken Hegemonies*, 4, 514, 601, 609. Furthermore, just two years after the 1969 thesis, Schürmann concludes "Meister Eckhart, Expert in Itinerancy" not with the Martha-

matter less of biographical curiosity or theoretical fascination than of exhibiting detachment and letting-be—or what Schürmann also simply calls "conversion"—as "the condition for the origin to manifest itself as a call [*appel*]."[135]

§8. The Logic of Conversion

> There was no one who showed me what I ought to do, but the Sovereign himself revealed to me that I ought to live according to the form of the Holy Gospel.
> —Francis of Assisi[136]

This brings us to the second difference between Schürmann's interpretation of Eckhart in 1969 and his interpretation in 1972. It concerns the logic of conversion, which is crucial in Schürmann's thesis on Eckhart but almost entirely drops out of *Maître Eckhart ou la joie errante*. As we saw with Eckhart's Christology, there is only one important reference to conversion in the French version of *Wandering Joy*, which Schürmann modified for the 1978 English publication. Here, again, is a literal translation of the French, followed by Schürmann's later English rendering:

> To learn the conversion that is ordained [*ordonnée*] and to comprehend the perfect identity with God that is already given [*donnée*]—these are the two faces, legislative and manifestative, of detachment [*détachement*].[137]
> For Eckhart, learning how to give up everything and understanding perfect identity with God, which is already given, are the two aspects, legislative and manifestative, of releasement.[138]

Releasement is at once the prescription to let go of, that is, to detach ourselves from, all distinction in ourselves and in God and the

---

Mary sermon but with a Zen tale, thereby suggesting, if not their equivalence, then at least a shared underlying experience. In this volume, 133.
135 In this volume, 114.
136 Cited in this volume, 114.
137 Schürmann, *Maître Eckhart ou la joie errante*, 13.
138 Schürmann, *Wandering Joy*, xix–xx.

description of the selfsame essence of ourselves and of God. This essence or way of being (Middle High German *wesen*) is less a static state than a process that essentially holds sway (*west*) 'before' and 'beneath' not just the dichotomies of activity and passivity, immanence and transcendence, subject and object, time and eternity, but any and all ends by which action is directed (whence Eckhart's anarchic appeal to life "without principle" [*sine principio*] or "without why" [*sunder warumbe*][139]).

Now, in *Maître Eckhart ou la joie errante*, the practical side of detachment—i.e., what Schürmann calls in the thesis "the apprenticeship of the craft [*métier*] of living"[140]—and the hermeneutical one—i.e., understanding one's existence by means of interpreting the word that addresses one as a call—are both maintained as its essential aspects. However, in *Maître Eckhart ou la joie errante*, 'conversion,' a term whose religious connotation suits a thesis in theology, makes way instead for a more secular paraphrase of detachment: 'give up everything.' In the thesis, on the contrary, conversion plays a key role, denoting as it does a double, joint and thorough (*con-*) movement of turning (*vertere*): not only that of the human toward the origin, but also and above all of the origin to the human. It is the origin that, in the first place, converts to "the detached man" in order for existence to take up a path that will lead it "to renew itself entirely."[141] Nevertheless, for the origin to be able to convert to the human being, and to be heard as a call to him to undertake "identical conversion to himself and to it,"[142] the human being has to abandon himself and even God. He must be—as Schürmann says after Eckhart—totally detached. Using, with Schürmann, a non-subjective transcendental vocabulary, we could say that if the condition of possibility for human conversion is listening to a call—i.e., to the call of the origin that converts to the human—the condition of possibility for the human's listening to the call, and for the origin's call to be able to resound, is detachment.

Exhibiting his debt to the Augustinian tradition, Schürmann first shows that conversion is always, at the same time, aversion. In the

---

[139] LW 3: 16, n. 19 (*In Ioh.*). DW 1: 90,11–91,2 (Pr. 5b, "In hoc apparuit").
[140] In this volume, 107.
[141] In this volume, 114.
[142] In this volume, 112.

fashion of a boustrophedon, one who undergoes conversion turns toward that from which one had, from time immemorial, turned away and turns away from that toward which one has long since turned. Conversion, writes Schürmann, "is an about-face that brings about the rehabilitation of something forgotten, so that the rehabilitated thing is now invested with predilection,"[143] i.e., with pre-eminent love. Yet what is it that has been forgotten? Hinging on Eckhart's notion of identity between the ground of the soul and the ground of God—i.e. the human being's origin—Schürmann declares that what has been forgotten, and therefore must be rehabilitated via conversion, is one's 'perfect identity with God.'

Interestingly, in *Peregrine Identity* but in none of the later versions of *Wandering Joy*, Schürmann turns to Francis of Assisi to exemplify the Eckhartian conversion to "serenity" (*sérénité*—one of the various ways in which Schürmann, as noted, translates *Gelassenheit* in his early work). A century before Meister Eckhart preached detachment, Francis had lived it. Drawing on the earlier *Vitae* of St. Francis, Schürmann recounts the latter's conversion "to liv[ing] according to the form of the Holy Gospel."[144] He finds in this conversion a paradigm of 'peregrine identity,' i.e. of the wandering self-sameness, by way of conversion, of the human with the origin.

Let us linger, for a moment, on Schürmann's reading of Francis's *exemplum*, as it will help us to understand what is at stake in the conversion of a detached human being. First, we note that the episode of Francis's conversion perfectly exhibits the 'kairological' time structure and hermeneutics of listening to the call and setting out on a path to the origin. Conversion only knows the now of a turning in which one's former existence—until *now*—is totally abandoned and existence is—from *now* on—entirely renewed. The decisive now of conversion thus splits Francis's life into two radically heterogenous existences: "Until now ... and from now on."[145] Schürmann carefully underlines that once conversion happens, a revelation of a call to leave oneself so as to turn toward the origin has already been comprehended. When conversion comes to

---

143 In this volume, 111.
144 Quoted in this volume, 114.
145 In this volume, 116.

language and appears "as suddenly evident,"[146] one has already taken the path of detachment. All previously established relations, to oneself and to others, are, in the decisive now of conversion, destituted as binding and thus emptied of their former meaning. Suddenly, existence "becomes significant for itself."[147] Francis, by divesting himself not only of his clothes but of his former existence as a whole, simultaneously goes the way of the Cross and lives with perfect detachment.[148]

Recall that Schürmann had reservations about the essentially Christian character of Eckhart's Christology and of his teaching of "the *kenōsis* of the Christian" through detachment and letting-be.[149] Now, if one can legitimately wonder whether these aspects of Eckhart's thought are to be considered "profoundly Christian" or whether they can instead be derived "from the universal experience that men have of the mystery of being in general,"[150] the same can be asked about 'conversion.' This question arises with respect to Schürmann's efforts to retrieve a logic of conversion at work in its different 'epochal' modes.

For Schürmann, the phenomenon of conversion is governed by a constant kairological and hermeneutical logic. This can also be inferred from an earlier draft of his thesis work titled *Dieu et l'homme, son symbol* (*God and Man, His Symbol*). In the draft, however, Schürmann's understanding of the universal logic of conversion is pushed even further. In this draft—wherein conversion is now called "philosophical conversion" (not a "conversion to philosophy" but "a conversion of existence to its authenticity for which philosophy only attempts to account"[151])—Schürmann

---

146 Ibid.

147 In this volume, 111.

148 Inversely, Schürmann will sometimes translate the Eckhartian language of detachment with terms reminiscent of Francis, such as despoilment (*spoliatio*) and divestment (*denudatio*). Early on in *Wandering Joy*, for example, Schürmann translates one of his French phrases for detachment, namely, *(se) dépouiller*, as 'detach' (xx), 'be devoid of' (7), 'rid (oneself) of' (16), 'let (oneself) be' (27), 'be deprived of' (19), and 'be despoiled of' (35).

149 In this volume, 51, 120.

150 In this volume, 120.

151 Reiner Schürmann, "Dieu et l'homme, son symbole: Une interprétation de Maître Eckhart," Reiner Schürmann papers, NA.0006.01, The New School Archives and Special

reiterates that the modes of such logic are given according to time period and vary according to the cultural conditions under which conversion happens. If, as in *Peregrine Identity*, Francis's conversion functions as paradigmatic, in *God and Man, His Symbol* such exemplarity seems to be assumed not because of its religious character but, significantly, *in spite of it*:

> According to the destiny of the history of being, it is clear that such a conversion [namely, of St. Francis] at the epoch in which it is attested to us, i.e., at the beginning of the High Middle Ages, could not but be religious; yet this changes nothing about the phenomenon.[152]

Although religiously inflected, Francis's detachment simply *instantiates* the cross-cultural, trans-epochal, and hence not specifically Christian logic of conversion to one's own 'authentic' existence. By losing its specifically Christian character, Francis's *exemplum* appears to lose its exemplarity as well. No longer serving as a paradigmatic case of releasement, Francis's conversion is thus left aside and finds no place in *Maître Eckhart ou la joie errante*.

§9. Hermeneutics of the Symbol

> We are the originary word.
> —Reiner Schürmann[153]

Why, however, is the turning through detachment so essential in Schürmann's early reading of Eckhart, and how are we to grasp the distance in which the movement from immemorial aversion to sudden conversion can happen? In order to think of an existence that, by learning the path of conversion, is able to understand its 'perfect identity with God,' Schürmann has to think of something that, by exhibiting both identity and difference, would recollect in itself what is dispersed in the distance, namely, the 'peregrine identity' of the human and the origin. What serves this purpose, for Schürmann, is

---

Collections, The New School, New York City, USA, Box 2, Folder 23, p. 125, note **.
152 Schürmann, "Dieu et l'homme, son symbole," 130.
153 Schürmann, "Dieu et l'homme, son symbole," 109.

the 'symbol.' The symbol has a twofold sense, referring both to itself and to something that exceeds and is concealed in it. In contrast to the image, the symbol brings about what it signifies; it makes one engage on the path of conversion. Alongside 'peregrine identity,' the symbol offers Schürmann another way to name and conceptualize Eckhart's notion of an identity between the human and God:

> Meister Eckhart violently defends himself against this [Platonic and Neoplatonic] theology of the image; one could say that his whole project is an attempt to think not the similarity but the identity between man and God—it was this project, which has been misunderstood, that earned him the charge of pantheism.
>
> The advantage of the image is, to be sure, that it establishes a certain continuity between the signifier and the signified. Yet, on the one hand, the tradition has recourse to images in a context of 'knowledge': the Creator is known through the creature because in it his properties, which are essentially unknowable, are reflected. Thus, for St. Augustine, the soul, thanks to its faculties of memory, intelligence, and will (De Trin. X and XI), or the cosmos, thanks to its beauty and order (e.g. Conf. XIII), are 'images' of God, but when he turns to these images, he admits: *"nec illic inveni te"* ["I did not find you there either"] (Conf. X.25.36). Knowledge through images remains imperfect. On the other hand, the reflection is not what it reflects. Man, the image of God, is not God, but he must take 'paths' that lead to him. *If it were possible to say that man is the symbol of God, it would say more than 'image of God': such a proposition would signify that man is identical to God in some way. The symbol has the task of determining this way.* The image reflects, it does not realize what it means.[154]

It is not incidental, then, that in his thesis work as Schürmann had originally conceived it, Eckhart was only meant to play a complementary part in a much more ambitious project of hermeneutic semiology, the aforementioned *God and Man, His Symbol*, whose subtitle reads *Une interprétation de Maître Eckhart* (*An Interpretation of Meister Eckhart*). The first part of this project, which Schürmann mostly drafted but never published as such, totals to

---

154 Schürmann, "Dieu et l'homme, son symbole," 50–51; emphasis added.

nearly two hundred typescript pages.[155] Although the bibliography of the extant draft is dated January 1968, Schürmann was still working on the project as late as December of that year, at which point he had at least drafted the second part on Eckhart (although this is not to be found in the typescript). One can get a sense of the scope of the project by perusing its table of contents, which ends on an open "Etc.!":

Introduction
FIRST PART: *Approaches to the Symbol*
    Chapter I: *The Symbol, a Given*
        A) A Complex Given
            1) The Symbolism of Water
            2) The Symbolism of Wandering
                a) The Wandering of Parsifal
                b) Romantic Wandering
        B) A Structured Given
            1) An Option: The Reception of Meaning
            2) The Mystery, the Sacred
            3) Myth, Allegory, Metaphor, Analogy,
                Image, Cipher, Ideogram, Sign, and Symbol
    Chapter II: *Symbol and Interpretation*
        A) The Ontological Place of the Symbol
            1) Meaning and Language
            2) Language and Being
        B) Hermeneutics and Existence
            1) From Interpretation to Conversion
            2) From Ontological Difference to
               Symbolic Difference

---

[155] Portions of it would later appear as "La différence symbolique," *Cahiers Internationaux de Symbolisme* 21 (1972): 51–77 / "Symbolic Difference," trans. Charles T. Wolfe, *Graduate Faculty Philosophy Journal* 19/20, nos. 2/1 (1997): 9–38, and "La praxis symbolique," *Cahiers Internationaux de Symbolisme* 29/30 (1976): 145–70 / "Symbolic Praxis," trans. Charles T. Wolfe, *Graduate Faculty Philosophy Journal* 19/20, nos. 2/1 (1997): 39–72. These and other texts on the symbol are also forthcoming in Reiner Schürmann, *The Place of the Symbolic*, ed. Kieran Aarons and Nicolas Schneider (Zurich: Diaphanes).

Chapter III: *The Achievement of the Symbol*
    A) The Achievement of the Symbol in a Poetics
        1) Festival
        2) Song
        3) The Work of Art
        4) Labor
    B) The Achievement of the Symbol in the Sacrament
        1) Philosophy and Theology
        2) A Theological Option: The Ratification of Time
        3) The Celebration of the New Birth
SECOND PART: *The Symbolic Theology of Meister Eckart* [sic]
    Introduction: What Does It Mean to Interpret an Ancient Author?
    Chapter I: The Symbolic Path: *Abgeschiedenheit*
        1) From Negative Theology to Abnegative Theology
        2) The Stages of the Path of Detachment
    Chapter II: Symbolic Identity
        1) Man, the Place of the Difference:
            a) The Difference between Nothing and Being
            b) The Difference between *Ens* and *Esse*
            c) The *Symballein* of the Ground of the Soul and the Ground of God
        2) Meister Eckart's Understanding of Being
                                Etc.!

The surviving draft only goes up through "Chapter III, A" of the First Part (i.e. through 'Labor' in 'The Achievement of the Symbol in a Poetics'). Later portions, such as the section on 'abnegative theology,' can be found in the Easter 1969 thesis, which also reproduces some of the material from the First Part. The 1969 thesis can accordingly be considered the only complete document approximating what Schürmann had initially envisioned for the entirety of his first major work.

It is unclear why Schürmann ultimately decided, for his 1971 dissertation at the Sorbonne (which, recall, would become *Maître Eckhart ou la joie errante*), to separate his work on Eckhart from the larger hermeneutic context of conversion via symbols in which it was supposed to appear. We know that Pierre Hadot, who served on Schürmann's dissertation committee and who would later become famous for his work on philosophy as a way of life, supported the larger project, indeed exactly as Schürmann had conceived it.[156] Bernhard Welte seems instead to have been the one to have convinced Schürmann to proceed otherwise. In a letter to Schürmann from December 1968 (in appendix 4 in this volume), Welte gives a couple of reasons for splitting up the project. Since, in the process, he also provides a helpful summary of it, we will cite Welte at length.

> As regards your interpretation of Meister Eckhart's thought [...] I will repeat my reservations about this plan. Essentially, these are based on two considerations. First, your thought of a symbolic ontology is, as I said, so self-contained, so impressive, and in many respects also so surprising that it does not need to be supplemented [*ergänzt*], as it were, with reference to Meister Eckhart. I fear that this would not be an organic appendix for the reader. And that would be a shame.
> My other reservation concerns Meister Eckhart. I see several essential difficulties in the application of your very impressive thoughts on the symbol to Meister Eckhart's formulations of identity. The symbol, as you interpret it, is a being [*ein Seiendes*], insofar as we observe it as such and, so to speak, as an external formation [*Gebilde*]. Language and existence also become symbols by being observed and interpreted by thinking. What is at issue in Meister Eckhart, however, is something entirely different. Not observation and interpretation, but rather a path of experience. His formulations of identity, at least the most decisive of them, describe entirely precise and concrete experiences, toward which the Meister again and again offers the path of detachment [*Abgeschiedenheit*]. [...] This seems to me to be a fundamental difference, even if it must be admitted that there is an interplay here. But, on account of this difference, I would always have reservations about characterizing the Meister's formulations of identity as formulations of a symbolic identity. I fear that this would not be able to lead the reader down the path that the Meister recommends, but rather distance the reader from that path.[157]

---

156 Information found in a letter, dated November 16, 1968, from Schürmann to Claude Geffré (Diaphanes Verlag, unprocessed private files, Zurich, Switzerland, and Berlin, Germany). See also Pierre Hadot, *The Present Alone Is Our Happiness*, 2nd ed., trans. Marc Djaballah and Michael Chase (Stanford: Stanford University Press, 2001), 7.
157 In this volume, 326–27.

Although, within the scope of his dissertation, Schürmann seems to have taken his professor's suggestion regarding his hermeneutics of symbols quite seriously, he did not forsake a 'symbolic hermeneutics' and went on to develop a hermeneutics of the symbol, namely the gathering of the human, God, and the world or of what he simply calls "the Three."[158] Nor did he abandon his interpretation of Eckhart's identity as a 'symbolic identity,' not even in the published version of his dissertation, where it is defined instead as 'operative' or 'energetic' identity to highlight its event-like character. Indeed, Welte's judgment about the independent status of what he calls Schürmann's 'symbol-ontology' and his apprehension about its applicability to Eckhart's 'formulations of identity' certainly exhibit a genuine professorial concern to set his young student on the right exegetical path; however, it is questionable whether the teacher's suggestion to separate the initial plan into two research projects of a hermeneutics of symbols and of an interpretation of the Meister is entirely justified.

Schürmann's description of the symbol in Eckhart suggests the legitimacy of applying his conception of symbolic hermeneutics to the Meister's teaching and preaching. The following passage from *Maître Eckhart ou la joie errante* (which also appears in a slightly different form in the body of the 1969 thesis) should suffice to clarify what is at stake for Schürmann in interpreting Eckhart's 'formulations of identity' as signifying 'symbolic identity':

> The Greek verb *symballein*, origin of the word "symbol," literally means "to throw together." The anonymity of what imparts itself to you and me unites us in the same operation, that is, it "throws together." The operative or energetic identity is thus "symbolic identity."
>
> Symbolic identity is opposed to the identity of substances. This latter identity is the one that metaphysics and its offspring, pantheism, deal with. It is quite clear that Eckhart had overcome representation of substances. Because he preached out of another form of thought, he was condemned as a heretic. Metaphysical representation admits of no other identity than that of substances with themselves: the ontic identity of a thing that remains itself. In objection to our interpretation of symbolic identity as the rise of the "we" in the event of a dialogue or of the harmony between the soloist

---

158 In this volume, 113.

and his hearer, representational thought would reply: substances are *"simpliciter diversa,"* otherness remains the first and inescapable fact in any relation. To Eckhart's teaching of the simultaneous begetting of the Word it has been objecting for six centuries that God and man are ontologically distinct beings. From the foregoing it results that there are two conflicting ways or orders of understanding identity: that of being as a process and that of being as substance. We have already hit upon this conflict. In a "verbal" understanding of being, one will emphasize symbolic identity, while in a "nominal" understanding of being, one will speak of substantial or ontic identity. Meister Eckhart's understanding of being is "verbal" and that of identity, "symbolic."[159]

Peregrine or symbolic identity hence denotes, for Schürmann, the energetic or event-like character of the human's 'perfect identity with God.' However, this identity, to be comprehended as such, must be experienced through a peregrine or symbolic 'difference,' which leads us to our next point.

§10. Ontological Difference, Peregrine Difference

The bearing out [of the difference] is a circling, the circling-around-one-another of being and beings.
—Martin Heidegger[160]

The fourth and last issue we want to highlight in Schürmann's reading of Eckhart in the late 1960s/early 1970s is his outlining, in *Peregrine Identity*, of what can be described as a practical radicalization of the ontological difference among being, beingness, and beings, which is less explicit in *Wandering Joy*. This practical radicalization Schürmann calls a "peregrine difference"[161] or, in *God and Man, His Symbol*, a "symbolic difference."[162] Taking recourse to Heidegger's

---

159 Schürmann, *Maître Eckhart ou la joie errante*, 171–72 / *Wandering Joy*, 102–103. Cf. Schürmann, "Identité pérégrinale: Le concept de détachement dans les sermons allemands de Maître Eckhart," 108–109.
160 GA 11: 75.
161 In this volume, 110.
162 Schürmann, "Dieu et l'homme, son symbole," 120ff.

famous philosopheme of the *ontologische Differenz* and to the cleft between God and Godhead in Eckhart, Schürmann sets sail to interrogate the existential implications of this difference.

Schürmann first stresses how both Eckhart and Heidegger conceive of a triadic ontological difference. The ontological difference is not to be apprehended as a difference between two beings or entities given to representation and susceptible to comparison by degree. But neither should it be reduced to the metaphysical difference between beings (*das Seiende, l'étant*) and their being (*Sein, être*) or what Heidegger sometimes calls their beingness (*Seiendheit; étantité* in French). Stepping back from this latter difference, Schürmann maintains that the ontological difference is instead to be grasped as an opening between the being of beings (their beingness) and being itself (*das Sein selbst, l'être lui-même*) as the 'clearing' that allows the former to be.[163] Schürmann detects a similar ontological difference in Eckhart. For the Meister, there is an ontological chasm not only between creatures and their origin but also between their status as entities (*iht*) (which is nothing in itself) and the essential unfolding of the origin itself (*wesen*). We can also find in Eckhart a related threefold difference at the level of the divine, which can be conceived as a relatable God (*ho theos*), as being (*on*), and an abyssal Godhead (*to theion*). (Eckhart's thinking is thus not solely 'ontotheological,' as Heidegger, despite his sweeping critique of Western metaphysics, himself once admitted in a letter to Welte.[164] That is, it does not simply understand being as a being or in terms of beings or as the being of those beings.) What Schürmann underlines, however, is that, in order not just to rationally apprehend but to existentially comprehend the ontological difference as such, one has to set out on a path whereby "being lets itself be experienced and tested anew [*l'être se laisse à nouveau éprouver*]."[165] Faithful to the insight that "whoever wants to understand his [Eckhart's] teaching on 'detachment' must

---

163 For this 'double step backward' that Schürmann takes following Heidegger, see Schürmann, *Le Principe d'anarchie*, 36 et passim / *Heidegger on Being and Acting*, 20 et passim. Schürmann speaks of Eckhart's "two steps back" in *Des Hégémonies brisées*, 326 / *Broken Hegemonies*, 274.

164 In Bernhard Welte and Martin Heidegger, *Briefe und Begegnungen*, ed. Alfred Denker and Holger Zaborowski (Stuttgart: Klett-Cotta, 2003), 29–30.

165 In this volume, 107

himself already be highly 'detached,'"[166] Schürmann thus feels the need to supplement a noetic apprehension of the 'difference' (be it spelled out in Heideggerian terms as 'ontological'—between being "as foundation for beings" and being as "truth or clearing"[167]—or in Eckhartian terms as 'the(i)ological'—between God and Godhead or "being-with-God [*l'être-auprès de Dieu*]" and "being-in-God [*l'être-en Dieu*]"[168]) with a practical comprehension of it.

What happens when one takes upon oneself not only to apprehend such an ontological difference in theory but to comprehend it in praxis, thus engaging existentially on the path of detachment? It happens that one finds oneself wandering in what Schürmann calls a 'peregrine difference':

> We call peregrine difference the itinerancy [*itinérance*] under which the existence experiences Being [*l'Être*] as that which converts itself to it in order to send it on the way of its own conversion. The peregrine difference is the distance that joins man to his origin, in a detached existence.[169]

Peregrine difference is, then, for Schürmann, nothing other than ontological difference experienced by the human as wandering. It is how Schürmann understands Eckhart's famous appeal to life without why. A couple of years later, Schürmann will call it a 'wandering joy':

> A detached man, Eckhart says, experiences such a joy that no one would be able to tear it away from him. But such a man remains unsettled. He who has let himself be, and who has let God be, lives in wandering joy, or joy without a cause.[170]

We have shown a few remarkable shifts that Reiner Schürmann's original reading of Eckhart underwent from its first renditions to publication in his famous book *Wandering Joy*. We focused on four key issues in Schürmann's early work on the Dominican Master: the status of Eckhart's Christianity, the logic of conversion, the herme-

---

166 In this volume, 102.
167 Schürmann, "Dieu et l'homme, son symbole," 127.
168 In this volume, 113.
169 In this volume, 112.
170 Schürmann, *Maître Eckhart ou la joie errante*, 13 / *Wandering Joy*, xx.

neutics of the symbol as facilitating realization of peregrine identity, and the peregrine difference beyond the ontological difference. Our intention in this portion of the afterword has been to highlight how, even at an initial stage, Schürmann's exegesis illuminated certain aspects of Eckhart's thinking which still demand interpretive attention and existential engagement. By casting Eckhart's crucial questions over our time of "organized reduction of the earth to a corpse," Schürmann provokes his readers to follow him down the "path without a path."[171] For he, too, as a young Dominican, found himself listening to a call resounding in the 'peregrine difference' and turned to Eckhart's preaching, thus 'converting' to the latter's teaching of detachment and letting-be. Perhaps, in the company of such a great 'expert in itinerancy,' he experienced that:

> The word that is the most intimate to us is at the same time the word in which we recognize ourselves as similar. Only two existences that each realize, according to their own word, the origin that they signify are capable of communication.[172]

In any case, the lines of communication in and through the "single Origin"[173] would soon be broken.

§11. Origin(s) Asunder

Quand s'ébranla le barrage de l'homme, aspiré par la faille géante de l'abandon du divin, des mots dans le lointain, des mots qui ne voulaient pas se perdre, tentèrent de résister à l'exorbitante poussée.
When man's dam was shaken, sucked in by the giant rift of the desertion of the divine, words afar, words that did not want to get lost, tried to resist the exorbitant thrust.
—René Char[174]

---

171 In this volume, 120.
172 Schürmann, "Dieu et l'homme, son symbole," 133.
173 In this volume, 150.
174 René Char, *Arrière-Histoire du Poème pulvérisé* (Paris: Jean Hugues, 1972), 29; Schürmann's translation in "Situating René Char: Hölderlin, Heidegger, Char, and the 'There Is,'" *boundary 2* 4, no. 2 (1976): 513-34 (520).

Eigentlich nämlich kann das Ursprüngliche nur in seiner Schwäche erscheinen.
The originary can actually appear only in its weakness.
—Friedrich Hölderlin[175]

Throughout the 1970s, one can see, in Schürmann's reflections, an acceleration in the aforementioned movement toward 'de-theologization.' To be sure, the holy and the mystery are still at the center of what could be described as his 'symbolic period.'[176] However, they now yield to a new reconfiguration of thinking wherein they are disjointed from the anthropomorphic, addressable God of the Christian tradition. During these fervid years, to the alembic in which Eckhart and Heidegger had already been melting so as to distill an unprecedented thinking of the 'principle of anarchy,' Schürmann adds a new, explosive element: Nietzsche.[177] The reading of Nietzsche—and of the French 'Nietzsche-renaissance' thinkers such as Michel Foucault, Gilles Deleuze, and Pierre Klossowski—marks a decisive shift from Schürmann's early, still-monotheistic desire in the 1970s that "all would be one"[178] to the later polymorphous desire to say yes to the "complex forms of relative life-duration within the flux of becoming,"[179] i.e., the desire to affirm—against what he would come to see as the unifying, principle-based power of the *archē*—the

---

[175] Friedrich Hölderlin, "Die Bedeutung der Tragödien," in *Sämtliche Werke*, 6 vols., ed. Friedrich Beissner (Stuttgart: Cotta, 1962), 4:286.

[176] In addition to "Symbolic Difference" and "Symbolic Practice," both of which stem from "Dieu et l'homme, son symbole," see "Il y a dans le poème…," *Cahiers Internationaux de Symbolisme* 24/25 (1973): 99–118 and its updated English version "Situating René Char," as well as "Du luxe d'exister: Karl Jaspers et le Sacré," *Cahiers Internationaux de Symbolisme* 27/28 (1975): 103–20, "The Ontological Difference and Political Philosophy," and "Politique et déconstruction: Heidegger et les fondements de la philosophie pratique," §48, pp. 615–36.

[177] In a 1977 interview about *Les Origines* Schürmann is clear about the coincidence he sees between Eckhart's *joie errante* and Nietzsche's *fröhliche Wissenschaft*: "To let-be—that is an errant joy. What Nietzsche called the 'gay science' is precisely the errant joy: accept chaos and set joy there." "Reiner Schürmann: Entretien avec un jeune écrivain allemand," *La Croix* (September 30, 1977): 2–3 (2). Schürmann's translation in "An Interview with Reiner Schürmann," Reiner Schürmann papers, NA.0006.01, The New School Archives and Special Collections, The New School, New York City, USA, Box 1, Folders 10–11.

[178] In this volume, 150.

[179] Friedrich Nietzsche, cited in Reiner Schürmann, *The Philosophy of Nietzsche*, ed. Francesco Guercio (Zurich: Diaphanes, 2020), 75.

manifold, ever-changing, and ultimately an-archic emergence and passing away of phenomenal constellations.

Yet, in 1973, Schürmann published a text in *La Vie spirituelle* in which his desire for the "single Origin"—perhaps the same desire for what Hegel, Schelling, and Hölderlin once celebrated as the *hen kai pan*, or even for the eschatological God who St. Paul proclaimed would one day be "all in all" (1 Corinthians 15:28)—and his contempt for "the multiplicity into which we are thrown by forgetfulness and exile"[180] are still very much perceptible. This text, titled "Trouver, enfin, l'origine" ("To Find, at Last, the Origin" [chapter 12 in this volume]), is an embryo of what would become his only novel, the prizewinning *Les Origines*. For those unacquainted with *Les Origines*—a disquieted and, at times, disquieting story whose aim is to unearth "the zone preserved in oneself from which a life arises"[181]—Schürmann's decision to publish an early précis of it in a Dominican journal, in an issue significantly dedicated to 'initiation,' would perhaps appear as an odd publishing choice on his part. The truth is that this prelude to Schürmann's 'autobiographical' novel (scare quotes are in this particular case, a must)[182] cannot be read as a scholarly essay on theology or even as fitting comfortably in a Dominican journal on spiritual life. However, those who have attentively read *Origins* and have found it to be not an anodyne, literary side project of an otherwise professional philosopher but rather Schürmann's *fourth* great work might not be so surprised by this decision. This is because *Origins*—and "To Find, at Last, the Origin," for its part, which condenses the novel's core ideas and avows its hidden ambitions—is first of all an attempt at accounting for an initiation "into the originary life,"[183] or, in other words, at recounting, in writing, an *experience of releasement*.

More precisely, "To Find, at Last..." is Schürmann's attempt at writing down Reiner Schürmann's *own* experience of releasement,

---

[180] In this volume, 153.
[181] "Reiner Schürmann: Entretien avec un jeune écrivain allemand," 2 / "An Interview with Reiner Schürmann."
[182] In a private conversation with Francesco Guercio, Ferruccio Scabbia, friend of Schürmann's and translator into Italian of *Les Origines*, recounted that Schürmann, when asked about his novel, did not like to talk of it as an 'autobiography.'
[183] In this volume, 149.

i.e, of responding, in praxis, to Eckhart's exhortation to live *gelassen*: of submitting, existentially, to the imperative to live 'released' (in the twofold sense of *Abgeschiedenheit* and *Abschied nehmen*, to be detached and to take leave). "To Find, at Last..." can thus be read as an *essai* in *Gelassenheit*, or better, as Schürmann's own *Gelassenheit-essai*, as both a trial of himself and a writing exercise recollecting that very trial.

There are many paths in "To Find, at Last..." worth exploring, from the text's apocalyptic undertone of *Selbstentfremdung*, to the question concerning the limits of language—and the *German* language in particular, irreparably "sullied"[184] as it was by the Nazis.[185] The origin*s* that the narrator in "To Find, at Last..." is, in fact, 'initiating' and 'initiated' to *let go of* and *let be* are, at the same time singular, historiographic, and historical. It is true that "To Find, at Last..."— and to a greater extent, *Origins*—inserts itself in a more general critical trend in post-WWII German intellectual life, namely, what is usually referred to as the *Vergangenheitsbewältigung* or 'coming to terms with the past' of Nazi Germany. In Reiner Schürmann, however, this coming to terms with both a 'singular,' i.e., familial, and a national-'historiographic' (*historisch*) past rises to the dimension of a thorough reconsideration—and one would dare say 'deconstruction'—of the 'historical-destinal' (*geschichtlich-geschicklich*) past of the West—which, for the tradition Schürmann situates himself in, is irredeemably an onto-theo-logical past. Reading "To Find, at Last..." closely, it becomes evident that, in contrast to what is often found in Heidegger, for Schürmann the historiographic and the historical-destinal cannot be altogether disjointed, nor can they be tackled separately if one is to unclench oneself from "the pointed finger of the past."[186] For the factual, historiographic past is rooted in the historical-destinal and only by detaching oneself from the latter one can attempt to come to terms with, or 'release,' the former. But this is only one of the possible readings of "To Find, at Last...."

---

184 Schürmann, *Origins*, 120 / *Les Origines*, 100.
185 For more on *Origins*, see Francesco Guercio, "Introduzione: Su *Le origini* di Reiner Schürmann," in *Le origini*, trans. Ferruccio Scabbia, ed. F. Guercio (Roma: Efesto, 2020), v–xxxi.
186 In this volume, 148.

For the sake of space, and in view of the scope of this afterword, we will limit ourselves to indicating how Schürmann's response to the Eckhartian imperative of releasement to and from the aforementioned threefold origin*s* unfolds as a process of *Ent-bildung*, i.e., as a de-figuration of the 'I,' of the first person singular. *Origins* could thus be defined as an *Ent-bildungsroman*. What interests us here is, in other words, the practical application of *Gelassenheit* to Reiner Schürmann's own existence. In his text, Schürmann notes that the "encounter with oneself that would not come to speech would be the most miserable of defeats."[187] But how can anyone *speak* or even *write* of such a singular experience of releasement, or, and this is equally crucial, of releasement *as singular experience*? Only as 'I.' "Je *suis laissé—I* am released"[188] writes the nameless narrator of "To Find, at Last...." No one but 'I' is released and can "testify," says Schürmann, even "signify"—and this is another element which directly resonates with our previous discussion of his explicitly theological writings—the single Origin that lies "beyond our mutilated origin*s*."[189]

That the guiding thread of Schürmann's first-person account was indeed Eckhartian had already been sensed by the respected scholar and translator of the Thuringian Master into French, Jeanne Ancelet-Hustache, to whom Schürmann would dedicate *Wandering Joy*. In her 1976 review of *Les Origins*, Ancelet-Hustache had suggested that

> those who are acquainted with Meister Eckhart know that, like many others before and after him, he often refers to God as the origin or the One. Isn't it this origin beyond origins that "I" [the nameless 'I' that is the narrator of *Origins*] seeks to rejoin? [...] [B]ut can this One designate a reality other than God?[190]

---

187 In this volume, 152.
188 In this volume, 153.
189 In this volume, 150.
190 Jeanne Ancelet-Hustache, "Un livre, une voix: *Les Origines* de Reiner Schürmann," *Documents* (Septempber 1976): 176–83 (182, 181). Schürmann's dedication is in *Wandering Joy*, xxi. See also Schürmann's reviews of her translations in chapter 11 in this volume.

However, if Ancelet-Hustache is correct in pointing out that the "single Origin" could well be signaling Eckahrt's Godhead beyond God, as well as in stressing the pivotal role played by releasement and detachment in Schürmann's *Origins*, more elements can be drawn from "To Find, at Last..." that would justify viewing this text as Schürmann's account of his own attempt at—to modify a title of one of his later writings—'constituting himself as a released subject.'

We note that such recounted self-constitution is at the same time, for Schürmann following Eckhart, a self-*destitution*. The 'I' to which "I am *released*" is, in Schürmann's account, an 'I' which has unclenched itself from all instances of *Ich-Bindung*,[191] i.e., of all ego-attachments and properties, and which has dispossessed itself even of itself, as first-person singular, in order to be 'translated' into an "originary freedom."[192] It is when Schürmann's detachment from *his* 'I' happens through the sheer exposition—*denudatio* or divestment—of *the* 'I' which binds itself to itself that "the false oppositions collapse" and "a more fundamental knowledge [*savoir*] takes over."[193] This is what ultimately makes Schürmann's "apprenticeship,"[194] i.e., the apprenticeship of his 'I' into detachment—despite the call for "the abolition of language"[195]—a *communicable* experience, *viable* to all *viatores*, to all peregrine 'I's on the wayless way of releasement. Already Albert-Marie Besnard, O.P., Schürmann's former teacher at Le Saulchoir, had grasped that what he had called, with a theologically loaded term, Schürmann's "testimony"—the releasement of the 'I' which can be only *singularly* owned up to—would, were one to let it *say* what it will, "speak also of *you*."[196]

But this was in 1973. *Origins* was still being written and would not be published until 1976. It marks a break in Schürmann's 'coming to terms with the past.' Whether his attempt at self-releasement succeeded, it is up to the readers of his novel to assess. In any case,

---

[191] This is Josef Quint's translation of Eckhart's Middle High German key term *eigenschaft*, 'property' or 'quality.'
[192] In this volume, 107 et passim.
[193] In this volume, 149
[194] In this volume, 148 et passim.
[195] In this volume, 152.
[196] In this volume, 147.

in his obituary notice, Bernard Flynn recalls that Schürmann considered *Les Origins* to be "a work of exorcism"—and that "it worked."[197]

In a 1977 interview with the Roman Catholic newspaper *La Croix*, Schürmann would talk instead of his 'monotheistic' quest for a single Origin as "vain" and finally link the anarchic 'neither-nor' of releasement to a wandering joy that is now gaily built on unstable ground, on the *fundamentum concussum* of self-less self-identity:

> Neither insurrection nor submission, but what I call "letting be," to give to each thing in the present the weight which is appropriate to it. After a time of flight, the vain search for a unique, viable origin—a basis of things which would be stable, as if that existed!—I ended up discovering this: it is in the absence of stable identity, in dislocation, that one must locate one's joy.[198]

In the following years, the origin that Schürmann once believed he had found will again split into different origins: *Ursprung* and *archē*—the bursting forth or the sheer emergence of phenomena through *phuein* and the dominating stronghold of the *principium* and the *princeps*. Schürmann will soon come to focus on targeting and dissecting the latter origin—the origin that, if one were to live released, 'without why,' would be ultimately lost.

§12. Intensities of Releasement on the Wayless Way

> Thus speaks master Eckhart: a master of life [*lebemeister*] would be a better guide than a thousand masters of learning [*lesemeister*], but learning and living prior to God—this, no one can achieve. If I were looking for a master of Scripture, I would look for him in Paris and in the schools of higher education on account of the higher knowledge there. But if I wanted to ask about the perfect life, he couldn't tell me. Where, then, should I go? Always nowhere else than into a nature that is naked and void—*it* could show me what I asked for so anxiously. People, what are

---

[197] Bernard Flynn, "Reiner Schürmann 1941–1993," *Social Research* 60, no. 4 (Winter 1993): v–vii (vi).
[198] "Reiner Schürmann: Entretien avec un jeune écrivain allemand," 3 / "An Interview with Reiner Schürmann."

you seeking in dead bones? Why aren't you seeking the living relic that can give you eternal life? For the dead can neither give nor take. And if the angel were to seek God prior to God, he would seek him nowhere except in a creature that is void, naked, and detached. All perfection consists in willingly, joyfully, emptily, eagerly, calmly and unmovingly suffering poverty and disgrace and misery and contempt and adversity and everything that may befall you and weigh on you, and enduring them to the point of death, without any why [*âne allez warumbe*].
—Proverb[199]

lâ stat, lâ zit,
ouch bilde mît
genk âne wek
den smalen stek
sô kums du an der wûste spor.
Leave place, leave time,
Avoid even image!
Go forth without a way
On the narrow path,
Then you will find the desert track.
—Anonymous, "Granum sinapis"[200]

Despite the differences we highlighted in §§7–10, above, crucial aspects of Schürmann's interpretation of Eckhart in *Wandering Joy* were already in place in his first substantial treatment of the Meister in the 1967 paper "The Philosophical Presuppositions of Meister Eckhart's Christology." For example, Schürmann had already recognized that Eckhart's "fundamental intuition" consists in the "identity with the divinity in view of which man must detach himself and let that which is be"—an identity that, moreover, "has nothing static or 'metaphysical' about it in the sense of a substantial coincidence" but on the contrary is "an accomplishment and an event."[201] Schür-

---

199 In Franz Pfeiffer, ed., *Meister Eckhart* (Deutsche Mystiker des vierzehnten Jahrhunderts, Vol. 2) (Leipzig: Göschen, 1857), 599.
200 Cited in McGinn, *The Mystical Thought of Meister Eckhart*, 114. McGinn also cites Eckhart's Pr. 5b: "'Go forth without a way,' because '[w]hoever is seeking God by ways is finding ways and losing God, who in ways is hidden'" (115).
201 In this volume, 46.

mann had also recognized that, although one can readily discern and name this intuition about the event-like identity of the ground of the soul and the ground of God, it means little if one does not follow it out in one's own existence. Indeed, the condition for understanding Eckhart's teaching of releasement is that we become released ourselves (a condition that Schürmann will later formalize and use to define 'mysticism' and philosophies dependent on a 'practical *a priori*'[202]). Eckhart does, to be sure, give us something of an itinerary. And, already in "The Philosophical Presuppositions...," Schürmann identifies the three main stretches of this itinerary as detachment from dissimilarity to God, appropriation of similarity to and identity with God, and breaking through to the Godhead. But only in *Wandering Joy* and in later essays, where however he divides the second stretch into two, does Schürmann recognize the profound paradox of Eckhart's way: the itinerary is supposed to end in itinerancy, for the way is ultimately wayless. To live without why, the pilgrim 'must' become a nomad, yet this transformation will never occur unless the command is itself released along the way.

Schürmann is accordingly more careful about describing Eckhart's "wayless way"[203] in subsequent texts (even if he did note, in "The Philosophical Presuppositions...," that these stretches or "stages" should not be understood "chronologically, but in the order of discovery[204]). In *Wandering Joy*, for example, Schürmann refers to the "four intensities of releasement,"[205] conceiving them not as "an ascent through degrees [...] by which the mind rises towards God," nor as "the road itself that the detached man travels," but rather as "the air, the fire, the water, the earth, which he needs for each instant of walking."[206] Dissimilarity is thus not abandoned in the

---

202 Schürmann, *Wandering Joy*, xx–xxi (absent from the corresponding material in *Maître Eckhart ou la joie errante*, 14). Schürmann, *Le Principe d'anarchie / Heidegger on Being and Acting*, §40.
203 "Wec âne wec." DW 3: 486,13 (Pr. 86, "Intravit Iesus in quoddam castellum etc.")
204 In this volume, 43.
205 Schürmann, *Wandering Joy*, 118. The earlier French version, like "The Philosophical Presuppositions...," speaks instead of "stages" (*étapes*) here. *Maître Eckhart ou la joie errante*, 199.
206 Schürmann, *Wandering Joy*, 57 / *Maître Eckhart ou la joie errante*, 99. Earlier, Schürmann described them as "determin[ing] existence here and now, like the four cardinal directions." In this volume, 127.

breakthrough. Nor (as Schürmann's work of the 1990s will make plain) can there be a simple "progression towards anarchy," as the more utopian 1978 essay "The Loss of the Origin in Soto Zen and Meister Eckhart" (chapter 15 in this volume) puts it, and as Schürmann himself suggests at various points in his career.[207]

It will be helpful to briefly summarize these four intensities of releasement, as they both distill the essence of Eckhart's message and of Schürmann's distinctive interpretation of it in the 70s and 80s and afford Schürmann the opportunity to make point-by-point comparisons with Zen. In this section, we will focus on Eckhart, and in the next we will turn to a comparison with Zen.

In "The Loss of the Origin...," Schürmann cites one of Eckhart's rare programmatic statements, delivered in a homily for the Nativity of John the Baptist:

> Whenever I preach I usually speak of detachment and that man must become bereft of himself and of all things; secondly that one should be remodeled into the image of the simple good which is God; thirdly that one should remember the great nobility which God has deposited in the mind in order for man to reach God through it; fourthly of the purity of the divine nature.[208]

This passage encapsulates the four intensities of releasement, which we will discuss in turn. Only the vocabulary for the headings is different: (1) instead of dissimilarity, Schürmann refers to the process of detaching from it; (2) instead of similarity to the divine, he highlights the activity of remodeling oneself; (3) instead of identity with God, he speaks of the soul's nobility; and (4) instead of the breakthrough to the Godhead and its subsequent dehiscence or 'bursting open,' he describes its pure nature.

---

207 Quotation in this volume, 231 et passim. This essay contains the first use of the oxymoronic notion of a "principle of anarchy" (page 229), later to be applied to the borderline of the end of metaphysics in Schürmann's eponymous book on Heidegger, *Le Principe d'anarchie* (in English as *Heidegger on Being and Acting*).
208 Cited in this volume, 231.

(1) Detachment from Dissimilarity

For Eckhart, creatures are nothing in themselves. To the extent that we are creatures, we, too, are nothing. Creatures depend entirely on God, who constantly infuses them with being. If God were to refrain from giving, they would cease to exist. In Eckhart's words:

> What does not possess being is nothingness. But no creature has being, for its being depends on the presence of God. Were God to withdraw, for an instant, from all creatures, they would be annihilated.[209]

This means that when we try to hold onto creatures independently from God, we are literally grasping at nothing. We attach ourselves to what is not. But nothing is really ours.

The first task is accordingly to detach ourselves from any and all creatureliness. While this may have material implications (recall our earlier discussion of St. Francis), it is first of all a spiritual task. As Schürmann explains in a discussion of Eckhart's Middle High German terminology for detachment:

> The word itself that Eckhart uses for detachment expresses the idea of riddance: *abegescheidenheit*, in modern German *Abgeschiedenheit*, is formed from the prefix *ab-* which designates a separation (*abetuon:* to rid oneself of something; *abekêre:* turning away, apostasy) and of the verb *scheiden* or *gescheiden*. In its transitive form, this verb means "to isolate," "to split," "to separate," and in its intransitive form "to depart," "to die." The word *abegescheidenheit*, "detachment" or "renunciation," and related verbs of deliverance evoke, in the allusive thought of Meister Eckhart, a mind that is on the way to dispossessing itself of all exteriority which might spoil its serenity.[210]

(2) Assimilation through Remodeling

Detachment to what end, though? Answer: to be more like God than like creatures. Or rather: to choose being over nothing. Eckhart uses several metaphors to describe this process. For example, we are wood that must assimilate to the burning fire that is God. We must

---

209 Cited in this volume, 234 et passim.
210 In this volume, 232–33.

become *bîworte* (or ad-verbs) to the divine Word (*Verbum*), that is to say, we must be *bî*, 'with,' the Son as the Son is with the Father. We are images of God, but we have become disfigured by presuming that images, properly speaking, are not wholly dependent on that which they image. We must accordingly 'remodel' ourselves.

(3) Noble Identity

Eckhart does not stop with likeness, however. It is not enough to become adopted children of God (Romans 8:14-17). Indeed, it is not enough for the Son to be born in our souls or even for us to become the Son. We must become identical with God the Father and thus give birth with him (or *as* him) to the Son. Affiliation must give way to paternity. As Schürmann had already explained in "The Philosophical Presuppositions...," quoting Eckhart:

> The birth of the Son is not the last word Meister Eckhart has to say within the framework of Christianity; he speaks of it only in order to prepare for the mystery of paternity in the soul: [...] "*In principio*": this word makes us understand that we are an only Son whom the Father has eternally engendered in the hidden darkness of the eternal 'concealment' and who is nonetheless immanent at the first commencement of the emptiness which is a plenitude of all emptiness. Here I have reposed eternally and slept in the hidden knowledge of the eternal Father, immanent and not emerging out of it. Out of this emptiness he has eternally engendered me as his only Son in the image of his eternal paternity, that I might be Father and engender him from whom I was birthed."[211]

More precisely, we must recognize that we *already are* identical with God the Father and must live out this recognition here and now. True nobility consists in this identity, shared by all, and in its realization, not in social standing.

But, as noted in §3, above, we must also be careful not to misunderstand this identity with God, as Eckhart's inquisitors did in the late 1320s. (Whether their miscomprehension was due to their fear of the practical implications of the anti-hierarchical element in Eckhart's understanding of nobility, which, to cite the the old anar-

---

211 In this volume, 47-48.

chist slogan with Schürmann, "tolerates neither lord nor master,"[212] is another matter.) We are not dealing with a substantial identity here, or with related "metaphysical titles such as prime analogate, supreme being, first cause, etc."[213] Eckhart is *not* saying that we, qua embodied, desirous, temporal and mortal humans, are of the same substance as the incorporeal, impassive, eternal and immortal God. Rather, we are dealing with an identity of process or operation, such as sometimes happens when the audience and the performer are taken outside of themselves in a concert, becoming absorbed in the event that is not simply more than the sum of the parts, but renders the common notions or part and whole meaningless in the moment of its happening. Schürmann writes, again quoting Eckhart:

> In such moments two existences are determined as identical: identical in the *gewürke*, that is, in the event. When applied to the realm of deification this scheme shows man living no longer "with" God but "in" him: "God is not found in distinction. When the soul reaches the original image [of which it is a reflection, R.S.] and finds itself alone in it, then it finds God. Finding itself and finding God is one single process, outside of time. As far as it penetrates into him, it is identical with God [..., R.S.] not included, nor united, but more: identical."[214]

(4) Breaking through to Pure Nature and Bursting Forth

Yet even God is not enough for Eckhart, nor is their noble identity. For, despite Eckhart's apophaticism and 'evental' ontology, there is still a danger that we would treat God and our deepest selves 'entitatively' and hence in terms of creatures (hence, too, in terms of the way in which we organize creatures according to rank). God would still be our 'why,' and we would still, on some level, be "serfs and mercenaries," as Eckhart characterizes those who "seek something with their works, those who act for a why."[215] Instead, we must break through to the Godhead beyond God, to the 'purity of the divine nature' that is without why. Only then will we too be able to release this imperative itself and live a joyous life without

---

212 In this volume, 256.
213 Ibid.
214 In this volume, 253.
215 Cited in this volume, 191.

why (which just *is* life, according to Eckhart[216]). Only then will the dark core of the Godhead break open into the light of day (or, to shift metaphors, only then will his fruit 'dehisce,' i.e., gape open to spread its seed). Only then will the 'this-worldly' character of Eckhart's preaching come to the fore and the active Martha, rather than the contemplative Mary, be accorded the 'better part.'[217] Perhaps only then, when the wayless way of releasement has been taken, will the cleft with Zen have been bridged.

§13. 'The Narrowest Cleft': Eckhart and Zen

Try to return to the time of your birth, when you could not understand which way was East and which way was West, and come tell me about it.
—From a Zen tale[218]

The narrowest cleft is the last to be bridged.
—Friedrich Nietzsche[219]

It is unclear when precisely Schürmann began to be interested in Buddhism, in particular zazen (seated meditation). Perhaps Heidegger's occasional commendations of Eastern thinking provided inspiration. More likely was the proliferation of comparative work on Eckhart and Zen in the 1950s and 1960s (some of which was also inspired by Heidegger).[220] For example, in the conclusion of his above-mentioned lecture course on Eckhart, Bernhard Welte raised the possibility that only now, at the end of metaphysics, has the time come for Eckhart. By 'the end of metaphysics,' Welte means,

---

216 LW 3: 16, no. 19 (*In Ioh.*).
217 See Pr. 86, "Intravit Iesus in quoddam castellum etc."
218 Cited in *Le bol et le bâton: 120 Contes Zen racontés par Maître Taisen Deshimaru* (Paris: Albin Michel, 1980), 14–15.
219 Cited in this volume, 267.
220 For instance, it is likely not a coincidence that Heidegger's friends Kochi Tsujimura and Hartmut Buchner, who were also involved with the Japanese edition of the philosopher's complete works, translated the famous commentary on the Ten Oxherding Pictures from Japanese into German. See Kôichi Tsushimura and Hartmut Buchner, trans., *Der Ochs und sein Hirte: Eine altchinesische Zen-Geschichte* (Pfullingen: Neske, 1958). See also Schürmann's commentary in "Three Thinkers of Releasement," §1.2.

among other things, no longer needing to conceive of God either as *an* entity (*ein Seiendes*), which is the highest *cause* of all other entities, or as being (*das Sein*), which is, despite its difference from them, nevertheless understood *in terms of entities*. Welte means, in short, the exhaustion of what Heidegger had called 'ontotheology.' This exhaustion not only enables us to read certain thinkers of the past with new eyes but also opens up the possibility of a more fruitful dialogue between Western and Eastern thought, a dialogue in which the name 'Meister Eckhart' was often, and would continue to be, heard. Writes Welte:

> If it should be correct, as one can also read in Heidegger [...], that the time of metaphysics is over, then perhaps the time of a master who in his time and in his own manner wanted to transcend metaphysics could only just be coming. [...] This is supported by the atypical role played by Meister Eckhart in the encounter of Western and Asian religious thought. There is, as far as I know, no other example of such a rank and intensity, where religious thoughts that lie far apart and that emerged independently of one another are so analogous, and where such a concrete dialogue has become possible on the basis of this analogy, as in this case; where Japanese, that is, Buddhist thinkers have intensively engaged with Meister Eckhart. This could be a sign of the times.[221]

We should mention two of these 'incisive engagements,' since both were, in different ways, important for Schürmann and reflect a tension in his own comparative work. At one end of the spectrum is

---

221 Welte, "Gedanke des Meisters Eckhart," 107–108. Here, we cite from a 1972 transcript that we assume resembles the 1965-1966 iteration that Schürmann attended. Cf., in any case, Welte's "[Review of] Shizuteru Ueda: *Die Gottesgeburt in der Seele und der Durchbruch zur Gottheit*," *Theologische Revue* 63 (1967): 86-89. It should also be noted that Schürmann was already citing the Buddha before studying with Welte. His earliest extant reference can be found in an Easter 1965 paper on anxiety in Kierkegaard and Heidegger, which begins: "'All is suffering': this is the central message of the Buddha's preaching." Reiner Schürmann, "Le sentiment d'angoisse comme constitutif de l'existence authentique: Une étude du 'Concept d'Angoisse' de Kierkegaard et de 'L'Être et le Temps' de Heidegger," Reiner Schürmann papers, NA.0006.01, The New School Archives and Special Collections, The New School, New York City, USA, Box 3, Folder 41–42.

D. T. Suzuki's "maximalist interpretation"[222] of the Eckhart/Zen relation. Schürmann criticizes Suzuki's hasty syncretism in chapter 13 in this volume, even as he recognizes that Suzuki is, in his own way, a profound thinker of the way of releasement.[223] The problem was not so much that Suzuki considered Eckhart to be speaking from the same depths as the great Zen masters. Schürmann, for his part, makes similar claims on and off throughout his career. The problem, for Schürmann, was more Suzuki's extension of this insight about the shared depths of Eckhart and Zen into numerous questions of detail. This extension obscured differences in, for example, the status of things (are they reflections of God or valid in their own right? should we relate to them theocentrically or with our ordinary state of mind?), and between the nothingness of the Godhead, with which the ground or spark of the soul is a sheer undifferentiated oneness (*ein einic ein ungescheiden*),[224] and Zen 'emptiness.' As Suzuki writes in his 1957 classic *Mysticism: Eastern and Buddhist*:

> When I first read [...] a little book containing a few of Meister Eckhart's sermons, they impressed me profoundly, for I never expected that any Christian thinker ancient or modern could or would cherish such daring thoughts as expressed in those sermons. [...] [T]he ideas expounded there closely approached Buddhist thoughts, so closely indeed, that one could stamp them almost definitely as coming out of Buddhist speculations. [...] Eckhart is in perfect accord with the Buddhist doctrine of śūnyatā, when he advances the notion of Godhead as "pure nothingness" (*ein bloss niht*).[225]

At the other end of the spectrum is the "minimalistic [...] interpretation"[226] offered by the third-generation Kyoto School philosopher Ueda Shizuteru, who, like Schürmann, was not content with Suzu-

---

222 In this volume, 269.
223 "Three Thinkers of Releasement," especially §4. Cf. Schürmann's expanded account in the appendix to *Wandering Joy* (not in *Maître Eckhart ou la joie errante*). 'Hasty syncretism' was also, by the way, the charge that Schürmann leveled against John Caputo's early work on Heidegger and Eckhart. See chapter 14 in this volume.
224 DW 1: 381,1 (Pr. 22, "Ave, gratia plena").
225 Daisetz Teitaro Suzuki, *Mysticism: Christian and Buddhist* (New York: Harper & Brothers, 1957), 3–4, 16.
226 In this volume, 269.

ki's syncretism, but felt it necessary to draw some subtle, indeed irreconcilable distinctions when advised by his doctoral advisor to undertake a now-famous comparative study of Eckhart and Zen Buddhism and to append it to his 1965 dissertation *Die Gottesgeburt in der Seele und der Durchbruch zur Gottheit: Die mystische Anthropologie Meister Eckharts und ihre Konfrontation mit der Mystik des Zen-Buddhismus* (*The Birth of God in the Soul and the Breakthrough to the Godhead: Meister Eckhart's Mystical Anthropology and Its Confrontation with the Mysticism of Zen-Buddhism*).[227] Schürmann translated excerpts from this appendix for a 1971 special issue of the aforementioned Dominican journal *La Vie spirituelle* on Eckhart (in which Schürmann's "Meister Eckhart, Expert in Itinerancy" [chapter 10 in this volume] would also appear).[228] Although, writes Ueda, "in Meister Eckhart's German-language sermons one repeatedly finds statements which could be valid word-for-word translations from Zen texts," Ueda nevertheless argues for the "inseparability of Meister Eckhart's theistically colored mysticism of infinity from its theistic foundation," in fact to such an extent that the "similarities become completely meaningless."[229] Buddhism, in Ueda's estimation, goes further than Eckhart in both its negative and affirmative thrusts. Whereas there are still theological, personal, and substantialist residues in the Eckhart's understanding of the divine (where, in short, the nothingness of the Godhead = pure being as *no* thing), Buddhist emptiness is atheological, impersonal, and in no sense a substance. This has implications for how one's unity with God is lived out *in vita*. According to Ueda, in Eckhartian releasement *to* things, "Jesus is painted small," as in the famous oil painting of Mary and Martha by Joachim Beuckelaer, "but he is still there."[230] Not so in Zen, where God completely "un-becomes" in the performance of

---

227 Gütersloh: Mohn, 1965.
228 Ueda Shizuteru, "Maître Eckhart et le bouddhisme zen," translated and with a preface by Reiner Schürmann, *La Vie spirituelle* 124, no. 578 (January 1971): 33–42. Schürmann's preface is available in chapter 11 of the present volume. Ueda's appendix is available in English under the title "Meister Eckhart's Mysticism in Comparison with Zen Buddhism," trans. Gregory S. Moss, *Comparative and Continental Philosophy* 14, no. 2 (2022): 128–52.
229 Ueda, "Meister Eckhart's Mysticism in Comparison with Zen Buddhism," 130–31.
230 Ueda, "Meister Eckhart's Mysticism in Comparison with Zen Buddhism," 130.

an everyday activity like cutting bamboo, as Ueda explains in reference to a Zen painting by Ryōkai.[231]

We will soon see Schürmann waver in his assessment of the relation between Eckhart and Zen, but first it is important to note that Schürmann, unlike many other Western scholars, did not confine his engagement with Zen to the academic level. Rather, he recognized that "the master-student relationship is the only way to learn Zen" and made it a point to announce that his remarks on this topic in "The Loss of the Origin..." were based on such a relationship: "an implicit reference is made throughout this paper to a period of time that I spent with Master Deshimaru from Kyoto, who also lives part of the time in France."[232] Later in the essay, he explains that his subsequent remarks on the Zen parallel to the last step or intensity of releasement are little more than a transcript: "Let me simply render here some notes taken at Deshimaru's *mondos* (sessions of questions and answers) on this last step of the way of releasement."[233] These sessions presumably took place in the late 1960s, after Deshimaru's arrival in France at the end of 1967 and prior to the start of Schürmann's teaching in the U.S. in 1971.[234]

Earlier, we noted that developing the four intensities of releasement in Eckhart would allow Schürmann to make point-by-point comparisons with Zen. This is true but insufficient. For, as Schürmann repeatedly stresses, it is solely on the *experiential* level, and not on the intellectual one, that the space for the encounter between the two can open up: "The true realm of encounter between such foreign traditions as a far-Eastern Buddhist sect of the twelfth century and our Medieval German late Scholastic is after all *my own*

---

231 Ueda, "Meister Eckhart's Mysticism in Comparison with Zen Buddhism," 132. For more on the Eckhart-reception in twentieth-century Japanese philosophy, see Johannes Brachtendorf, "Meister Eckhart zwischen Avignon und Kyoto: Zur Rezeption seines Denkens in der buddhistischen Philosophie Japans," *Theologische Quartalschrift* 201, no. 2 (2021): 120–50.
232 In this volume, 228.
233 In this volume, 258.
234 Taïsen Deshimaru, *Questions à un maître zen* (Paris: Albin Michel, 1981), 9. Schürmann relates that he studied with Deshimaru in Lodève (located in southern France), in this volume, 228[n373]. Deshimaru also had a center in Paris, although we do not know whether Schürmann studied *zazen* there.

existence."[235] The only way in which to genuinely compare the two traditions is, as Schürmann did, to test them out by putting one's existence at stake.[236] In other words:

> Such point-by-point comparisons as are sometimes undertaken [by, for example, Suzuki] do not lead very far here. Rather, some hypothesis of interpretation is needed for a re-seizure, *at one's own risk*, of the matter itself, that is, of the experience to which both Zen and Eckhart testify. Let me call this experience the way of releasement. [...] [T]here is no other way of responsibly dealing with the convergence [with Eckhart] noticed by [...] Japanese authors [such as Suzuki] than to *somehow involve oneself in the way of releasement.*[237]

Still, in this afterword, which is, after all, centered on appreciating Schürmann's path, it behooves us to recount the results of his attempt at dealing with the Eckhart/Zen convergence by involving himself in the way of releasement.[238]

Although, in his early period, Schürmann wondered about the possible overlaps between the Godhead and śūnyatā and about their common practical implications (is there not but "one charity"?, he asks in a 1971 review of Masumi Shibata's *Les maîtres du zen au Japon* [*The Masters of Zen in Japan*][239]), and although he did not hesitate to adduce examples from Buddhism, Schürmann would also stress subtle differences, especially concerning Eckhart's 'theocentrism.' For example, in his preface to his translation of Ueda (published, recall, in *La Vie spirituelle*), he notes:

---

235 In this volume, 226; emphasis added.
236 And Schürmannn clearly means this 'existential ordeal' in the most literal sense when, in a lecture version of his "The Loss of the Origin..." delivered before the Lindisfarne association in Manhattan, he relates that, one day when Deshimaru was meditating in Lodève, a fire started on a different floor of the dojo; Deshimaru commanded his students to remain sitting regardless of the approaching danger. In this volume, 243[n433].
237 In this volume, 227; emphases added.
238 On the relation between Schürmann's ontological *anarché*, as well as anarchic praxis, and Zen—especially Dōgen and the Kyoto School philosopher Nishida Kitarō—see John W. M. Krummel, "Zen and Anarchy in Reiner Schürmann," *Philosophy Today* 66, no. 1 (2022): 115–32.
239 In this volume, 144.

The Buddhist cannot follow Meister Eckhart all the way. The pages that you will read here, although they trace the stages of a fundamental spiritual experience of man, nevertheless also make evident the irreducible originality of the Christian revelation.[240]

Or, in the more neutral "Three Thinkers of Releasement," Schürmann emphasizes that "[i]t is once again that Eckhart's theocentrism which here resists syncretism."[241] Later in his career, the question of Eckhart's theocentrism again comes up, this time in Schürmann's final treatment of Zen in the "The Law of Nature and Pure Nature" (chapter 16 in this volume), which Schürmann first gave in German as a lecture in Kyoto in 1984 and then translated into English for a 1987 publication; only, it is now less Zen that cannot follow Eckhart than Eckhart who cannot follow Zen:

> As much as Zen and Eckhart resemble each other in [their] transgressions of the limits set by representational thought, it is clear that Eckhart, in the transition from laws of nature to pure nature, puts into question the metaphysics of *order* only to gain access to a more radically theistic thinking.[242]

The major exception to this assessment of Eckhart's theocentrism vis-à-vis Zen (whether cast more positively, as in the early Schürmann, or more negatively, in the later Schürmann), is the 1978 essay "The Loss of the Origin...." To be sure, Schürmann begins by noting the principal gap that seems to divide Eckhart from Zen. At issue here, as elsewhere, is Eckhart's lingering theological com-

---

240 In this volume, 141.
241 In this volume, 215. Schürmann is blunter in an updated version of the material on Eckhart and Suzuki, published as an appendix to *Wandering Joy* (not in *Maître Eckhart ou la joie errante*): "God's nothingness is his 'super-being,' *hyper-on*. As Eckhart's vocabulary and thinking remain thoroughly theocentric, there seems to be a pure equivocity of nothingness as between Suzuki and Eckhart" (218).
242 In this volume, 295. For a different critique of Eckhart in the 1980s, see Schürmann's last extant interview "On the Philosophers' Release from Civil Service: An Interview with Reiner Schürmann," *Kairos* 2 (1988): 133–45, where he stresses, not Eckhart's theocentrism, but rather the insufficiency of a doctrine of releasement that, being still "a luxury that makes to much of interiority" (137), would—in some extreme cases, such as life under a totalitarian regime—end up playing "into the hands of that of which it is meant to hasten the closure or withering" (139). This interview will be republished in *The Place of the Symbolic*.

mitment: "The profound cleavage that I see at this first stage of releasement [namely, detachment from dissimilarity] is that Eckhart negates attachment for the sake of God."[243] However, in this essay, Schürmann considers the possibility that Eckhart does not just move beyond the 'principial,' 'arche-teleocratic' God for the sake of a Godhead that is *sine principio,* 'an-archic,' and 'a-teleocratic' (a move that, despite its radicality, is nevertheless still indexed to a notion of the divine), but that, with Eckhart's call to *Gelassenheit,* his "theocentrism, which distinguishes him on this first level from Zen, will perhaps collapse under the implacable logic of releasement which teaches one to let everything be."[244] Toward the end of the essay, Schürmann is more direct, noting that his "reservations" about Eckhart's intellectualism and theocentrism "will both collapse" "the more we discover now the anarchic element in Eckhart."[245]

In any case, Schürmann's experience studying both Zen and his Dominican predecessor led him to conclude that they both went the way of releasement. Even the stretches or 'intensities' (dissimilarity, similarity, identity, and breakthrough/dehiscence) are alike. Eckhart exhorted his congregations to detach themselves—i.e., to cut themselves off—from the multiplicity, temporality, and corporeality of creatures, which are nothing independently of the simplicity, eternity, and incorporeality of the being of God. Zen, for its part, also begins with the "deadly seriousness" of violent imperatives: kill your ego, void your mind. Focus only on your posture. If you must will, will not to will. Your preoccupations are nothing.

Second, as Eckhart taught assimilation—i.e., likening oneself—to God, so Zen teaches becoming like the Buddha through a variety of stages, which need not be sequential. Relying on "several authors of

---

[243] In this volume, 237.
[244] Ibid.
[245] In this volume, 248. See also the following comments from the lecture version of the essay, where Schürmann declares that, "[A]t the end, this theistic framework will be totally disrupted, also in Meister Eckhart." "God not only changes in face or in appearance but in the end [...] vanishes." "[T]he difference between origin and originated, has totally disappeared. So, this is a state of identity. And there Eckhart ceases to be theocentric at all. And here I think we leave the schemes of thought of the inherited Christian metaphysics of the West." In this volume, 237[n412], 238[n417], 249[n455].

the tradition,"²⁴⁶ Schürmann names ten stages, which we recapitulate as follows:

1. Hell, or the extreme discomfort of seated meditation, especially at first;
2. Avidity, or the eagerness for enlightenment;
3. Sensuality, or the excessive focus on sensations, be they hunger or a sense of oneness with the universe;
4. Battle, or competitiveness with other practitioners;
5. Concern, or worry about daily affairs and one's past;
6. Light, or extraordinary (and thus improper) joy;
7. Dogmatism, or overemphasis on correct ideas;
8. Immobility, or retreat from others;
9. Compassion, or being amidst others, displaying enlightenment without yearning for it, being a living Buddha.
10. Nothingness, or being *hotoke*, which is a name for Buddha that "means to untie, release, set free, disentangle, divest, lay bare, become nothing."²⁴⁷

While steps nine and ten seem to overlap with the third and fourth intensities of releasement, in his discussion of the Zen parallels to the intensities, Schürmann stresses that identification with the Buddha is also an identification with oneself. This resembles the stage of identity in Eckhart when we recognize that an aspect of us is always already at one in operation with God. Furthermore, as Eckhart preached both a breakthrough into the nothingness of the Godhead and a bursting forth into the world, so too do steps nine and ten here seem to be joined in the final stage of Zen practice. As Schürmann writes, now in reference to the final Oxherding Picture:

> the experience of nothingness [as depicted in the eighth picture, for example] here leads man back "among the drunkards and the beggars": "Carrying a gourd he goes out into the market; leaning against a stick he comes home. He is found in company of wine-bibbers and butchers; he and they are all converted into Buddhas."²⁴⁸

---

246 In this volume, 240^{n425}.
247 In this volume, 242.
248 In this volume, 259.

§14. From Wandering Joy to Tragic Happiness: On the Eckhartian Double Bind

Viele versuchten umsonst das Freudigste freudig zu sagen
Hier spricht endlich es mir, hier in der Trauer sich aus.
Many have sought in vain to say the most joyful with joy,
Here it is spoken at last, here in the grandeur of grief.
—Hölderlin, "Sophokles"[249]

In "The Law of Nature and Pure Nature" (German 1984, English 1987), Schürmann seemed to fault Eckhart for the theocentrism and intellectualism that prevented him from bridging the 'narrowest cleft' with Zen. Schürmann's comments in "The Loss of the Origin..." aside, Eckhart could never quite silence the "inkling" of a theocentric 'thou.' He failed, in other words, to go as far as the Zen masters of the Far East, even though he did supposedly "cancel"[250] the metaphysics of natural law for the sake of the pure nature of the Godhead. By the early 1990s, however, Schürmann had come to see Eckhart's restraint as a virtue and efforts to simply cancel metaphysics as liable to reinforce its sway. For the very late Schürmann, Eckhart becomes a paradigmatic thinker, not of wandering joy or of an-archy as life without why, but of the tragic double bind. Schürmann takes the notion of the double bind from Gregory Bateson, extending its reach from psychology (where it is used to describe situations such as when someone tells you they love you but in a tone that suggests the opposite) to the ultimate traits of human being and further to the ultimate traits of being as such. As developed in his posthumous magnum opus *Broken Hegemonies*, Schürmann sees the human as irreparably torn between the thrusts of natality (or universalization) and mortality (or singularization), and being itself as irreparably torn between the thrusts of appropriation (or phenomenalization) and expropriation (or dephenomenalization). Both sets of thrusts are inescapable. In Schürmann's language, natality and mortality are "in differend" (i.e., in *irresolvable* contradiction) with another, as are appropriation and expropriation.

---

[249] Friedrich Hölderlin, *Sämtliche Werke und Briefwechsel in drei Bänden*, ed. Michael Knaupp (Munich: Hanser, 2019), 1: 271.
[250] In this volume, 268.

This constitutes the tragic. But we can learn, through suffering and its recollection, to live in view of twofold, tragic legislation and perhaps thereby avoid the worst consequences of tragic blindness. This constitutes tragic wisdom.

Now, what makes Eckhart so remarkable for the Schürmann of *Broken Hegemonies* is precisely his ability to sustain the tragic double bind. This is, to be sure, a peculiar claim to make of the erstwhile teacher of serene, 'peregrine identity,' a claim that, to our knowledge, has never been made of Eckhart elsewhere.[251] But it is nevertheless a claim that is based on a more comprehensive view of the Meister's writings. Instead of speculating, as he had in 1967, about whether "Meister Eckhart should be the first thinker to have abandoned the schema—so convenient for representation—of a hierarchical cosmos,"[252] Schürmann sees Eckhart as attempting to maintain, *at the same time*, both a hierarchical, theocratic order that institutes natural law *and* a leveling, 'theolytic' disorder that destitutes it. In the introduction (chapter 17 in this volume) to his Spring 1993 lecture course on Eckhart—a course that had to be interrupted due to complications from AIDS, of which Schürmann would die a few months later—Schürmann explains that, on the one hand, "[Eckhart] constantly speaks as an advocate of a highly stratified universe, obviously indebted in this to Neoplatonist constructs—as well as to a feudal view of the world which it would never occur to him to put into question." On the other hand, "there is another conceptual strategy that [Eckhart] pursues throughout his writings [...]. No hierarchy here any more, but a deliberate and vehement gesture to erase hierarchies." It is "the conflict between the two argumentative lines" that "goes to the heart of the matter in Meister Eckhart."[253] If, however, the introduction still suggests a primacy of the second strategy over the first and hence the anarchic wandering (*errance*) that Schürmann develops in his earlier work on Eckhart, *Broken Hegemonies* tries to hold both together in such a way that wandering yields to an "erratic or intermittent relation"

---

251 For the history of the reception of Eckhart, see Ingeborg Degenhardt, *Studien zum Wandel des Eckhartbildes* (Leiden: Brill, 1967), and Schürmann's review of this book in chapter 11 in this volume.
252 In this volume, 55.
253 In this volume, 299.

(*l'erratique*)²⁵⁴ to the conflicting claims of the natural law of God and the pure nature of the Godhead, and anarchy, understood as altogether without *archē*, yields to a distinctive conception of anarchy as the irreconcilable conflict of ultimates, hence as the double bind.²⁵⁵

At the end of *Broken Hegemonies*, Schürmann notes that it is "possible to think for itself the double bind that we know." He then wonders whether we might be able to love this bind: "With eyes opened by the hubristic sufferings that our age has inflicted on itself— as Oedipus at Colonus wants [*veut*] his eyes open and who thought of [*se veut*] his eyes as open—is it possible to love the ultimates in differend?"²⁵⁶ It would seem that Eckhart, as Schürmann reads him in *Broken Hegemonies*, would be able to say yes. At any rate, he becomes the teacher of happiness—not, to be sure, a happiness that is found in addressing God or in knowing or loving him as the highest object (as the Dominicans and Franciscans long debated), nor a happiness that consists in liberation from all legislation, but a happiness that happens in embracing the double bind as "the legislative tragic"²⁵⁷ (or at least, in Eckhart's case, the 'the(i)ological' version of it). As Schürmann explains in an earlier section of *Broken Hegemonies* (which may well have been the final section he composed and hence one of the last substantial things he wrote before his death in August 1993²⁵⁸):

> The double bind of the nominative [i.e., natural law, God as ground (*Grund*)] and infinitive [i.e., pure nature or "naturing," the Godhead as abyss (*Abgrund*)] expresses the secret of happiness [*bonheur*] (tragic, in the sense of incongruous ultimates), just as it first expresses the mystery of being (agonal, in the sense of being and beings in a differend). Neither happiness nor being is designated simply, plainly, by name.²⁵⁹

---

254 Schürmann, *Des Hégémonies brisées*, 327 / *Broken Hegemonies*, 274; translation modified.
255 See Schürmann, *Des Hégémonies brisées*, 344, 722 / *Broken Hegemonies*, 289, 629.
256 Schürmann, *Des Hégémonies brisées*, 724 / *Broken Hegemonies*, 631.
257 *Le Tragique légiférant* was an earlier title for *Des Hégémonies brisées*.
258 Evidence for this chronology and further discussion of Eckhart's role in Schürmann's magnum opus are provided in Ian Alexander Moore, "On the Rise and Fall of Natural Law in Schürmann's *Broken Hegemonies*: For the Love of the Tragic Double Bind," forthcoming in a volume edited by Marcia Sá Cavalcante Schuback (Södertörn University / Diaphanes Press).
259 Schürmann, *Des Hégémonies brisées*, 395 / *Broken Hegemonies*, 335.

Although, presumably because of the prominence accorded to the tragic, Schürmann's interest in Zen had faded in his final years (Buddhism is not even mentioned in *Broken Hegemonies*, for example), a death poem by the Japanese poet Ome Shushiki, which serves as an epigraph to Schürmann's final work, complements this secret of happiness by turning our attention to the fleeting singulars of everyday life. However, after hegemony has been shown to have always been broken and the phantasms of its inverse—i.e., the end of metaphysics, the celebration of sheer dislocation, difference, and dissolution—have also ultimately been traced back to the "megalomania of desire,"[260] what appears is not the divine in all things (Eckhart) or the rose that blooms without why (Silesius), nor the fourfold of earth, sky, divinities and mortals (Heidegger), but the water iris, *as it is*, in its sheer such-ness and thus-ness, caught in an exorbitant embrace of life and death revolving one around the other:

> Dead my old fine hopes,
> And dry my dreaming
> But still—
> Iris, blue each spring.

---

[260] Reiner Schürmann, "'Only Proteus Can Save Us Now': On Anarchy and Broken Hegemonies," ed. Francesco Guercio and Ian Alexander Moore, *Graduate Faculty Philosophy Journal* 42, no. 1 (2021): 53–90 (80).

Acknowledgments

Many people have assisted in the production of this book. We would like to thank, in addition to those who helped prepare the translations: Kieran Aarons, Benjamin Acree, Marcia Sá Cavalcante Schuback, Joseph de Almeida Monteiro, O.P., Weian Ding, Markus Enders, Jean-Miguel Garrigues, O.P., Michael Heitz, John Krummel, David McCullough, Chet Mlcek, Marianne Nouveau, Jean-Michel Potin, O.P., Hendrik Rohlf, Joeri Schrijvers, Nicolas Schneider, and Duane Williams. Finally, our gratitude goes to our families for their love and support.

Index nominum

Albert the Great, 41, 109, 300, 328
Al-Farabi, 302
Agnes of Austria, Queen of Hungary, 145
Ancelet-Hustache, Jeanne, 142, 145–46, 162[n197], 395–96
Angelus Silesius (Johann Scheffler), 105, 105[n141], 121[n162], 141, 162, 162[n197], 171–172[n216], 177[n231], 182[n243], 189[n261], 207[n303], 218, 233[n396], 246[n443], 255[n482], 260[n517], 260–61[n518], 252[n526], 263[n536], 352, 416
Anselm of Canterbury, 261[n520]
Aquinas, Thomas, 18[n22], 41, 49–50, 53–57, 66, 73[n107], 81–85, 87[n130], 109, 111, 136, 139[n178], 161[n193], 166, 167–168[n207], 176, 176[n228], 176[n229], 281, 287, 293, 300, 318, 322–24, 326, 328, 367–68
Arendt, Hannah, 336
Aristotle, 48, 161, 161[n195], 164, 176, 228, 252, 252[n472], 285–86, 287, 294, 300, 302, 318, 326
Aubenque, Pierre, 169[n212]
Augustine of Hippo, 30, 54, 67, 73[n107], 83[n126], 93, 168[n208], 172, 172[n219], 187, 222, 239[n420], 249, 249[n452], 270, 273, 290, 293, 300, 323, 362, 379, 383
Averroes (Ibn-Rushd), 302
Avicenna (Ibn-Sina), 302
Bakunin, Mikhail, 230
Barrett, William, 196
Bernardone, Pietro, 115–16

Besnard, Albert-Marie, 147, 396
Bassui, Tokushō, 144
Beuckelaer, Joachim, 407
Bloch, Ernst, 256, 256[n493]
Bonhoeffer, Dietrich, 340
Brandt, Willy, 149, 149[n183]
Buber, Martin, 21, 26[n35], 348, 351, 358
Buchner, Hartmut, 404[n220]
Buddha, 143, 144, 157, 159, 181, 226, 240, 242, 250, 259, 259[n509]
Bultmann, Rudolf, 11, 53, 340, 363
Camelot, Pierre Thomas, 85[n129]
Caputo, John, 155, 217–24, 339[n15], 406[n223]
Char, René, 391, 391[n174], 392[n176]
Chenu, Marie-Dominique, 58[n86], 84[n127], 323, 323[n580]
Cicero, Marcus Tullius, 267, 270[n540], 276
Clark, James M., 108[n146]
Cognet, Louis, 143
Congar, Yves, 58, 172[n217]
Comte, Auguste, 196
Degenhardt, Ingeborg, 120[n160], 135, 138–41, 259[n515], 414[n251]
Della Volpe, Galvano, 168[n209]
Deleuze, Gilles, 392
Denifle, Heinrich, 139–40
Descartes, René, 204[n291], 217
Deshimaru, Taisen, 225, 228, 232, 243[n433], 250[n457], 258, 404, 408, 408[n234], 409[n236]
De Spira, Iulianus, 116[n156]

Dōgen Zenji, 133, 242, 250, 258, 273[n544], 409[n238]
Dominic, Saint, 10, 10[n4], 340
Donatello, 248[n449]
Dubilet, Alex, 372
Dumoulin, Heinrich, 139, 225[n359]
Duns Scotus, 267
Eckhart, Johannes (von Hochheim), 9, 14, 16, 18, 23, 41–57, 74, 84, 87–89, 95, 102–146, 155–222, 225–304, 312, 314[n572], 317–19, 321–24, 326, 328, 334–40, 342–48, 350–58, 361, 367, 370–416
Enomiya, Hugo M., 139, 225[n359]
Feist-Hirsch, Elisabeth, 207, 207[n305]
Flynn, Bernard, 397
Foucault, Michel, 392
Freud, Sigmund, 99, 150
Francis of Assisi, 25, 25[n33], 95, 114–16, 130, 363, 372, 378, 380–82, 401
Gadamer, Hans-Georg, 345
Garrigues, Jean-Miguel, 350–51
Geffré, Claude, 12, 13, 18[n22], 41, 139[n178], 317–319, 322, 339, 345, 353, 357, 363, 375[n124], 386[n156]
Gilbert of Poitiers, 168[n208]
Gilson, Étienne, 140, 142, 166, 166[n204]
Hadot, Pierre, 111[n149], 385, 386[n156]
Hakuin, Ekaku, 149
Hemingway, Ernest, 38
Hegel, Georg Wilhelm Friedrich, 66, 68[n96], 98[n139], 228, 256[n493], 259, 259[n513], 259[n515], 333, 393
Heidegger, Martin, 9–10, 13–19, 42, 54, 57, 59, 66–80, 84, 87[n130], 90–92, 105, 111–12[n149], 141, 155, 171, 194–211, 217–19, 222–24, 240[n424], 260[n517], 286, 297, 334[n3], 335–40, 342–55, 357, 360, 363, 367–70, 373–74, 376, 388–92, 394, 400[n207], 404, 405, 406[n223], 416
Heinrich, W., 225[n359]
Henry, Michel, 110
Heraclitus, 71–74, 200
Hitler, Adolf, 148
Hölderlin, Friedrich, 17, 63, 75–79, 88, 342, 349, 368–69, 392–93, 413, 413[n249]
Ishin, Seigen, 194[n265], 274
Jaspers, Karl, 81[n123], 392[n176]
Jesus of Nazareth, 10–11, 25, 27, 38, 39, 49, 51, 52, 58, 83, 86, 89, 90, 91, 99, 110, 118–21, 121[n162], 130, 132, 137, 194, 277, 310, 315, 341, 342, 350, 361, 362, 363, 375–77, 407
Job, 58, 117–118
John the Baptist, 400
John the Evangelist, 21, 24, 28, 33, 36, 39, 49, 51, 54, 58, 80, 91–92, 136, 246–247, 289, 315, 348[n37], 355[n56], 356, 361, 368
John XXII, Pope, 110
Kant, Immanuel, 61, 66, 68[n96], 73, 150, 273, 334[n3], 338
Karl the Bald, 288–289
Kierkegaard, Søren, 53, 98[n140], 344[n3], 367, 405[n221]
Kleiber, Morand, 370
Klossowski, Pierre, 392
Koch, Joseph, 166[n205], 168[n208], 204[n292], Krummel, John W. M., 409[n238]
Lao-Tzu, 181[n241], 213, 213[n331]
Le Guillou, Marie-Joseph, 366[n93]
Le Saux, Dom Henri, 225[n359]
Lévinas, Emmanuel, 197, 197[n278]

Lossky, Vladimir, 138, 138[n176], 139, 140, 142, 143, 163[n199], 166[n203], 171, 171[n214], 184[n247], 204[n292], 254[n479], 318, 318[n574]
Ludwig the German, 288–289
Luke the Evangelist, 21, 28, 33, 92, 120[n159], 122[n165], 133, 315, 355
Martha of Bethany, 39, 122, 132–33, 194, 268, 377, 378[n134], 404, 407
Marx, Karl, 107, 107[n144], 150, 245[n439], 365
Mary of Bethany, 39, 122, 133, 194, 268, 377, 377–78[n134], 404, 407
Mary of Nazareth, 136
McGinn, Bernard, 165[n201], 354[n54], 355[n57], 372, 372[n112], 398[n200]
Meisner, Helmut, 29, 29[n40]
Mechthild of Magdeburg, 171[n216], 221, 221[n353]
Menenius, Agrippa 230, 230[n388]
Merton, Thomas, 225[n359]
Morrison, Jim 106[n143], 124, 124[n166], 126
Monroe, Marylin, 38
Nambara, Minoru, 139, 225[n359],
Nietzsche, Friedrich, 66–78, 199–200, 240[n424], 259, 259[n513], 267, 268, 290, 338, 350, 350[n44], 351[n45], 367, 392, 392[n177], 392[n179], 404
Nishitani, Keiji, 225[n359], 274, 279, 290
Nouveau, Philippe, 57, 367
Ott, Heinrich, 90[n134]
Otto, Rudolf, 225[n359]
Otto of Freising, 168[n208]
Paul, Saint, 31, 84, 91, 92, 353, 354, 356, 368, 376, 377, 393
Plato, 59, 60, 72, 73, 200, 230, 254[n477], 285

Peter, Saint, 54, 342
Plotinus, 111[n149], 249[n453], 251[n464], 273, 302
Proclus, 57, 59, 60, 62, 63, 65–67, 69–71, 74, 83, 86, 88, 178[n232], 351, 367
Proudhon, Pierre-Joseph, 230
Pseudo-Dionysius the Areopagite, 302, 303, 354, 356
Pöggeler, Otto, 66[n92]
Quelquejeu, Bernard, 57
Quint, Josef, 23[n30], 42[n44], 51, 51[n74], 87[n131], 167[n206], 396[n191]
Rahner, Karl, 84, 90, 90[n134]
Raison du Cleuziou, Yann, 364[n88]
Ricœur, Paul, 323, 323[n579]
Rilke, Rainer Maria, 75, 75[n112], 80
Rinzai, 226[n364], 227
Robinson, John A. T. 9, 340
Rousset, Jean, 141
Rosenberg, Alfred, 138
Rosenzweig, Franz, 77[n118]
Ryōkai (Liang Kai), 408
Saichi, Asahara, 143
Scabbia, Ferruccio, 393[n182]
Schelling, Friedrich Wilhelm Joseph, 393
Schlier, Heinrich, 90[n134]
Schomerus, H. W., 225[n359]
Sergius of Radonezh, Saint, 95, 95[n137]
Sekida, Katsuki, 274[n575], 294
Shibata, Masumi, 133[n173], 143, 144, 409
Shin'ichi, Hisamatsu, 143
Shirakawa, 143
Shushiki, Ome, 416
Spinoza, Baruch, 252[n467]

421

Suzuki, Daisetz Teitaro, 143, 155, 160, 173, 178–216, 225[n359], 226, 226[n364], 226[n365], 250, 269, 330, 406, 409, 410[n241]
Teilhard de Chardin, Pierre, 30, 35, 35[n41], 314, 314[n571], 356
Teixeira-Leite Penido, Maruílo, 169[n211]
Tetsugen, Doko, 144
Théry, Gabriel, 163[n200]
Thérèse of Lisieux, 30
Thomas à Kempis, 27[n39], 30
Tillich, Paul, 340
Tokushō, Bassui, 144
Tsushimura, Kôichi, 157, 404[n220]
Ueda, Shizuteru, 139, 141, 187, 193[n264], 203[n290], 207[n304], 225[n359], 269, 291, 291[n561], 328, 330, 405[n221], 406, 407, 407[n228], 408, 409

Vaysse, Jean-Marie, 13[n9], 344[n31]
Von Balthasar, Hans Urs, 15
Von Baader, Franz, 259[n515]
Weil, Eric, 197
Weiss, Bardo, 135, 371
Weiss, Konrad, 108[n145]
Welte, Bernhard, 11, 11[n7], 12, 12[n8], 13, 14, 18, 18[n22], 41, 53, 53[n78], 87[n130], 89[n134], 161[n196], 204[n293], 321–328, 339, 339[n14], 342, 343, 343[n29], 344[n31], 345, 351, 363, 363[n86], 386, 387, 389, 389[n164], 404, 405, 405[n221]
Wittgenstein, Ludwig, 111[n149]
Woods, Richard, 372
Yeats, William Butler, 70
Yôsai, Kikuchi, 143, 144

Index compiled by Weian Ding